**OFFICE OF POPULATION CENSUSES AND SURVEYS**

# Classification of occupations

## and coding index

London: Her Majesty's Stationery Office

ISBN 0 11 690728 2*

# CONTENTS

**Classification of occupations**

# CLASSIFICATION OF OCCUPATIONS

## Introduction

### Types of economic activity classification

A fourfold classification of the economically active or former active population will be used in the analyses of the information collected at the Census of Population to be taken in 1981 namely, by:

(1) Occupation,
(2) Industry,
(3) Employment status,
(4) Economic position.

These four classifications are independent and relate to four separate aspects of the employment or former employment of a person.

**Occupation**. The occupation of a person is the kind of work which he or she performs, due regard being paid to the conditions under which it is performed; and this alone determines the particular group in an occupation classification to which the person is assigned. The nature of the factory, business, or service in which the person is employed has no bearing upon the classification of his occupation, except to the extent that it enables the nature of his duties to be more clearly defined. This perhaps will be made clearer by an example. A crane driver may be employed in a shipyard, an engineering works or in building and construction, but this has no bearing upon his occupation and all crane drivers should be classified to the same occupation group.

**Industry**. The industry in which an individual is engaged is determined (whatever may be his occupation) by reference to the business or economic activity in which his occupation is followed. As a single business may employ a number of individuals of widely varying occupations for the purpose of affording a particular service or creating a particular product, it will be seen that the industrial classification differs essentially from the occupational in that the latter takes account only of the nature of the work performed by the individual, while the former has regard only to the nature of the service or product to which his labour contributes. The man who is occupationally a carpenter or a carman, for instance, is classified industrially to building, if employed by a builder, but to brewing, if employed by a brewer.

**Employment status**. This is primarily a distinction between the 'employed' and the 'self-employed'. The 'employee' category is sub-divided to indicate relative levels within an occupation, e.g. apprentices or foremen.

**Economic position**. This distinguishes those economically active from the inactive and among the latter those previously active. Among the active population separate groups are provided for those in employment and various categories of those seeking employment.
Further details of the classification are given on pp. ix−x.

### Application of the classification to the total enumerated populations

The fourfold classification is applicable to all persons enumerated in the Census who are working in the United Kingdom. The Classification by Industry provides a separate code to distinguish those whose employment is outside the United Kingdom.

### Time reference for coding economic activity

The economic activity to which these codes will apply will be that of the main work for pay or profit during the week before Census and no lower limit to the hours worked will be specified. No questions on usual occupation will be asked. As regards those seeking work, disabled and/or retired, the reference will be to the most recent employment.

# Classification of occupations

## General

The OPCS Classification of Occupations 1980 is based on the Classification of Occupations and Directory of Occupational Titles (CODOT) published by the Department of Employment. The groups in the Key Occupations for Statistical Purposes (KOS), CODOT, Vol. 1, pp. 89−103 (HMSO, 1972), have been aggregated and form the basis of the OPCS classification. The relationship between KOS and the aggregated or condensed KOS is shown in Appendix A on pp. lxxi−lxxxi. The OPCS classification is summarised on pp. xiv−xxix. A definition of each group and its relationship to CODOT is shown on pp. xxx−lxx. It has been necessary to create four groups within the OPCS classification but outside the condensed KOS structure, to cover cases where there is insufficient information to allocate more satisfactorily. These four groups are:

| | |
|---|---|
| −.1 Foremen (engineering and allied trades) | appearing between condensed KOS groups 131 and 132 |
| −.2 Trainee craftsmen (engineering and allied trades) | |
| −.1 Inadequately described occupations | appearing after condensed KOS group 161 |
| −.2 Occupations not stated | |

The current classification has been designed to maintain a high degree of comparability with the OPCS Classification of Occupations 1970. A tabulation showing the relationship between the 1970 and 1980 classifications is in course of preparation and will be available free of charge from OPCS, on application.

## Basis of the classification

The main purpose has been to provide groups with at least one common characteristic. The basic common factor of all groups is the kind of work done and the nature of the operation performed. But if, by reason of the material worked in, the degree of skill involved, the physical energy required, the environmental conditions, the social and economic status associated with the occupation, or any combination of these factors, unit groups based solely on kind of work done seemed too comprehensive they were further broken down on the basis of these other factors in order to identify what are substantially separate occupations.

Certain limiting conditions have also operated, e.g. that the number of individuals likely to be included in a unit is sufficiently large to be worth separate identification on a 10% sample basis, that the identification of a unit group is likely to be tolerably complete and accurate from the limited information obtained from a Census, that there is sufficient potential interest in the group to justify separate identification, and that statistics for the group could not be obtained from the cross-classification of occupation by industry.

## Certain principles of the classification

Certain groups of persons in employment, in particular the self-employed and the managers give rise to difficult conceptual problems.

**Self-employed.** In certain cases the self-employed are treated as managers because they have independent responsibility which involves the performance of managerial functions. This can apply even though they may not have supervisors under their control. Thus owners of wholesale and retail establishments, catering and lodging establishments and farms, for example, are classified under managerial occupations. Self-employed travel agents, employment agents and ticket agents are assigned to 037.2. However, owners of small undertakings who exercise a professional or craft function, and whose management role is clearly subordinate to the application of specialist skills are classified to those skills; for example self-employed accountants, bakers and electricians are classified as accountants, bakers and electricians, and not as managers. All professional and semi-professional workers are classified to that profession. There are instances where the proprietor may not carry out the functions e.g. a nursing home proprietor or even a proprietor of a dental practice. Because of the small number involved and the impossibility of determining whether they actually perform the professional duties, these persons are included in the professions. Self-employed forestry workers and minor agricultural workers e.g. bee keepers, maggot breeders, hedgers and ditchers and gardeners are classified as workers. Self-employed manufacturers are classified with the workers, thus a proprietor of a silk weaving business is classified as a weaver. The proprietor of more general functions e.g. textile manufacturer is assigned to the appropriate not elsewhere classified (n.e.c.) group. Owners of firms providing services, such as a typewriting bureau or photographic agency with regard to whom there is no evidence that they perform the actual work associated with such services are classified in group 057.6 unless specifically mentioned elsewhere. Self-employed builders and contractors will be assigned to group 140.6.

**Managers**. The growing recognition of management as an occupation in itself which is to a certain extent independent of the particular field in which it is exercised, has led to managers being included in specific groups. There are however, exceptions to this. In some fields, mainly services, the title of manager is given to persons with comparatively limited responsibilities and also because in some cases the main activity is that of an occupation other than management. Managers of professional activities whose work chiefly comprises maintaining the professional or technical quality of the work done are assigned to the relevant professional or technical group. Therefore such persons as chief accountants, Borough engineers, headmasters and editors are classified within the groups for accountants, civil engineers, teachers and writers respectively.*

**Supervisors/Foremen**. Generally supervisors are classified in separate groups which can be related to the type of work supervised. Where a foreman controls a variety of workers or is identified only by branch of industry he is classified in the group relating to workers n.e.c. most appropriate to the branch of industry. Thus a clothing factory foreman is classified in 101.6 and a food factory foreman is classified in 090.6. Such foremen in the engineering industries are however allocated to -.1 Foremen (engineering and allied trades). Works, general and senior foremen in manufacturing and construction are considered managers and coded accordingly to groups 034.0 and 035.1 respectively.

**Labourers**. The groups 159.1−159.8, 160.1−160.8 assigned to labourers are strictly limited to persons performing occupations requiring little or no training or experience and for this reason certain groups of persons who have some degree of skill but are returned as labourers, e.g. fitters' labourers, are excluded.
Allocation of these groups is on a strictly industrial basis, thus departing from the general basis of classification elsewhere; the industry concerned is that of the 'establishment'† taken as a whole. This split is purely for convenience and, with the exception that foundry labourers are separated into groups 159.5 and 160.5, the resulting information could also be obtained from a cross-classification by industry.

**Apprentices, articled pupils and learners** are classified to the group appropriate to those whose training is completed. Graduate and student apprentices are classified to the professional occupation for which they are training.

**Armed Forces**. For the various economic activity and social classifications it is intended to keep distinct all uniformed members of the Services and officers are in separate groups from the men. Medical officers and chaplains are accordingly assigned to the groups for Armed Forces officers, 041.0, 042.0.


## Classification of industries

The Industrial Classification for use in the Census of Population will be based on the Standard Industrial Classification.§ A list of the groups to be used in 1981 is given in Appendix D.


## Classification by employment status

The classification by Employment status used in 1970 has been continued, with the exception that the family worker status is no longer separately identified but is included within 'employees n.e.c.'.

---

* For a more extended discussion see *CODOT* vol. 1 pp. 14−15, HMSO 1972
† For definition of 'establishment' see *Standard Industrial Classification* HMSO 1980 page 4 paragraph 23 (a)
§ *Standard Industrial Classification* HMSO 1980

The classification by Employment status divides the 'employee' from the 'self-employed' and further sub-divides these groups as follows:

A. Self-employed
  (1) Without employees
  (2) With employees
    (a) Large establishments
    (b) Small establishments

B. Employees
  (1) Managers
    (a) Large establishments
    (b) Small establishments
  (2) Foremen and Supervisors
    (a) Manual
    (b) Non-manual
  (3) Apprentices, articled pupils, formal trainees
  (4) Employees n.e.c. (not elsewhere classified).

The definitions of the Employment status codes are:

### A. Self-employed

Persons not employed by any person or company and persons working in their own home for an employer (out-workers).

*Note*: As far as practicable all Class II insured persons are included here.

The following, for example, are included:

Proprietors of businesses (including members of partnerships).

Medical practitioners who are principals in the National Health Service and in private practice (but see below).

The following, for example, are excluded:

Directors and Managers of limited companies.

All persons in national and local government and nationalised undertakings.

Medical practitioners in private practice who are also employed as National Health Service consultants.

### (1) Without employees

Persons included above who work without paid assistance.

The following are included:

Out-workers

Members of a partnership without paid employee(s).

### (2) With employees

All self-employed persons not included in (1)

  (a) Large establishments

  Employers (except farmers) whose establishments number 25 or more persons.

  (b) Small establishments

  Other (including all farmers).

### B. Employees

All persons not self-employed.

### (1) Managers

Includes all persons classified to occupation groups 002.5, 005.3, 005.4, 007.1, 007.2, 008.0, 035.1, 036.1−4, 037.1, 039.4, 041.0, 042.0, 043.1−3; all persons not being self-employed classified to occupation groups 002.6, 002.7, 003.1, 005.1, 005.2, 009.1, 009.3, 032.3, 037.2, 038.2−4, 039.1−3, 039.5, 040.0, 044.1−4, 057.1, 057.3, 075.4, 075.5; persons occupied as managers, persons returned as managers and other persons of equivalent status whose occupation code is preceded by an 'M' in the occupation index.

Excludes professional workers classified in groups 001.0, 002.1, 004.1, 009.6, 010.1, 012.2, 012.3, 014.0, 015.1, 015.2, 017.1, 017.3, 018.2, 024.1−3, 025.0, 026.1, 026.2, 027.1, 027.2, 028.1−6, 031.1 even if returned as managers.

    (a) Large establishments

        Managers in establishments, except farms, employing 25 or more persons including all civil servants, local government officials and ships' officers coded as managers, and aircraft captains.

    (b) Small establishments

        Others including farmers, trawler skippers and foresters.

**(2) Foremen and Supervisors**

Persons returned as foremen or equivalent as defined in the notes on coding occupations, and other persons with supervisory functions not equivalent to management, whose occupation code number is preceded by an 'F' in the occupation index.

    (a) Manual supervisors

        Persons as above, supervising manual occupations

    (b) Non-manual supervisors

        Others

**(3) Apprentices and trainees**

    Apprentices

    Articled clerks

    Articled pupils

    Graduate apprentices

    Management trainees

    Student apprentices

    Trainee craftsmen

    Trainee technicians

i.e. persons undergoing training for a period fixed in advance, leading to recognition as a skilled worker or technician and/or to a recognised technical, commercial or professional qualification or management post.

**(4) Employees n.e.c.**

All occupied or retired persons not elsewhere classified.

## Classification by economic position

The Classification by Economic Position divides the economically active from the inactive and provides further sub-division of these groups as follows:

A.  Economically active

    (1) Persons in employment

    (2) Persons out of employment

        (a) Waiting to take up a job already accepted

        (b) Seeking work

        (c) Prevented by temporary sickness from seeking work

B.  Economically inactive

    (1) Permanently sick or disabled

    (2) Housewife

    (3) Wholly retired from employment

    (4) Full time student at an educational establishment not provided by an employer

    (5) Other persons economically inactive

In addition the codes provide the facilities for counting the number of students who were also in employment during the week before Census.

The groups are defined as follows:

### A. Economically active

#### (1) Persons in employment

Persons with a paid job or self-employed or working in a family business. Temporary, part-time, or casual employment is included. Persons absent from their employment due to holidays, strikes, lockouts, short time working or temporary stoppage are regarded as in employment. Persons off work sick are regarded as 'in employment' if their job is waiting for them on their return.

#### (2) Persons out of employment

Persons without a paid job:

    (a) Waiting to take up a job already accepted

    (b) Seeking work

    (c) Prevented by temporary sickness from seeking work

### B. Economically inactive

#### (1) Permanently sick or disabled

Persons, whether or not previously in employment not now seeking employment because of permanent sickness or disability. Persons also included are those who have spent more than six months in a chronic sick or psychiatric hospital and are returned as out of employment.

#### (2) Housewives

Persons engaged entirely in unpaid domestic duties.

#### (3) Retired

Formerly occupied persons who have ceased working are no longer seeking further employment. Females engaged on unpaid domestic duties even though previously employed are treated as 'other economically inactive'.

#### (4) Students in educational establishments

Persons aged 16 and over who are or will be attending full time, during the next term, at an educational establishment not provided by an employer:

    (a) those with a paid job

    (b) those without a paid job

#### (5) Others economically inactive

All persons who have never been in employment and are not now seeking employment, and those who have spent more than six months in a prison and are returned as out of employment. Persons also included are those of independent means or engaged entirely on unpaid domestic duties even though they may have had paid work at some time.

In the 1981 Census the economic position will relate to the week ending 5 April 1981.

## Social and socio-economic classifications

To provide a convenient summary of economic activity information for many social and medical purposes the structure of the two separate classifications, namely by 'Social Class' and by 'Socio-economic group' used in the 1971 Census are retained unchanged. In the allocation of individual occupations changes have been necessitated by the revision of the Classification of Occupations.

### Social Class

Since the 1911 Census it has been customary, for certain analytical purposes, to arrange the large number of groups of the occupational classification into a small number of broad categories called Social Classes* as follows:

---

* The present Social Class grouping follows the same general lines adopted in 1921, 1931 and 1951, although the allocation of occupations to the five groups has varied from Census to Census in accordance with changes in economic conditions and with the intention of preserving the gradient rather than literal continuity. Fuller details of all earlier classifications can be found in the Registrar General's Annual Report, 1911, pp. xl, xli, Decennial Supplement, 1921, Part II, p. viii, Decennial Supplement, 1931, Part IIA, pp. 7, 8, Census 1951, Classification of Occupations, p. vii, Classification of Occupations 1970, p. x, Population Trends 8, pp. 1–7. A paper by Dr. T.H.C. Stevenson, C.B.E., M.D., then Statistical Officer at the General Register Office, and a discussion on the origins of this form of social classification will be found in the *Journal of the Royal Statistical Society*, Volume XCI. (1928), pp. 207–230.

I   **Professional, etc. occupations**
II   **Intermediate occupations**
III   **Skilled occupations**
     (N)  non-manual
     (M)  manual
IV   **Partly skilled occupations**
V   **Unskilled occupations**

The occupation groups included in each of these categories have been selected in such a way as to bring together, so far as is possible, people with similar levels of occupational skill. In general each occupation group is assigned as a whole to one or another social class and no account is taken of differences between individuals in the same occupation group e.g. differences of education or level of remuneration. However persons of a particular employment status within occupation groups are allocated to the appropriate Social Classes as derived by the following rules:

(a) each occupation is given a basic Social Class

(b) persons of foreman status whose basic Social Class is IV or V are allotted to Social Class III

(c) persons of manager status are allocated to Social Class II except for the following:

    Social Class I for group 007.1

    Social Class III for groups 039.4 and 057.3 and if the basic class is IV or V.


**Socio-economic groups**

Classification by socio-economic groups was introduced in 1951 and extensively amended in 1961. The classification aims to bring together people with jobs of similar social and economic status. The allocation of occupied persons to socio-economic groups is determined by considering their employment status and occupation (and industry, though for practical purposes no direct reference is made since it is possible in Great Britain to use classification by occupation as a means of distinguishing effectively those engaged in agriculture).

The socio-economic groups with brief definitions are:

(1) **Employers and managers in central and local government, industry, commerce, etc.—large establishments**

    1.1  Employers in industry, commerce, etc.

        Persons who employ others in non-agricultural enterprises employing 25 or more persons.

    1.2  Managers in central and local government, industry, commerce, etc.

        Persons who generally plan and supervise in non-agricultural enterprises employing 25 or more persons.

(2) **Employers and managers in industry, commerce, etc.—small establishments**

    2.1  Employers in industry, commerce, etc.—small establishments. As in 1.1 but in establishments employing fewer than 25 persons.

    2.2  Managers in industry, commerce, etc.—small establishments. As in 1.2 but in establishments employing fewer than 25 persons.

(3) **Professional workers—self-employed**

Self-employed persons engaged in work normally requiring qualifications of university degree standard.

(4) **Professional workers—employees**

Employees engaged in work normally requiring qualifications of university degree standard.

(5) **Intermediate non-manual workers**

    5.1  Ancillary workers and artists

        Employees engaged in non-manual occupations ancillary to the professions, not normally requiring qualifications of university degree standard; persons engaged in artistic work and not employing others therein. Self-employed nurses, medical auxiliaries, teachers, work study engineers and technicians are included.

5.2   Foremen and supervisors non-manual

Employees (other than managers) engaged in occupations included in group 6, who formally and immediately supervise others engaged in such occupations.

**(6)   Junior non-manual workers**

Employees, not exercising general planning or supervisory powers, engaged in clerical, sales and non-manual communications occupations, excluding those who have additional and formal supervisory functions (these are included in group 5.2).

**(7)   Personal service workers**

Employees engaged in service occupations caring for food, drink, clothing and other personal needs.

**(8)   Foremen and supervisors—manual**

Employees (other than managers) who formally and immediately supervise others engaged in manual occupations, whether or not themselves engaged in such occupations.

**(9)   Skilled manual workers**

Employees engaged in manual occupations which require considerable and specific skills.

**(10)   Semi-skilled manual workers**

Employees engaged in manual occupations which require slight but specific skills.

**(11)   Unskilled manual workers**

Other employees engaged in manual occupations.

**(12)   Own account workers (other than professional)**

Self-employed persons engaged in any trade, personal service or manual occupation not normally requiring training of university degree standard and having no employees other than family workers.

**(13)   Farmers—employers and managers**

Persons who own, rent or manage farms, market gardens or forests, employing people other than family workers in the work of the enterprise.

**(14)   Farmers—own account**

Persons who own or rent farms, market gardens or forests and having no employees other than family workers.

**(15)   Agricultural workers**

Persons engaged in tending crops, animals, game or forests, or operating agricultural or forestry machinery.

**(16)   Members of armed forces**

**(17)   Inadequately described and not stated occupations**


**Classification by size of establishment**

It is not practicable to include in the Census questions on the degree of responsibility exercised by employers and managers. An indirect, and necessarily rather crude distinction between greater and lesser responsibility is therefore provided by further classifying employers and managers by the size of the establishment in which they work. All civil servants, local authority officials and ships' officers coded as managers and aircraft captains are conventionally regarded as managers in large establishments. Farmers, trawler skippers, and foresters are conventionally regarded as working in small establishments.


**Detailed allocation**

The detailed allocation of the occupation/employment status groups to the social class and socio-economic groups and details of the socio-economic groups and social classes in terms of the occupation and employment status groups are shown in Appendix B.

**Application of the socio-economic classification to the whole population**
The 17 socio-economic groups detailed above may be applied to the economically active or retired population either combined or independently. For some purposes, however, it is more appropriate to treat retired persons as a separate socio-economic group and assign only the economically active population to the individual groups.
If it is desired to extend the socio-economic groups to include the remaining categories of the economically inactive, the following groups are recommended:

    (1)   **Inactive residents in non-private households**

    (2)   **Students and children under 16**

    (3)   **Other economically inactive persons**

**Socio-economic class**
The classifications by Socio-economic group and by Social Class are not interconvertible. In order to meet a need for a classification from which both Socio-economic group and Social Class can be derived some tables in the 1981 Census series will be produced for a series of groups formed from a complete cross-classification of Socio-economic group by Social Class. For convenience this classification is referred to as the 'Socio-economic class' classification and details are shown in Appendix C.

**European Economic Community Socio-economic status groups**
In order to increase the comparability of international statistics the EEC has devised a Socio-economic classification based on the International Standard Classification of Occupations* and employment status. This classification will be used by OPCS for the purpose of international comparison. Details of this classification and its relationship to the OPCS Classification of Occupations are given in Appendix E.

---

* International Labour Office. *International Standard Classification of Occupations, Geneva* 1968

# Summary of the OPCS 1980 occupation groups with condensed KOS headings

**Order  1   Professional and related supporting management; senior national and local government managers**

001   Judges, barristers, advocates, solicitors
  0   Judges, barristers, advocates, solicitors

002   Accountants, valuers, finance specialists
  1   Chartered and certified accountants
  2   Cost and works accountants
  3   Estimators
  4   Valuers, claims assessors
  5   Financial managers
  6   Underwriters, brokers, investment analysts
  7   Taxation experts

003   Personnel and industrial relations managers; O and M, work study and operational research officers
  1   Personnel and industrial relations officers
  2   O and M, work study and OR officers

004   Economists, statisticians, systems analysts, computer programmers
  1   Economists, statisticians, actuaries
  2   Systems analysts, computer programmers

005   Marketing, sales, advertising, public relations and purchasing managers
  1   Marketing and sales managers and executives
  2   Advertising and PR executives
  3   Buyers (retail trade)
  4   Buyers and purchasing officers (not retail)

006   Statutory and other inspectors
  1   Environmental health officers
  2   Building inspectors
  3   Inspectors (statutory and similar)

007   General administrators—national government
  1   General administrators—national government (Assistant Secretary level and above)
  2   General administrators—national government (HEO to Senior Principal level)

008   Local government officers (administrative and executive functions)
  0   Local government officers (administrative and executive functions)

009   All other professional and related supporting management and administration
  1   Company secretaries
  2   Officials of trade associations, trade unions, professional bodies and charities
  3   Property and estate managers
  4   Librarians, information officers
  5   Legal service and related occupations
  6   Management consultants
  7   Managers' personal assistants
  8   Professional workers and related supporting management and administration n.e.c.

---

Note: n.e.c. = not elsewhere classified

**Order 2 Professional and related in education, welfare and health**

010 Teachers in higher education
  1 University academic staff
  2 Teachers in establishments for further and higher education

011 Teachers n.e.c.
  0 Teachers n.e.c.

012 Vocational and industrial trainers, education officers, social and behavioural scientists
  1 Vocational and industrial trainers
  2 Education officers, school inspectors
  3 Social and behavioural scientists

013 Welfare workers
  1 Matrons, houseparents
  2 Playgroup leaders
  3 Welfare occupations n.e.c.

014 Clergy, ministers of religion
  0 Clergy, ministers of religion

015 Medical and dental practitioners
  1 Medical practitioners
  2 Dental practitioners

016 Nurse administrators, nurses
  0 Nurse administrators, nurses

017 Pharmacists, radiographers, therapists n.e.c.
  1 Pharmacists
  2 Medical radiographers
  3 Ophthalmic and dispensing opticians
  4 Physiotherapists
  5 Chiropodists
  6 Therapists n.e.c.

018 All other professional and related in education, welfare and health
  1 Medical technicians, dental auxiliaries
  2 Veterinarians
  3 Driving instructors (not HGV)
  4 Professional and related in education, welfare and health n.e.c.

**Order 3 Literary, artistic and sports**

019 Authors, writers, journalists
  0 Authors, writers, journalists

020 Artists, designers, window dressers
  1 Artists, commercial artists
  2 Industrial designers (not clothing)
  3 Clothing designers
  4 Window dressers

021 Actors, musicians, entertainers, stage managers
  1 Actors, entertainers, singers, stage managers
  2 Musicians

022 Photographers, cameramen, sound and vision equipment operators
  1 Photographers, cameramen
  2 Sound and vision equipment operators

Note: n.e.c. = not elsewhere classified

023   All other literary, artistic and sports
   1   Professional sportsmen, sports officials
   2   Literary, artistic and sports workers n.e.c.

**Order  4  Professional and related in science, engineering, technology and similar fields**

024   Scientists, physicists, mathematicians
   1   Biological scientists, biochemists
   2   Chemical scientists
   3   Physical and geological scientists, mathematicians

025   Civil, structural, municipal, mining and quarrying engineers
   0   Civil, structural, municipal, mining and quarrying engineers

026   Mechanical and aeronautical engineers
   1   Mechanical and aeronautical engineers
   2   Design and development engineers (mechanical)

027   Electrical and electronic engineers
   1   Electrical engineers
   2   Electronic engineers

028   Engineers and technologists n.e.c.
   1   Chemical engineers
   2   Production engineers
   3   Planning and quality control engineers
   4   Engineers n.e.c.
   5   Metallurgists
   6   Technologists n.e.c.

029   Draughtsmen
   0   Draughtsmen

030   Laboratory and engineering technicians, technician engineers
   1   Laboratory technicians
   2   Engineering technicians, technician engineers

031   Architects, town planners, quantity, building and land surveyors
   1   Architects, town planners
   2   Quantity surveyors
   3   Building, land and mining surveyors

032   Officers (ships and aircraft), air traffic planners and controllers
   1   Aircraft flight deck officers
   2   Air traffic planners and controllers
   3   Deck, engineering and radio officers and pilots, ship

033   Professional and related in science, engineering and other technologies and similar fields
       n.e.c.
   1   Architectural and town planning technicians
   2   Building and civil engineering technicians
   3   Technical and related workers n.e.c.

**Order  5  Managerial**

034   Production, works and maintenance managers, works foremen
   0   Production, works and maintenance managers, works foremen

035   Site and other managers, agents and clerks of works, general foremen (building and civil
       engineering)
   1   Managers in building and contracting
   2   Clerks of works

---

Note: n.e.c. = not elsewhere classified

036 Managers in transport, warehousing, public utilities and mining
  1 Managers in mining and public utilities
  2 Transport managers
  3 Stores controllers
  4 Managers in warehousing and materials handling n.e.c.

037 Office managers
  1 Credit controllers
  2 Office managers n.e.c.

038 Managers in wholesale and retail distribution
  1 Garage proprietors
  2 Butchers (managers and proprietors)
  3 Fishmongers (managers and proprietors)
  4 Other proprietors and managers (sales)

039 Managers of hotels, clubs, etc., and in entertainment and sport
  1 Hotel and residential club managers
  2 Publicans
  3 Restaurateurs
  4 Club stewards
  5 Entertainment and sports managers

040 Farmers, horticulturists, farm managers
  0 Farmers, horticulturists, farm managers

041 Officers, UK armed forces
  0 Officers, UK armed forces

042 Officers, foreign and Commonwealth armed forces
  0 Officers, foreign and Commonwealth armed forces

043 Senior police, prison and fire service officers
  1 Prison officers (chief officers and above)
  2 Police officers (inspectors and above)
  3 Fire service officers

044 All other managers
  1 Proprietors and managers, service flats, holiday flats, caravan sites, etc.
  2 Managers of laundry and dry cleaning receiving shops
  3 Hairdressers' and barbers' managers and proprietors
  4 Managers n.e.c.

**Order 6 Clerical and related**

045 Supervisors of clerks, civil service executive officers
  1 Civil service executive officers
    Supervisors of—
  2   Stores and despatch clerks
  3   Tracers, drawing office assistants
  4   Other clerks and cashiers (not retail)
  5   Retail shop cashiers, check-out and cash and wrap operators

046 Clerks
  1 Stores and despatch clerks
  2 Tracers, drawing office assistants
  3 Other clerks and cashiers (not retail)

047 Retail shop cashiers, check-out and cash and wrap operators
  0 Retail shop cashiers, check-out and cash and wrap operators

---

Note: n.e.c. = not elsewhere classified

048 Supervisors of typists, office machine operators, telephonists, etc.
  Supervisors of—
 1  Typists, shorthand writers, secretaries
 2  Office machine operators
 3  Telephone operators
 4  Radio and telegraph operators

049 Secretaries, shorthand typists, receptionists
 1 Receptionists
 2 Typists, shorthand writers, secretaries

050 Office machine operators
 0 Office machine operators

051 Telephonists, radio and telegraph operators
 1 Telephonist receptionists
 2 Telephone operators
 3 Radio and telegraph operators

052 Supervisors of postmen, mail sorters, messengers
  Supervisors of—
 1  Postmen, mail sorters
 2  Messengers

053 Postmen, mail sorters, messengers
 1 Postmen, mail sorters
 2 Messengers

**Order 7 Selling**

054 Sales supervisors
  Supervisors of—
 1  Shop salesmen and assistants
 2  Petrol pump, forecourt attendants
 3  Roundsmen, van salesmen

055 Salesmen, sales assistants, shop assistants, shelf fillers, petrol pump, forecourt attendants
 1 Shop salesmen and assistants
 2 Shelf fillers
 3 Petrol pump, forecourt attendants

056 Roundsmen, van salesmen
 0 Roundsmen, van salesmen

057 Sales representatives and agents
 1 Importers, exporters, commodity brokers
 2 Market and street traders and assistants
 3 Scrap dealers, general dealers, rag and bone merchants
 4 Credit agents, collector salesmen
 5 Sales representatives
 6 Sales representatives (property and services), other agents

**Order 8 Security and protective service**

058 NCOs and other ranks, UK armed forces
 0 NCOs and other ranks, UK armed forces

059 NCOs and other ranks, foreign and Commonwealth armed forces
 0 NCOs and other ranks, foreign and Commonwealth armed forces

---

Note: n.e.c. = not elsewhere classified

060 Supervisors (police sergeants, fire fighting and related)
  1  Police sergeants
  2  Fire service supervisors
  3  Prison service principal officers
     Supervisors of—
  4    Security guards and officers, patrolmen, watchmen
  5    Traffic wardens
  6    Security and protective service workers n.e.c.

061 Policemen, firemen, prison officers
  1  Policemen (below sergeant)
  2  Firemen
  3  Prison officers (below principal officer)

062 Other security and protective service workers
  1  Security guards and officers, patrolmen, watchmen
  2  Traffic wardens
  3  Security and protective service workers n.e.c.

**Order 9 Catering, cleaning, hairdressing and other personal service**

063 Catering supervisors
     Supervisors of—
  1    Chefs, cooks
  2    Waiters, waitresses
  3    Barmen, barmaids
  4    Counter hands, assistants

064 Chefs, cooks
  0  Chefs, cooks

065 Waiters and bar staff
  1  Waiters, waitresses
  2  Barmen, barmaids

066 Counter hands, assistants, kitchen porters, hands
  1  Counter hands, assistants
  2  Kitchen porters, hands

067 Supervisors—housekeeping and related
  1  Housekeepers (non-domestic)
     Supervisors of—
  2    Other domestic and school helpers
  3    Travel stewards and attendants
  4    Hospital porters
  5    Hotel porters
  6    Ambulancemen
  7    Hospital, ward orderlies

068 Domestic staff and school helpers
  1  Domestic housekeepers
  2  Nursery nurses
  3  Other domestic and school helpers

069 Travel stewards and attendants, hospital and hotel porters
  1  Travel stewards and attendants
  2  Hospital porters
  3  Hotel porters

Note: n.e.c. = not elsewhere classified

070 Ambulancemen, hospital orderlies
1 Ambulancemen
2 Hospital, ward orderlies

071 Supervisors, foremen—caretaking, cleaning and related
Supervisors of—
1 Caretakers
2 Cleaners, window cleaners, chimney sweeps, road sweepers
3 Railway stationmen
4 Lift and car park attendants

072 Caretakers, road sweepers and other cleaners
1 Caretakers
2 Cleaners, window cleaners, chimney sweeps, road sweepers

073 Hairdressing supervisors
0 Hairdressing supervisors

074 Hairdressers, barbers
0 Hairdressers, barbers

075 All other in catering, cleaning and other personal service
1 Railway stationmen
2 Lift and car park attendants
3 Launderers, dry cleaners, pressers
4 Undertakers
5 Bookmakers, betting shop managers
6 Service workers n.e.c.

**Order 10   Farming, fishing and related**

076 Foremen—farming, horticulture, forestry
1 Farm foremen
2 Horticultural foremen
3 Foremen gardeners and groundsmen
4 Agricultural machinery foremen
5 Forestry foremen
6 Other foremen in farming and related

077 Farm workers
0 Farm workers

078 Horticultural workers, gardeners, groundsmen
1 Horticultural workers
2 Gardeners, groundsmen

079 Agricultural machinery drivers, operators
0 Agricultural machinery drivers, operators

080 Forestry workers
0 Forestry workers

081 Supervisors, mates—fishing
0 Supervisors, mates—fishing

082 Fishermen
0 Fishermen

083 All other in farming and related
0 All other in farming and related

---

Note: n.e.c. = not elsewhere classified

**Order 11  Materials processing; making and repairing (excluding metal and electrical)**

084  Foremen—tannery and leather (including leather substitutes) working
      Foremen—
  1    Tannery production workers
  2    Shoe repairers
  3    Leather cutters and sewers, footwear lasters, makers, finishers
  4    Other making and repairing, leather

085  Tannery and leather (including leather substitutes) workers
  1  Tannery production workers
  2  Shoe repairers
  3  Leather cutters and sewers, footwear lasters, makers, finishers

086  Foremen—textile processing
      Foremen—
  1    Preparatory fibre processors
  2    Spinners, doublers, twisters
  3    Winders, reelers
  4    Warp preparers
  5    Weavers
  6    Knitters
  7    Bleachers, dyers, finishers
  8    Menders, darners
  9    Other material processing, textiles

087  Textile workers
  1  Preparatory fibre processors
  2  Spinners, doublers, twisters
  3  Winders, reelers
  4  Warp preparers
  5  Weavers
  6  Knitters
  7  Bleachers, dyers, finishers
  8  Menders, darners

088  Foremen—chemical processing
  0  Foremen—chemical processing

089  Chemical, gas and petroleum process plant operators
  0  Chemical, gas and petroleum process plant operators

090  Foremen—food and drink processing
      Foremen—
  1    Bakers, flour confectioners
  2    Butchers, meat cutters
  3    Fishmongers, poultry dressers
  4    Brewery and vinery process workers
      Other material processing—
  5      Bakery and confectionery workers
  6      Food and drink n.e.c.

091  Bakers, flour confectioners
  0  Bakers, flour confectioners

092  Butchers
  1  Butchers, meat cutters
  2  Fishmongers, poultry dressers

---

Note: n.e.c. = not elsewhere classified

093    Foremen—paper and board making and paper products
       Foremen—
   1       Paper, paperboard and leatherboard workers
   2       Bookbinders and finishers
   3       Cutting and slitting machine operators (paper and paper products making)
   4       Other material processing, wood and paper
   5       Other making and repairing, paper goods and printing

094    Paper, board and paper product makers, bookbinders
   1    Paper, paperboard and leatherboard workers
   2    Bookbinders and finishers
   3    Cutting and slitting machine operators (paper and paper products making)

095    Foremen—glass, ceramics, rubber, plastics, etc.
       Foremen—
   1       Glass and ceramics furnacemen, kilnsetters
   2       Glass formers and shapers, finishers, decorators
   3       Casters and other pottery makers
   4       Rubber process workers, moulding machine operators, tyre builders
   5       Calendar and extruding machine operators, moulders (plastics)
   6       Man-made fibre makers
   7       Washers, screeners and crushers in mines and quarries
           Other making and repairing—
   8           Glass and ceramics
   9           Rubber
  10           Plastics

096    Glass and ceramics furnacemen and workers
   1    Glass and ceramics furnacemen, kilnsetters
   2    Glass formers and shapers, finishers, decorators
   3    Casters and other pottery makers

097    Rubber and plastics workers
   1    Rubber process workers, moulding machine operators, tyre builders
   2    Calendar and extruding machine operators, moulders (plastics)

098    All other in processing materials (other than metal)
   1    Man-made fibre makers
   2    Brewery and vinery process workers
   3    Washers, screeners and crushers in mines and quarries
        Other material processing—
   4       Textiles
   5       Bakery and confectionery workers
   6       Tobacco
   7       Food and drink n.e.c.
   8       Wood and paper
   9       All other (excluding metal) n.e.c.

099    Foremen—printing
       Foremen—
   1       Compositors
   2       Electrotypers, stereotypers, printing plate and cylinder preparers
   3       Printing machine minders and assistants
   4       Screen and block printers
   5       Printers (so described)

---

Note: n.e.c. = not elsewhere classified

100 Printing workers, screen and block printers
  1 Compositors
  2 Electrotypers, stereotypers, printing plate and cylinder preparers
  3 Printing machine minders and assistants
  4 Screen and block printers
  5 Printers (so described)

101 Foremen—textile materials working
    Foremen—
  1 Tailors, tailoresses, dressmakers
  2 Clothing cutters, milliners, furriers
  3 Sewers, embroiderers
  4 Coach trimmers, upholsterers, mattress makers
  5 Carpet fitters
  6 Other making and repairing, clothing and related products

102 Tailors, dressmakers and other clothing workers
  1 Tailors, tailoresses, dressmakers
  2 Clothing cutters, milliners, furriers
  3 Sewers, embroiderers

103 Coach trimmers, upholsterers, mattress makers
  0 Coach trimmers, upholsterers, mattress makers

104 Foremen—woodworking
    Foremen—
  1 Carpenters, joiners
  2 Cabinet makers
  3 Case and box makers
  4 Pattern makers (moulds)
  5 Sawyers, veneer cutters, woodworking machinists
  6 Other making and repairing, wood

105 Woodworkers, pattern makers
  1 Carpenters, joiners
  2 Cabinet makers
  3 Case and box makers
  4 Pattern makers (moulds)

106 Sawyers, veneer cutters, woodworking machinists
  0 Sawyers, veneer cutters, woodworking machinists

107 All other in making and repairing (excluding metal and electrical)
  1 Labourers and mates to woodworking craftsmen
  2 Dental technicians
  3 Carpet fitters
  4 Musical instrument makers, piano tuners
    Other making and repairing—
  5 Glass and ceramics
  6 Wood
  7 Leather
  8 Clothing and related products
  9 Paper goods and printing
  10 Rubber
  11 Plastics
  12 All other (excluding metal and electrical) n.e.c.

---

Note: n.e.c. = not elsewhere classified

**Order 12   Processing, making, repairing and related (metal and electrical)**

108   Foremen—metal making and treating
    Foremen—
  1    Furnace operating occupations (metal)
  2    Rollermen
  3    Smiths, forgemen
  4    Metal drawers
  5    Moulders, coremakers, die casters
  6    Electroplaters
  7    Annealers, hardeners, temperers (metal)
  8    Galvanizers, tin platers, dip platers
  9    Metal making and treating workers n.e.c.

109   Furnacemen (metal), rollermen, smiths, forgemen
  1    Furnace operating occupations (metal)
  2    Rollermen
  3    Smiths, forgemen

110   Metal drawers, moulders, die casters, electroplaters, annealers
  1    Metal drawers
  2    Moulders, coremakers, die casters
  3    Electroplaters
  4    Annealers, hardeners, temperers (metal)

111   Foremen—engineering machining
    Foremen—
  1    Press and machine tool setters
  2    Centre lathe turners
  3    Machine tool setter operators
  4    Machine tool operators
  5    Press, stamping and automatic machine operators
  6    Metal polishers
  7    Fettlers, dressers
  8    Shot blasters

112   Press and machine tool setter operators and operators, turners
  1    Press and machine tool setters
  2    Centre lathe turners
  3    Machine tool setter operators
  4    Machine tool operators

113   Machine attendants, minders, press and stamping machine operators, metal polishers, fettlers, dressers
  1    Press, stamping and automatic machine operators
  2    Metal polishers
  3    Fettlers, dressers

114   Foremen—production fitting (metal)
    Foremen—
  1    Tool makers, tool fitters, markers-out
  2    Precision instrument makers and repairers
  3    Watch and chronometer makers and repairers
  4    Metal working production fitters and fitter/machinists
  5    Motor mechanics, auto engineers
  6    Maintenance fitters (aircraft engines)
  7    Office machinery mechanics

115   Tool makers, tool fitters, markers-out
  0    Tool makers, tool fitters, markers-out

Note: n.e.c. = not elsewhere classified

116 Instrument and watch and clock makers and repairers
   1   Precision instrument makers and repairers
   2   Watch and chronometer makers and repairers

117 Metal working production fitters and fitter/machinists
   0   Metal working production fitters and fitter/machinists

118 Motor vehicle and aircraft mechanics
   1   Motor mechanics, auto engineers
   2   Maintenance fitters (aircraft engines)

119 Office machinery mechanics
   0   Office machinery mechanics

120 Foremen—production fitting and wiring (electrical)
      Foremen—
   1      Production fitters (electrical, electronic)
   2      Electricians, electrical maintenance fitters
   3      Plant operators and attendants n.e.c.
   4      Telephone fitters
   5      Cable jointers, linesmen
   6      Radio and TV mechanics
   7      Other electronic maintenance engineers

121 Production fitters, electricians, electricity power plant operators, switchboard attendants
   1   Production fitters (electrical, electronic)
   2   Electricians, electrical maintenance fitters
   3   Electrical engineers (so described)
   4   Plant operators and attendants n.e.c.

122 Telephone fitters, cable jointers, linesmen
   1   Telephone fitters
   2   Cable jointers, linesmen

123 Radio, TV and other electronic maintenance fitters and mechanics
   1   Radio and TV mechanics
   2   Other electronic maintenance engineers

124 Foremen—metal working, pipes, sheets, structures
      Foremen—
   1      Plumbers, heating and ventilating fitters, gas fitters
   2      Sheet metal workers
   3      Metal plate workers, shipwrights, riveters
   4      Steel erectors, benders, fixers
   5      Scaffolders, stagers
   6      Welders
   7      Riggers

125 Plumbers, heating and ventilating fitters, gas fitters
   0   Plumbers, heating and ventilating fitters, gas fitters

126 Sheet metal workers, platers, shipwrights, riveters, etc.
   1   Sheet metal workers
   2   Metal plate workers, shipwrights, riveters

127 Steel erectors, scaffolders, steel benders, fixers
   1   Steel erectors, benders, fixers
   2   Scaffolders, stagers

---

Note: n.e.c. = not elsewhere classified

128 Welders
 0 Welders

129 Foremen—other processing, making and repairing (metal and electrical)
    Foremen—
  1   Goldsmiths, silversmiths, precious stone workers
  2   Engravers, etchers (printing)
  3   Coach and vehicle body builders
  4   Oilers, greasers, lubricators
  5   Electronics wiremen
  6   Coil winders

130 Goldsmiths, silversmiths, etc., engravers, etchers
  1   Goldsmiths, silversmiths, precious stone workers
  2   Engravers, etchers (printing)

131 All other in processing, making and repairing (metal and electrical)
  1   Coach and vehicle body builders
  2   Galvanizers, tin platers, dip platers
  3   Metal making and treating workers n.e.c.
  4   Oilers, greasers, lubricators
  5   Riggers
  6   Electronics wiremen
  7   Coil winders
  8   Shot blasters
  9   Other metal, jewellery, electrical production workers

  —
  1   Foremen (engineering and allied trades)
  2   Trainee craftsmen (engineering and allied trades)

**Order 13   Painting, repetitive assembling, product inspecting, packaging and related**

132 Foremen—painting and similar coating
    Foremen—
  1   Pottery decorators
  2   Coach painters (so described)
  3   Other spray painters
  4   Painters and decorators n.e.c., french polishers

133 Painters, decorators, french polishers
  1   Pottery decorators
  2   Coach painters (so described)
  3   Other spray painters
  4   Painters and decorators n.e.c., french polishers

134 Foremen—product assembling (repetitive)
    Foremen assemblers—
  1   Electrical, electronic
  2   Instruments
  3   Vehicles and other metal goods
  4   Paper production, processing and printing
  5   Plastics goods

135 Repetitive assemblers (metal and electrical goods)
  1   Assemblers (electrical, electronic)
  2   Instrument assemblers
  3   Assemblers (vehicles and other metal goods)

---

Note: n.e.c. = not elsewhere classified

136 Foremen—product inspection and packaging
     Foremen inspectors, viewers, examiners—
  1    Metal, electrical goods
  2    Textiles
  3    Food
  4    Rubber goods
  5    Plastics goods
  6    Woodwork
     Foremen—
  7    Packers, bottlers, canners, fillers
  8    Laboratory assistants
  9    Inspectors, sorters in paper production, processing and printing
 10    Weighers
 11    Graders, sorters, selectors n.e.c.

137 Inspectors, viewers, testers, packers, bottlers, etc.
  1  Inspectors, viewers (metal, electrical goods)
  2  Packers, bottlers, canners, fillers

138 All other in painting, repetitive assembling, product inspection, packaging and related
  1  Laboratory assistants
     Inspectors, viewers, examiners—
  2    Textiles
  3    Food
  4    Rubber goods
  5    Plastics goods
  6    Woodwork
  7  Inspectors, sorters in paper production, processing and printing
  8  Assemblers in paper production, processing and printing
  9  Assemblers (plastics goods)
 10  Weighers
 11  Graders, sorters, selectors n.e.c.
 12  Painting, assembling and related occupations n.e.c.

## Order 14  Construction, mining and related not identified elsewhere

139 Foremen—building and civil engineering n.e.c.
     Foremen—
  1    Bricklayers, tile setters
  2    Masons, stone cutters
  3    Plasterers
  4    Roofers, glaziers
  5    Handymen, general building workers
  6    Railway lengthmen
  7    Road surfacers, concreters
  8    Roadmen
  9    Paviors, kerb layers
 10    Sewage plant attendants
 11    Mains and service layers, pipe jointers
 12    Construction workers n.e.c.

140 Building and construction workers
  1  Bricklayers, tile setters
  2  Masons, stone cutters
  3  Plasterers
  4  Roofers, glaziers
  5  Handymen, general building workers
  6  Builders (so described)

---

Note: n.e.c. = not elsewhere classified

141 Concreters, road surfacers, railway lengthmen
  1  Railway lengthmen
  2  Road surfacers, concreters
  3  Roadmen
  4  Paviors, kerb layers

142 Sewage plant attendants, sewermen (maintenance), mains and service layers, pipe jointers
     (gas, water, drainage, oil), inspectors (water supply), turncocks
  1  Sewage plant attendants
  2  Mains and service layers, pipe jointers

143 Civil engineering labourers, craftsmen's mates and other builders' labourers n.e.c.
  1  Craftsmen's mates
  2  Building and civil engineering labourers

144 Foremen/deputies—coalmining
  0  Foremen/deputies—coalmining

145 Face-trained coalmining workers
  0  Face-trained coalmining workers

146 All other in construction, mining, quarrying, well drilling and related n.e.c.
  1  Miners (not coal), quarrymen, well drillers
  2  Construction workers n.e.c.

**Order 15   Transport operating, materials moving and storing and related**

147 Foremen—ships, lighters and other vessels
  0  Foremen—ships, lighters and other vessels

148 Deck, engine-room hands, bargemen, lightermen, boatmen
  0  Deck, engine-room hands, bargemen, lightermen, boatmen

149 Foremen—rail transport operating
    Foremen—
  1    Railway guards
  2    Signalmen and crossing keepers, railway
  3    Shunters, pointsmen
  4    Other foremen rail transport

150 Rail transport operating staff
  1  Drivers, motormen, secondmen, railway engines
  2  Railway guards
  3  Signalmen and crossing keepers, railway
  4  Shunters, pointsmen

151 Foremen—road transport operating, bus inspectors
  1  Bus inspectors
    Foremen—
  2    Drivers of road goods vehicles
  3    Other foremen road transport

152 Bus, coach, lorry drivers, etc.
  1  Bus and coach drivers
  2  Drivers of road goods vehicles
  3  Other motor drivers

153 Bus conductors, drivers' mates
  1  Bus conductors
  2  Drivers' mates

---

Note: n.e.c. = not elsewhere classified

154 Foremen—civil engineering plant operating, materials handling equipment operating
    Foremen—
  1    Mechanical plant drivers, operators (earth moving and civil engineering)
  2    Crane drivers, operators
  3    Fork lift, mechanical truck drivers
  4    Slingers

155 Mechanical plant, fork lift, mechanical truck drivers, crane drivers, operators
  1  Mechanical plant drivers, operators (earth moving and civil engineering)
  2  Crane drivers, operators
  3  Fork lift, mechanical truck drivers

156 Foremen—materials moving and storing
    Foremen—
  1    Storekeepers, warehousemen
  2    Stevedores, dockers
  3    Goods porters
  4    Refuse collectors, dustmen

157 Storekeepers, stevedores, warehouse, market and other goods porters
  1  Storekeepers, warehousemen
  2  Stevedores, dockers
  3  Goods porters
  4  Refuse collectors, dustmen

158 All other in transport operating, materials moving and storing and related n.e.c.
  1  Slingers
  2  Workers in transport operating, materials moving and storing and related n.e.c.

**Order 16  Miscellaneous**
159 Foremen—miscellaneous
    Foremen—
    Labourers and unskilled workers n.e.c.—
  1    Textiles (not textile goods)
  2    Chemicals and allied trades
  3    Coke ovens and gas works
  4    Glass and ceramics
  5    Foundries in engineering and allied trades
  6    Engineering and allied trades
  7    Coal mines
  8    Other
  9  Boiler operators

160 General labourers
    Labourers and unskilled workers n.e.c.—
  1    Textiles (not textile goods)
  2    Chemicals and allied trades
  3    Coke ovens and gas works
  4    Glass and ceramics
  5    Foundries in engineering and allied trades
  6    Engineering and allied trades
  7    Coal mines
  8    Other

161 All other in miscellaneous occupations n.e.c.
  1  Boiler operators
  2  All other in miscellaneous occupations n.e.c.

**Order 17  Inadequately described and not stated**
  —
  1  Inadequately described occupations
  2  Occupations not stated

Note: n.e.c. = not elsewhere classified

# Occupation groups with short descriptions of contents and CODOT definitions

Please note that the CODOT occupations with numbers ending in .98, trainees, have been omitted from these definitions (see item Apprentices, articled pupils and learners on page vii). The CODOT equivalent of KOS group 002 (i.e. CODOT unit group 002 except 002.65) has been omitted because its individual occupations are divided between groups under condensed KOS headings 034–040 and 044 as appropriate.


**001.0  Judges, barristers, advocates, solicitors**
Persons qualified as barristers, solicitors or advocates (Scotland) drawing up legal documents, giving legal advice, pleading in court, presiding over judicial proceedings.
CODOT
021, 022


**002.1  Chartered and certified accountants**
Persons with professional qualifications performing accountancy services; auditors and assistant auditors in the Department of the Environment. Local authority treasurers and investment advisers are excluded and classified in 002.5 and 002.6 respectively.
CODOT
032.10 pt. Remainder in 002.5
032.99


**002.2  Cost and works accountants**
Persons with professional qualifications performing accountancy duties that assist management in the planning and control of an undertaking's income and expenditure. Qualified management accountants are included.
CODOT
032.20


**002.3  Estimators**
Persons calculating probable costs of projects and products, including rates and charges officers (transport).
CODOT
033.00 pt., 033.99 pt. Remainders in 002.4
033.10, 033.20, 033.30, 033.40


**002.4  Valuers, claims assessors**
Persons assessing values of real and other property; investigating, assessing liability and calculating monetary settlements in respect of insurance claims and marine losses. Rating and valuation surveyors, rent officers and Inland Revenue examiners are included.
CODOT
033.00 pt., 033.99 pt. Remainders in 002.3
033.50, 033.60, 033.70


**002.5  Financial managers**
Persons dealing with the financial aspects of a company. Local authority treasurers, trust officers and managers of merchant banks are included.
CODOT
032.00
032.10 pt. Remainder in 002.1
034.40
034.99 pt. Remainder in 002.6


**002.6  Underwriters, brokers, investment analysts**
Persons dealing in stocks and shares and bills of exchange, advising on investment and insurance; underwriting insurance. Advance advisers (banking), foreign exchange brokers and stockbrokers' attachés are included.
CODOT
034 pt. Excludes—034.40, 034.99 pt. included in 002.5


**002.7  Taxation experts**
Persons advising on tax matters. Inspectors of taxes are included.
CODOT
039.40, 039.50


**003.1  Personnel and industrial relations officers**
Persons administering personnel and industrial relations policies. Conciliation officers are included.
CODOT
041


**003.2  O and M, work study and OR officers**
Persons advising on and implementing methods to improve the efficient and economic use of manpower, materials, equipment and other resources, including organisation and methods officers and operational research officers. Safety officers, progress engineers and work study assistants are excluded and classified in 013.3, 028.3 and 046.3 respectively.
CODOT
042

**004.1  Economists, statisticians, actuaries**
Persons working in economic, statistical and actuarial specialist occupations.
CODOT
043

**004.2  Systems analysts, computer programmers**
Persons planning and controlling computer installations; developing procedures and preparing programmes for the processing of data automatically. Systems engineers are included.
CODOT
044

**005.1  Marketing and sales managers and executives**
Persons determining and implementing sales policy; executives in charge of headquarters' sales organisation in industry, commerce and services. Persons managing local teams of sales representatives such as field sales managers, area managers and regional managers are excluded and classified in 057.5.
CODOT
051.05, 051.10, 051.15

**005.2  Advertising and PR executives**
Persons planning and organising advertising campaigns and similar activities and promoting the public relations of an organisation.
CODOT
051 pt. Excludes—051.05, 051.10, 051.15

**005.3  Buyers (retail trade)**
Persons buying merchandise from manufacturers, importers, wholesalers and other sources for resale through retail distribution.
CODOT
061.00 pt., 061.99 pt. Remainders in 005.4
061.10

**005.4  Buyers and purchasing officers (not retail)**
Persons buying merchandise, materials, equipment and other items and services on behalf of an industrial, commercial or public undertaking, or for wholesale distribution.
CODOT
061 pt. Excludes—061.00 pt., 061.10, 061.99 pt. included in 005.3

**006.1  Environmental health officers**
Persons working as environmental health officers.
CODOT
064.05

**006.2  Building inspectors**
Persons inspecting plans and buildings to ensure compliance with regulations.
CODOT
064.30

**006.3  Inspectors (statutory and similar)**
Persons undertaking investigations authorised by Acts, orders, regulations, etc., including inspectors of factories, public utilities, trading standards; Customs and Excise officers, driving examiners, immigration officers, ships' surveyors, water bailiffs. Housing and planning inspectors, inspectors of schools and traffic wardens are excluded and classified in 009.5, 012.2 and 062.2 respectively.
CODOT
064 pt. Excludes—064.05, 064.30

**007.1  General administrators—national government (Assistant Secretary level and above)**
Persons of Assistant Secretary or equivalent rank and above in the Civil Service; Members of Parliament not classifiable elsewhere and foreign and Commonwealth diplomatic representatives. Inspectors of taxes are excluded and classified in 002.7.
CODOT
001 pt. Excludes—001.40 included in 008.0
002.65
069.20 pt. Remainder in 007.2

**007.2  General administrators—national government (HEO to Senior Principal level)**
Persons returned as senior principal, principal, senior and higher executive officers or equivalent rank in the Civil Service. Managers of government Job Centres and Social Security offices are included. Government service intelligence officers and managers of government training centres are excluded and classified in 009.4 and 012.1 respectively.
CODOT
069.20 pt. Remainder in 007.1
281.02 pt. Remainder in 008.0, 037.2 and 045.1
281.28, 281.30, 281.32

**008.0  Local government officers (administrative and executive functions)**
Persons of administrative or executive rank in local authority employ. Local authority treasurers, statutory inspectors, directors of education, and housing managers are excluded and classified in 002.5, 006.3, 012.2 and 013.3 respectively.
CODOT
001.40
031.20
069.30
281.02 pt. Remainder in 007.2, 037.2 and 045.1
281.34

**009.1  Company secretaries**
Persons having responsibility for all work connected with the meetings with the board of directors and shareholders; giving advice on company law and practise; acting as legal representatives of the company. Company registrars are excluded and classified in 009.8.
CODOT
031.10

**009.2    Officials of trade associations, trade unions, professional bodies and charities**
Persons working as paid officials of trade or political associations, trade unions, professional bodies and charities. Secretaries of health authorities and boards are excluded and classified in 009.8.
CODOT
031.30, 031.40, 031.50, 031.60
031.99 pt. Remainder in 009.8

**009.3    Property and estate managers**
Persons managing estates and buying and selling real property on behalf of clients and employers. Estate agents are included. Property negotiators are excluded and classified in 057.6.
CODOT
062

**009.4    Librarians, information officers**
Persons organising and controlling library services, collecting and disseminating information. Government service intelligence officers are included.
CODOT
063.10, 063.30, 063.40

**009.5    Legal service and related occupations**
Persons undertaking legal service and related functions not elsewhere classified. Housing and planning inspectors, legal executives and barristers' and solicitors' managing clerks are included. Qualified solicitors are excluded and classified in 001.0.
CODOT
023, 029

**009.6    Management consultants**
Persons advising industrial, commercial, governmental and other organisations on various management and technical matters.
CODOT
049

**009.7    Managers' personal assistants**
Persons assisting with tasks or functions which form part of the duties of a director or manager.
CODOT
069.10

**009.8    Professional workers and related supporting management and administration n.e.c.**
Persons in professional and related occupations supporting management and administration not elsewhere classified including archivists, bursars, company registrars, curators, secretaries of health authorities and boards, trade-mark agents.
CODOT
031.99 pt. Remainder in 009.2
039 pt. Excludes—039.40, 039.50 included in 002.7
063.20, 063.50, 063.99
069.40, 069.50, 069.99

**010.1    University academic staff**
Persons lecturing or teaching at universities or university colleges.
CODOT
091

**010.2    Teachers in establishments for further and higher education**
Persons lecturing or teaching at technical colleges, colleges of education and further education.
CODOT
092, 093

**011.0    Teachers n.e.c.**
Persons teaching at nursery, primary and secondary schools. Teachers of physical training, diversionary activities; private tutors; private dancing and music teachers are excluded and classified in 018.4. Private driving instructors and sports instructors are excluded and classified in 018.3 and 023.1 respectively.
CODOT
094, 095, 096, 097

**012.1    Vocational and industrial trainers**
Persons giving instruction in manual, manipulative and other vocational skills and organising, controlling and advising on instruction within industrial, commercial and similar undertakings. Persons teaching people to drive heavy goods and public service vehicles and managers of government training centres are included.
CODOT
098

**012.2    Education officers, school inspectors**
Persons organising educational activities within a local education authority area. Inspectors of schools employed by central government are included.
CODOT
099.00, 099.01, 099.10

**012.3    Social and behavioural scientists**
Persons working as social and behavioural scientists including sociologists, historians, psychologists and geographers.
CODOT
101

**013.1    Matrons, houseparents**
Persons managing welfare institutions such as day or residential nurseries; working as houseparents in children's homes or establishments for young offenders; matrons or wardens of old people's homes. Matrons of schools and hospitals, hostels and lodging houses are excluded and classified in 016.0, and 044.4 respectively.
CODOT
102.18, 102.20, 102.22, 102.24

**013.2    Playgroup leaders**

Persons supervising play and other activities for pre-school age children. Persons assisting playgroup leaders are excluded and classified in 075.6.

CODOT

102.99 pt. Remainder in 013.3

**013.3    Welfare occupations n.e.c.**

Persons engaged in social welfare and related services, including housing managers, probation officers, safety engineers and officers, social workers, community workers, home help organisers and youth leaders.

CODOT

102 pt. Excludes—102.18, 102.20, 102.22, 102.24
               —102.99 pt. included in 013.2

**014.0    Clergy, ministers of religion**

Clergy, ministers of religion and members of religious communities. Persons engaged in other professional or technical occupations, e.g. teaching, are excluded.

CODOT

103

**015.1    Medical practitioners**

Qualified persons diagnosing, prescribing and giving medical and surgical treatment for physical and mental disorders of the human body. Medical administrators and radiotherapists are included. Bacteriologists, pathologists and physiologists are excluded and classified in 024.1.

CODOT

111

**015.2    Dental practitioners**

Qualified persons treating by medicine or surgery dental or oral diseases and disorders.

CODOT

112

**016.0    Nurse administrators, nurses**

Persons providing, or training to provide, nursing or midwifery care. Hospital sisters and matrons, and school matrons are included. Nursery nurses and assistants; ward orderlies and first-aid attendants are excluded and classified in 068.2; and 070.2 respectively.

CODOT

113

**017.1    Pharmacists**

Qualified persons compounding and dispensing medicines. Pharmacists owning or managing retail chemists' shops are included. Dispensers are excluded and classified in 018.1.

CODOT

114

**017.2    Medical radiographers**

Persons employed as medical radiographers. Radiotherapists and industrial radiographers are excluded and classified in 015.1 and 030.2 respectively.

CODOT

115

**017.3    Ophthalmic and dispensing opticians**

Qualified persons testing eye sight and/or dispensing spectacles. Opticians owning or managing retail establishments are included. Orthoptists are excluded and classified in 017.6.

CODOT

116

**017.4    Physiotherapists**

Persons working as physiotherapists.

CODOT

117.10

**017.5    Chiropodists**

Persons working as chiropodists.

CODOT

119.10

**017.6    Therapists n.e.c.**

Persons carrying out therapeutic treatments and activities, not elsewhere classified, including occupational therapists, orthoptists, osteopaths, remedial gymnasts and speech therapists.

CODOT

117 pt. Excludes—117.10

**018.1    Medical technicians, dental auxiliaries**

Persons undertaking a variety of medical, dental, pharmaceutical and related tasks, including artificial limb fitters; dental auxiliaries and hygienists; dispensers; prosthetists; audiology, cardiological, encephalographic and pharmacy technicians. Dietitians, laboratory technicians and dental technicians are excluded and classified in 018.4, 030.1 and 107.2 respectively.

CODOT

119 pt. Excludes—119.05
               —119.10 included in 017.5

**018.2    Veterinarians**

Professionally qualified persons treating and preventing animal diseases; treating animal ailments and injuries.

CODOT

121

**018.3  Driving instructors (not HGV)**
Persons teaching people to drive cars and light commercial vehicles who are included in the Register of Approved Driving Instructors.
Persons teaching people to drive heavy goods and public service vehicles are excluded and classified in 012.1.

CODOT
099.05 pt. Remainder in 018.4
099.80

**018.4  Professional and related in education, welfare and health n.e.c.**
Persons employed in a variety of occupations in education, welfare and health, not elsewhere classified, including teachers of physical
training and diversionary activities; private tutors; private dancing and music teachers; careers officers and vocational guidance
specialists; dietitians, and animal health attendants and technicians.

CODOT
099 pt. Excludes—099.00, 099.01, 099.10 included in 012.2
        —099.05 pt., 099.80 included in 018.3
109
119.05
129

**019.0  Authors, writers, journalists**
Persons writing original works of fiction or non-fiction; collecting news items and presenting them in a form for publication; writing
advertising copy, plays, radio, film and television scripts, song lyrics, criticisms of artistic, etc. works. Book editors, translators,
interpreters, literary agents and press officers are included. Public relations officers are excluded and classified in 005.2.

CODOT
151, 159

**020.1  Artists, commercial artists**
Persons creating artistic works by painting, drawing, engraving, sculpting, etc.; drawing cartoons and illustrations for advertisements;
designing interior decorations, shop window displays and stage settings; restoring paintings, etc.. Window dressers and technical illu-
strators are excluded and classified in 020.4 and 029.0 respectively.

CODOT
161

**020.2  Industrial designers (not clothing)**
Persons creating non-technical designs for industrial and commercial products.

CODOT
162 pt. Excludes—162.00 pt., 162.20 included in 020.3

**020.3  Clothing designers**
Persons creating designs for clothing and fashion accessories.

CODOT
162.00 pt. Remainder in 020.2
162.20

**020.4  Window dressers**
Persons displaying merchandise in shop windows.

CODOT
179.40

**021.1  Actors, entertainers, singers, stage managers**
Persons directing or producing film, radio, television or stage plays or other shows; chief cameramen (films) and lighting managers;
film editors; acting; dancing; entertaining; singing; announcing radio and television programmes; creating or arranging dances.
Private dancing teachers are excluded and classified in 018.4.

CODOT
171
172.30, 172.99
173 pt. Excludes—173.10, 173.20
179.10, 179.20, 179.30

**021.2  Musicians**
Persons playing a musical instrument; writing or arranging music; conducting musical performances. Private music teachers are
excluded and classified in 018.4.

CODOT
172.10, 172.20
173.10, 173.20

**022.1  Photographers, cameramen**
Persons operating still, television and cine cameras. Self-employed photographers are included. Chief cameramen (films) are excluded
and classified in 021.1.

CODOT
174

**022.2  Sound and vision equipment operators**
Persons operating equipment, other than cameras, to record or project sound and/or vision.

CODOT
175

**023.1  Professional sportsmen, sports officials**
Persons managing teams, participating in and controlling sporting events and training sportsmen. Teachers of physical training are
excluded and classified in 018.4.

CODOT
181

**023.2  Literary, artistic and sports workers n.e.c.**

Persons not elsewhere classified in literary, artistic and sporting occupations. Florists (including retail florists) are included.

CODOT

179.50, 179.60, 179.70, 179.99

**024.1  Biological scientists, biochemists**

Persons planning, directing and undertaking research, development, technical advisory, consultancy and related work in the field of biological science and the chemistry of living organisms. Only persons performing work normally requiring training of university degree standard are included, including biologists, botanists, entomologists, geneticists, microbiologists, pathologists, pharmacologists, physiologists and zoologists.

CODOT

211

219.00 pt. Remainder in 024.2 and 024.3

219.10

**024.2  Chemical scientists**

Persons planning, directing and undertaking research, development, analysis, technical advisory, consultancy and related work in the field of chemical science or in relation to the physical aspects of chemical structure and chemical change. Only persons performing work normally requiring training of university degree standard are included.

CODOT

212

219.00 pt. Remainder in 024.1 and 024.3

219.30

**024.3  Physical and geological scientists, mathematicians**

Persons planning, directing and undertaking research, development, technical advisory, consultancy and related work in the fields of physics, mathematics, the physics of living organisms and geology. Only persons performing work normally requiring training of university degree standard are included, including meteorologists, mineralogists and physicists.

CODOT

213

214

215

219.00 pt. Remainder in 024.1 and 024.2

219.20, 219.99

**025.0  Civil, structural, municipal, mining and quarrying engineers**

Persons planning, organising and technically supervising the construction and repair of roads, bridges, santitation systems, reservoirs, other structures, mines and quarries or acting as adviser for such projects. Only persons performing work normally requiring training of university degree standard are included. Building inspectors are excluded and classified in 006.2.

CODOT

221, 222

**026.1  Mechanical and aeronautical engineers**

Persons planning and technically supervising the production or repair and maintenance of engines, machines, vehicles and other mechanical products or acting as adviser, including marine engineers and naval architects. Only persons performing work normally requiring training of university degree standard are included. Estimators are excluded and classified in 002.3.

CODOT

223 pt. Excludes—223.00 pt., 223.31, 223.32, 223.33, 223.34, 223.35, 223.36, 223.37, 223.39, 223.99 pt. included in 026.2

**026.2  Design and development engineers (mechanical)**

Persons originating, from product ideas or requirements, engineering designs in the field of general mechanical engineering.

CODOT

223.00 pt., 223.99 pt. Remainders in 026.1

223.31, 223.32, 223.33, 223.34, 223.35, 223.36, 223.37, 223.39

**027.1  Electrical engineers**

Persons designing, planning and technically supervising the production or repair and maintenance of electrical and telephonic equipment, technically supervising the operation of power stations or acting as adviser in electrical engineering matters. Only persons performing work normally requiring training of university degree standard are included. Systems engineers are excluded and classified in 004.2.

CODOT

224.12, 224.15, 224.22, 224.25, 224.32, 224.35, 224.42, 224.45, 224.52, 224.55, 224.62, 224.65, 224.72, 224.75

All remaining occupations of unit group 224 are divided between 027.1 and 027.2

**027.2  Electronic engineers**

Persons designing, planning and technically supervising the production or repair and maintenance of electronic equipment, including radio communication, radar and industrial electronic equipment. Only persons performing work normally requiring training of university degree standard are included.

CODOT

224 pt. Excludes—224.12, 224.15, 224.22, 224.25, 224.32, 224.35, 224.42, 224.45, 224.52, 224.55, 224.62, 224.65, 224.72, 224.75

All remaining occupations of unit group 224 are divided between 027.1 and 027.2

**028.1  Chemical engineers**

Persons planning, directing, undertaking research and development and related work in respect of chemical manufacture. Only persons performing work normally requiring training of university degree standard are included.

CODOT

225

**028.2  Production engineers**

Persons overseeing the technical aspects of production programmes. Only persons performing work normally requiring training of university degree standard are included.

CODOT

226

**028.3 Planning and quality control engineers**

Persons planning production schedules and work procedures in production fields; planning procedures for the maintenance of standards. Only persons performing work normally requiring training of university degree standard are included.

CODOT
259.10, 259.40

**028.4 Engineers n.e.c.**

Engineers performing work normally requiring training of university degree standard developing, etc., all types of industrial processes not elsewhere classified. Environmental and traffic engineers are included. Ships' surveyors and naval architects are excluded and classified in 006.3 and 026.1 respectively.

CODOT
229

**028.5 Metallurgists**

Persons studying the properties of metals, developing, etc. processes for the production of metals from their ores and advising on their utilisation. Only persons performing work normally requiring training of university degree standard are included.

CODOT
231.05

**028.6 Technologists n.e.c.**

Persons planning, directing, undertaking research and development, and related work in particular materials products and processes, other than in engineering; including textile and rubber technologists, fuel technologists, brewers and technologists not elsewhere classified. Only persons performing work normally requiring training of university degree standard are included.

CODOT
231 pt. Excludes—231.05

**029.0 Draughtsmen**

Persons preparing technical drawings, plans, maps, charts and similar items, including technical illustrators. Tracers and drawing office assistants are excluded and classified in 046.2.

CODOT
253

**030.1 Laboratory technicians**

Persons carrying out technical functions requiring the application of established or prescribed procedures in physical, chemical, biological, botanical, medical and other laboratories. Laboratory assistants are excluded and classified in 138.1.

CODOT
254

**030.2 Engineering technicians, technician engineers**

Persons performing a variety of engineering technical functions, (excluding architectural, constructional and related functions); technically controlling the installation and testing of engineering systems, diagnosing and correcting complex faults. Industrial radiographers are included.

CODOT
256

**031.1 Architects, town planners**

Professionally qualified persons designing buildings; planning the layout of urban and rural areas or acting as adviser in these matters. Housing and planning inspectors, and architectural and town planning assistants are excluded and classified in 009.5, and 033.1 respectively.

CODOT
251

**031.2 Quantity surveyors**

Persons advising on financial and contractual matters relating to, and preparing bills of quantities for, construction projects; including technical assistants to quantity surveyors.

CODOT
255.10, 255.20

**031.3 Building, land and mining surveyors**

Persons conducting building, land and mining surveys. Insurance surveyors are excluded and classified in 033.3.

CODOT
252.10, 252.30, 252.40

**032.1 Aircraft flight deck officers**

Persons flying and navigating aircraft and servicing them in flight. Hovercraft pilots and navigators are excluded and classified in 033.3.

CODOT
241

**032.2 Air traffic planners and controllers**

Persons preparing flight plans, authorising flight departures and maintaining contact with aircraft to provide safe and orderly movement of air traffic. Air traffic control assistants are excluded and classified in 051.3.

CODOT
242

**032.3 Deck, engineering and radio officers and pilots, ship**

Persons commanding and navigating seagoing ships and craft operating in coastal and inland waters; organising, directing and supervising the activities of deck ratings, advising ships' masters on the navigation of ships in hazardous waters. Pilots and navigators of hovercraft and skippers of fishing vessels are excluded and classified in 033.3 and 044.4 respectively.

CODOT
243, 244

**033.1  Architectural and town planning technicians**
Persons assisting architects and town planners by carrying out technical functions related to the design of buildings and the planning of urban and rural areas.
CODOT
255.30, 255.40

**033.2  Building and civil engineering technicians**
Persons performing a variety of functions requiring the application of prescribed engineering procedures in the field of civil engineering, including structural engineering and building.
CODOT
255.50, 255.99

**033.3  Technical and related workers n.e.c.**
Persons carrying out a variety of technical and scientific occupations not elsewhere classified including hovercraft pilots and navigators, marine surveyors, insurance surveyors and patent agents and examiners.
CODOT
249
252.20, 252.50, 252.99
259.20, 259.30, 259.50, 259.60, 259.70, 259.99

**034.0  Production, works and maintenance managers, works foremen**
Persons managing the work and resources necessary for such industrial operations as production, processing and maintenance. Post Office area engineers and engineers directly responsible for production and maintenance in factories and maintenance in transport undertakings, mines, etc. and works, general and senior foremen in manufacturing are included.
CODOT
271
272
273 pt. Excludes—273.20 pt. included in 038.1

**035.1  Managers in building and contracting**
Managers in construction, including works, general and senior foremen and persons responsible for civil engineering work on the railways and building maintenance.
CODOT
274 pt. Excludes—274.35

**035.2  Clerks of works**
Persons representing clients on construction projects to ensure contractors' compliance with design specifications and standards.
CODOT
274.35

**036.1  Managers in mining and public utilities**
Managers in mining, quarrying, and in the production and supply of electricity, gas and water. Mining overmen are included.
CODOT
275, 276

**036.2  Transport managers**
Persons managing activities and resources necessary for the transportation of passengers and freight.
CODOT
277 pt. Excludes—277.32, 277.34, 277.36, 277.38, 277.40

**036.3  Stores controllers**
Persons managing activities and resources for maintaining stocks of material, products or commodities and for storing and issuing such items. Stores managers are included.
CODOT
277.34, 277.36

**036.4  Managers in warehousing and materials handling n.e.c.**
Persons organising and directing activities for the receipt, warehousing and despatch of goods, commodities, products and other items. Freight managers and wharf managers are included.
CODOT
277.32, 277.38, 277.40

**037.1  Credit controllers**
Persons organising offices responsible for credit control and debt collection.
CODOT
281.06

**037.2  Office managers n.e.c.**
Persons managing offices carrying out clerical and related functions; including computer operations managers, medical records officers, sales office managers, bank managers, building society managers. Owners and managers of travel agencies and private employment agencies are included. Insurance office managers are included but managers of local agents are excluded and classified in 057.6. Sub-postmasters are included except the self-employed who are excluded and classified in 038.4.
CODOT
281 pt. Excludes—281.02 pt. included in 007.2, 008.0 and 045.1
              —281.28, 281.30, 281.32 included in 007.2
              —281.34 included in 008.2

**038.1  Garage proprietors**
Persons owning garages and filling stations.
CODOT
273.20 pt. Remainder in 034.0
283.99 pt. Remainder in 038.4 and 044.2

**038.2 Butchers (managers and proprietors)**
Persons owning and managing butchers' shops.
CODOT
283.40 pt., 283.60 pt. Remainders in 038.3 and 038.4

**038.3 Fishmongers (managers and proprietors)**
Persons owning and managing fishmongers' shops.
CODOT
283.40 pt., 283.60 pt. Remainders in 038.2 and 038.4

**038.4 Other proprietors and managers (sales)**
Persons owning or managing wholesale and retail establishments. Pawnbrokers, self-employed sub-postmasters and managers of mail order establishments and trading stamp redemption offices are included. Pharmacists, opticians (ophthalmic and dispensing) and managers of laundry and dry cleaning receiving shops are excluded and classified in 017.1, 017.3 and 044.2 respectively.
CODOT
282
283 pt. Excludes—283.40 pt., 283.60 pt. included in 038.2 and 038.3
          —283.99 pt. included in 038.1 and 044.2

**039.1 Hotel and residential club managers**
Persons owning or managing boarding houses, hotels and residential clubs. Pursers are included.
CODOT
284.05, 284.10, 284.15

**039.2 Publicans**
Persons owning or managing public houses. 'Innkeepers' so described are excluded and classified in 044.4.
CODOT
284.70

**039.3 Restaurateurs**
Persons owning or managing restaurants and canteens.
CODOT
284.30, 284.35, 284.40, 284.45, 284.50, 284.55, 284.60, 284.65

**039.4 Club stewards**
Persons organising the bar and catering services at non-residential clubs.
CODOT
284.80

**039.5 Entertainment and sports managers**
Persons owning or managing sporting, recreational and amenity services including cinemas and theatres, including park superintendents. Producers and directors of stage, television, radio and film productions are excluded and classified in 021.1.
CODOT
285

**040.0 Farmers, horticulturists, farm managers**
Persons owning or managing farms or market gardens including fruit farmers, poultry farmers, agricultural contractors and tenants of a croft or holding under, and in terms of, the Crofters (Scotland) Act, 1955, not elsewhere classified. Fish farmers and trainers of horses are excluded and classified in 044.4.
CODOT
286 pt. Excludes—286.40, 286.50, 286.55, 286.60, 286.99 pt. included in 044.4

**041.0 Officers, UK armed forces**
All full time commissioned officers of the armed forces of the United Kingdom.
CODOT
287.10 pt. Remainder in 042.0

**042.0 Officers, foreign and Commonwealth armed forces**
All full time commissioned officers of the armed forces of foreign and Commonwealth countries.
CODOT
287.10 pt. Remainder in 041.0

**043.1 Prison officers (chief officers and above)**
Governors and chief officers in prisons or similar institutions. Wardens of detention centres are included.
CODOT
288.40

**043.2 Police officers (inspectors and above)**
Persons organising a specific geographical or functional area of general or specialised police work.
CODOT
288.10

**043.3 Fire service officers**
Persons organising a specific physical or functional area of a statutory or private fire brigade. Salvage corps senior officers are included.
CODOT
288.20, 288.30

**044.1 Proprietors and managers, service flats, holiday flats, caravan sites, etc.**
Persons owning or managing service flats, holiday flats and chalets, holiday camps, and camping and caravan sites.
CODOT
284.99 pt. Remainder in 044.4

**044.2   Managers of laundry and dry cleaning receiving shops**
Managers of launderettes and premises used for the receipt and despatch of items for laundering and dry cleaning.
CODOT
283.99 pt. Remainder in 038.1 and 038.4

**044.3   Hairdressers' and barbers' managers and proprietors**
Persons owning and managing hairdressing, beauty treatment or similar establishments.
CODOT
289.40

**044.4   Managers n.e.c.**
Managers not elsewhere classified, including managers of gardening/grounds keeping services; tree surgeons; managers of animal establishments (other than farm livestock); head housekeepers of large hotels, hospitals, institutions or residential buildings; managers of residential hostels for students, hikers or wanderers; registrars of educational establishments; skippers of fishing vessels; fish farmers; fieldmen; ambulance station superintendents; innkeepers; administration and general service managers. Owners and managers of laundries, dry cleaning works (not receiving shops) and firms hiring or servicing machinery and equipment, undertaking cleaning and related services are included.
CODOT
279
284.20, 284.25, 284.75
284.99 pt. Remainder in 044.1
286.40, 286.50, 286.55, 286.60
286.99 pt. Remainder in 040.0
288.50, 288.99
289 pt. Excludes—289.40

**045.1   Civil Service executive officers**
Persons of the basic grade of executive officer in the Civil Service or of equivalent rank. Customs and Excise Officers, waterguards, preventive officers, immigration officers are excluded and classified in 006.3.
CODOT
281.02 pt. Remainder in 007.2, 008.0 and 037.2
310.80 pt. Remainder in 045.3 and 045.4

**045.2   Supervisors of stores and despatch clerks**
Supervisors of persons classified in 046.1.
CODOT
310.50 pt. Remainder in 045.4

**045.3   Supervisors of tracers, drawing office assistants**
Supervisors of persons classified in 046.2.
CODOT
310.80 pt. Remainder in 045.1 and 045.4

**045.4   Supervisors of other clerks and cashiers (not retail)**
Supervisors of persons classified in 046.3.
CODOT
310 pt. Excludes—310.20 pt. included in 045.5
            —310.50 pt. included in 045.2
            —310.80 pt. included in 045.1 and 045.3

**045.5   Supervisors of retail shop cashiers, check-out and cash and wrap operators**
Supervisors of persons classified in 047.0.
CODOT
310.20 pt. Remainder in 045.4

**046.1   Stores and despatch clerks**
Persons checking and recording details of stock movements, preparing requisitions or despatch documents for ordered goods.
CODOT
314.15, 314.20

**046.2   Tracers, drawing office assistants**
Persons employed as tracers or drawing office assistants.
CODOT
319.28

**046.3   Other clerks and cashiers (not retail)**
Persons keeping records of cash; collecting cash or issuing tickets at theatres, etc., taking readings of meters and emptying coin boxes; performing all types of office work. Proof readers, ADP tape librarians, library clerks and assistants, debt and rent collectors are included but credit agents and collector salesmen are excluded and classified in 057.4. Civil Servants and local government officers, etc., so described are included.
CODOT
311
312 pt. Excludes—312.90, 312.91 included in 047.0
313
314 pt. Excludes—314.15, 314.20
315
316
319 pt. Excludes—319.28
            —319.56, 319.58, 319.60 included in 049.1

**047.0   Retail shop cashiers, check-out and cash and wrap operators**
Persons employed as cashiers, check-out and cash and wrap operators in retail shops and cafés.
CODOT
312.90, 312.91

**048.1** **Supervisors of typists, shorthand writers, secretaries**
Supervisors of persons classified in 049.2.

CODOT
320

**048.2** **Supervisors of office machine operators**
Supervisors of persons classified in 050.0.

CODOT
330

**048.3** **Supervisors of telephone operators**
Supervisors of persons classified in 051.2.

CODOT
340.10

**048.4** **Supervisors of radio and telegraph operators**
Supervisors of persons classified in 051.3.

CODOT
340.20, 340.30
340.99 pt. Remainder in 052.2

**049.1** **Receptionists**
Persons receiving callers at commercial, industrial and other establishments. Hotel, dental and medical receptionists are included.

CODOT
319.56, 319.58, 319.60

**049.2** **Typists, shorthand writers, secretaries**
Persons typing; taking shorthand records; acting as personal secretary. 'Secretaries' so described are included. Proprietors and managers of typewriting bureaux, if not typists, are excluded and classified in 057.6 and 044.4 respectively.

CODOT
321, 322

**050.0** **Office machine operators**
Persons operating office machines, including photo and blue printers; duplicator, key punch, computer and peripheral equipment operators. Offset duplicating machine operators are excluded and classified in 107.9.

CODOT
331, 332, 333, 334, 339

**051.1** **Telephonist receptionists**
Persons combining the functions of operating a telephone switchboard and receiving callers at commercial, industrial and other establishments.

CODOT
341.20 pt. Remainder in 051.2

**051.2** **Telephone operators**
Persons operating telephone switchboards.

CODOT
341.10
341.20 pt. Remainder in 051.1

**051.3** **Radio and telegraph operators**
Persons operating radio, telegraph and teleprinter equipment to transmit and receive signals and messages. Air traffic control assistants are included.

CODOT
342

**052.1** **Supervisors of postmen, mail sorters**
Supervisors of persons classified in 053.1.

CODOT
340.40 pt. Remainder in 052.2

**052.2** **Supervisors of messengers**
Supervisors of persons classified in 053.2.

CODOT
340.40 pt. Remainder in 052.1
340.99 pt. Remainder in 048.4

**053.1** **Postmen, mail sorters**
Persons collecting, delivering and sorting mail.

CODOT
343.10, 343.50

**053.2** **Messengers**
Persons collecting and distributing correspondence within an establishment or delivering messages, etc., elsewhere as instructed. Delivery and errand boys are included.

CODOT
343.90, 343.99

**054.1** **Supervisors of shop salesmen and assistants**
Supervisors of persons included in 055.1.

CODOT
360.10 pt. Remainder in 054.2
360.99

**054.2 Supervisors of petrol pump, forecourt attendants**
Supervisors of persons included in 055.3.

CODOT
360.10 pt. Remainder in 054.1

**054.3 Supervisors of roundsmen, van salesmen**
Supervisors of persons included in 056.0.

CODOT
360.20

**055.1 Shop salesmen and assistants**
Persons selling goods and services to customers in shops and similar establishments. Sub-post office assistants, programme sellers and assistants in take-away food shops are included. Cash and wrap operators are excluded and classified in 047.0.

CODOT
361 pt. Excludes—361.92
369.99 pt. Remainder in 055.2

**055.2 Shelf fillers**
Persons replenishing stocks of goods in self service stores and, where required, marking prices on goods before displaying.

CODOT
369.99 pt. Remainder in 055.1

**055.3 Petrol pump, forecourt attendants**
Persons selling petrol, etc., at a petrol service station or garage.

CODOT
361.92

**056.0 Roundsmen, van salesmen**
Persons delivering and selling food, drink and other goods and collecting and delivering laundry. Mobile shop salesmen are included. Coal delivery drivers are excluded and classified in 152.2.

CODOT
362
363.10

**057.1 Importers, exporters, commodity brokers**
Persons acting as agents in the purchase, sale, import and export of commodities in bulk, including ship and air brokers, and principals and managers of import and export agencies.

CODOT
379.10, 379.20, 379.30, 379.40, 379.50
379.99 pt. Remainder in 057.6

**057.2 Market and street traders and assistants**
Persons selling goods, other than refreshments, from a stall or barrow in a market place or street (including self-employed traders); hawkers. Trolleymen selling refreshments are excluded and classified in 066.1.

CODOT
363.20
363.99 pt. Remainder in 057.3 and 057.4

**057.3 Scrap dealers, general dealers, rag and bone merchants**
Persons trading in scrap metal, rags, waste materials, etc. (including self-employed traders).

CODOT
363.99 pt. Remainder in 057.2 and 057.4

**057.4 Credit agents, collector salesmen**
Persons visiting private households to solicit orders and collect payments for goods and services. Debt and rent collectors are excluded and classified in 046.3.

CODOT
363.99 pt. Remainder in 057.2 and 057.3
379.90, 379.95

**057.5 Sales representatives**
Persons soliciting orders for machinery, equipment and materials; the wholesale provision of food, drink, clothing and other consumer goods. Manufacturers' agents are included.

CODOT
371, 372

**057.6 Sales representatives (property and services), other agents**
Persons selling property and soliciting orders for insurance, financial, security, cleaning and other services. Auctioneers, demonstrators, way-leave officers, telephone canvassers and property negotiators are included. Estate agents are excluded and classified in 009.3.

CODOT
369.10
373
379.99 pt. Remainder in 057.1

**058.0 NCOs and other ranks, UK armed forces**
All full time members of the armed forces of the United Kingdom, except commissioned officers who are excluded and classified in 041.0.

CODOT
400.10 pt., 401.10 pt. Remainders in 059.0

**059.0**  **NCOs and other ranks, foreign and Commonwealth armed forces**
All full time members of the armed forces of foreign and Commonwealth countries, except commissioned officers who are excluded and classified in 042.0.

CODOT
400.10 pt., 401.10 pt. Remainders in 058.0

**060.1**  **Police sergeants**
Sergeants employed by statutory police authorities, including railway, dock and airport police.

CODOT
410.10, 410.20

**060.2**  **Fire service supervisors**
Supervisors of persons included in 061.2.

CODOT
410.30

**060.3**  **Prison service principal officers**
Principal officers in the prison service.

CODOT
410.40
410.99 pt. Remainder in 060.4, 060.5 and 060.6

**060.4**  **Supervisors of security guards and officers, patrolmen, watchmen**
Supervisors of persons included in 062.1.

CODOT
410.50
410.99 pt. Remainder in 060.3, 060.5 and 060.6

**060.5**  **Supervisors of traffic wardens**
Supervisors of persons included in 062.2.

CODOT
410.99 pt. Remainder in 060.3, 060.4 and 060.6

**060.6**  **Supervisors of security and protective service workers n.e.c.**
Supervisors of persons included in 062.3.

CODOT
410.99 pt. Remainder in 060.3, 060.4 and 060.5

**061.1**  **Policemen (below sergeant)**
Uniformed members and detectives employed by statutory police authorities, including railway, dock and airport police.

CODOT
411

**061.2**  **Firemen**
Persons fighting fires, advising on fire hazards and salvaging goods during or after fires as members of public or private fire brigades. Woodland fire fighting patrols are excluded and classified in 080.0.

CODOT
412

**061.3**  **Prison officers (below principal officer)**
Persons, below principal officers, guarding inmates in prisons, borstals, detention centres or young offenders' institutions.

CODOT
419.20

**062.1**  **Security guards and officers, patrolmen, watchmen**
Persons employed in protecting persons, premises and property from injury, damage or theft. Store, hotel and private detectives, gate-keepers, park keepers and estate rangers are included.

CODOT
419 pt. Excludes—419.10, 419.30, 419.99 pt. included in 062.3
                —419.20 included in 061.3
                —419.93

**062.2**  **Traffic wardens**
Persons patrolling areas to detect and prevent infringements of local parking regulations. Parking meter attendants are included.

CODOT
419.93

**062.3**  **Security and protective service workers n.e.c.**
Persons engaged in security services not elsewhere classified. Coastguards, bailiffs, life guards, museum and art gallery attendants and road crossing attendants are included.

CODOT
419.10, 419.30
419.99 pt. Remainder in 062.1

**063.1**  **Supervisors of chefs, cooks**
Supervisors of persons classified in 064.0.

CODOT
430.10, 430.20, 430.30

**063.2**  **Supervisors of waiters, waitresses**
Supervisors of persons classified in 065.1.

CODOT
430.40, 430.50

**063.3  Supervisors of barmen, barmaids**
Supervisors of persons classified in 065.2.

CODOT
430.60

**063.4  Supervisors of counter hands, assistants**
Supervisors of persons classified in 066.1.

CODOT
430.70

**064.0  Chefs, cooks**
Persons preparing and cooking meals. Persons peeling vegetables, washing dishes, etc.; cook-housekeepers; and cooks employed in food products manufacturing are excluded and classified in 066.2; 068.1; and 098.7 respectively.

CODOT
431

**065.1  Waiters, waitresses**
Persons guiding diners to tables; serving food and refreshments at tables.

CODOT
432

**065.2  Barmen, barmaids**
Persons serving drinks at or from the licensed bars of clubs, hotels, public houses and similar establishments; including bar stewards. Club stewards and wine waiters are excluded and classified in 039.4 and 065.1 respectively.

CODOT
433

**066.1  Counter hands, assistants**
Persons serving food and other refreshments from counters of self service restaurants, buffets, cafés, canteens and similar establishments. Trolleymen selling refreshments and school meals assistants and attendants are included. School helpers, mid-day assistants and school meals supervisors are excluded and classified in 068.3.

CODOT
434

**066.2  Kitchen porters, hands**
Persons preparing vegetables, washing crockery, etc. and performing various cleaning, fetching, carrying and similar tasks in kitchens.

CODOT
435.10, 435.20, 435.30

**067.1  Housekeepers (non-domestic)**
Persons acting as housekeepers in hotels, schools and similar non-private establishments.

CODOT
440.10 pt. Remainder in 067.2

**067.2  Supervisors of other domestic and school helpers**
Supervisors of persons included in 068.3.

CODOT
440.10 pt. Remainder in 067.1
440.20

**067.3  Supervisors of travel stewards and attendants**
Supervisors of persons included in 069.1.

CODOT
440.30, 440.40
440.99 pt. Remainder in 067.4 and 067.5

**067.4  Supervisors of hospital porters**
Supervisors of persons included in 069.2.

CODOT
440.99 pt. Remainder in 067.3 and 067.5

**067.5  Supervisors of hotel porters**
Supervisors of persons included in 069.3.

CODOT
440.99 pt. Remainder in 067.3 and 067.4

**067.6  Supervisors of ambulancemen**
Supervisors of persons included in 070.1.

CODOT
440.50 pt. Remainder in 067.7

**067.7  Supervisors of hospital, ward orderlies**
Supervisors of persons included in 070.2.

CODOT
440.50 pt. Remainder in 067.6

**068.1  Domestic housekeepers**
Persons acting as housekeepers in private homes. Cook-housekeepers are included.

CODOT
441.05

**068.2**   **Nursery nurses**

Persons caring for healthy children in day or residential nurseries, children's homes, maternity hospitals or units or similar establishments, including nursery assistants. Nannies and children's nurses employed in private households are excluded and classified in 068.3.

CODOT
441.25, 441.30

**068.3**   **Other domestic and school helpers**

Persons attending to the personal needs and comforts of others, cleaning and tidying living quarters in private households, hotels, hospitals and similar establishments; assisting teachers with non-teaching activities and supervising children in playgrounds and dining rooms. Companions, domestics, nannies and children's nurses in private housholds and ward maids are included. Playgroup leaders are excluded and classified in 013.2.

CODOT
441 pt. Excludes—441.05, 441.25, 441.30
             —441.35, 441.50, 441.99 included in 075.6

**069.1**   **Travel stewards and attendants**

Persons attending to the needs and comforts of travellers and conducting or assisting tourists on holiday.

CODOT
442

**069.2**   **Hospital porters**

Persons working as porters in hospitals.

CODOT
449.30

**069.3**   **Hotel porters**

Persons employed as porters in hotels or similar residential establishments including hall porters and page boys.

CODOT
449 pt. Excludes—449.30
             —449.99 included in 075.6

**070.1**   **Ambulancemen**

Persons transporting sick, injured or convalescent persons by ambulance; giving first aid during journey. Ambulance station superintendents and first aid attendants are excluded and classified in 044.4 and 070.2 respectively.

CODOT
443.20

**070.2**   **Hospital, ward orderlies**

Persons working as orderlies or attendants in hospitals and similar institutions; first aid attendants; care assistants in homes for the elderly or infirm. Ward maids are excluded and classified in 068.3.

CODOT
443 pt. Excludes—443.20

**071.1**   **Supervisors of caretakers**

Supervisors of persons included in 072.1.

CODOT
450.30 pt. Remainder in 071.4

**071.2**   **Supervisors of cleaners, window cleaners, chimney sweeps, road sweepers**

Supervisors of persons included in 072.2.

CODOT
450.10, 450.99

**071.3**   **Supervisors of railway stationmen**

Supervisors of persons included in 075.1.

CODOT
450.20

**071.4**   **Supervisors of lift and car park attendants**

Supervisors of persons included in 075.2.

CODOT
450.30 pt. Remainder in 071.1

**072.1**   **Caretakers**

Persons taking care of premises and keeping them in a clean and orderly condition.

CODOT
451

**072.2**   **Cleaners, window cleaners, chimney sweeps, road sweepers**

Persons cleaning interiors of aircraft, buildings, road vehicles, ships and trains; cleaning chimneys and windows; manually cleaning streets and washing down vehicle exteriors. Mechanical road sweeper drivers and vehicle washing plant attendants are excluded and classified in 152.3 and 161.2 respectively.

CODOT
452

**073.0**   **Hairdressing supervisors**

Supervisors of persons classified in 074.0.

CODOT
470.10

**074.0  Hairdressers, barbers**

Persons cutting, styling and shampooing hair. Manicurists and beauticians are excluded and classified in 075.6.

CODOT
471.05, 471.10

**075.1  Railway stationmen**

Persons performing various duties on railway station platforms, including ticket collectors, porters, stationmen and railmen (so described).

CODOT
453

**075.2  Lift and car park attendants**

Persons operating passenger or goods lifts; controlling parking of vehicles in public or private parking areas.

CODOT
459.30, 459.45

**075.3  Launderers, dry cleaners, pressers**

Persons washing, dry cleaning, ironing and pressing clothing, household linen, carpets and similar articles; including persons directly supervising these activities. 'Dyers and cleaners' are included but job dyers are excluded and classified in 087.7.

CODOT
460, 461

**075.4  Undertakers**

Persons owning or managing funeral services.

CODOT
470.20

**075.5  Bookmakers, betting shop managers**

Persons offering odds and accepting bets on the results of sporting or other events or directly supervising these activities. Turf accountants and owners and managers of betting establishments are included.

CODOT
470.40

**075.6  Service workers n.e.c.**

Persons performing manual tasks in mortuaries; assisting with funerals; giving beauty treatments; attending baths and toilets; operating entertainments such as amusement arcades, bingo halls, cinemas, dance halls, fairgrounds, ice rinks and theatres; providing personal services not elsewhere classified. Playgroup assistants, pest control operators, wardrobe mistresses, commissionaires, ushers and usherettes are included.

CODOT
430.99
435.40, 435.99
439
441.35, 441.50, 441.99
449.99
459 pt. Excludes—459.30, 459.45
470.30, 470.99
471 pt. Excludes—471.05, 471.10 included in 074.0
472
479

**076.1  Farm foremen**

Supervisors of persons included in 077.0.

CODOT
500.10, 500.20, 500.30

**076.2  Horticultural foremen**

Supervisors of persons included in 078.1.

CODOT
500.50

**076.3  Foremen gardeners and groundsmen**

Supervisors of persons included in 078.2.

CODOT
500.60

**076.4  Agricultural machinery foremen**

Supervisors of persons included in 079.0.

CODOT
500.70

**076.5  Forestry foremen**

Supervisors of persons included in 080.0.

CODOT
500.80

**076.6  Other foremen in farming and related**

Supervisors of persons included in 083.0.

CODOT
500.40, 500.99

**077.0**   **Farm workers**

Persons carrying out general farm duties in the cultivation of arable crops and in tending and breeding farm animals. Agricultural workers, cowmen, pigmen, poultrymen, shepherds and farm stockmen are included. Hatchery workers and persons tending horses, dogs, mink and zoo animals are excluded and classified in 083.0.

CODOT

501

502.02, 502.04, 502.06, 502.08, 502.10, 502.50

**078.1**   **Horticultural workers**

Persons cultivating plants and crops grown in glass houses, nurseries, market gardens and orchards. Propagators and persons employed as bulb, mushroom or watercress growers are included.

CODOT

503

**078.2**   **Gardeners, groundsmen**

Persons laying out and tending public or private gardens (excluding market gardens) and sports grounds, landscape gardeners, turf layers and cutters and green keepers are included. Managers of gardening/grounds keeping services and park superintendents are excluded and classified in 044.4 and 039.5 respectively.

CODOT

504

**079.0**   **Agricultural machinery drivers, operators**

Persons driving and operating agricultural tractors, implements and machines. Agricultural contractors and managers are excluded and classified in 040.0.

CODOT

505

**080.0**   **Forestry workers**

Persons carrying out tasks related to the cultivation and harvesting of trees, guarding against fire or other damage. Forest rangers, osier growers, tree fellers, woodcutters and woodmen are included. Persons tending fruit trees and peat cutters are excluded and classified in 078.1 and 083.0 respectively.

CODOT

506

509.20

**081.0**   **Supervisors, mates—fishing**

Supervisors of persons included in 082.0.

CODOT

510

**082.0**   **Fishermen**

Persons engaged in catching fish at sea; cultivating and harvesting shellfish; breeding and rearing fish. Trawlermen, oyster bed workers, fish hatchers, harpooners (whales), seaweed and mussel gatherers are included. Fishing vessel skippers are excluded and classified in 044.4.

CODOT

511, 519

**083.0**   **All other in farming and related**

Persons performing various tasks related to farming, horticulture and forestry; tending horses, dogs, mink and zoo animals; including gamekeepers, beekeepers, hatchery workers, canine beauticians, huntsmen, inseminators, livestock classifiers, peat cutters, seasonal crop harvesters and mushroom pickers.

CODOT

502 pt. Excludes—502.02, 502.04, 502.06, 502.08, 502.10, 502.50 included in 077.0

509 pt. Excludes—509.20 included in 080.0

**084.1**   **Foremen—Tannery production workers**

Foremen of persons included in 085.1.

CODOT

530

**084.2**   **Foremen—Shoe repairers**

Foremen of persons included in 085.2.

CODOT

660.60

**084.3**   **Foremen—Leather cutters and sewers, footwear lasters, makers, finishers**

Foremen of persons included in 085.3.

CODOT

660 pt. Excludes—660.40, 660.60

**084.4**   **Foremen—Other making and repairing, leather**

Foremen of persons included in 107.7.

CODOT

660.40

**085.1**   **Tannery production workers**

Persons treating hides, skins and pelts to prepare them for making up into leather, skin and fur products.

CODOT

531

**085.2**   **Shoe repairers**

Persons repairing worn and damaged footwear.

CODOT

666

**085.3**  **Leather cutters and sewers, footwear lasters, makers, finishers**
Persons cutting out component parts, sewing, making up and decorating footwear (including leather substitute and rubber), and leather and leather substitute goods, other than garments; performing finishing tasks in the manufacture of footwear, including footwear examiners. Persons moulding rubber footwear, and assemblers of footwear and leather goods are excluded and classified in 097.1 and 138.12 respectively.

CODOT
661, 662, 663, 665
669.14, 669.60, 669.62, 669.64, 669.66, 669.94

**086.1**  **Foremen—Preparatory fibre processors**
Foremen of persons included in 087.1.

CODOT
540.05

**086.2**  **Foremen—Spinners, doublers, twisters**
Foremen of persons included in 087.2.

CODOT
540.10
540.15 pt. Remainder in 086.3

**086.3**  **Foremen—Winders, reelers**
Foremen of persons included in 087.3.

CODOT
540.15 pt. Remainder in 086.2

**086.4**  **Foremen—Warp preparers**
Foremen of persons included in 087.4.

CODOT
540.20

**086.5**  **Foremen—Weavers**
Foremen of persons included in 087.5.

CODOT
540.25
540.99 pt. Remainder in 086.9

**086.6**  **Foremen—Knitters**
Foremen of persons included in 087.6.

CODOT
540.30

**086.7**  **Foremen—Bleachers, dyers, finishers**
Foremen of persons included in 087.7.

CODOT
540.35, 540.40

**086.8**  **Foremen—Menders, darners**
Foremen of persons included in 087.8.

CODOT
540.45

**086.9**  **Foremen—Other material processing, textiles**
Foremen of persons included in 098.4.

CODOT
540.50, 540.55, 540.60
540.99 pt. Remainder in 086.5

**087.1**  **Preparatory fibre processors**
Persons preparing fibres for spinning into yarn and making into non-woven fabric; dressing bristles and fibres for use as brush fillings. Carders, combers, drawers, fibre openers and rag grinders are included. Carbonisers, washers, driers and fur fibre mixers; persons maintaining textile fibre preparing machinery, card grinders; and wool sorters are excluded and classified in 098.4; 131.9; and 138.11 respectively.

CODOT
541

**087.2**  **Spinners, doublers, twisters**
Persons operating spinning and doubling (twisting) machines in the manufacture of yarn and thread, including chenille makers and piecers. Setter fitter-mechanics of textile machinery are excluded and classified in 117.0.

CODOT
542 pt. Excludes—542.65, 542.80, 542.90, 542.92, 542.99 pt. included in 087.3

**087.3**  **Winders, reelers**
Persons operating machines which wind yarn and thread from one package to another, including yarn curlers and openers, twine ballers and spoolers. Setter fitter-mechanics of textile machinery are excluded and classified in 117.0.

CODOT
542.65, 542.80, 542.90, 542.92
542.99 pt. Remainder in 087.2

**087.4**  **Warp preparers**
Persons operating machines which wind warp yarn on to packages and beams; arranging warp threads ready for dyeing, knitting or weaving. Setter fitter-mechanics of textile machinery are excluded and classified in 117.0.

CODOT
543

**087.5 Weavers**

Persons weaving yarn of natural and man-made fibres into carpets and fabric; including lace weavers and net makers. Warp lace makers and setter fitter-mechanics of textile machinery are excluded and classified in 087.6 and 117.0 respectively.

CODOT
544

**087.6 Knitters**

Persons operating knitting machines or knitting by hand, including warp lace makers. Setter fitter-mechanics of textile machinery are excluded and classified in 117.0.

CODOT
545

**087.7 Bleachers, dyers, finishers**

Persons bleaching, dyeing and otherwise treating textile fabrics, yarn, cloth and goods including gassers, calenderers, stenterers and dyers of piece goods. Carbonisers, driers, fullers, washers; and textile printers are excluded and classified in 098.4; and 107.9 respectively.

CODOT
546 pt. Excludes—546.50, 546.85, 546.86, 546.89 included in 098.4

**087.8 Menders, darners**

Persons rectifying faults arising during the course of manufacture of textile goods; repairing worn garments and other used articles by invisible mending. Burlers are included.

CODOT
547

**088.0 Foremen—Chemical processing**

Foremen of persons included in 089.0.

CODOT
560

**089.0 Chemical, gas and petroleum process plant operators**

Persons operating plant to process chemical and related materials by heat treatment, chemical reaction, crushing, milling, mixing and mechanically separating. Persons evaporating brine, calcining and sintering metallic ores, distilling alcoholic beverages, softening water; coal gas and coke oven furnacemen are included. Man-made fibre spinners; mineral crushers at mines and quarries; millers of ceramic materials and colour mixers; and fillers of cartridges, detonators and fireworks are excluded and classified in, 098.1; 098.3; 098.9; and 107.12 respectively.

CODOT
561

**090.1 Foremen—Bakers, flour confectioners**

Foremen of persons included in 091.0.

CODOT
570.10

**090.2 Foremen—Butchers, meat cutters**

Foremen of persons included in 092.1.

CODOT
570.20

**090.3 Foremen—Fishmongers, poultry dressers**

Foremen of persons included in 092.2.

CODOT
570.30

**090.4 Foremen—Brewery and vinery process workers**

Foremen of persons included in 098.2.

CODOT
570.40 pt., 570.70 pt. Remainders in 090.5 and 090.6
570.99 pt. Remainder in 090.6

**090.5 Foremen—Other material processing—Bakery and confectionery workers**

Foremen of persons included in 098.5.

CODOT
570.40 pt., 570.70 pt. Remainders in 090.4 and 090.6
570.50 pt. Remainder in 090.6

**090.6 Foremen—Other material processing—Food and drink n.e.c.**

Foremen of persons included in 098.7.

CODOT
570.40 pt., 570.70 pt. Remainders in 090.4 and 090.5
570.50 pt. Remainder in 090.5
570.60
570.99 pt. Remainder in 090.4

**091.0 Bakers, flour confectioners**

Persons making bread and flour confectionery; finishing flour confectionery products by hand. Ovensmen, mixers, machine operators and minders and biscuit makers are excluded and classified in 098.5.

CODOT
571

**092.1 Butchers, meat cutters**

Persons slaughtering animals and preparing carcasses for processing and sales. Butchers' shop managers and proprietors are excluded and classified in 038.2.

CODOT
572.10, 572.20, 572.30
572.99 pt. Remainder in 092.2

**092.2 Fishmongers, poultry dressers**
Persons cleaning, cutting and preparing fish and poultry carcasses for processing and sales. Fishmongers' managers and proprietors are excluded and classified in 038.3.
CODOT
572.50, 572.60, 572.90
572.99 pt. Remainder in 092.1

**093.1 Foremen—Paper, paperboard and leatherboard workers**
Foremen of persons included in 094.1.
CODOT
580.20 pt., 580.40 pt. Remainders in 093.4

**093.2 Foremen—Bookbinders and finishers**
Foremen of persons included in 094.2.
CODOT
640.10

**093.3 Foremen—Cutting and slitting machine operators (paper and paper products making)**
Foremen of persons included in 094.3.
CODOT
640.20 pt. Remainder in 093.5

**093.4 Foremen—Other material processing, wood and paper**
Foremen of persons included in 098.8.
CODOT
580.10, 580.30, 580.99
580.20 pt., 580.40 pt. Remainders in 093.1

**093.5 Foremen—Other making and repairing, paper goods and printing**
Foremen of persons included in 107.9.
CODOT
630.30 pt., 630.99 pt. Remainders in 099.3
630.50
640.20 pt. Remainder in 093.3

**094.1 Paper, paperboard and leatherboard workers**
Persons operating machinery to beat and mix fluid pulps, to dry and to finish, to impart a glaze and to wind and rewind in the process of the production of paper, paperboard and leatherboard. Beatermen, calendermen, dryermen, reelermen, refinermen and winder operators are included. Spoolers are excluded and classified in 107.9.
CODOT
582.10, 582.50
584.05, 584.10, 584.65, 584.80

**094.2 Bookbinders and finishers**
Persons engaged in book binding occupations.
CODOT
641

**094.3 Cutting and slitting machine operators (paper and paper products making)**
Persons operating machinery to cut or slit paper or similar materials. Paper pattern cutting machine operators are excluded and classified in 107.9.
CODOT
642.54, 642.56

**095.1 Foremen—Glass and ceramics furnacemen, kilnsetters**
Foremen of persons included in 096.1.
CODOT
590.10 pt. Remainder in 098.9
590.99 pt. Remainder in 095.7 and 098.9

**095.2 Foremen—Glass formers and shapers, finishers, decorators**
Foremen of persons included in 096.2.
CODOT
610

**095.3 Foremen—Casters and other pottery makers**
Foremen of persons included in 096.3.
CODOT
620.10 pt. Remainder in 095.8

**095.4 Foremen—Rubber process workers, moulding machine operators, tyre builders**
Foremen of persons included in 097.1.
CODOT
590.20 pt. Remainder in 095.7
680.10 pt. Remainder in 095.5, 095.9 and 095.10
680.20 pt. Remainder in 095.9

**095.5 Foremen—Calender and extruding machine operators, moulders (plastics)**
Foremen of persons included in 097.2.
CODOT
680.10 pt. Remainder in 095.4, 095.9 and 095.10
680.30 pt. Remainder in 095.10

**095.6 Foremen—Man-made fibre makers**
Foremen of persons included in 098.1.

CODOT
590.40 pt. Remainder in 095.7 and 098.9

**095.7 Foremen—Washers, screeners and crushers in mines and quarries**
Foremen of persons included in 098.3.

CODOT
590.20 pt. Remainder in 095.4
590.30 pt. Remainder in 139.10
590.40 pt. Remainder in 095.6 and 098.9
590.99 pt. Remainder in 095.1 and 098.9

**095.8 Foremen—Other making and repairing—Glass and ceramics**
Foremen of persons included in 107.5.

CODOT
620.10 pt. Remainder in 095.3
620.20, 620.99

**095.9 Foremen—Other making and repairing—Rubber**
Foremen of persons included in 107.10.

CODOT
680.10 pt. Remainder in 095.4, 095.5 and 095.10
680.20 pt. Remainder in 095.4

**095.10 Foremen—Other making and repairing—Plastics**
Foremen of persons included in 107.11.

CODOT
680.10 pt. Remainder in 095.4, 095.5 and 095.9
680.30 pt. Remainder in 095.5

**096.1 Glass and ceramics furnacemen, kilnsetters**
Persons operating furnaces and kilns in the production of glass and ceramics, positioning articles ready for firing in kilns, including carriers-in, kiln placers and brick kiln attendants. Saggar packers are excluded and classified in 098.9.

CODOT
591.10, 591.50, 591.52, 591.54, 591.58, 591.62, 591.90
599.10, 599.50
599.99 pt. Remainder in 098.9

**096.2 Glass formers and shapers, finishers, decorators**
Persons forming glassware and glass products by blowing, moulding and pressing; finishing glassware by removing surplus glass; grinding and polishing; decorating glassware by cutting, acid etching and sandblasting.

CODOT
611, 612, 613, 614

**096.3 Casters and other pottery makers**
Persons forming ceramic ware (including porcelain, pottery, stoneware and refractory goods) by casting, extruding, moulding, pressing and shaping. Brick makers, crucible makers, furnace moulders, plaster casters and saggar makers are excluded and classified in 107.5.

CODOT
621.06, 621.08, 621.10, 621.16, 621.18, 621.26, 621.50, 621.52, 621.54, 621.58, 621.60, 621.90

**097.1 Rubber process workers, moulding machine operators, tyre builders**
Persons operating machines to masticate raw or reclaimed rubber; preparing rubber compound, dough or solution; building tyres. Calenderers and extruders (rubber), masticating millmen and press and vacuum moulding machinists are included.

CODOT
592.55, 592.70
594.60 pt., 594.62 pt. Remainders in 097.2
681.06
681.60 pt., 681.90 pt., 681.92 pt. Remainders in 097.2

**097.2 Calender and extruding machine operators, moulders (plastics)**
Persons operating calendering, extruding and moulding machines in the processing of plastics.

CODOT
594.60 pt., 594.62 pt.
681.60 pt., 681.90 pt., 681.92 pt. } Remainders in 097.1

**098.1 Man-made fibre makers**
Persons employed in the manufacturing process producing man-made fibres, including rayon spinners.

CODOT
594.58

**098.2 Brewery and vinery process workers**
Persons producing malt liquors, beers, wines and related products by crushing, mixing, malting, cooking and fermenting grains and fruits; producing yeast and vinegar.

CODOT
573.20, 573.25, 573.66, 573.68
573.50 pt., 573.80 pt.
574.50 pt., 574.58 pt. } Remainders in 098.7
575.99 pt.
576.76
579.25, 579.30, 579.50, 579.55

1

**098.3  Washers, screeners and crushers in mines and quarries**
Persons washing, dry cleaning, crushing or screening coal, stone or ores.
CODOT
592.50 pt., 592.60 pt., 592.90 pt. ⎫
593.35 pt., 593.99 pt.              ⎬ Remainders in 098.9
593.05, 593.10, 593.15, 593.20, 593.25, 593.30, 593.40
594.99 pt. Remainder in 098.9

**098.4  Other material processing—Textiles**
Persons making braid, plait, line and rope from yarn. Persons performing various textile processing, fabricating and finishing tasks
including back washers, battery fillers, braiders, carbonisers, colour matchers, creelers, doffers, driers, fullers, harness builders,
lappers, line and rope makers, loom cleaners, plaiters, scourers, textile machine operators' assistants, twine spinners and twisters,
tufters and washers.
CODOT
546.50, 546.85, 546.86, 546.89
548
549
592.05 pt. Remainder in 098.9

**098.5  Other material processing—Bakery and confectionery workers**
Persons employed in the processing of bread and flour confectionery including ovensmen, mixers, machine operators and minders and
biscuit makers. Bakers and flour confectioners are excluded and classified in 091.0.
CODOT
573.72
574.54
576.50
576.85 pt. Remainder in 098.7

**098.6  Other material processing—Tobacco**
Persons employed in processing tobacco leaves and making cigarettes and other tobacco products by hand or machine.
CODOT
550, 551

**098.7  Other material processing—Food and drink n.e.c.**
Persons crushing, grinding, blending grains, spices, seeds; refining sugar; making glucose, sugar and chocolate confectionery; making
animal feeding stuffs; curing, freezing, cooling foodstuffs; processing milk and cream; producing butter, cheese and ice cream;
making sausages; making non-alcoholic beverages; making macaroni and similar products; making ice; extracting juice from fruit;
shelling, cleaning, etc. nuts.
CODOT
573 pt. Excludes—573.20, 573.25, 573.50 pt., 573.66, 573.68, 573.80 pt. included in 098.2
              —573.72
574 pt. Excludes—574.50 pt., 574.58 pt. included in 098.2
              —574.54
575 pt. Excludes—575.99 pt. included in 098.2
576 pt. Excludes—576.50, 576.85 pt. included in 098.5
              —576.76
579 pt. Excludes—579.25, 579.30, 579.50, 579.55

**098.8  Other material processing—Wood and paper**
Persons in wood processing and paper, paperboard and leatherboard making not elsewhere classified; operating kilns to season wood;
attending wood mills; operating filtering and straining and other separating equipment; operating machines to coat or impregnate
paper and paperboard. Beatermen, calendermen, dryermen, reelermen, refinermen and winder operators are excluded and classified
in 094.1.
CODOT
581
582.60, 582.90, 582.99
583
584 pt. Excludes—584.05, 584.10, 584.65, 584.80 included in 094.1
589
594.56

**098.9  Other material processing—All other (excluding metal) n.e.c.**
Paint colour matchers, concrete mixer drivers, kiln burners (cement), ceramic glaze makers, liquor men (leather tanning), mica split-
ters, dough preparers (artificial teeth), saggar packers; persons operating kilns to fire abrasive and carbon products, operating
machines to produce slurry for making asbestos-cement goods, operating equipment to make and dry plasterboard, making pipes and
sheets of asbestos-cement; persons in material processing (excluding metal) not elsewhere classified.
CODOT
590.10 pt. Remainder in 095.1
590.40 pt. Remainder in 095.6 and 095.7
590.99 pt. Remainder in 095.1 and 095.7
591 pt. Excludes—591.10, 591.50, 591.52, 591.54, 591.58, 591.62, 591.90 included in 096.1
592 pt. Excludes—592.05 pt. included in 098.4
              —592.50 pt., 592.60 pt., 592.90 pt. included in 098.3
              —592.55, 592.70 included in 097.1
593.35 pt., 593.99 pt. Remainders in 098.3
594 pt. Excludes—594.56, 594.58
              —594.60, 594.62 included in 097.1 and 097.2
              —594.99 pt. Remainder in 098.3
599 pt. Excludes—599.10, 599.50, 599.99 pt. included in 096.1

**099.1  Foremen—Compositors**
Foremen of persons included in 100.1.
CODOT
630.10 pt. Remainder in 099.5

**099.2 Foremen—Electrotypers, stereotypers, printing plate and cylinder preparers**
Foremen of persons included in 100.2.

CODOT
630.20

**099.3 Foremen—Printing machine minders and assistants**
Foremen of persons included in 100.3.

CODOT
630.30 pt., 630.99 pt. Remainders in 093.5

**099.4 Foremen—Screen and block printers**
Foremen of persons included in 100.4.

CODOT
630.40

**099.5 Foremen—Printers (so described)**
Foremen of persons included in 100.5.

CODOT
630.10 pt. Remainder in 099.1

**100.1 Compositors**
Persons setting up printing type by hand or machine. Lay-out men and make-up hands are included.

CODOT
632

**100.2 Electrotypers, stereotypers, printing plate and cylinder preparers**
Persons in printing plate and cylinder preparing occupations. Engravers of metal printing plates and rollers are excluded and classified in 130.2.

CODOT
633

**100.3 Printing machine minders and assistants**
Persons setting, operating and assisting in operating letterpress, lithographic, photogravure and web-offset printing machines. Offset duplicating machine operators are excluded and classified in 107.9.

CODOT
634.05, 634.10, 634.15, 634.20
639.50, 639.52, 639.54

**100.4 Screen and block printers**
Persons printing lettering and designs on fabric and other materials by screen and block method.

CODOT
635

**100.5 Printers (so described)**
Persons returned as 'printer', 'general printer', 'master printer', 'printer and stationer' without more specific description, including principals of printing firms.

CODOT
631

**101.1 Foremen—Tailors, tailoresses, dressmakers**
Foremen of persons included in 102.1.

CODOT
650.05
650.10 pt. Remainder in 101.6

**101.2 Foremen—Clothing cutters, milliners, furriers**
Foremen of persons included in 102.2.

CODOT
650.20, 650.25
650.30 pt. Remainder in 101.6

**101.3 Foremen—Sewers, embroiderers**
Foremen of persons included in 102.3.

CODOT
650.35, 650.40

**101.4 Foremen—Coach trimmers, upholsterers, mattress makers**
Foremen of persons included in 103.0.

CODOT
650.15 pt. Remainder in 101.6

**101.5 Foremen—Carpet fitters**
Foremen of persons included in 107.3.

CODOT
650.99 pt. Remainder in 101.6

**101.6 Foremen—Other making and repairing, clothing and related products**
Foremen of persons included in 107.8.

CODOT
650.10 pt. Remainder in 101.1
650.15 pt. Remainder in 101.4
650.30 pt. Remainder in 101.2
650.45
650.99 pt. Remainder in 101.5

**102.1    Tailors, tailoresses, dressmakers**
Persons making or fitting and altering tailored garments, dresses and other articles of light clothing. Persons described as tailors, tailors' assistants and tailors' fitters in manufacturing or retail trade are included. Corset makers are excluded and classified in 107.8.
CODOT
651
652.10, 652.30, 652.40

**102.2    Clothing cutters, milliners, furriers**
Persons cutting out, shaping and trimming material, including fur, for the manufacture of garments; making women's, girls' and children's hats throughout.
CODOT
654, 655
656.10, 656.12, 656.14, 656.16, 656.18, 656.20, 656.50, 656.52, 656.54, 656.56, 656.58

**102.3    Sewers, embroiderers**
Persons sewing and embroidering either by hand or machine, garments and other products made from textile fabric, fur and skin.
CODOT
657, 658

**103.0    Coach trimmers, upholsterers, mattress makers**
Persons upholstering vehicle and aircraft seating; fixing trimmings to the interiors of vehicles and aircraft; upholstering furniture; making mattresses, curtains and other soft furnishings.
CODOT
653 pt. Excludes—653.50, 653.99 included in 107.8

**104.1    Foremen—Carpenters, joiners**
Foremen of persons included in 105.1.
CODOT
670.10
670.30 pt. Remainder in 104.3 and 104.6

**104.2    Foremen—Cabinet makers**
Foremen of persons included in 105.2.
CODOT
670.20

**104.3    Foremen—Case and box makers**
Foremen of persons included in 105.3.
CODOT
670.30 pt. Remainder in 104.1 and 104.6

**104.4    Foremen—Pattern makers (moulds)**
Foremen of persons included in 105.4.
CODOT
670.60

**104.5    Foremen—Sawyers, veneer cutters, woodworking machinists**
Foremen of persons included in 106.0.
CODOT
670.40, 670.50

**104.6    Foremen—Other making and repairing, wood**
Foremen of persons included in 107.6.
CODOT
670.30 pt. Remainder in 104.1 and 104.3
670.99

**105.1    Carpenters, joiners**
Persons constructing, erecting, installing and repairing wooden structures and fittings on site and on board ship; building and repairing small wooden craft and preparing launchways; making wooden internal fittings for aircraft, scenic equipment for theatres and film studios. Scale model makers and template makers are included.
CODOT
671
673.05, 673.10, 673.15, 673.20, 673.25, 673.30

**105.2    Cabinet makers**
Persons performing the more highly skilled tasks in making and repairing wooden furniture and piano and cabinet cases. Assemblers of wood products are excluded and classified in 138.12.
CODOT
672

**105.3    Case and box makers**
Persons cutting and assembling wood to make packing cases, crates or similar articles. Coopers are included.
CODOT
673.40, 673.45

**105.4    Pattern makers (moulds)**
Persons making patterns of wood, metal or other materials for moulds used in metal casting.
CODOT
677

**106.0 Sawyers, veneer cutters, woodworking machinists**

Persons setting and/or operating all types of wood cutting or woodworking machinery, including wood turners.

CODOT
674, 675, 676
799.06

**107.1 Labourers and mates to woodworking craftsmen**

Persons assisting woodworking craftsmen and woodworking machine operators.

CODOT
679.90, 679.92

**107.2 Dental technicians**

Persons engaged in making and repairing dentures.

CODOT
692.20

**107.3 Carpet fitters**

Persons laying carpets on customers' premises. Carpet planners are excluded and classified in 107.8.

CODOT
659.40

**107.4 Musical instrument makers, piano tuners**

Persons making, repairing, adjusting, stringing and tuning musical instruments; fitting and regulating piano action parts and making bows for stringed instruments.

CODOT
690.10
691

**107.5 Other making and repairing—Glass and ceramics**

Brick makers, crucible makers, furnace moulders, plaster casters, saggar makers and persons performing various tasks n.e.c. in glass, clay and stone working and ceramics forming and finishing.

CODOT
619
621.02, 621.04, 621.12, 621.14, 621.20, 621.22, 621.24, 621.28, 621.56, 621.62, 621.92, 621.99
622
629

**107.6 Other making and repairing—Wood**

Persons carving and bending wood; laying hardwood strip and wood block floors; matching, joining and repairing veneers and performing various tasks not elsewhere classified. Makers of handcarts, ladders, picture frames, sports equipment, textile bobbins and shuttles, timber fences; stockers (bespoke guns) and wheelwrights are included.

CODOT
673.35, 673.50, 673.55, 673.60, 673.99
679 pt. Excludes—679.90, 679.92

**107.7 Other making and repairing—Leather**

Persons engaged in the manufacture of footwear, leather and leather substitute goods other than garments and gloves, not elsewhere classified. Harness makers and saddlers are included. Upholsterers and leather goods assemblers are excluded and classified in 103.0 and 138.12 respectively.

CODOT
664
669 pt. Excludes—669.14, 669.60, 669.62, 669.64, 669.66, 669.94 included in 085.3

**107.8 Other making and repairing—Clothing and related products**

Persons making patterns for the manufacture of garments and upholstery; marking and cutting out parts of articles other than garments; making canvas goods such as awnings, boat covers, flags, sails and tents; performing various tasks in the manufacture of fabric bags and sacks. Carpet planners, corset makers, hood and apron makers (perambulators) and persons shaping hats by hand or machine are included.

CODOT
652.20, 652.99
653.50, 653.99
656 pt. Excludes—656.10, 656.12, 656.14, 656.16, 656.18, 656.20, 656.50, 656.52, 656.54, 656.56, 656.58 included in 102.2
659 pt. Excludes—659.40

**107.9 Other making and repairing—Paper goods and printing**

Persons engaged in setting and operating die stamping and embossing machines; processing, printing and finishing still and cine film; performing various tasks in printing, photographic processing and manufacture of paper and paperboard products not elsewhere classified. Printers (textile and wallpaper), offset duplicating machine operators, paper pattern cutting machine operators, provers, spoolers and upper markers (footwear) are included. All other cutting and slitting machine operators (paper goods and printing) are excluded and classified in 094.3.

CODOT
634 pt. Excludes—634.05, 634.10, 634.15, 634.20 included in 100.3
636
639 pt. Excludes—639.50, 639.52, 639.54 included in 100.3
642 pt. Excludes—642.54, 642.56 included in 094.3

**107.10 Other making and repairing—Rubber**

Persons making and repairing articles of rubber material not elsewhere classified; sheathing cables and wires; lining and covering industrial plant, equipment and products. Tyre repairers and restorers are included but tyre builders are excluded and classified in 097.1.

CODOT
681.02, 681.04, 681.50, 681.52, 681.70, 681.72, 681.74, 681.76, 681.78, 681.80, 681.96
681.08 pt., 681.10 pt., 681.56 pt., 681.58 pt., 681.62 pt., 681.64 pt., 681.66 pt., 681.94 pt., 681.99 pt. Remainders in 107.11

**107.11**  **Other making and repairing—Plastics**
Persons making and repairing articles of plastics materials, including glass fibre reinforced plastics, not elsewhere classified; sheathing cables and wires. Artificial eye makers and spectacle frame makers are included.

CODOT
681.12, 681.14, 681.16, 681.54, 681.68
681.08 pt., 681.10 pt., 681.56 pt., 681.58 pt., 681.62 pt., 681.64 pt., 681.66 pt., 681.94 pt., 681.99 pt. Remainders in 107.10

**107.12**  **Other making and repairing—All other (excluding metal and electrical) n.e.c.**
Persons forming and finishing concrete, asbestos-cement, abrasive stone and related products; making and repairing orthopaedic and orthodontic appliances; brush makers; wicker product makers; wig makers and racket stringers. Fillers of cartridges, detonators and fireworks are included. Persons operating machines producing pipes and sheets of asbestos-cement, and dental technicians are excluded and classified in 098.9 and 107.2 respectively.

CODOT
620.30
623
690.20, 690.99
692.10, 692.30, 692.40, 692.99
699

**108.1**  **Foremen—Furnace operating occupations (metal)**
Foremen of persons included in 109.1.

CODOT
710.10

**108.2**  **Foremen—Rollermen**
Foremen of persons included in 109.2.

CODOT
710.20 pt. Remainder in 108.4 and 108.9

**108.3**  **Foremen—Smiths, forgemen**
Foremen of persons included in 109.3.

CODOT
710.40 pt. Remainder in 108.9

**108.4**  **Foremen—Metal drawers**
Foremen of persons included in 110.1.

CODOT
710.20 pt. Remainder in 108.2 and 108.9

**108.5**  **Foremen—Moulders, core makers, die casters**
Foremen of persons included in 110.2.

CODOT
710.30 pt. Remainder in 108.9

**108.6**  **Foremen—Electroplaters**
Foremen of persons included in 110.3.

CODOT
710.50 pt. Remainder in 108.8

**108.7**  **Foremen—Annealers, hardeners, temperers (metal)**
Foremen of persons included in 110.4.

CODOT
710.60

**108.8**  **Foremen—Galvanizers, tin platers, dip platers**
Foremen of persons included in 131.2.

CODOT
710.50 pt. Remainder in 108.6

**108.9**  **Foremen—Metal making and treating workers n.e.c.**
Foremen of persons included in 131.3.

CODOT
710.20 pt. Remainder in 108.2 and 108.4
710.30 pt. Remainder in 108.5
710.40 pt. Remainder in 108.3
710.99

**109.1**  **Furnace operating occupations (metal)**
Persons operating furnaces, etc. to smelt metalliferous ores, refine metal, melt metal for casting, reheat metal for further working. Persons heating metal for annealing, etc. and ladlemen are excluded and classified in 110.4 and 131.3 respectively.

CODOT
711

**109.2**  **Rollermen**
Persons operating or directing the operation of steel rolling mill to roll slabs, blooms, billets, bars, rods, strip, sheet, plates, sections or tubes. Assistant rollers are included but rolling mill assistants, third and fourth hand rollers, and bar, etc. straighteners are excluded and classified in 131.3.

CODOT
712.05, 712.10

**109.3**  **Smiths, forgemen**
Persons shaping heated metal by hand hammering on an anvil; by power hammer or forging press. Chain makers (forging) are included. Forge assistants and smiths' strikers are excluded and classified in 131.3.

CODOT
714 pt. Excludes—714.50, 714.55, 714.60, 714.65, 714.70, 714.75, 714.99 pt. included in 131.3

**110.1    Metal drawers**
Persons setting up and operating machines to draw wire, tubes, rods or bars.
CODOT
712.70, 712.75

**110.2    Moulders, coremakers, die casters**
Persons making moulds or cores either by hand or machine for use in casting molten metal; pouring metal into dies or operating die casting machinery.
CODOT
713.05, 713.10, 713.15, 713.20, 713.25, 713.50, 713.52, 713.54, 713.68, 713.70, 713.92

**110.3    Electroplaters**
Persons coating articles or parts electrolytically, in tanks or vats, with chromium, copper, nickel, or other non-ferrous metal. Anodisers and electroformers are excluded and classified in 131.2.
CODOT
715.05

**110.4    Annealers, hardeners, temperers (metal)**
Persons heat treating metal to anneal, harden or temper.
CODOT
716

**111.1    Foremen—Press and machine tool setters**
Foremen of persons included in 112.1.
CODOT
720.10 pt. Remainder in 111.2, 111.3 and 111.4
720.20 pt. Remainder in 111.5

**111.2    Foremen—Centre lathe turners**
Foremen of persons included in 112.2.
CODOT
720.10 pt. Remainder in 111.1, 111.3 and 111.4

**111.3    Foremen—Machine tool setter operators**
Foremen of persons included in 112.3.
CODOT
720.10 pt. Remainder in 111.1, 111.2 and 111.4

**111.4    Foremen—Machine tool operators**
Foremen of persons included in 112.4.
CODOT
720.10 pt. Remainder in 111.1, 111.2 and 111.3

**111.5    Foremen—Press, stamping and automatic machine operators**
Foremen of persons included in 113.1.
CODOT
720.20 pt. Remainder in 111.1
720.30

**111.6    Foremen—Metal polishers**
Foremen of persons included in 113.2.
CODOT
720.40 pt. Remainder in 111.7, 111.8 and 131.9

**111.7    Foremen—Fettlers, dressers**
Foremen of persons included in 113.3.
CODOT
720.40 pt. Remainder in 111.6, 111.8 and 131.9

**111.8    Foremen—Shot blasters**
Foremen of persons included in 131.8.
CODOT
720.40 pt. Remainder in 111.6, 111.7 and 131.9

**112.1    Press and machine tool setters**
Persons setting up press and machine tool and metal working machines.
CODOT
721

**112.2    Centre lathe turners**
Persons setting up and operating centre lathes. Roll turners and 'fitters and turners' are excluded and classified in 112.4 and 117.0 respectively.
CODOT
722.04

**112.3    Machine tool setter operators**
Persons setting up and operating boring, drilling, grinding and milling machines (except centre lathes). Metal spinners are included.
CODOT
722 pt. Excludes—722.04

**112.4** **Machine tool operators**

Persons operating previously set up machine tools to cut, shape and otherwise machine metal workpieces. Roll turners and persons returned as 'engineer' or 'mechanical engineer', without further information, are included.

CODOT
723


**113.1** **Press, stamping and automatic machine operators**

Persons operating presses and preset machines for shaping of cold metal parts. Press bending machinists are included.

CODOT
724, 725


**113.2** **Metal polishers**

Persons polishing metal including jewellery polishers, die polishers and barrel polishers.

CODOT
726.20, 726.50, 726.55, 726.60


**113.3** **Fettlers, dressers**

Persons removing surplus metal and rough surfaces from castings, forgings or components with hand and power tools. Shot blasters, and chippers and grinders (steel dressing) are excluded and classified in 131.8, and 131.9 respectively.

CODOT
726.90


**114.1** **Foreman—Tool makers, tool fitters, markers-out**

Foremen of persons included in 115.0.

CODOT
730.10


**114.2** **Foremen—Precision instrument makers and repairers**

Foremen of persons included in 116.1.

CODOT
730.20 pt., 740.40 pt. Remainders in 114.3


**114.3** **Foremen—Watch and chronometer makers and repairers**

Foremen of persons included in 116.2.

CODOT
730.20 pt., 740.40 pt. Remainders in 114.2


**114.4** **Foremen—Metal working production fitters and fitter/machinists**

Foremen of persons included in 117.0.

CODOT
730.30, 730.40, 730.50
740.10


**114.5** **Foremen—Motor mechanics, auto engineers**

Foremen of persons included in 118.1.

CODOT
740.20


**114.6** **Foremen—Maintenance fitters (aircraft engines)**

Foremen of persons included in 118.2.

CODOT
740.30


**114.7** **Foremen—Office machinery mechanics**

Foremen of persons included in 119.0.

CODOT
740.50


**115.0** **Tool makers, tool fitters, markers-out**

Persons making, maintaining and repairing press tools, dies, gauges, jigs and fixtures; marking out metal for machine tool working.

CODOT
731


**116.1** **Precision instrument makers and repairers**

Persons making and repairing precision and optical instruments including calibrators. Office machinery mechanics; dental and surgical instrument makers and repairers; and instrument assemblers are excluded and classified in 119.0; 131.9; and 135.2 respectively.

CODOT
732 pt. Excludes—732.15
744 pt. Excludes—744.30


**116.2** **Watch and chronometer makers and repairers**

Persons making, repairing, cleaning and adjusting watches, clocks and chronometers. Watch and clock assemblers are excluded and classified in 135.2.

CODOT
732.15
744.30

**117.0    Metal working production fitters and fitter/machinists**
Persons erecting, installing, repairing and servicing engineering and mechanical plant and industrial machinery, including ship machinery and related fittings, airframes, coin operated machines, locks and railway rolling stock. Engine fitters, maintenance fitters, setter fitter-mechanics and 'fitters and turners' (so described) are included. Persons maintaining and repairing aircraft engines are excluded and classified in 118.2.

CODOT
733, 734, 741
799.02, 799.04

**118.1    Motor mechanics, auto engineers**
Persons repairing and servicing mechanical parts of motor vehicles. Oilers and greasers of motor vehicles are included. Engine fitters are excluded and classified in 117.0.

CODOT
742
746.10

**118.2    Maintenance fitters (aircraft engines)**
Persons repairing and servicing aircraft engines; repairing and servicing both aircraft engines and frames. Persons repairing and servicing airframes but not engines are excluded and classified in 117.0.

CODOT
743
749.05, 749.35

**119.0    Office machinery mechanics**
Persons repairing and servicing mechanical office machinery, cash tills and registers. Electrical office machinery service engineers and electronic office machinery service engineers are excluded and classified in 121.2 and 123.2 respectively.

CODOT
745

**120.1    Foremen—Production fitters (electrical, electronic)**
Foremen of persons included in 121.1.

CODOT
750.10, 750.20

**120.2    Foremen—Electricians, electrical maintenance fitters**
Foremen of persons included in 121.2.

CODOT
750.30
760.10 pt., 760.20 pt., 760.30 pt. Remainders in 120.3

**120.3    Foremen—Plant operators and attendants n.e.c.**
Foremen of persons included in 121.4.

CODOT
760.10 pt., 760.20 pt., 760.30 pt. Remainders in 120.2
970.10 pt. Remainder in 159.9

**120.4    Foremen—Telephone fitters**
Foremen of persons included in 122.1.

CODOT
760.40 pt., 760.50 pt. Remainders in 120.6 and 120.7

**120.5    Foremen—Cable jointers, linesmen**
Foremen of persons included in 122.2.

CODOT
760.60

**120.6    Foremen—Radio and TV mechanics**
Foremen of persons included in 123.1.

CODOT
760.40 pt., 760.50 pt. Remainders in 120.4 and 120.7

**120.7    Foremen—Other electronic maintenance engineers**
Foremen of persons included in 123.2.

CODOT
760.40 pt., 760.50 pt. Remainders in 120.4 and 120.6

**121.1    Production fitters (electrical, electronic)**
Persons fitting and assembling parts and sub-assemblies in the manufacture of electrical and electronic equipment. Electrical and electronic fitters not otherwise specified are included.

CODOT
751

**121.2    Electricians, electrical maintenance fitters**
Persons installing, maintaining and repairing electrical wiring systems, electrical plant, machinery and other equipment, including electrical wiremen. Electricity board inspectors, power switchboard operators and wirers of electronic equipment are excluded and classified in 006.3, 121.4 and 131.6 respectively.

CODOT
752
761.10 pt., 761.20 pt., 761.30 pt., 761.40 pt., 761.50 pt., 761.60 pt. Remainders in 121.3
761.70, 761.80, 761.99
762.10 pt., 762.20 pt., 762.30 pt. Remainders in 121.3
762.40, 762.99

**121.3**   **Electrical engineers (so described)**
Persons returned as 'electrical engineer' without more specific description.
CODOT
761.10 pt., 761.20 pt., 761.30 pt., 761.40 pt., 761.50 pt., 761.60 pt., 762.10 pt., 762.20 pt., 762.30 pt. Remainders in 121.2

**121.4**   **Plant operators and attendants n.e.c.**
Persons operating and attending machinery, plant and equipment such as compressors, electrical substations and switchboards, turbines, nuclear generating stations.
CODOT
971 pt. Excludes—971.15, 971.92 included in 161.1
          —971.91, 971.93 included in 161.2
973
979.10

**122.1**   **Telephone fitters**
Persons installing and maintaining public and private telephone systems.
CODOT
763.10

**122.2**   **Cable jointers, linesmen**
Persons installing, maintaining and repairing overhead lines for electricity supply, electric traction and telecommunications; jointing underground, submarine and surface electric and telecommunications cables.
CODOT
764

**123.1**   **Radio and TV mechanics**
Persons repairing and maintaining domestic radios and television receivers.
CODOT
763.65, 763.70

**123.2**   **Other electronic maintenance engineers**
Persons installing, maintaining and repairing electronic equipment other than domestic radio and television receivers. Installers and fitters of computer systems are included.
CODOT
763 pt. Excludes—763.10 included in 122.1
          —763.65, 763.70

**124.1**   **Foremen—Plumbers, heating and ventilating fitters, gas fitters**
Foremen of persons included in 125.0.
CODOT
770.10 pt. Remainder in 131.9

**124.2**   **Foremen—Sheet metal workers**
Foremen of persons included in 126.1.
CODOT
770.20

**124.3**   **Foremen—Metal plate workers, shipwrights, riveters**
Foremen of persons included in 126.2.
CODOT
770.30 pt. Remainder in 131.9

**124.4**   **Foremen—Steel erectors, benders, fixers**
Foremen of persons included in 127.1.
CODOT
770.40 pt. Remainder in 124.5

**124.5**   **Foremen—Scaffolders, stagers**
Foremen of persons included in 127.2.
CODOT
770.40 pt. Remainder in 124.4

**124.6**   **Foremen—Welders**
Foremen of persons included in 128.0.
CODOT
770.50

**124.7**   **Foremen—Riggers**
Foremen of persons included in 131.5.
CODOT
770.99 pt. Remainder in 131.9

**125.0**   **Plumbers, heating and ventilating fitters, gas fitters**
Persons installing, maintaining and repairing plumbing fixtures, heating and ventilating systems, pipe systems and lead, lead lined and lead covered plant.
CODOT
771 pt. Excludes—771.40, 771.99 included in 131.9

**126.1**   **Sheet metal workers**
Persons marking out, cutting, shaping and fitting sheet metal to make and repair products and components. Metal spinners, press operators, and sheet metal bending and rolling machine operators are excluded and classified in 112.3, 113.1, and 131.9 respectively.
CODOT
772

**126.2 Metal plate workers, shipwrights, riveters**
Persons marking off, drilling, bending, positioning and riveting metal plates and girders and sealing joints in metal plate. Shipwrights and shipyard steelworkers are included. Holders-up and shipyard frame benders are excluded and classified in 131.9.
CODOT
773 pt. Excludes—773.50, 773.99 included in 131.9

**127.1 Steel erectors, benders, fixers**
Persons fitting and erecting structural metal work, making up metal framework by hand to form reinforcing core for concrete structures or products. Metal shuttering erectors are excluded and classified in 131.5.
CODOT
774.20, 774.50

**127.2 Scaffolders, stagers**
Persons erecting and dismantling scaffolding, and temporary working platforms for use in ship construction and repair.
CODOT
774.25, 774.30

**128.0 Welders**
Persons joining metal parts and fabrications by welding, brazing and soldering; cutting metal to specifications and removing defects by means of gas flame and oxygen jet, electric arc or laser beam. Assemblers of vehicles and other metal goods are excluded and classified in 135.3.
CODOT
775

**129.1 Foremen—Goldsmiths, silversmiths, precious stone workers**
Foremen of persons included in 130.1.
CODOT
790.10

**129.2 Foremen—Engravers, etchers (printing)**
Foremen of persons included in 130.2.
CODOT
790.20 pt. Remainder in 131.9

**129.3 Foremen—Coach and vehicle body builders**
Foremen of persons included in 131.1.
CODOT
790.30

**129.4 Foremen—Oilers, greasers, lubricators**
Foremen of persons included in 131.4.
CODOT
740.99 pt. Remainder in 131.9

**129.5 Foremen—Electronics wiremen**
Foremen of persons included in 131.6.
CODOT
750.99 pt. Remainder in 129.6

**129.6 Foremen—Coil winders**
Foremen of persons included in 131.7.
CODOT
750.99 pt. Remainder in 129.5

**130.1 Goldsmiths, silversmiths, precious stone workers**
Persons making and repairing jewellery and precious metal ware; cutting, polishing and setting precious and semi-precious stones; making jewellery patterns. Precious metal spinners and jewellery engravers are excluded and classified in 112.3 and 131.9 respectively.
CODOT
791

**130.2 Engravers, etchers (printing)**
Persons engraving and etching metal printing cylinders, plates and rollers; engraving metal dies and punches.
CODOT
792 pt. Excludes—792.18, 792.20, 792.50, 792.99 included in 131.9

**131.1 Coach and vehicle body builders**
Persons constructing and repairing vehicle bodies (including railway coaches and wagons) and fixing fittings to vehicle and aircraft bodies. Vehicle body assemblers are excluded and classified in 135.3.
CODOT
793

**131.2 Galvanizers, tin platers, dip platers**
Persons coating articles, sheet, wire, etc. with metal, including anodisers and electroformers. Electroplaters are excluded and classified in 110.3.
CODOT
715 pt. Excludes—715.05 included in 110.3

**131.3   Metal making and treating workers n.e.c.**

Persons making and treating metal in operations n.e.c. including rolling mill assistants, core turners, casters (not die casters), ladlemen, smiths' strikers, forge assistants, and bar, etc. straighteners. Persons returned as labourers are excluded and classified in groups 160.1–160.8.

CODOT

712 pt. Excludes—712.05, 712.10 included in 109.2
             —712.70, 712.75 included in 110.1
713 pt. Excludes—713.05, 713.10, 713.15, 713.20, 713.25, 713.50, 713.52, 713.54, 713.68, 713.70, 713.92 included in 110.2
714 pt. Excludes—714.05, 714.10, 714.15, 714.20, 714.25, 714.30, 714.35, 714.99 pt. included in 109.3
719 pt. Excludes—719.84, 719.85, 719.86, 719.87, 719.88, 719.99 pt. included in 160.5
             —719.89 included in 160.6

**131.4   Oilers, greasers, lubricators**

Persons lubricating moving parts of stationary engines, rolling stock, other machinery and mechanical equipment. Oilers and greasers of motor vehicles are excluded and classified in 118.1.

CODOT

746 pt. Excludes—746.10 included in 118.1
             —746.60

**131.5   Riggers**

Persons preparing, installing, repairing and splicing ropes, wires and cables, setting up lifting equipment. Metal shuttering erectors are included.

CODOT

774 pt. Excludes—774.20, 774.50 included in 127.1
             —774.25, 774.30 included in 127.2

**131.6   Electronics wiremen**

Persons wiring up prepared parts and/or sub-assemblies in the manufacture of various types of electronic equipment. Electrical wiremen are excluded and classified in 121.2.

CODOT

759.05, 759.10, 759.15

**131.7   Coil winders**

Persons making coils and wiring harnesses for electrical and electronic equipment. Cable formers and neon sign assemblers are included.

CODOT

759 pt. Excludes—759.05, 759.10, 759.15

**131.8   Shot blasters**

Persons cleaning and/or smoothing metal surfaces by the use of vapour jet or compressed air and abrasive material.

CODOT

726.92

**131.9   Other metal, jewellery, electrical production workers**

Chippers and grinders (steel dressing), dental and surgical instrument makers and repairers, sheet metal bending and rolling machine operators, holders-up and shipyard frame benders, jewellery engravers, mates to metal working craftsmen, strippers and grinders (card clothing); persons engaged in metal, jewellery, engineering electrical and electronics products and parts making or repairing not elsewhere classified.

CODOT

720.40 pt. Remainder in 111.6, 111.7 and 111.8
720.99
726 pt. Excludes—726.20, 726.50, 726.55, 726.60 included in 113.2
             —726.90 included in 113.3
             —726.92
729
730.99
739
740.99 pt. Remainder in 129.4
746.60
749 pt. Excludes—749.05, 749.35 included in 118.2
760.99
769
770.10 pt. Remainder in 124.1
770.30 pt. Remainder in 124.3
770.99 pt. Remainder in 124.7
771.40, 771.99
773.50, 773.99
776
779
790.20 pt. Remainder in 129.2
790.99
792.18, 792.20, 792.50, 792.99
799 pt. Excludes—799.02, 799.04 included in 117.0
             —799.06 included in 106.0

**—.1   Foremen (engineering and allied trades)**

Persons returned as foremen in engineering and allied trades (S.I.C. Division 3) and not associated with a specific occupation. Technical supervisors employed in government factories are included. Works, general and senior foremen are excluded and classified in 034.0.

CODOT

—

**—.2   Trainee craftsmen (engineering and allied trades)**

Persons returned as trainee craftsmen or apprentices in engineering and allied trades not associated with a specific occupation.

CODOT

—

**132.1  Foremen—Pottery decorators**
Foremen of persons included in 133.1.

CODOT
810.20 pt. Remainder in 132.4 and 138.12
810.30 pt. Remainder in 132.2 and 132.3
810.40 pt., 810.99 pt. Remainders in 138.12

**132.2  Foremen—Coach painters (so described)**
Foremen of persons included in 133.2.

CODOT
810.30 pt. Remainder in 132.1 and 132.3

**132.3  Foremen—Other spray painters**
Foremen of persons included in 133.3.

CODOT
810.30 pt. Remainder in 132.1 and 132.2

**132.4  Foremen—Painters and decorators n.e.c., french polishers**
Foremen of persons included in 133.4.

CODOT
810.10, 810.50
810.20 pt. Remainder in 132.1 and 138.12

**133.1  Pottery decorators**
Persons dipping and spraying ceramics with glaze, painting ceramics and applying transfers. Ground layers are included. Ceramic stencillers are excluded and classified in 138.12.

CODOT
812 pt. Excludes—812.05
              —812.10, 812.70, 812.99 included in 138.12
813.50, 813.90
814.10
819.10, 819.55, 819.92

**133.2  Coach painters (so described)**
Persons returned as 'coach painter' without more specific description.

CODOT
813.20 pt. Remainder in 133.3
819.20

**133.3  Other spray painters**
Persons applying paint, enamel or lacquer by spraying, but persons spraying ceramics are excluded and classified in 133.1.

CODOT
813 pt. Excludes—813.20 pt. included in 133.2
              —813.50, 813.90

**133.4  Painters and decorators n.e.c., french polishers**
Persons preparing surfaces and applying paint, wallpaper and other protective materials, not elsewhere classified; staining, waxing and french polishing wood surfaces. Signwriters are included.

CODOT
811
812.05
815

**134.1  Foremen assemblers—Electrical, electronic**
Foremen of persons included in 135.1.

CODOT
820.10 pt. Remainder in 134.2, 134.3, 134.5 and 138.12

**134.2  Foremen assemblers—Instruments**
Foremen of persons included in 135.2.

CODOT
820.10 pt. Remainder in 134.1, 134.3, 134.4, 134.5 and 138.12

**134.3  Foremen assemblers—Vehicles and other metal goods**
Foremen of persons included in 135.3.

CODOT
820.10 pt. Remainder in 134.1, 134.2, 134.4, 134.5 and 138.12

**134.4  Foremen assemblers—Paper production, processing and printing**
Foremen of persons included in 138.8.

CODOT
820.10 pt. Remainder in 134.1, 134.2, 134.3, 134.5 and 138.12

**134.5  Foremen assemblers—Plastics goods**
Foremen of persons included in 138.9.

CODOT
820.10 pt. Remainder in 134.1, 134.2, 134.3, 134.4 and 138.12

**135.1  Assemblers (electrical, electronic)**
Persons engaged in the semi-skilled or repetitive assembly of electrical and electronic equipment.

CODOT
821.45

**135.2    Instrument assemblers**
Persons engaged in the routine assembly of precision instruments such as gauges, meters, watches and clocks, etc..
CODOT
821.35 pt., 821.40 pt. Remainders in 135.3

**135.3    Assemblers (vehicles and other metal goods)**
Persons engaged in the routine assembly of vehicles and other metal and engineering products.
CODOT
821.35 pt., 821.40 pt. Remainders in 135.2

**136.1    Foremen inspectors, viewers, examiners—Metal, electrical goods**
Foremen of persons included in 137.1.
CODOT
830.10, 830.20

**136.2    Foremen inspectors, viewers, examiners—Textiles**
Foremen of persons included in 138.2.
CODOT
830.30 pt. Remainder in 136.3, 136.4, 136.5, 136.6 and 136.9

**136.3    Foremen inspectors, viewers, examiners—Food**
Foremen of persons included in 138.3.
CODOT
830.30 pt. Remainder in 136.2, 136.4, 136.5, 136.6 and 136.9

**136.4    Foremen inspectors, viewers, examiners—Rubber goods**
Foremen of persons included in 138.4.
CODOT
830.30 pt. Remainder in 136.2, 136.3, 136.5, 136.6 and 136.9

**136.5    Foremen inspectors, viewers, examiners—Plastics goods**
Foremen of persons included in 138.5.
CODOT
830.30 pt. Remainder in 136.2, 136.3, 136.4, 136.6 and 136.9

**136.6    Foremen inspectors, viewers, examiners—Woodwork**
Foremen of persons included in 138.6.
CODOT
830.30 pt. Remainder in 136.2, 136.3, 136.4, 136.5 and 136.9

**136.7    Foremen—Packers, bottlers, canners, fillers**
Foremen of persons included in 137.2.
CODOT
840.10

**136.8    Foremen—Laboratory assistants**
Foremen of persons included in 138.1.
CODOT
830.99 pt. Remainder in 136.10

**136.9    Foremen—Inspectors, sorters in paper production, processing and printing**
Foremen of persons included in 138.7.
CODOT
830.30 pt. Remainder in 136.2, 136.3, 136.4, 136.5 and 136.6

**136.10    Foremen—Weighers**
Foremen of persons included in 138.10.
CODOT
830.99 pt. Remainder in 136.8

**136.11    Foremen—Graders, sorters, selectors n.e.c.**
Foremen of persons included in 138.11.
CODOT
830.40

**137.1    Inspectors, viewers (metal, electrical goods)**
Persons inspecting or testing metal, engineering and electrical products or parts. Industrial radiographers are excluded and classified in 030.2.
CODOT
831, 832

**137.2    Packers, bottlers, canners, fillers**
Persons packing, wrapping, filling, labelling, sealing, containers by hand or machine.
CODOT
841, 842

**138.1    Laboratory assistants**
Persons carrying out routine procedures, not requiring professional training, in physical, chemical, biological, botanical, medical and other laboratories. Laboratory technicians are excluded and classified in 030.1.
CODOT
839.30

**138.2 Inspectors, viewers, examiners—Textiles**

Persons inspecting or testing textile materials or products for processing or manufacturing defects. Yarn straighteners are included.

CODOT
833.05, 833.10, 833.35
833.55 pt. Remainder in 138.12
833.99 pt. Remainder in 138.3 and 138.12

**138.3 Inspectors, viewers, examiners—Food**

Persons inspecting or examining food for processing defects. Egg candlers and foodstuffs samplers are included.

CODOT
833.90
833.99 pt. Remainder in 138.2 and 138.12

**138.4 Inspectors, viewers, examiners—Rubber goods**

Persons inspecting or examining rubber material or goods, for processing or manufacturing defects.

CODOT
833.45 pt. Remainder in 138.5

**138.5 Inspectors, viewers, examiners—Plastics goods**

Persons inspecting or examining plastics materials or goods, for processing or manufacturing defects.

CODOT
833.45 pt. Remainder in 138.4

**138.6 Inspectors, viewers, examiners—Woodwork**

Persons inspecting or examining wood or wood products, for processing or manufacturing defects.

CODOT
833.20

**138.7 Inspectors, sorters in paper production, processing and printing**

Persons inspecting, examining or sorting paper, paper products or printed matter, for processing or manufacturing defects.

CODOT
833.25

**138.8 Assemblers in paper production, processing and printing**

Persons engaged in routine assembly in paper production, processing and printing. Paper pattern folders are included.

CODOT
821.10
821.99 pt. Remainder in 138.12

**138.9 Assemblers (plastics goods)**

Persons engaged in routine assembly of plastics goods or components.

CODOT
821.30 pt. Remainder in 138.12

**138.10 Weighers**

Persons weighing and measuring materials, goods and products. Weighbridgemen and weighbridge clerks are included.

CODOT
835

**138.11 Graders, sorters, selectors n.e.c.**

Persons sorting and grading materials, products and other articles. Mail sorters are excluded and classified in 053.1.

CODOT
834

**138.12 Painting, assembling and related occupations n.e.c.**

Ceramic stencillers, wallpaper grounders, jewellery enamellers, mottlers (ceramics), glass examiners, footwear assemblers, fishing rod pluggers, fence assemblers, windscreen fitters, goods vehicle testers, cask smellers, leaf inspectors (tobacco) and persons engaged in painting, routine assembly and product inspection and related occupations not elsewhere classified.

CODOT
810.20 pt. Remainder in 132.1 and 132.4
810.40 pt., 810.99 pt. Remainders in 132.1
812.10, 812.70, 812.99
814 pt. Excludes—814.10 included in 133.1
819 pt. Excludes—819.10, 819.55, 819.92 included in 133.1
               —819.20 included in 133.2
820.10 pt. Remainder in 134.1, 134.2, 134.3, 134.4 and 134.5
821.05, 821.15, 821.20, 821.25
821.30 pt. Remainder in 138.9
821.99 pt. Remainder in 138.8
833.15, 833.30, 833.40, 833.50
833.55 pt. Remainder in 138.2
833.99 pt. Remainder in 138.2 and 138.3
839 pt. Excludes—839.30

**139.1 Foremen—Bricklayers, tile setters**

Foremen of persons included in 140.1.

CODOT
860.05, 860.20

**139.2 Foremen—Masons, stone cutters**

Foremen of persons included in 140.2.

CODOT
620.40
860.10

**139.3 Foremen—Plasterers**
Foremen of persons included in 140.3.

CODOT
860.15

**139.4 Foremen—Roofers, glaziers**
Foremen of persons included in 140.4.

CODOT
860.25, 860.30

**139.5 Foremen—Handymen, general building workers**
Foremen of persons included in 140.5.

CODOT
860.99 pt. Remainder in 139.7, 139.10, 139.11 and 139.12

**139.6 Foremen—Railway lengthmen**
Foremen of persons included in 141.1.

CODOT
860.40, 860.45, 860.50

**139.7 Foremen—Road surfacers, concreters**
Foremen of persons included in 141.2.

CODOT
860.35 pt. Remainder in 139.8 and 139.9
860.55
860.99 pt. Remainder in 139.5, 139.10, 139.11 and 139.12

**139.8 Foremen—Roadmen**
Foremen of persons included in 141.3.

CODOT
860.35 pt. Remainder in 139.7 and 139.9

**139.9 Foremen—Paviors, kerb layers**
Foremen of persons included in 141.4.

CODOT
860.35 pt. Remainder in 139.7 and 139.8

**139.10 Foremen—Sewage plant attendants**
Foremen of persons included in 142.1.

CODOT
590.30 pt. Remainder in 095.7
860.99 pt. Remainder in 139.5, 139.7, 139.11 and 139.12

**139.11 Foremen—Mains and service layers, pipe jointers**
Foremen of persons included in 142.2.

CODOT
860.99 pt. Remainder in 139.5, 139.7, 139.10 and 139.12

**139.12 Foremen—Construction workers n.e.c.**
Foremen of persons included in 146.2.

CODOT
860.99 pt. Remainder in 139.5, 139.7, 139.10 and 139.11

**140.1 Bricklayers, tile setters**
Persons building and repairing brick structures, setting wall and floor tiles and mosaics, laying and finishing granolithic and terrazzo mixtures, building fireplaces. Terrazzo and mosaic tile casters are excluded and classified in 107.12.

CODOT
861 pt. Excludes—861.40
863

**140.2 Mason, stone cutters**
Persons building and repairing stone structures; facing brick, cement or steel backing with stone; cutting, shaping and finishing, granite, marble, slate and other stone. Stone engravers and monumental masons are included.

CODOT
624
861.40

**140.3 Plasterers**
Persons applying plaster or cement mixtures to walls and ceilings; casting and fixing ornamental plaster work, carrying out other plastering tasks.

CODOT
862

**140.4 Roofers, glaziers**
Persons covering roofs with felt, slates, tiles and thatch; cutting, fitting and setting glass in windows, doors, etc..

CODOT
864, 865

**140.5 Handymen, general building workers**
Persons engaged in a combination of operations in the construction, alteration, maintenance and repair of buildings. Tunnellers and well sinkers are included. Handymen in residential buildings are excluded and classified in 146.2.

CODOT
869.02 pt. Remainder in 140.6
872.20
872.99 pt. Remainder in 145.0

**140.6 Builders (so described)**

Persons returned as 'builder', 'builder and decorator', 'building contractor', 'builder and contractor' without more specific description.

CODOT
869.02 pt. Remainder in 140.5

**141.1 Railway lengthmen**

Persons laying and maintaining railway tracks.

CODOT
866.20, 866.30

**141.2 Road surfacers, concreters**

Persons spreading, sealing and smoothing newly laid asphalt road or similar surface; pouring and levelling concrete in the construction of buildings and roads. Persons driving and operating asphalt spreading machines and concrete paving machines are excluded and classified in 155.1.

CODOT
866.60, 866.90
867
869.54

**141.3 Roadmen**

Persons carrying out a variety of tasks in the construction or repair of roads; road lengthmen, chippers, road markers.

CODOT
866.50, 866.92, 866.99

**141.4 Paviors, kerb layers**

Persons laying paving slabs and kerbstones to form pavements and street gutters.

CODOT
866.10

**142.1 Sewage plant attendants**

Persons attending plant in which sewage is treated; maintaining main sewerage system. Turncocks are included.

CODOT
593.45
869.20
972.60

**142.2 Mains and service layers, pipe jointers**

Persons laying or jointing pipes for drainage, gas, water or similar piping systems. Water supply waste inspectors are included.

CODOT
869.28, 869.30, 869.32, 869.34

**143.1 Craftsmen's mates**

Persons returned as labourers, assistants and mates to building craftsmen.

CODOT
868 pt. Excludes—868.50, 868.60, 860.70, 868.99 pt. included in 143.2

**143.2 Building and civil engineering labourers**

Labourers and unskilled workers n.e.c., in building and civil engineering. Trenchmen and street light erectors are included.

CODOT
868.50, 868.60, 868.70
868.99 pt. Remainder in 143.1

**144.0 Foremen/deputies—Coalmining**

Foremen, deputies and deputy overmen supervising the working of an underground district of a coal mine. Overmen are excluded and classified in 036.1.

CODOT
870.30

**145.0 Face-trained coalmining workers**

Coal mine face workers; including rippers, drillers, shotfirers, packers, timberers, wastemen, manhole makers, linesmen and roof bolters. Onsetters, haulage men and conveyor operators, and coal miners not otherwise specified are excluded and classified in 155.2, 158.2 and 160.7 respectively.

CODOT
871.05, 871.15
872.10
872.99 pt. Remainder in 140.5
873
879.20 pt., 879.99 pt. Remainders in 146.1
879.30

**146.1 Miners (not coal), quarrymen, well drillers**

Persons extracting minerals, other than coal, from underground workings and quarries; setting up and operating equipment, including wirelines to drill wells. Stone and ore crushers and washers are excluded and classified in 098.3.

CODOT
870 pt. Excludes—870.30 included in 144.0
871 pt. Excludes—871.05, 871.15 included in 145.0
879 pt. Excludes—879.20 pt., 879.30, 879.99 pt. included in 145.0

**146.2 Construction workers n.e.c.**

Persons performing various tasks in building and civil engineering; working under water, cleaning and restoring exteriors of buildings, laying composition floors and linoleum; steeplejacks, demolition workers, fence erectors, handymen in residential buildings, grave diggers, building insulators, other building and construction workers not elsewhere classified.

CODOT
869 pt. Excludes—869.02 included in 140.5 and 140.6
    —869.20 included in 142.1
    —869.28, 869.30, 869.32, 869.34 included in 142.2
    —869.54 included in 141.2

**147.0  Foremen—Ships, lighters and other vessels**
Foremen of persons included in 148.0.
CODOT
910 pt. Excludes—910.50, 910.99 pt. included in 158.2

**148.0  Deck, engine-room hands, bargemen, lightermen, boatmen**
Persons carrying out deck and engine-room duties on board ships and craft operating at sea and in coastal and inland waters;
including ferrymen. Fishermen and dredgermen are excluded and classified to 082.0 and 155.1.
CODOT
911

**149.1  Foremen—Railway guards**
Foremen of persons included in 150.2.
CODOT
920.10 pt. Remainder in 149.4

**149.2  Foremen—Signalmen and crossing keepers, railway**
Foremen of persons included in 150.3.
CODOT
920.30

**149.3  Foremen—Shunters, pointsmen**
Foremen of persons included in 150.4.
CODOT
920.20

**149.4  Other foremen rail transport**
Foremen of workers in the operation of rail transport not elsewhere classified. Station foremen are excluded and classified in 071.3.
CODOT
920.10 pt. Remainder in 149.1
920.40, 920.99

**150.1  Drivers, motormen, secondmen, railway engines**
Persons driving railway engines, driving or acting as assistant to the driver on all types of locomotives on surface and underground
railways.
CODOT
921

**150.2  Railway guards**
Persons in charge of passenger and goods trains on surface and underground railways.
CODOT
922

**150.3  Signalmen and crossing keepers, railway**
Persons operating signals to control the movements of trains; opening and closing gates at level crossings.
CODOT
923.60, 923.99

**150.4  Shunters, pointsmen**
Persons operating manual points; guiding and linking wagons and coaches to form complete trains.
CODOT
923.10, 923.50

**151.1  Bus inspectors**
Persons supervising activities of drivers and conductors of public service vehicles.
CODOT
930.10

**151.2  Foremen—Drivers of road goods vehicles**
Foremen of persons included in 152.2.
CODOT
930.20 pt., 930.99 pt. Remainders in 151.3

**151.3  Other foremen road transport**
Foremen of workers in the operation of road transport, other than vehicle maintenance workers, not elsewhere classified. Traffic
foremen and yard foremen are included.
CODOT
930.20 pt., 930.99 pt. Remainders in 151.2
930.30

**152.1  Bus and coach drivers**
Persons driving road passenger carrying vehicles such as buses, coaches, mini buses, trolley buses and trams.
CODOT
931

**152.2  Drivers of road goods vehicles**
Persons driving motor vehicles to transport goods or animals by road. Coal delivery drivers are included but roundsmen are excluded
and classified in 056.0.
CODOT
932
933.10

**152.3** **Other motor drivers**

Persons driving taxis; chauffeurs, mechanical road sweeper drivers, road patrolmen. Ambulance drivers are excluded and classified in 070.1.

CODOT
933 pt. Excludes—933.10

**153.1** **Bus conductors**

Persons collecting fares, issuing tickets and controlling passengers on buses.

CODOT
934

**153.2** **Drivers' mates**

Persons accompanying drivers of road vehicles and assisting with loading and unloading.

CODOT
935

**154.1** **Foremen—Mechanical plant drivers, operators (earth moving and civil engineering)**

Foremen of persons included in 155.1.

CODOT
940.10

**154.2** **Foremen—Crane drivers, operators**

Foremen of persons included in 155.2.

CODOT
940.20 pt. Remainder in 154.3, 154.4 and 158.2

**154.3** **Foremen—Fork lift, mechanical truck drivers**

Foremen of persons included in 155.3.

CODOT
940.20 pt. Remainder in 154.2, 154.4 and 158.2

**154.4** **Foremen—Slingers**

Foremen of persons included in 158.1.

CODOT
940.20 pt. Remainder in 154.2, 154.3 and 158.2

**155.1** **Mechanical plant drivers, operators (earth moving and civil engineering)**

Persons operating machines to excavate, level and compact earth, gravel, sand and similar materials, drive piles into the ground, lay surfaces of asphalt and concrete, dredge rivers, canals, etc.. Concrete mixer drivers and dumper drivers are excluded and classified in 098.9 and 155.3 respectively.

CODOT
941

**155.2** **Crane drivers, operators**

Persons driving and operating cranes and hoists (including winding engines at mines). Mine onsetters are included.

CODOT
942.05, 942.10, 942.30, 942.50, 942.52, 942.54, 942.56, 942.58, 942.60

**155.3** **Fork lift, mechanical truck drivers**

Persons driving and operating fork lift and similar trucks in factories, warehouses and on sites to transfer goods or materials. Coal chargers and coke carmen (coal-gas ovens, coke ovens), and dumper drivers are included.

CODOT
942.62, 942.64, 942.66, 942.74

**156.1** **Foremen—Storekeepers, warehousemen**

Foremen of persons included in 157.1.

CODOT
950.10
950.99 pt. Remainder in 156.3, 156.4 and 158.2

**156.2** **Foremen—Stevedores, dockers**

Foremen of persons included in 157.2.

CODOT
950.20

**156.3** **Foremen—Goods porters**

Foremen of persons included in 157.3.

CODOT
950.99 pt. Remainder in 156.1, 156.4 and 158.2

**156.4** **Foremen—Refuse collectors, dustmen**

Foremen of persons included in 157.4.

CODOT
950.99 pt. Remainder in 156.1, 156.3 and 158.2

**157.1** **Storekeepers, warehousemen**

Persons storing, selecting and issuing materials, goods, etc. and maintaining stock records; including cellarmen, timber tallymen, linen keepers, lampmen (mining).

CODOT
951

**157.2     Stevedores, dockers**
Persons loading and discharging ships' cargoes; supplying berthed ships with water and performing related tasks.
CODOT
952


**157.3     Goods porters**
Persons loading, unloading and moving goods, materials and equipment about warehouses, stores, goods depots, shops, markets or slaughterhouses; loading and unloading goods, etc. on to and from vehicles and aircraft; moving furniture; carrying baggage at docks and air terminals.
CODOT
959.10, 959.50, 959.65, 959.70


**157.4     Refuse collectors, dustmen**
Persons collecting refuse from premises.
CODOT
959.85


**158.1     Slingers**
Persons placing wires, chains or ropes round articles to be lifted; signaling instructions to crane operators.
CODOT
942.76


**158.2     Workers in transport operating, materials moving and storing and related n.e.c.**
Conveyor operators, haulage men (coalmine), horse drawn vehicle drivers; persons handling ships in docks and aircraft on the ground, operating locks and lighthouses, carrying out transport and material handling occupations not elsewhere classified.
CODOT
910.50
910.99 pt. Remainder in 147.0
919
939
940.20 pt. Remainder in 154.2, 154.3 and 154.4
940.99
942.15, 942.20, 942.25, 942.68, 942.70, 942.72, 942.78, 942.80, 942.82, 942.99
949
950.99 pt. Remainder in 156.1, 156.3 and 156.4
959.55, 959.60, 959.75, 959.80, 959.99


## Labourers and unskilled workers n.e.c.

Persons performing occupations not elsewhere classified requiring little or no training. 'Factory workers' not otherwise specified and maintenance hands n.e.c. and maintenance workers n.e.c. are included. Assignment to the various groups 159.1–159.8 and 160.1–160.8 is in accordance with the industry of the establishment in which they are employed.

**159.1     Foremen—Labourers and unskilled workers n.e.c.—Textiles (not textile goods)**
Foremen of persons included in 160.1.
CODOT
990.00 pt., 990.10 pt., 990.20 pt. Remainders in 159.2, 159.3, 159.4, 159.5, 159.6, 159.7 and 159.8


**159.2     Foremen—Labourers and unskilled workers n.e.c.—Chemicals and allied trades**
Foremen of persons included in 160.2.
CODOT
990.00 pt., 990.10 pt., 990.20 pt. Remainders in 159.1, 159.3, 159.4, 159.5, 159.6, 159.7 and 159.8


**159.3     Foremen—Labourers and unskilled workers n.e.c.—Coke ovens and gas works**
Foremen of persons included in 160.3.
CODOT
990.00 pt., 990.10 pt., 990.20 pt. Remainders in 159.1, 159.2, 159.4, 159.5, 159.6, 159.7 and 159.8


**159.4     Foremen—Labourers and unskilled workers n.e.c.—Glass and ceramics**
Foremen of persons included in 160.4.
CODOT
990.00 pt., 990.10 pt., 990.20 pt. Remainders in 159.1, 159.2, 159.3, 159.5, 159.6, 159.7 and 159.8


**159.5     Foremen—Labourers and unskilled workers n.e.c.—Foundries in engineering and allied trades**
Foremen of persons included in 160.5.
CODOT
990.00 pt., 990.10 pt., 990.20 pt. Remainders in 159.1, 159.2, 159.3, 159.4, 159.6, 159.7 and 159.8


**159.6     Foremen—Labourers and unskilled workers n.e.c.—Engineering and allied trades**
Foremen of persons included in 160.6.
CODOT
990.00 pt., 990.10 pt., 990.20 pt. Remainders in 159.1, 159.2, 159.3, 159.4, 159.5, 159.7 and 159.8


**159.7     Foremen—Labourers and unskilled workers n.e.c.—Coal mines**
Foremen of persons included in 160.7.
CODOT
990.00 pt., 990.10 pt., 990.20 pt. Remainders in 159.1, 159.2, 159.3, 159.4, 159.5, 159.6 and 159.8


**159.8     Foremen—Labourers and unskilled workers n.e.c.—Other**
Foremen of persons included in 160.8.
CODOT
990.00 pt., 990.10 pt., 990.20 pt. Remainders in 159.1, 159.2, 159.3, 159.4, 159.5, 159.6 and 159.7

**159.9**     **Foremen—Boiler operators**
Foremen of persons included in 161.1.

CODOT
970.10 pt. Remainder in 120.3

**160.1**     **Labourers and unskilled workers n.e.c.—Textiles (not textile goods)**
Labourers, etc. in establishments assigned to S.I.C. Class 43. 'Textile operatives', 'cotton operatives' and 'textile workers' so described are included.

CODOT
991.10 pt., 991.20 pt. Remainders in 160.2, 160.3, 160.4, 160.5, 160.6, 160.7 and 160.8

**160.2**     **Labourers and unskilled workers n.e.c.—Chemicals and allied trades**
Labourers, etc. in establishments assigned to S.I.C. Classes 14, 15, 25 and 26.

CODOT
991.10 pt., 991.20 pt. Remainders in 160.1, 160.3, 160.4, 160.5, 160.6, 160.7 and 160.8

**160.3**     **Labourers and unskilled workers n.e.c.—Coke ovens and gas works**
Labourers, etc. in establishments assigned to S.I.C. Class 12 and Group 162.

CODOT
991.10 pt., 991.20 pt. Remainders in 160.1, 160.2, 160.4, 160.5, 160.6, 160.7 and 160.8

**160.4**     **Labourers and unskilled workers n.e.c.—Glass and ceramics**
Labourers, etc. in establishments assigned to S.I.C. Groups 241, 243, 247 and 248.

CODOT
991.10 pt., 991.20 pt. Remainders in 160.1, 160.2, 160.3, 160.5, 160.6, 160.7 and 160.8

**160.5**     **Labourers and unskilled workers n.e.c.—Foundries in engineering and allied trades**
Labourers, etc. in foundries in the engineering and allied trades (S.I.C. Class 22 and Division 3).

CODOT
719.84, 719.85, 719.86, 719.87, 719.88
719.99 pt. Remainder in 131.3
991.10 pt., 991.20 pt. Remainders in 160.1, 160.2, 160.3, 160.4, 160.6, 160.7 and 160.8

**160.6**     **Labourers and unskilled workers n.e.c.—Engineering and allied trades**
Labourers, etc. in establishments assigned to S.I.C. Class 22 and Division 3. 'Steelworkers' and 'metal workers' so described are included. Unskilled workers in foundries are excluded and classified in 160.5.

CODOT
719.89
991.10 pt., 991.20 pt. Remainders in 160.1, 160.2, 160.3, 160.4, 160.5, 160.7 and 160.8

**160.7**     **Labourers and unskilled workers n.e.c.—Coal mines**
Labourers, etc. in coal mines assigned to S.I.C. Activity Heading 1113. 'Coal miners' not otherwise specified are included.

CODOT
991.10 pt., 991.20 pt. Remainders in 160.1, 160.2, 160.3, 160.4, 160.5, 160.6 and 160.8

**160.8**     **Labourers and unskilled workers n.e.c.—Other**
Labourers, etc. in industries not elsewhere classified. Building and civil engineering labourers are excluded and classified in 143.2.

CODOT
991.10 pt., 991.20 pt. Remainders in 160.1, 160.2, 160.3, 160.4, 160.5, 160.6 and 160.7

**161.1**     **Boiler operators**
Persons operating boilers to produce steam or hot water for central heating systems and industrial use.

CODOT
971.15, 971.92

**161.2**     **All other in miscellaneous occupations n.e.c.**
Person carrying out various tasks not classified elsewhere including crematorium attendants, incinerator operators, pumpmen, gas cylinder preparers, vehicle washing plant attendants, stage hands (entertainment).

CODOT
970.20, 970.30, 970.99
971.91, 971.93
972.10, 972.50, 972.99
979.50, 979.55, 979.60, 979.65, 979.99
991.30
999.99

**—.1**     **Inadequately described occupations**
Persons with inadequately described occupations including persons described as 'Foremen', 'Manager', 'Workman' without further information.

CODOT
—

**—.2**     **Occupations not stated**
Persons in employment, seeking work, permanently sick or retired with no statement of occupation.

CODOT
—

# Appendix A

## Condensed KOS headings and associated KOS groups

Con.
KOS KOS

001     Judges, barristers, advocates, solicitors
    003     Judges, barristers, advocates and solicitors

002     Accountants, valuers, finance specialists
    007     Accountants
    008     Estimators, valuers and assessors
    009     Finance, investment, insurance and tax specialists

003     Personnel and industrial relations managers; O and M, work study and operational research officers
    010     Personnel and industrial relations officers and managers
    011     Organisation and Methods, work study and operational research officers

004     Economists, statisticians, systems analysts, computer programmers
    012     Economists, statisticians, actuaries
    013     Systems analysts and computer programmers

005     Marketing, sales, advertising, public relations and purchasing managers
    014     Marketing and sales managers and executives
    015     Advertising and public relations managers and executives
    016     Purchasing officers and buyers

006     Statutory and other inspectors
    019     Environmental health officers
    020     Other statutory and similar inspectors

007     General administrators—national government
    001 pt.     Top managers—national government and other non-trading organisations
    021     Civil servants (administrative and executive functions) not identified elsewhere
    094 pt.     Office managers—national government

008     Local government officers (administrative and executive functions)
    001 pt.     Top managers—national government and other non-trading organisations
    005     Town Clerks and other clerks to local authorities
    022     Local government officers (administrative and executive functions) not identified elsewhere
    095     Office managers—local government

009     All other professional and related supporting management and administration
    004     Company secretaries
    006     Secretaries of trade associations, trade unions, professional bodies and charities
    017     Property and estate managers
    018     Librarians and information officers
    023     All other professional and related supporting management and administration

010     Teachers in higher education
    024     University academic staff
    025     Teachers in establishments for further and higher education

011     Teachers n.e.c.
    026     Secondary teachers
    027     Primary teachers
    028     Pre-primary teachers
    029     Special education teachers

012     Vocational and industrial trainers, education officers, social and behavioural scientists
    030     Vocational/industrial trainers
    031     Directors of education, education officers, school inspectors
    032     Social and behavioural scientists

013     Welfare workers
    033     Welfare workers (social, medical, industrial, educational and moral)

014     Clergy, ministers of religion
    034     Clergy, ministers of religion

031     **Architects, town planners, quantity, building and land surveyors**
    078     Architects and town planners
    080     Quantity surveyors
    081     Building, land and mining surveyors

032     **Officers (ships and aircraft), air traffic planners and controllers**
    082     Aircraft flight deck officers
    083     Air traffic planners and controllers
    084     Ships' masters, deck officers and pilots
    085     Ships' engineer officers
    086     Ships' radio officers

033     **Professional and related in science, engineering and other technologies and similar fields n.e.c.**
    079     Town planning, architectural and building technicians
    087     All other professional and related in science, engineering and other technologies and similar fields

034*     **Production, works and maintenance managers, works foremen**
    088     Production managers, works managers, works foremen
    089     Engineering maintenance managers

035*     **Site and other managers, agents and clerks of works, general foremen (building and civil engineering)**
    090     Site and other managers, agents and clerks of works, general foremen (building and civil engineering)

036*     **Managers in transport, warehousing, public utilities and mining**
    091     Managers—underground mining and public utilities
    092     Transport managers—air, sea, rail, road, harbour
    093     Managers—warehousing and materials handling

037*     **Office managers**
    096     Other office managers

038*     **Managers in wholesale and retail distribution**
    097     Managers—wholesale distribution
    098     Managers—department store, variety chain store, supermarket and departmental managers
    099     Branch managers of shops other than above
    100     Managers of independent shops (employees)
    101     Shop keepers (employers and self-employed)

039*     **Managers of hotels, clubs, etc., and in entertainment and sport**
    102     Hotel and residential club managers
    103     Publicans (employers and self-employed)
    104     Publicans (employees)
    105     Catering and non-residential club managers
    106     Entertainment and sports managers

040*     **Farmers, horticulturists, farm managers**
    107     Farmers and horticulturists (employers and self-employed)
    108     Farm managers (employees)

041     **Officers, UK armed forces**
    109 pt.     Officers (Armed Forces) not identified elsewhere
    (i.e. service officers with no civilian occupational counterpart)

042     **Officers, foreign and Commonwealth armed forces**
    109 pt.     Officers (Armed Forces) not identified elsewhere
    (i.e. service officers with no civilian occupational counterpart)

043     **Senior police, prison and fire service officers**
    110     Police officers (inspectors and above)
    111     Prison officers (chief officers and above)
    112     Fire service officers

044*     **All other managers**
    113     All other managers

045     **Supervisors of clerks, civil service executive officers**
    094 pt.     Office managers—national government
    114     Supervisors of clerks

046     **Clerks**
    115     Clerks

---

* And KOS 002—General, central, divisional managers—trading organisations, as appropriate

142     **Sewage plant attendants, sewermen (maintenance), mains and service layers, pipe jointers (gas, water, drainage, oil), inspectors (water supply), turncocks**

     211     Sewage plant attendants
     362     Sewermen (maintenance)
     363     Mains and service layers and pipe jointers (gas, water, drainage, oil)
     364     Waste inspectors (water supply)
     401     Turncocks (water supply)

143     **Civil engineering labourers, craftsmen's mates and other builders' labourers n.e.c.**

     365     Craftsmen's mates and other builders' labourers not identified elsewhere
     366     Civil engineering labourers

144     **Foremen/deputies—coalmining**

     367     Foremen/deputies—coalmining

145     **Face-trained coalmining workers**

     368     Face-trained coalmining workers

146     **All other in construction, mining, quarrying, well drilling and related n.e.c.**

     370     All other in construction, mining, quarrying, well drilling and related, not identified elsewhere

147     **Foremen—ships, lighters and other vessels**

     371     Foremen—ships, lighters and other vessels

148     **Deck, engine-room hands, bargemen, lightermen, boatmen**

     372     Deck and engine-room hands (sea-going)
     373     Bargemen, lightermen, boatmen, tugmen

149     **Foremen—rail transport operating**

     374     Foremen—rail transport operating

150     **Rail transport operating staff**

     375     Railway engine drivers, motormen
     376     Secondmen (railways)
     377     Railway guards
     378     Railway signalmen and shunters

151     **Foremen—road transport operating, bus inspectors**

     379     Foremen—road transport operating
     380     Bus inspectors

152     **Bus, coach, lorry drivers, etc.**

     381     Bus and coach drivers
     382     Heavy goods drivers (over 3 tons unladen weight)
     383     Other goods drivers
     384     Other motor drivers

153     **Bus conductors, drivers' mates**

     385     Bus conductors
     386     Drivers' mates

154     **Foremen—civil engineering plant operating, materials handling equipment operating**

     387     Foremen—civil engineering plant operating
     389     Foremen—materials handling equipment operating

155     **Mechanical plant, fork lift, mechanical truck drivers, crane drivers, operators**

     388     Mechanical plant drivers/operators (earth moving and civil engineering)
     390     Crane drivers/operators
     391     Fork lift and other mechanical truck drivers/operators

156     **Foremen—materials moving and storing**

     392     Foremen—materials moving and storing

157     **Storekeepers, stevedores, warehouse, market and other goods porters**

     393     Storekeepers, warehousemen
     394     Stevedores and dockers
     395     Furniture removers
     396     Warehouse, market and other goods porters
     397     Refuse collectors/dustmen

158     **All other in transport operating, materials moving and storing and related n.e.c.**

     398     All other in transport operating, materials moving and storing and related not identified elsewhere

# Appendix B

## Social Classes and Socio-economic groups

The following appendices show the allocation of the groups arising from the cross-classification of Occupation and Employment status to the Social Classes and Socio-economic groups (details of which are given on pages x–xii).

Persons with Employment status 'Apprentices, articled pupils, etc.' are included with Employees not elsewhere classified (n.e.c.) except management trainees who are included with Managers.

Appendix B.1 is intended primarily as a key to the allocation of persons to Social Class or Socio-economic group when their occupation code and employment status group have been determined.

Appendix B.2 provides details of the composition of the Social Classes and Socio-economic groups in terms of the individual occupation and employment status groups.

Where no distinction is made in these appendices between Socio-economic groups 1.1 and 2.1 or 1.2 and 2.2 allocation is determined by the size of the establishment which the person owns or manages. For details see pages xi–xii.

**Appendix B.1**

**Socio-economic Group and Social Class allocations of Occupation and Employment Status Groups**

| Occupation | Manual Non-manual | Self-employed with employees | | Self-employed without employees | | Managers | | Foremen | | Apprentices, etc., Employees n.e.c. | |
|---|---|---|---|---|---|---|---|---|---|---|---|
| | | S.E.G. | Social Class | S.E.G. | Social Class | S.E.G. | Social Class | S.E.G. | Social Class | S.E.G. | Social Class |
| 001 Judges, barristers, advocates, solicitors | | | | | | | | | | | |
| 0 Judges, barristers, advocates, solicitors | NM | 3 | I | 3 | I | — | — | — | — | 4 | I |
| 002 Accountants, valuers, finance specialists | | | | | | | | | | | |
| 1 Chartered and certified accountants | NM | 3 | I | 3 | I | — | — | — | — | 4 | I |
| 2 Cost and works accountants | NM | 5.1 | II | 5.1 | II | — | — | — | — | 5.1 | II |
| 3 Estimators | NM | 5.1 | II | 5.1 | II | 1.2, 2.2 | II | — | — | 5.1 | II |
| 4 Valuers, claims assessors | NM | 5.1 | II | 5.1 | II | 1.2, 2.2 | II | — | — | 5.1 | II |
| 5 Financial managers | NM | — | — | — | — | 1.2, 2.2 | II | — | — | — | — |
| 6 Underwriters, brokers, investment analysts | NM | 1.1, 2.1 | II | 5.1 | II | 1.2, 2.2 | II | — | — | — | — |
| 7 Taxation experts | NM | 5.1 | II | 5.1 | II | 1.2, 2.2 | II | — | — | — | — |
| 003 Personnel and industrial relations managers; O and M, work study and operational research officers | | | | | | | | | | | |
| 1 Personnel and industrial relations officers | NM | 5.1 | II | 5.1 | II | 1.2, 2.2 | II | — | — | — | — |
| 2 O and M, work study and OR officers | NM | 5.1 | II | 5.1 | II | 1.2, 2.2 | II | — | — | 5.1 | II |
| 004 Economists, statisticians, systems analysts, computer programmers | | | | | | | | | | | |
| 1 Economists, statisticians, actuaries | NM | 3 | I | 3 | I | — | — | — | — | 4 | I |
| 2 Systems analysts, computer programmers | NM | 5.1 | II | 5.1 | II | 1.2, 2.2 | II | — | — | 5.1 | II |
| 005 Marketing, sales, advertising, public relations and purchasing managers | | | | | | | | | | | |
| 1 Marketing and sales managers and executives | NM | 1.1, 2.1 | II | 5.1 | II | 1.2, 2.2 | II | — | — | — | — |
| 2 Advertising and PR executives | NM | 1.1, 2.1 | II | 5.1 | II | 1.2, 2.2 | II | — | — | — | — |
| 3 Buyers (retail trade) | NM | — | — | — | — | 1.2, 2.2 | II | — | — | — | — |
| 4 Buyers and purchasing officers (not retail) | NM | — | — | — | — | 1.2, 2.2 | II | — | — | — | — |
| 006 Statutory and other inspectors | | | | | | | | | | | |
| 1 Environmental health officers | NM | — | — | — | — | — | — | — | — | 5.1 | II |
| 2 Building inspectors | NM | — | — | — | — | — | — | — | — | 5.1 | II |
| 3 Inspectors (statutory and similar) | NM | — | — | — | — | — | — | — | — | 5.1 | II |
| 007 General administrators—national government | | | | | | | | | | | |
| 1 General administrators—national government (Assistant Secretary level and above) | NM | — | — | — | — | 1.2 | I | — | — | — | — |
| 2 General administrators—national government (HEO to Senior Principal level) | NM | — | — | — | — | 1.2 | II | — | — | — | — |
| 008 Local government officers (administrative and executive functions) | | | | | | | | | | | |
| 0 Local government officers (administrative and executive functions) | NM | — | — | — | — | 1.2 | II | — | — | — | — |

| | Occupation | | | | | | | | | | | |
|---|---|---|---|---|---|---|---|---|---|---|---|---|
| 009 | All other professional and related supporting management and administration | | | | | | | | | | | |
| 1 | Company secretaries | NM | 5.1 | II | 5.1 | II | 1.2, 2.2 | II | — | — | — | — |
| 2 | Officials of trade associations, trade unions, professional bodies and charities | NM | — | — | — | — | 1.2, 2.2 | II | — | — | 5.1 | II |
| 3 | Property and estate managers | NM | 5.1 | II | 5.1 | II | 1.2, 2.2 | II | — | — | — | — |
| 4 | Librarians, information officers | NM | — | — | — | — | 1.2, 2.2 | II | — | — | 5.1 | II |
| 5 | Legal service and related occupations | NM | 5.1 | II | 5.1 | II | 1.2, 2.2 | II | — | — | 5.1 | II |
| 6 | Management consultants | NM | 3 | I | 3 | I | — | — | — | — | 4 | I |
| 7 | Managers' personal assistants | NM | — | — | — | — | — | — | — | — | 6 | III N |
| 8 | Professional workers and related supporting management and administration n.e.c. | NM | 5.1 | II | 5.1 | II | 1.2, 2.2 | II | — | — | 5.1 | II |
| 010 | Teachers in higher education | | | | | | | | | | | |
| 1 | University academic staff | NM | — | — | — | — | — | — | — | — | 4 | I |
| 2 | Teachers in establishments for further and higher education | NM | 5.1 | II | 5.1 | II | 1.2, 2.2 | II | — | — | 5.1 | II |
| 011 | Teachers n.e.c. | | | | | | | | | | | |
| 0 | Teachers n.e.c.... | NM | 5.1 | II | 5.1 | II | 1.2, 2.2 | II | — | — | 5.1 | II |
| 012 | Vocational and industrial trainers, education officers, social and behavioural scientists | | | | | | | | | | | |
| 1 | Vocational and industrial trainers | NM | 5.1 | II | 5.1 | II | 1.2, 2.2 | II | — | — | 5.1 | II |
| 2 | Education officers, school inspectors | NM | — | — | — | — | — | — | — | — | 4 | I |
| 3 | Social and behavioural scientists | NM | 3 | I | 3 | I | — | — | — | — | 4 | I |
| 013 | Welfare workers | | | | | | | | | | | |
| 1 | Matrons, houseparents | NM | 1.1, 2.1 | II | 12 | II | 1.2, 2.2 | II | — | — | 7 | II |
| 2 | Playgroup leaders | NM | 2.1 | III N | 12 | III N | — | — | — | — | 6 | III N |
| 3 | Welfare occupations n.e.c. | NM | — | — | — | — | 1.2, 2.2 | II | — | — | 5.1 | II |
| 014 | Clergy, ministers of religion | | | | | | | | | | | |
| 0 | Clergy, ministers of religion | NM | 3 | I | 3 | I | — | — | — | — | 4 | I |
| 015 | Medical and dental practitioners | | | | | | | | | | | |
| 1 | Medical practitioners | NM | 3 | I | 3 | I | — | — | — | — | 4 | I |
| 2 | Dental practitioners | NM | 3 | I | 3 | I | — | — | — | — | 4 | I |
| 016 | Nurse administrators, nurses | | | | | | | | | | | |
| 0 | Nurse administrators, nurses | NM | 5.1 | II | 5.1 | II | 1.2, 2.2 | II | 5.1 | II | 5.1 | II |
| 017 | Pharmacists, radiographers, therapists n.e.c. | | | | | | | | | | | |
| 1 | Pharmacists | NM | 3 | I | 3 | I | — | — | — | — | 4 | I |
| 2 | Medical radiographers | NM | 5.1 | II | 5.1 | II | 1.2, 2.2 | II | 5.1 | II | 5.1 | II |
| 3 | Ophthalmic and dispensing opticians | NM | 3 | I | 3 | I | — | — | — | — | 4 | I |
| 4 | Physiotherapists | NM | 5.1 | II | 5.1 | II | 1.2, 2.2 | II | 5.1 | II | 5.1 | II |
| 5 | Chiropodists | NM | 5.1 | II | 5.1 | II | 1.2, 2.2 | II | — | — | 5.1 | II |
| 6 | Therapists n.e.c. | NM | 5.1 | II | 5.1 | II | 1.2, 2.2 | II | 5.1 | II | 5.1 | II |

| Occupation | Manual Non-manual | Self-employed | | | | Managers | | Foremen | | Apprentices, etc., Employees n.e.c. | |
|---|---|---|---|---|---|---|---|---|---|---|---|
| | | with employees | | without employees | | | | | | | |
| | | S.E.G. | Social Class | S.E.G. | Social Class | S.E.G. | Social Class | S.E.G. | Social Class | S.E.G. | Social Class |
| **018 All other professional and related in education, welfare and health** | | | | | | | | | | | |
| 1 Medical technicians, dental auxiliaries | NM | 5.1 | II | 5.1 | II | 1.2, 2.2 | II | 5.1 | II | 5.1 | II |
| 2 Veterinarians | NM | 3 | I | 3 | I | — | — | — | — | 4 | I |
| 3 Driving instructors (not HGV) | NM | 2.1 | III N | 12 | III N | 2.2 | II | — | — | 6 | III N |
| 4 Professional and related in education, welfare and health n.e.c. | NM | 5.1 | II | 5.1 | II | 1.2, 2.2 | II | — | — | 5.1 | II |
| **019 Authors, writers, journalists** | | | | | | | | | | | |
| 0 Authors, writers, journalists | NM | 1.1, 2.1 | II | 5.1 | II | 1.2, 2.2 | II | — | — | 5.1 | II |
| **020 Artists, designers, window dressers** | | | | | | | | | | | |
| 1 Artists, commercial artists | NM | 1.1, 2.1 | II | 5.1 | II | 1.2, 2.2 | II | 5.1 | II | 5.1 | II |
| 2 Industrial designers (not clothing) | NM | 1.1, 2.1 | II | 5.1 | II | 1.2, 2.2 | II | — | — | 5.1 | II |
| 3 Clothing designers | NM | 1.1, 2.1 | II | 5.1 | II | 1.2, 2.2 | II | — | — | 5.1 | II |
| 4 Window dressers | NM | 1.1, 2.1 | II | 5.1 | II | 1.2, 2.2 | II | — | — | 5.1 | II |
| **021 Actors, musicians, entertainers, stage managers** | | | | | | | | | | | |
| 1 Actors, entertainers, singers, stage managers | NM | 1.1, 2.1 | II | 5.1 | II | 1.2, 2.2 | II | — | — | 5.1 | II |
| 2 Musicians | NM | 1.1, 2.1 | II | 5.1 | II | 1.2, 2.2 | II | — | — | 5.1 | II |
| **022 Photographers, cameramen, sound and vision equipment operators** | | | | | | | | | | | |
| 1 Photographers, cameramen | NM | 1.1, 2.1 | III N | 12 | III N | 1.2, 2.2 | II | 5.2 | III N | 6 | III N |
| 2 Sound and vision equipment operators | NM | 1.1, 2.1 | III N | 12 | III N | 1.2, 2.2 | II | 5.2 | III N | 6 | III N |
| **023 All other literary, artistic and sports** | | | | | | | | | | | |
| 1 Professional sportsmen, sports officials | NM | 1.1, 2.1 | III N | 12 | III N | 1.2, 2.2 | II | — | — | 6 | III N |
| 2 Literary, artistic and sports workers n.e.c. | NM | 1.1, 2.1 | III N | 12 | III N | 1.2, 2.2 | II | — | — | 6 | III N |
| **024 Scientists, physicists, mathematicians** | | | | | | | | | | | |
| 1 Biological scientists, biochemists | NM | 3 | I | 3 | I | — | — | — | — | 4 | I |
| 2 Chemical scientists | NM | 3 | I | 3 | I | — | — | — | — | 4 | I |
| 3 Physical and geological scientists, mathematicians | NM | 3 | I | 3 | I | — | — | — | — | 4 | I |
| **025 Civil, structural, municipal, mining and quarrying engineers** | | | | | | | | | | | |
| 0 Civil, structural, municipal, mining and quarrying engineers | NM | 3 | I | 3 | I | — | — | — | — | 4 | I |
| **026 Mechanical and aeronautical engineers** | | | | | | | | | | | |
| 1 Mechanical and aeronautical engineers | NM | 3 | I | 3 | I | — | — | — | — | 4 | I |
| 2 Design and development engineers (mechanical) | NM | 3 | I | 3 | I | — | — | — | — | 4 | I |
| **027 Electrical and electronic engineers** | | | | | | | | | | | |
| 1 Electrical engineers | NM | 3 | I | 3 | I | — | — | — | — | 4 | I |
| 2 Electronic engineers | NM | 3 | I | 3 | I | — | — | — | — | 4 | I |

| | | | | | | | | | | | |
|---|---|---|---|---|---|---|---|---|---|---|---|
| 028 Engineers and technologists n.e.c. | | | | | | | | | | | |
| 1 Chemical engineers | NM | 3 | I | 3 | I | — | — | — | — | 4 | I |
| 2 Production engineers | NM | 3 | I | 3 | I | — | — | — | — | 4 | I |
| 3 Planning and quality control engineers | NM | 3 | I | 3 | I | — | — | — | — | 4 | I |
| 4 Engineers n.e.c. | NM | 3 | I | 3 | I | — | — | — | — | 4 | I |
| 5 Metallurgists | NM | 3 | I | 3 | I | — | — | — | — | 4 | I |
| 6 Technologists n.e.c. | NM | 3 | I | 3 | I | — | — | — | — | 4 | I |
| 029 Draughtsmen | | | | | | | | | | | |
| 0 Draughtsmen | NM | 1.1, 2.1 | III N | 12 | III N | 1.2, 2.2 | II | 5.2 | III N | 6 | III N |
| 030 Laboratory and engineering technicians, technician engineers | | | | | | | | | | | |
| 1 Laboratory technicians | NM | 5.1 | II | 5.1 | II | 2.2 | II | 5.1 | II | 5.1 | II |
| 2 Engineering technicians, technician engineers | NM | 5.1 | II | 5.1 | II | 1.2, 2.2 | II | 5.1 | II | 5.1 | II |
| 031 Architects, town planners, quantity, building and land surveyors | | | | | | | | | | | |
| 1 Architects, town planners | NM | 3 | I | 3 | I | — | — | — | — | 4 | I |
| 2 Quantity surveyors | NM | 5.1 | II | 5.1 | II | — | — | — | — | 5.1 | II |
| 3 Building, land and mining surveyors | NM | 3 | I | 3 | I | — | — | — | — | 4 | I |
| 032 Officers (ships and aircraft), air traffic planners and controllers | | | | | | | | | | | |
| 1 Aircraft flight deck officers | NM | 1.1 | II | 12 | II | 1.2 | II | — | — | 5.1 | II |
| 2 Air traffic planners and controllers | NM | — | — | — | — | — | — | — | — | 5.1 | II |
| 3 Deck, engineering and radio officers and pilots, ship | NM | 1.1 | II | 12 | II | 1.2 | II | — | — | — | — |
| 033 Professional and related in science, engineering and other technologies and similar fields n.e.c. | | | | | | | | | | | |
| 1 Architectural and town planning technicians | NM | — | — | 5.1 | II | — | — | — | — | 5.1 | II |
| 2 Building and civil engineering technicians | NM | — | — | — | — | — | — | — | — | 5.1 | II |
| 3 Technical and related workers n.e.c. | NM | 5.1 | II | 5.1 | II | 1.2, 2.2 | II | 5.1 | II | 5.1 | II |
| 034 Production, works and maintenance managers, works foremen | | | | | | | | | | | |
| 0 Production, works and maintenance managers, works foremen | NM | — | — | — | — | 1.2, 2.2 | II | 5.2 | III N | — | — |
| 035 Site and other managers, agents and clerks of works, general foremen (building and civil engineering) | | | | | | | | | | | |
| 1 Managers in building and contracting | NM | — | — | — | — | 1.2, 2.2 | II | — | — | — | — |
| 2 Clerks of works | NM | — | — | — | — | — | — | — | — | 6 | III N |
| 036 Managers in transport, warehousing, public utilities and mining | | | | | | | | | | | |
| 1 Managers in mining and public utilities | NM | — | — | — | — | 1.2, 2.2 | II | — | — | — | — |
| 2 Transport managers | NM | — | — | — | — | 1.2, 2.2 | II | — | — | — | — |
| 3 Stores controllers | NM | — | — | — | — | 1.2, 2.2 | II | — | — | — | — |
| 4 Managers in warehousing and materials handling n.e.c. | NM | — | — | — | — | 1.2, 2.2 | II | — | — | — | — |
| 037 Office managers | | | | | | | | | | | |
| 1 Credit controllers | NM | — | — | — | — | 1.2, 2.2 | II | — | — | — | — |
| 2 Office managers n.e.c. | NM | 1.1, 2.1 | II | 12 | II | 1.2, 2.2 | II | — | — | — | — |

| Occupation | Manual Non-manual | Self-employed | | | | Managers | | Foremen | | Apprentices, etc., Employees n.e.c. | |
|---|---|---|---|---|---|---|---|---|---|---|---|
| | | with employees | | without employees | | | | | | | |
| | | S.E.G. | Social Class | S.E.G. | Social Class | S.E.G. | Social Class | S.E.G. | Social Class | S.E.G. | Social Class |
| **038 Managers in wholesale and retail distribution** | | | | | | | | | | | |
| 1 Garage proprietors | NM | 1.1, 2.1 | II | 12 | II | — | — | — | — | — | — |
| 2 Butchers (managers and proprietors) | NM | 1.1, 2.1 | III N | 12 | III N | 2.2 | II | — | — | — | — |
| 3 Fishmongers (managers and proprietors) | NM | 1.1, 2.1 | III N | 12 | III N | 2.2 | II | — | — | — | — |
| 4 Other proprietors and managers (sales) | NM | 1.1, 2.1 | II | 12 | II | 1.2, 2.2 | II | — | — | — | — |
| **039 Managers of hotels, clubs, etc., and in entertainment and sport** | | | | | | | | | | | |
| 1 Hotel and residential club managers | NM | 1.1, 2.1 | II | 12 | II | 1.2, 2.2 | II | — | — | — | — |
| 2 Publicans | NM | 1.1, 2.1 | II | 12 | II | 1.2, 2.2 | II | — | — | — | — |
| 3 Restaurateurs | NM | 1.1, 2.1 | III N | 12 | III N | 1.2, 2.2 | II | — | — | — | — |
| 4 Club stewards | NM | — | — | — | — | 2.2 | III N | — | — | — | — |
| 5 Entertainment and sports managers | NM | 1.1, 2.1 | III N | 12 | III N | 1.2, 2.2 | II | — | — | — | — |
| **040 Farmers, horticulturists, farm managers** | | | | | | | | | | | |
| 0 Farmers, horticulturists, farm managers | NM | 13 | II | 14 | II | 13 | II | — | — | — | — |
| **041 Officers, UK armed forces** | | | | | | | | | | | |
| 0 Officers, UK armed forces | — | — | — | — | — | 16 | — | — | — | — | — |
| **042 Officers, foreign and Commonwealth armed forces** | | | | | | | | | | | |
| 0 Officers, foreign and Commonwealth armed forces | — | — | — | — | — | 16 | — | — | — | — | — |
| **043 Senior police, prison and fire service officers** | | | | | | | | | | | |
| 1 Prison officers (chief officers and above) | NM | — | — | — | — | 1.2 | II | — | — | — | — |
| 2 Police officers (inspectors and above) | NM | — | — | — | — | 1.2 | II | — | — | — | — |
| 3 Fire service officers | NM | — | — | — | — | 1.2 | II | — | — | — | — |
| **044 All other managers** | | | | | | | | | | | |
| 1 Proprietors and managers, service flats, holiday flats, caravan sites, etc. | NM | 1.1, 2.1 | III N | 12 | III N | 1.2, 2.2 | II | — | — | — | — |
| 2 Managers of laundry and dry cleaning receiving shops | NM | 2.1 | IV | 12 | IV | 2.2 | III N | — | — | — | — |
| 3 Hairdressers' and barbers' managers and proprietors | NM | 1.1, 2.1 | III N | 12 | III N | 1.2, 2.2 | II | — | — | — | — |
| 4 Managers n.e.c. | NM | 1.1, 2.1 | II | 12 | II | 1.2, 2.2 | II | — | — | — | — |
| **045 Supervisors of clerks, civil service executive officers** | | | | | | | | | | | |
| 1 Civil service executive officers | NM | — | — | — | — | — | — | 5.1 | II | — | — |
| Supervisors of— | | | | | | | | | | | |
| 2 Stores and despatch clerks | NM | — | — | — | — | — | — | 5.2 | III N | — | — |
| 3 Tracers, drawing office assistants | NM | — | — | — | — | — | — | 5.2 | III N | — | — |
| 4 Other clerks and cashiers (not retail) | NM | — | — | — | — | — | — | 5.2 | III N | — | — |
| 5 Retail shop cashiers, check-out and cash and wrap operators | NM | — | — | — | — | — | — | 5.2 | III N | — | — |

| | | | | | | | | | | | |
|---|---|---|---|---|---|---|---|---|---|---|---|
| 046 | Clerks | | | | | | | | | | |
| 1 | Stores and despatch clerks | NM | — | — | — | — | — | — | — | — | 6 | III N |
| 2 | Tracers, drawing office assistants | NM | — | — | 12 | III N | — | — | — | — | 6 | III N |
| 3 | Other clerks and cashiers (not retail) | NM | 1.1, 2.1 | III N | 12 | III N | — | — | — | — | 6 | III N |
| 047 | Retail shop cashiers, check-out and cash and wrap operators | | | | | | | | | | |
| 0 | Retail shop cashiers, check-out and cash and wrap operators | NM | — | — | — | — | — | — | — | — | 6 | III N |
| 048 | Supervisors of typists, office machine operators, telephonists, etc. | | | | | | | | | | |
| | Supervisors of— | | | | | | | | | | |
| 1 | Typists, shorthand writers, secretaries | NM | — | — | — | — | — | — | 5.2 | III N | — | — |
| 2 | Office machine operators | NM | — | — | — | — | — | — | 5.2 | III N | — | — |
| 3 | Telephone operators | NM | — | — | — | — | — | — | 5.2 | III N | — | — |
| 4 | Radio and telegraph operators | NM | — | — | — | — | — | — | 5.2 | III N | — | — |
| 049 | Secretaries, shorthand typists, receptionists | | | | | | | | | | |
| 1 | Receptionists | NM | — | — | — | — | — | — | — | — | 6 | III N |
| 2 | Typists, shorthand writers, secretaries | NM | 1.1, 2.1 | III N | 12 | III N | — | — | — | — | 6 | III N |
| 050 | Office machine operators | | | | | | | | | | |
| 0 | Office machine operators | NM | 1.1, 2.1 | III N | 12 | III N | — | — | — | — | 6 | III N |
| 051 | Telephonists, radio and telegraph operators | | | | | | | | | | |
| 1 | Telephonist receptionists | NM | — | — | — | — | — | — | — | — | 6 | III N |
| 2 | Telephone operators | NM | — | — | — | — | — | — | — | — | 6 | IV |
| 3 | Radio and telegraph operators | NM | — | — | — | — | — | — | — | — | 6 | III N |
| 052 | Supervisors of postmen, mail sorters, messengers | | | | | | | | | | |
| | Supervisors of— | | | | | | | | | | |
| 1 | Postmen, mail sorters | M | — | — | — | — | — | — | 8 | III M | — | — |
| 2 | Messengers | M | — | — | — | — | — | — | 8 | III M | — | — |
| 053 | Postmen, mail sorters, messengers | | | | | | | | | | |
| 1 | Postmen, mail sorters | M | — | — | — | — | — | — | — | — | 10 | IV |
| 2 | Messengers | M | — | — | 12 | V | — | — | — | — | 11 | V |
| 054 | Sales supervisors | | | | | | | | | | |
| | Supervisors of— | | | | | | | | | | |
| 1 | Shop salesmen and assistants | NM | — | — | — | — | — | — | 5.2 | III N | — | — |
| 2 | Petrol pump, forecourt attendants | NM | — | — | — | — | — | — | 5.2 | III N | — | — |
| 3 | Roundsmen, van salesmen | NM | — | — | — | — | — | — | 5.2 | III N | — | — |
| 055 | Salesmen, sales assistants, shop assistants, shelf fillers, petrol pump, forecourt attendants | | | | | | | | | | |
| 1 | Shop salesmen and assistants | NM | — | — | — | — | — | — | — | — | 6 | III N |
| 2 | Shelf fillers | NM | — | — | — | — | — | — | — | — | 6 | IV |
| 3 | Petrol pump, forecourt attendants | NM | — | — | — | — | — | — | — | — | 6 | III N |
| 056 | Roundsmen, van salesmen | | | | | | | | | | |
| 0 | Roundsmen, van salesmen | M | 1.1, 2.1 | III M | 12 | III M | 1.2, 2.2 | II | — | — | 9 | III M |

| Occupation | Manual Non-manual | Self-employed | | | | Managers | | Foremen | | Apprentices, etc., Employees n.e.c. | |
| | | with employees | | without employees | | | | | | | |
| | | S.E.G. | Social Class | S.E.G. | Social Class | S.E.G. | Social Class | S.E.G. | Social Class | S.E.G. | Social Class |
|---|---|---|---|---|---|---|---|---|---|---|---|
| 057 Sales representatives and agents | | | | | | | | | | | |
| 1 Importers, exporters, commodity brokers ... ... ... ... ... | NM | 1.1, 2.1 | II | 12 | II | 1.2, 2.2 | II | — | — | — | — |
| 2 Market and street traders and assistants ... ... ... ... | NM | 1.1, 2.1 | IV | 12 | IV | 2.2 | III N | — | — | 6 | IV |
| 3 Scrap dealers, general dealers, rag and bone merchants ... ... ... | NM | 1.1, 2.1 | III N | 12 | III N | 1.2, 2.2 | III N | — | — | — | — |
| 4 Credit agents, collector salesmen ... ... ... ... ... | NM | 1.1, 2.1 | IV | 12 | IV | 2.2 | III N | — | — | 6 | IV |
| 5 Sales representatives ... ... ... ... ... ... | NM | 1.1, 2.1 | III N | 12 | III N | 2.2 | II | — | — | 6 | III N |
| 6 Sales representatives (property and services), other agents... ... ... | NM | 1.1, 2.1 | III N | 12 | III N | 1.2, 2.2 | II | — | — | 6 | III N |
| 058 NCOs and other ranks, UK armed forces | | | | | | | | | | | |
| 0 NCOs and other ranks, UK armed forces ... ... ... ... | — | — | — | — | — | — | — | — | — | 16 | — |
| 059 NCOs and other ranks, foreign and Commonwealth armed forces | | | | | | | | | | | |
| 0 NCOs and other ranks, foreign and Commonwealth armed forces ... | — | — | — | — | — | — | — | — | — | 16 | — |
| 060 Supervisors (police sergeants, fire fighting and related) | | | | | | | | | | | |
| 1 Police sergeants ... ... ... ... ... ... | NM | — | — | — | — | — | — | 5.2 | III N | — | — |
| 2 Fire service supervisors ... ... ... ... ... ... | NM | — | — | — | — | — | — | 5.2 | III N | — | — |
| 3 Prison service principal officers ... ... ... ... ... | NM | — | — | — | — | — | — | 5.2 | III N | — | — |
| Supervisors of— | | | | | | | | | | | |
| 4 Security guards and officers, patrolmen, watchmen ... ... ... | NM | — | — | — | — | — | — | 5.2 | III N | — | — |
| 5 Traffic wardens ... ... ... ... ... ... | NM | — | — | — | — | — | — | 5.2 | III N | — | — |
| 6 Security and protective service workers n.e.c. ... ... ... | NM | — | — | — | — | — | — | 5.2 | III N | — | — |
| 061 Policemen, firemen, prison officers | | | | | | | | | | | |
| 1 Policemen (below sergeant) ... ... ... ... ... | NM | — | — | — | — | — | — | — | — | 6 | III N |
| 2 Firemen ... ... ... ... ... ... | NM | — | — | — | — | — | — | — | — | 6 | III N |
| 3 Prison officers (below principal officer) ... ... ... ... | NM | — | — | — | — | — | — | — | — | 6 | IV |
| 062 Other security and protective service workers | | | | | | | | | | | |
| 1 Security guards and officers, patrolmen, watchmen ... ... ... | M | 1.1, 2.1 | IV | 12 | IV | — | — | — | — | 10 | IV |
| 2 Traffic wardens ... ... ... ... ... | M | — | — | — | — | — | — | — | — | 10 | IV |
| 3 Security and protective service workers n.e.c. ... ... ... | M | 1.1, 2.1 | IV | 12 | IV | — | — | — | — | 10 | IV |
| 063 Catering supervisors | | | | | | | | | | | |
| Supervisors of— | | | | | | | | | | | |
| 1 Chefs, cooks ... ... ... ... ... ... | M | — | — | — | — | — | — | 7 | III M | — | — |
| 2 Waiters, waitresses ... ... ... ... ... | M | — | — | — | — | — | — | 7 | III M | — | — |
| 3 Barmen, barmaids ... ... ... ... ... | M | — | — | — | — | — | — | 7 | III M | — | — |
| 4 Counter hands, assistants ... ... ... ... | M | — | — | — | — | — | — | 7 | III M | — | — |
| 064 Chefs, cooks | | | | | | | | | | | |
| 0 Chefs, cooks ... ... ... ... ... ... ... ... | M | 1.1, 2.1 | III M | 12 | III M | 1.2, 2.2 | II | — | — | 7 | III M |

| | | | | | | | | | | | |
|---|---|---|---|---|---|---|---|---|---|---|---|
| **065 Waiters and bar staff** | | | | | | | | | | | |
| 1 Waiters, waitresses | M | — | — | 12 | IV | — | — | — | — | 7 | IV |
| 2 Barmen, barmaids | M | — | — | 12 | IV | — | — | — | — | 7 | IV |
| **066 Counter hands, assistants, kitchen porters, hands** | | | | | | | | | | | |
| 1 Counter hands, assistants | M | — | — | — | — | — | — | — | — | 7 | IV |
| 2 Kitchen porters, hands | M | — | — | — | — | — | — | 8 | III M | 11 | V |
| **067 Supervisors—housekeeping and related** | | | | | | | | | | | |
| 1 Housekeepers (non-domestic) | M | — | — | — | — | — | — | 7 | III M | — | — |
| Supervisors of— | | | | | | | | | | | |
| 2 Other domestic and school helpers | M | — | — | — | — | — | — | 7 | III M | — | — |
| 3 Travel stewards and attendants | M | — | — | — | — | — | — | 7 | III M | — | — |
| 4 Hospital porters | M | — | — | — | — | — | — | 8 | III M | — | — |
| 5 Hotel porters | M | — | — | — | — | — | — | 8 | III M | — | — |
| 6 Ambulancemen | M | — | — | — | — | — | — | 8 | III M | — | — |
| 7 Hospital, ward orderlies | M | — | — | — | — | — | — | 8 | III M | — | — |
| **068 Domestic staff and school helpers** | | | | | | | | | | | |
| 1 Domestic housekeepers | M | — | — | — | — | — | — | — | — | 7 | III M |
| 2 Nursery nurses | M | 1.1, 2.1 | III M | 12 | III M | — | — | — | — | 7 | III M |
| 3 Other domestic and school helpers | M | — | — | 12 | IV | — | — | — | — | 7 | IV |
| **069 Travel stewards and attendants, hospital and hotel porters** | | | | | | | | | | | |
| 1 Travel stewards and attendants | M | — | — | 12 | III M | — | — | — | — | 7 | III M |
| 2 Hospital porters | M | — | — | — | — | — | — | — | — | 10 | IV |
| 3 Hotel porters | M | — | — | — | — | — | — | — | — | 10 | IV |
| **070 Ambulancemen, hospital orderlies** | | | | | | | | | | | |
| 1 Ambulancemen | M | — | — | — | — | — | — | — | — | 9 | III M |
| 2 Hospital, ward orderlies | M | — | — | — | — | — | — | — | — | 10 | IV |
| **071 Supervisors, foremen—caretaking, cleaning and related** | | | | | | | | | | | |
| Supervisors of— | | | | | | | | | | | |
| 1 Caretakers | M | — | — | — | — | — | — | 8 | III M | — | — |
| 2 Cleaners, window cleaners, chimney sweeps, road sweepers | M | — | — | — | — | — | — | 8 | III M | — | — |
| 3 Railway stationmen | M | — | — | — | — | — | — | 8 | III M | — | — |
| 4 Lift and car park attendants | M | — | — | — | — | — | — | 8 | III M | — | — |
| **072 Caretakers, road sweepers and other cleaners** | | | | | | | | | | | |
| 1 Caretakers | M | — | — | — | — | — | — | — | — | 10 | IV |
| 2 Cleaners, window cleaners, chimney sweeps, road sweepers | M | 1.1, 2.1 | V | 12 | V | 2.2 | III M | — | — | 11 | V |
| **073 Hairdressing supervisors** | | | | | | | | | | | |
| 0 Hairdressing supervisors | M | — | — | — | — | — | — | 7 | III M | — | — |
| **074 Hairdressers, barbers** | | | | | | | | | | | |
| 0 Hairdressers, barbers | M | — | — | — | — | — | — | — | — | 7 | III M |

| Occupation | Manual Non-manual | Self-employed with employees | | Self-employed without employees | | Managers | | Foremen | | Apprentices, etc., Employees n.e.c. | |
|---|---|---|---|---|---|---|---|---|---|---|---|
| | | S.E.G. | Social Class | S.E.G. | Social Class | S.E.G. | Social Class | S.E.G. | Social Class | S.E.G. | Social Class |
| 075 All other in catering, cleaning and other personal service | | | | | | | | | | | |
| 1 Railway stationmen | M | — | — | — | — | — | — | — | — | 11 | V |
| 2 Lift and car park attendants | M | — | — | — | — | — | — | — | — | 11 | V |
| 3 Launderers, dry cleaners, pressers | M | — | — | — | — | 1.2, 2.2 | III M | 8 | III M | 10 | IV |
| 4 Undertakers | M | 1.1, 2.1 | III M | 12 | III M | 1.2, 2.2 | II | — | — | — | — |
| 5 Bookmakers, betting shop managers | M | 1.1, 2.1 | III M | 12 | III M | 1.2, 2.2 | II | — | — | — | — |
| 6 Service workers n.e.c. | M | 1.1, 2.1 | IV | 12 | IV | 1.2, 2.2 | III M | 8 | III M | 10 | IV |
| 076 Foremen—farming, horticulture, forestry | | | | | | | | | | | |
| 1 Farm foremen | M | — | — | — | — | — | — | 15 | III M | — | — |
| 2 Horticultural foremen | M | — | — | — | — | — | — | 15 | III M | — | — |
| 3 Foremen gardeners and groundsmen | M | — | — | — | — | — | — | 8 | III M | — | — |
| 4 Agricultural machinery foremen | M | — | — | — | — | — | — | 15 | III M | — | — |
| 5 Forestry foremen | M | — | — | — | — | — | — | 15 | III M | — | — |
| 6 Other foremen in farming and related | M | — | — | — | — | — | — | 15 | III M | — | — |
| 077 Farm workers | | | | | | | | | | | |
| 0 Farm workers | M | 15 | IV | 15 | IV | — | — | — | — | 15 | IV |
| 078 Horticultural workers, gardeners, groundsmen | | | | | | | | | | | |
| 1 Horticultural workers | M | 15 | IV | 15 | IV | — | — | — | — | 15 | IV |
| 2 Gardeners, groundsmen | M | 1.1, 2.1 | IV | 12 | IV | 1.2, 2.2 | III M | — | — | 10 | IV |
| 079 Agricultural machinery drivers, operators | | | | | | | | | | | |
| 0 Agricultural machinery drivers, operators | M | 15 | IV | 15 | IV | — | — | — | — | 15 | IV |
| 080 Forestry workers | | | | | | | | | | | |
| 0 Forestry workers | M | 15 | IV | 15 | IV | — | — | — | — | 15 | IV |
| 081 Supervisors, mates—fishing | | | | | | | | | | | |
| 0 Supervisors, mates—fishing | M | — | — | — | — | — | — | 8 | III M | — | — |
| 082 Fishermen | | | | | | | | | | | |
| 0 Fishermen | M | 2.1 | IV | 12 | IV | 2.2 | III M | — | — | 10 | IV |
| 083 All other in farming and related | | | | | | | | | | | |
| 0 All other in farming and related | M | 15 | IV | 15 | IV | — | — | — | — | 15 | IV |

| Code | No. | Occupation | | | | | | | | | | | |
|---|---|---|---|---|---|---|---|---|---|---|---|---|---|
| 084 | | Foremen—tannery and leather (including leather substitutes) working | | | | | | | | | | | |
| | | Foremen— | | | | | | | | | | | |
| | 1 | Tannery production workers | M | — | — | — | — | — | — | 8 | III M | — | — |
| | 2 | Shoe repairers | M | — | — | — | — | — | — | 8 | III M | — | — |
| | 3 | Leather cutters and sewers, footwear lasters, makers, finishers | M | — | — | — | — | — | — | 8 | III M | — | — |
| | 4 | Other making and repairing, leather | M | — | — | — | — | — | — | 8 | III M | — | — |
| 085 | | Tannery and leather (including leather substitutes) workers | | | | | | | | | | | |
| | 1 | Tannery production workers | M | 1.1, 2.1 | III M | 12 | III M | 2.2 | II | — | — | 9 | III M |
| | 2 | Shoe repairers | M | 1.1, 2.1 | III M | 12 | III M | 2.2 | II | — | — | 9 | III M |
| | 3 | Leather cutters and sewers, footwear lasters, makers, finishers | M | 1.1, 2.1 | III M | 12 | III M | 2.2 | II | — | — | 9 | III M |
| 086 | | Foremen—textile processing | | | | | | | | | | | |
| | | Foremen— | | | | | | | | | | | |
| | 1 | Preparatory fibre processors | M | — | — | — | — | — | — | 8 | III M | — | — |
| | 2 | Spinners, doublers, twisters | M | — | — | — | — | — | — | 8 | III M | — | — |
| | 3 | Winders, reelers | M | — | — | — | — | — | — | 8 | III M | — | — |
| | 4 | Warp preparers | M | — | — | — | — | — | — | 8 | III M | — | — |
| | 5 | Weavers | M | — | — | — | — | — | — | 8 | III M | — | — |
| | 6 | Knitters | M | — | — | — | — | — | — | 8 | III M | — | — |
| | 7 | Bleachers, dyers, finishers | M | — | — | — | — | — | — | 8 | III M | — | — |
| | 8 | Menders, darners | M | — | — | — | — | — | — | 8 | III M | — | — |
| | 9 | Other material processing, textiles | M | — | — | — | — | — | — | 8 | III M | — | — |
| 087 | | Textile workers | | | | | | | | | | | |
| | 1 | Preparatory fibre processors | M | 1.1, 2.1 | IV | 12 | IV | 2.2 | III M | — | — | 10 | IV |
| | 2 | Spinners, doublers, twisters | M | 1.1, 2.1 | IV | 12 | IV | 2.2 | III M | — | — | 10 | IV |
| | 3 | Winders, reelers | M | 1.1, 2.1 | IV | 12 | IV | 2.2 | III M | — | — | 10 | IV |
| | 4 | Warp preparers | M | 1.1, 2.1 | III M | 12 | III M | 2.2 | II | — | — | 9 | III M |
| | 5 | Weavers | M | 1.1, 2.1 | III M | 12 | III M | 2.2 | II | — | — | 9 | III M |
| | 6 | Knitters | M | 1.1, 2.1 | III M | 12 | III M | 2.2 | II | — | — | 9 | III M |
| | 7 | Bleachers, dyers, finishers | M | 1.1, 2.1 | III M | 12 | III M | 2.2 | II | — | — | 9 | III M |
| | 8 | Menders, darners | M | 1.1, 2.1 | III M | 12 | III M | 2.2 | II | — | — | 9 | III M |
| 088 | | Foremen—chemical processing | | | | | | | | | | | |
| | 0 | Foremen—chemical processing | M | — | — | — | — | — | — | 8 | III M | — | — |
| 089 | | Chemical, gas and petroleum process plant operators | | | | | | | | | | | |
| | 0 | Chemical, gas and petroleum process plant operators | M | 1.1, 2.1 | IV | 12 | IV | 2.2 | III M | — | — | 10 | IV |
| 090 | | Foremen—food and drink processing | | | | | | | | | | | |
| | | Foremen— | | | | | | | | | | | |
| | 1 | Bakers, flour confectioners | M | — | — | — | — | — | — | 8 | III M | — | — |
| | 2 | Butchers, meat cutters | M | — | — | — | — | — | — | 8 | III M | — | — |
| | 3 | Fishmongers, poultry dressers | M | — | — | — | — | — | — | 8 | III M | — | — |
| | 4 | Brewery and vinery process workers | M | — | — | — | — | — | — | 8 | III M | — | — |
| | | Other material processing— | | | | | | | | | | | |
| | 5 | Bakery and confectionery workers | M | — | — | — | — | — | — | 8 | III M | — | — |
| | 6 | Food and drink n.e.c. | M | — | — | — | — | — | — | 8 | III M | — | — |

| Occupation | Manual Non-manual | Self-employed | | | | Managers | | Foremen | | Apprentices, etc., Employees n.e.c. | |
|---|---|---|---|---|---|---|---|---|---|---|---|
| | | with employees | | without employees | | | | | | | |
| | | S.E.G. | Social Class | S.E.G. | Social Class | S.E.G. | Social Class | S.E.G. | Social Class | S.E.G. | Social Class |
| 091 Bakers, flour confectioners | | | | | | | | | | | |
| 0 Bakers, flour confectioners | M | 1.1, 2.1 | III M | 12 | III M | 2.2 | II | — | — | 9 | III M |
| 092 Butchers | | | | | | | | | | | |
| 1 Butchers, meat cutters | M | — | — | — | — | — | — | — | — | 9 | III M |
| 2 Fishmongers, poultry dressers | M | — | — | — | — | — | — | — | — | 9 | III M |
| 093 Foremen—paper and board making and paper products | | | | | | | | | | | |
| Foremen— | | | | | | | | | | | |
| 1 Paper, paperboard and leatherboard workers | M | — | — | — | — | — | — | 8 | III M | — | — |
| 2 Bookbinders and finishers | M | — | — | — | — | — | — | 8 | III M | — | — |
| 3 Cutting and slitting machine operators (paper and paper products making) | M | — | — | — | — | — | — | 8 | III M | — | — |
| 4 Other material processing, wood and paper | M | — | — | — | — | — | — | 8 | III M | — | — |
| 5 Other making and repairing, paper goods and printing | M | — | — | — | — | — | — | 8 | III M | — | — |
| 094 Paper, board and paper product makers, bookbinders | | | | | | | | | | | |
| 1 Paper, paperboard and leatherboard workers | M | 1.1, 2.1 | III M | 12 | III M | — | — | — | — | 9 | III M |
| 2 Bookbinders and finishers | M | 1.1, 2.1 | III M | 12 | III M | 2.2 | II | — | — | 9 | III M |
| 3 Cutting and slitting machine operators (paper and paper products making) | M | — | — | — | — | — | — | — | | 9 | III M |
| 095 Foremen—glass, ceramics, rubber, plastics, etc. | | | | | | | | | | | |
| Foremen— | | | | | | | | | | | |
| 1 Glass and ceramics furnacemen, kilnsetters | M | — | — | — | — | — | — | — | — | — | — |
| 2 Glass formers and shapers, finishers, decorators | M | — | — | — | — | — | — | 8 | III M | — | — |
| 3 Casters and other pottery makers | M | — | — | — | — | — | — | 8 | III M | — | — |
| 4 Rubber process workers, moulding machine operators, tyre builders | M | — | — | — | — | — | — | 8 | III M | — | — |
| 5 Calender and extruding machine operators, moulders (plastics) | M | — | — | — | — | — | — | 8 | III M | — | — |
| 6 Man-made fibre makers | M | — | — | — | — | — | — | 8 | III M | — | — |
| 7 Washers, screeners and crushers in mines and quarries | M | — | — | — | — | — | — | 8 | III M | — | — |
| Other making and repairing— | | | | | | | | | | | |
| 8 Glass and ceramics | M | — | — | — | — | — | — | 8 | III M | — | — |
| 9 Rubber | M | — | — | — | — | — | — | 8 | III M | — | — |
| 10 Plastics | M | — | — | — | — | — | — | 8 | III M | — | — |
| 096 Glass and ceramics furnacemen and workers | | | | | | | | | | | |
| 1 Glass and ceramics furnacemen, kilnsetters | M | — | — | — | — | — | — | — | — | 9 | III M |
| 2 Glass formers and shapers, finishers, decorators | M | 1.1, 2.1 | III M | 12 | III M | 2.2 | II | — | — | 9 | III M |
| 3 Casters and other pottery makers | M | 1.1, 2.1 | III M | 12 | III M | 2.2 | II | — | — | 9 | III M |

| | | | | | | | | | | | |
|---|---|---|---|---|---|---|---|---|---|---|---|
| **097** | **Rubber and plastics workers** | | | | | | | | | | |
| 1 | Rubber process workers, moulding machine operators, tyre builders | M | 1.1, 2.1 | III M | 12 | III M | 2.2 | II | — | — | 9 | III M |
| 2 | Calender and extruding machine operators, moulders (plastics) | M | 1.1, 2.1 | IV | 12 | IV | 2.2 | III M | — | — | 10 | IV |
| **098** | **All other in processing materials (other than metal)** | | | | | | | | | | |
| 1 | Man-made fibre makers | M | — | — | — | — | — | — | — | — | 10 | IV |
| 2 | Brewery and vinery process workers | M | 1.1, 2.1 | III M | 12 | III M | 2.2 | II | — | — | 9 | III M |
| 3 | Washers, screeners and crushers in mines and quarries | M | — | — | — | — | — | — | — | — | 10 | IV |
| | Other material processing— | | | | | | | | | | |
| 4 | Textiles | M | 1.1, 2.1 | IV | 12 | IV | — | — | — | — | 10 | IV |
| 5 | Bakery and confectionery workers | M | 1.1, 2.1 | III M | 12 | III M | — | — | — | — | 9 | III M |
| 6 | Tobacco | M | — | — | — | — | — | — | 8 | III M | 10 | IV |
| 7 | Food and drink n.e.c. | M | 1.1, 2.1 | IV | 12 | IV | 2.2 | III M | — | — | 10 | IV |
| 8 | Wood and paper | M | 1.1, 2.1 | III M | 12 | III M | — | — | — | — | 9 | III M |
| 9 | All other (excluding metal) n.e.c. | M | 1.1, 2.1 | IV | 12 | IV | — | — | 8 | III M | 10 | IV |
| **099** | **Foremen—printing** | | | | | | | | | | |
| | Foremen— | | | | | | | | | | |
| 1 | Compositors | M | — | — | — | — | — | — | 8 | III M | — | — |
| 2 | Electrotypers, stereotypers, printing plate and cylinder preparers | M | — | — | — | — | — | — | 8 | III M | — | — |
| 3 | Printing machine minders and assistants | M | — | — | — | — | — | — | 8 | III M | — | — |
| 4 | Screen and block printers | M | — | — | — | — | — | — | 8 | III M | — | — |
| 5 | Printers (so described) | M | — | — | — | — | — | — | 8 | III M | — | — |
| **100** | **Printing workers, screen and block printers** | | | | | | | | | | |
| 1 | Compositors | M | 1.1, 2.1 | III M | 12 | III M | 2.2 | II | — | — | 9 | III M |
| 2 | Electrotypers, stereotypers, printing plate and cylinder preparers | M | 1.1, 2.1 | III M | 12 | III M | 2.2 | II | — | — | 9 | III M |
| 3 | Printing machine minders and assistants | M | 1.1, 2.1 | III M | 12 | III M | — | — | — | — | 9 | III M |
| 4 | Screen and block printers | M | 1.1, 2.1 | III M | 12 | III M | 2.2 | II | — | — | 9 | III M |
| 5 | Printers (so described) | M | 1.1, 2.1 | III M | 12 | III M | 2.2 | II | — | — | 9 | III M |
| **101** | **Foremen—textile materials working** | | | | | | | | | | |
| | Foremen— | | | | | | | | | | |
| 1 | Tailors, tailoresses, dressmakers | M | — | — | — | — | — | — | 8 | III M | — | — |
| 2 | Clothing cutters, milliners, furriers | M | — | — | — | — | — | — | 8 | III M | — | — |
| 3 | Sewers, embroiderers | M | — | — | — | — | — | — | 8 | III M | — | — |
| 4 | Coach trimmers, upholsterers, mattress makers | M | — | — | — | — | — | — | 8 | III M | — | — |
| 5 | Carpet fitters | M | — | — | — | — | — | — | 8 | III M | — | — |
| 6 | Other making and repairing, clothing and related products | M | — | — | — | — | — | — | 8 | III M | — | — |
| **102** | **Tailors, dressmakers and other clothing workers** | | | | | | | | | | |
| 1 | Tailors, tailoresses, dressmakers | M | 1.1, 2.1 | III M | 12 | III M | 2.2 | II | — | — | 9 | III M |
| 2 | Clothing cutters, milliners, furriers | M | 1.1, 2.1 | III M | 12 | III M | 2.2 | II | — | — | 9 | III M |
| 3 | Sewers, embroiderers | M | 1.1, 2.1 | IV | 12 | IV | — | — | — | — | 10 | IV |
| **103** | **Coach trimmers, upholsterers, mattress makers** | | | | | | | | | | |
| 0 | Coach trimmers, upholsterers, mattress makers | M | 1.1, 2.1 | III M | 12 | III M | 2.2 | II | — | — | 9 | III M |

| Occupation | Manual Non-manual | Self-employed | | | | Managers | | Foremen | | Apprentices, etc., Employees n.e.c. | |
| | | with employees | | without employees | | | | | | | |
| | | S.E.G. | Social Class | S.E.G. | Social Class | S.E.G. | Social Class | S.E.G. | Social Class | S.E.G. | Social Class |
|---|---|---|---|---|---|---|---|---|---|---|---|
| 104 Foremen—woodworking | | | | | | | | | | | |
| Foremen— | | | | | | | | | | | |
| 1 Carpenters, joiners | M | — | — | — | — | — | — | 8 | III M | — | — |
| 2 Cabinet makers | M | — | — | — | — | — | — | 8 | III M | — | — |
| 3 Case and box makers | M | — | — | — | — | — | — | 8 | III M | — | — |
| 4 Pattern makers (moulds) | M | — | — | — | — | — | — | 8 | III M | — | — |
| 5 Sawyers, veneer cutters, woodworking machinists | M | — | — | — | — | — | — | 8 | III M | — | — |
| 6 Other making and repairing, wood | M | — | — | — | — | — | — | 8 | III M | — | — |
| 105 Woodworkers, pattern makers | | | | | | | | | | | |
| 1 Carpenters, joiners | M | 1.1, 2.1 | III M | 12 | III M | 2.2 | II | — | — | 9 | III M |
| 2 Cabinet makers | M | 1.1, 2.1 | III M | 12 | III M | 2.2 | II | — | — | 9 | III M |
| 3 Case and box makers | M | 1.1, 2.1 | III M | 12 | III M | 2.2 | II | — | — | 9 | III M |
| 4 Pattern makers (moulds) | M | 1.1, 2.1 | III M | 12 | III M | 2.2 | II | — | — | 9 | III M |
| 106 Sawyers, veneer cutters, woodworking machinists | | | | | | | | | | | |
| 0 Sawyers, veneer cutters. woodworking machinists | M | 1.1, 2.1 | III M | 12 | III M | 2.2 | II | — | — | 9 | III M |
| 107 All other in making and repairing (excluding metal and electrical) | | | | | | | | | | | |
| 1 Labourers and mates to woodworking craftsmen | M | — | — | — | — | — | — | — | — | 9 | III M |
| 2 Dental technicians | M | 1.1, 2.1 | III M | 12 | III M | 2.2 | II | 8 | III M | 9 | III M |
| 3 Carpet fitters | M | 1.1, 2.1 | III M | 12 | III M | — | — | — | — | 9 | III M |
| 4 Musical instrument makers, piano tuners | M | 1.1, 2.1 | III M | 12 | III M | 2.2 | II | 8 | III M | 9 | III M |
| Other making and repairing— | | | | | | | | | | | |
| 5 Glass and ceramics | M | 1.1, 2.1 | III M | 12 | III M | — | — | — | — | 9 | III M |
| 6 Wood | M | 1.1, 2.1 | III M | 12 | III M | 2.2 | II | — | — | 9 | III M |
| 7 Leather | M | 1.1, 2.1 | III M | 12 | III M | 2.2 | II | — | — | 9 | III M |
| 8 Clothing and related products | M | 1.1, 2.1 | III M | 12 | III M | 2.2 | II | — | — | 9 | III M |
| 9 Paper goods and printing | M | 1.1, 2.1 | III M | 12 | III M | 2.2 | II | — | — | 9 | III M |
| 10 Rubber | M | 1.1, 2.1 | III M | 12 | III M | 2.2 | II | — | — | 9 | III M |
| 11 Plastics | M | 1.1, 2.1 | IV | 12 | IV | 2.2 | III M | — | — | 10 | IV |
| 12 All other (excluding metal and electrical) n.e.c. | M | 1.1, 2.1 | IV | 12 | IV | 2.2 | III M | 8 | III M | 10 | IV |
| 108 Foremen—metal making and treating | | | | | | | | | | | |
| Foremen— | | | | | | | | | | | |
| 1 Furnace operating occupations (metal) | M | — | — | — | — | — | — | 8 | III M | — | — |
| 2 Rollermen | M | — | — | — | — | — | — | 8 | III M | — | — |
| 3 Smiths, forgemen | M | — | — | — | — | — | — | 8 | III M | — | — |
| 4 Metal drawers | M | — | — | — | — | — | — | 8 | III M | — | — |
| 5 Moulders, coremakers, die casters | M | — | — | — | — | — | — | 8 | III M | — | — |
| 6 Electroplaters | M | — | — | — | — | — | — | 8 | III M | — | — |
| 7 Annealers, hardeners, temperers (metal) | M | — | — | — | — | — | — | 8 | III M | — | — |
| 8 Galvanizers, tin platers, dip platers | M | — | — | — | — | — | — | 8 | III M | — | — |
| 9 Metal making and treating workers n.e.c. | M | — | — | — | — | — | — | 8 | III M | — | — |

| | Occupation | | | | | | | | | | | |
|---|---|---|---|---|---|---|---|---|---|---|---|---|
| 109 | Furnacemen (metal), rollermen, smiths, forgemen | | | | | | | | | | | |
| 1 | Furnace operating occupations (metal) | M | 1.1, 2.1 | III M | 12 | III M | — | — | — | — | 9 | III M |
| 2 | Rollermen | M | 1.1, 2.1 | III M | 12 | III M | 2.2 | II | — | — | 9 | III M |
| 3 | Smiths, forgemen | M | 1.1, 2.1 | III M | 12 | III M | 2.2 | II | — | — | 9 | III M |
| 110 | Metal drawers, moulders, die casters, electroplaters, annealers | | | | | | | | | | | |
| 1 | Metal drawers | M | 1.1, 2.1 | III M | 12 | III M | — | — | — | — | 9 | III M |
| 2 | Moulders, coremakers, die casters | M | 1.1, 2.1 | III M | 12 | III M | — | — | — | — | 9 | III M |
| 3 | Electroplaters | M | 1.1, 2.1 | III M | 12 | III M | 2.2 | II | — | — | 9 | III M |
| 4 | Annealers, hardeners, temperers (metal) | M | 1.1, 2.1 | IV | 12 | IV | — | — | — | — | 10 | IV |
| 111 | Foremen—engineering machining | | | | | | | | | | | |
| | Foremen— | | | | | | | | | | | |
| 1 | Press and machine tool setters | M | — | — | — | — | — | — | 8 | III M | — | — |
| 2 | Centre lathe turners | M | — | — | — | — | — | — | 8 | III M | — | — |
| 3 | Machine tool setter operators | M | — | — | — | — | — | — | 8 | III M | — | — |
| 4 | Machine tool operators | M | — | — | — | — | — | — | 8 | III M | — | — |
| 5 | Press, stamping and automatic machine operators | M | — | — | — | — | — | — | 8 | III M | — | — |
| 6 | Metal polishers | M | — | — | — | — | — | — | 8 | III M | — | — |
| 7 | Fettlers, dressers | M | — | — | — | — | — | — | 8 | III M | — | — |
| 8 | Shot blasters | M | — | — | — | — | — | — | 8 | III M | — | — |
| 112 | Press and machine tool setter operators and operators, turners | | | | | | | | | | | |
| 1 | Press and machine tool setters | M | 1.1, 2.1 | III M | 12 | III M | 2.2 | II | — | — | 9 | III M |
| 2 | Centre lathe turners | M | 1.1, 2.1 | III M | 12 | III M | 2.2 | II | — | — | 9 | III M |
| 3 | Machine tool setter operators | M | 1.1, 2.1 | III M | 12 | III M | 2.2 | II | — | — | 9 | III M |
| 4 | Machine tool operators | M | 1.1, 2.1 | IV | 12 | IV | — | — | — | — | 10 | IV |
| 113 | Machine attendants, minders, press and stamping machine operators, metal polishers, fettlers, dressers | | | | | | | | | | | |
| 1 | Press, stamping and automatic machine operators | M | 1.1, 2.1 | IV | 12 | IV | 2.2 | III M | — | — | 10 | IV |
| 2 | Metal polishers | M | 1.1, 2.1 | III M | 12 | III M | 2.2 | II | — | — | 9 | III M |
| 3 | Fettlers, dressers | M | 1.1, 2.1 | IV | 12 | IV | — | — | — | — | 10 | IV |
| 114 | Foremen—production fitting (metal) | | | | | | | | | | | |
| | Foremen— | | | | | | | | | | | |
| 1 | Tool makers, tool fitters, markers-out | M | — | — | — | — | — | — | 8 | III M | — | — |
| 2 | Precision instrument makers and repairers | M | — | — | — | — | — | — | 8 | III M | — | — |
| 3 | Watch and chronometer makers and repairers | M | — | — | — | — | — | — | 8 | III M | — | — |
| 4 | Metal working production fitters and fitter/machinists | M | — | — | — | — | — | — | 8 | III M | — | — |
| 5 | Motor mechanics, auto engineers | M | — | — | — | — | — | — | 8 | III M | — | — |
| 6 | Maintenance fitters (aircraft engines) | M | — | — | — | — | — | — | 8 | III M | — | — |
| 7 | Office machinery mechanics | M | — | — | — | — | — | — | 8 | III M | — | — |
| 115 | Tool makers, tool fitters, markers-out | | | | | | | | | | | |
| 0 | Tool makers, tool fitters, markers-out | M | 1.1, 2.1 | III M | 12 | III M | 2.2 | II | — | — | 9 | III M |
| 116 | Instrument and watch and clock makers and repairers | | | | | | | | | | | |
| 1 | Precision instrument makers and repairers | M | 1.1, 2.1 | III M | 12 | III M | 2.2 | II | — | — | 9 | III M |
| 2 | Watch and chronometer makers and repairers | M | 1.1, 2.1 | III M | 12 | III M | 2.2 | II | — | — | 9 | III M |

| Occupation | Manual Non-manual | Self-employed | | | | Managers | | Foremen | | Apprentices, etc., Employees n.e.c. | |
|---|---|---|---|---|---|---|---|---|---|---|---|
| | | with employees | | without employees | | | | | | | |
| | | S.E.G. | Social Class | S.E.G. | Social Class | S.E.G. | Social Class | S.E.G. | Social Class | S.E.G. | Social Class |
| 117 Metal working production fitters and fitter/machinists | | | | | | | | | | | |
| 0 Metal working production fitters and fitter/machinists ... ... ... | M | 1.1, 2.1 | III M | 12 | III M | 2.2 | II | — | — | 9 | III M |
| 118 Motor vehicle and aircraft mechanics | | | | | | | | | | | |
| 1 Motor mechanics, auto engineers ... ... ... ... ... | M | 1.1, 2.1 | III M | 12 | III M | 2.2 | II | — | — | 9 | III M |
| 2 Maintenance fitters (aircraft engines) ... ... ... ... | M | — | — | 12 | III M | — | — | — | — | 9 | III M |
| 119 Office machinery mechanics | | | | | | | | | | | |
| 0 Office machinery mechanics ... ... ... ... ... ... ... | M | 1.1, 2.1 | III M | 12 | III M | 2.2 | II | — | — | 9 | III M |
| 120 Foremen—production fitting and wiring (electrical) | | | | | | | | | | | |
| Foremen— | | | | | | | | | | | |
| 1 Production fitters (electrical, electronic) ... ... ... | M | — | — | — | — | — | — | 8 | III M | — | — |
| 2 Electricians, electrical maintenance fitters ... ... ... | M | — | — | — | — | — | — | 8 | III M | — | — |
| 3 Plant operators and attendants n.e.c. ... ... ... ... | M | — | — | — | — | — | — | 8 | III M | — | — |
| 4 Telephone fitters ... ... ... ... ... ... | M | — | — | — | — | — | — | 8 | III M | — | — |
| 5 Cable jointers, linesmen ... ... ... ... ... | M | — | — | — | — | — | — | 8 | III M | — | — |
| 6 Radio and TV mechanics ... ... ... ... ... | M | — | — | — | — | — | — | 8 | III M | — | — |
| 7 Other electronic maintenance engineers ... ... ... | M | — | — | — | — | — | — | 8 | III M | — | — |
| 121 Production fitters, electricians, electricity power plant operators, switchboard attendants | | | | | | | | | | | |
| 1 Production fitters (electrical, electronic) ... ... ... | M | 1.1, 2.1 | III M | 12 | III M | 2.2 | II | — | — | 9 | III M |
| 2 Electricians, electrical maintenance fitters ... ... ... | M | 1.1, 2.1 | III M | 12 | III M | 2.2 | II | — | — | 9 | III M |
| 3 Electrical engineers (so described) ... ... ... ... | M | 1.1, 2.1 | III M | 12 | III M | 2.2 | II | — | — | 9 | III M |
| 4 Plant operators and attendants n.e.c. ... ... ... ... | M | — | — | — | — | — | — | — | — | 9 | III M |
| 122 Telephone fitters, cable jointers, linesmen | | | | | | | | | | | |
| 1 Telephone fitters ... ... ... ... ... ... | M | — | — | 12 | III M | — | — | — | — | 9 | III M |
| 2 Cable jointers, linesmen ... ... ... ... ... | M | — | — | 12 | III M | — | — | — | — | 9 | III M |
| 123 Radio, TV and other electronic maintenance fitters and mechanics | | | | | | | | | | | |
| 1 Radio and TV mechanics ... ... ... ... ... | M | 1.1, 2.1 | III M | 12 | III M | 2.2 | II | — | — | 9 | III M |
| 2 Other electronic maintenance engineers ... ... ... | M | 1.1, 2.1 | III M | 12 | III M | 2.2 | II | — | — | 9 | III M |
| 124 Foremen—metal working, pipes, sheets, structures | | | | | | | | | | | |
| Foremen— | | | | | | | | | | | |
| 1 Plumbers, heating and ventilating fitters, gas fitters ... ... ... | M | — | — | — | — | — | — | 8 | III M | — | — |
| 2 Sheet metal workers ... ... ... ... ... | M | — | — | — | — | — | — | 8 | III M | — | — |
| 3 Metal plate workers, shipwrights, riveters ... ... ... ... | M | — | — | — | — | — | — | 8 | III M | — | — |
| 4 Steel erectors, benders, fixers ... ... ... ... | M | — | — | — | — | — | — | 8 | III M | — | — |
| 5 Scaffolders, stagers ... ... ... ... | M | — | — | — | — | — | — | 8 | III M | — | — |
| 6 Welders ... ... ... ... ... ... | M | — | — | — | — | — | — | 8 | III M | — | — |
| 7 Riggers ... ... ... ... ... ... | M | — | — | — | — | — | — | 8 | III M | — | — |

| | | | | | | | | | | | |
|---|---|---|---|---|---|---|---|---|---|---|---|
| 125 Plumbers, heating and ventilating fitters, gas fitters | | | | | | | | | | | |
|   0 Plumbers, heating and ventilating fitters, gas fitters | M | 1.1, 2.1 | III M | 12 | III M | 2.2 | II | — | — | 9 | III M |
| 126 Sheet metal workers, platers, shipwrights, riveters, etc. | | | | | | | | | | | |
|   1 Sheet metal workers | M | 1.1, 2.1 | III M | 12 | III M | 2.2 | II | — | — | 9 | III M |
|   2 Metal plate workers, shipwrights, riveters | M | 1.1, 2.1 | III M | 12 | III M | 2.2 | II | — | — | 9 | III M |
| 127 Steel erectors, scaffolders, steel benders, fixers | | | | | | | | | | | |
|   1 Steel erectors, benders, fixers | M | 1.1, 2.1 | III M | 12 | III M | 2.2 | II | — | — | 9 | III M |
|   2 Scaffolders, stagers | M | 1.1, 2.1 | IV | 12 | IV | — | — | — | — | 10 | IV |
| 128 Welders | | | | | | | | | | | |
|   0 Welders | M | 1.1, 2.1 | III M | 12 | III M | 2.2 | II | — | — | 9 | III M |
| 129 Foremen—other processing, making and repairing (metal and electrical) | | | | | | | | | | | |
|     Foremen— | | | | | | | | | | | |
|   1 Goldsmiths, silversmiths, precious stone workers | M | — | — | — | — | — | — | 8 | III M | — | — |
|   2 Engravers, etchers (printing) | M | — | — | — | — | — | — | 8 | III M | — | — |
|   3 Coach and vehicle body builders | M | — | — | — | — | — | — | 8 | III M | — | — |
|   4 Oilers, greasers, lubricators | M | — | — | — | — | — | — | 8 | III M | — | — |
|   5 Electronics wiremen | M | — | — | — | — | — | — | 8 | III M | — | — |
|   6 Coil winders | M | — | — | — | — | — | — | 8 | III M | — | — |
| 130 Goldsmiths, silversmiths, etc., engravers, etchers | | | | | | | | | | | |
|   1 Goldsmiths, silversmiths, precious stone workers | M | 1.1, 2.1 | III M | 12 | III M | 2.2 | II | — | — | 9 | III M |
|   2 Engravers, etchers (printing) | M | 1.1, 2.1 | III M | 12 | III M | — | — | — | — | 9 | III M |
| 131 All other in processing, making and repairing (metal and electrical) | | | | | | | | | | | |
|   1 Coach and vehicle body builders | M | 1.1, 2.1 | III M | 12 | III M | 2.2 | II | — | — | 9 | III M |
|   2 Galvanizers, tin platers, dip platers | M | 1.1, 2.1 | III M | 12 | III M | — | — | — | — | 9 | III M |
|   3 Metal making and treating workers n.e.c. | M | 1.1, 2.1 | III M | 12 | III M | — | — | — | — | 9 | III M |
|   4 Oilers, greasers, lubricators | M | — | — | — | — | — | — | — | — | 9 | III M |
|   5 Riggers | M | 1.1, 2.1 | III M | 12 | III M | 2.2 | II | — | — | 9 | III M |
|   6 Electronics wiremen | M | — | — | 12 | III M | — | — | — | — | 9 | III M |
|   7 Coil winders | M | 1.1, 2.1 | III M | 12 | III M | 2.2 | II | — | — | 9 | III M |
|   8 Shot blasters | M | — | — | — | — | — | — | — | — | 10 | IV |
|   9 Other metal, jewellery, electrical production workers | M | 1.1, 2.1 | IV | 12 | IV | 2.2 | III M | 8 | III M | 10 | IV |
| — | | | | | | | | | | | |
|   1 Foremen (engineering and allied trades) | M | — | — | — | — | — | — | 8 | III M | — | — |
|   2 Trainee craftsmen (engineering and allied trades) | M | — | — | — | — | — | — | — | — | 9 | III M |
| 132 Foremen—painting and similar coating | | | | | | | | | | | |
|     Foremen— | | | | | | | | | | | |
|   1 Pottery decorators | M | — | — | — | — | — | — | 8 | III M | — | — |
|   2 Coach painters (so described) | M | — | — | — | — | — | — | 8 | III M | — | — |
|   3 Other spray painters | M | — | — | — | — | — | — | 8 | III M | — | — |
|   4 Painters and decorators n.e.c., french polishers | M | — | — | — | — | — | — | 8 | III M | — | — |

| Occupation | Manual Non-manual | Self-employed | | | | Managers | | Foremen | | Apprentices, etc., Employees n.e.c. | |
|---|---|---|---|---|---|---|---|---|---|---|---|
| | | with employees | | without employees | | | | | | | |
| | | S.E.G. | Social Class | S.E.G. | Social Class | S.E.G. | Social Class | S.E.G. | Social Class | S.E.G. | Social Class |
| 133 Painters, decorators, french polishers | | | | | | | | | | | |
| 1 Pottery decorators | M | 1.1, 2.1 | III M | 12 | III M | — | — | — | — | 9 | III M |
| 2 Coach painters (so described) | M | 1.1, 2.1 | III M | 12 | III M | 2.2 | II | — | — | 9 | III M |
| 3 Other spray painters | M | 1.1, 2.1 | IV | 12 | IV | 2.2 | III M | — | — | 10 | IV |
| 4 Painters and decorators n.e.c., french polishers | M | 1.1, 2.1 | III M | 12 | III M | 2.2 | II | — | — | 9 | III M |
| 134 Foremen—product assembling (repetitive) | | | | | | | | | | | |
| Foremen assemblers— | | | | | | | | | | | |
| 1 Electrical, electronic | M | — | — | — | — | — | — | 8 | III M | — | — |
| 2 Instruments | M | — | — | — | — | — | — | 8 | III M | — | — |
| 3 Vehicles and other metal goods | M | — | — | — | — | — | — | 8 | III M | — | — |
| 4 Paper production, processing and printing | M | — | — | — | — | — | — | 8 | III M | — | — |
| 5 Plastics goods | M | — | — | — | — | — | — | 8 | III M | — | — |
| 135 Repetitive assemblers (metal and electrical goods) | | | | | | | | | | | |
| 1 Assemblers (electrical, electronic) | M | 1.1, 2.1 | IV | 12 | IV | — | — | — | — | 10 | IV |
| 2 Instrument assemblers | M | — | — | 12 | III M | — | — | — | — | 9 | III M |
| 3 Assemblers (vehicles and other metal goods) | M | — | — | 12 | IV | — | — | — | — | 10 | IV |
| 136 Foremen—product inspection and packaging | | | | | | | | | | | |
| Foremen inspectors, viewers, examiners— | | | | | | | | | | | |
| 1 Metal, electrical goods | M | — | — | — | — | — | — | 8 | III M | — | — |
| 2 Textiles | M | — | — | — | — | — | — | 8 | III M | — | — |
| 3 Food | M | — | — | — | — | — | — | 8 | III M | — | — |
| 4 Rubber goods | M | — | — | — | — | — | — | 8 | III M | — | — |
| 5 Plastics goods | M | — | — | — | — | — | — | 8 | III M | — | — |
| 6 Woodwork | M | — | — | — | — | — | — | 8 | III M | — | — |
| Foremen— | | | | | | | | | | | |
| 7 Packers, bottlers, canners, fillers | M | — | — | — | — | — | — | 8 | III M | — | — |
| 8 Laboratory assistants | M | — | — | — | — | — | — | 8 | III M | — | — |
| 9 Inspectors, sorters in paper production, processing and printing | M | — | — | — | — | — | — | 8 | III M | — | — |
| 10 Weighers | M | — | — | — | — | — | — | 8 | III M | — | — |
| 11 Graders, sorters, selectors n.e.c. | M | — | — | — | — | — | — | 8 | III M | — | — |
| 137 Inspectors, viewers, testers, packers, bottlers, etc. | | | | | | | | | | | |
| 1 Inspectors, viewers (metal, electrical goods) | M | — | — | 12 | IV | — | — | — | — | 10 | IV |
| 2 Packers, bottlers, canners, fillers | M | 1.1, 2.1 | IV | 12 | IV | — | — | — | — | 10 | IV |

| No. |  | Sex | | | | | | | | | | |
|---|---|---|---|---|---|---|---|---|---|---|---|---|
| 138 | All other in painting, repetitive assembling, product inspection, packaging and related | | | | | | | | | | | |
| 1 | Laboratory assistants | M | — | — | — | — | — | — | — | — | 9 | III M |
|  | Inspectors, viewers, examiners— | | | | | | | | | | | |
| 2 | Textiles | M | — | — | — | — | — | — | — | — | 9 | III M |
| 3 | Food | M | — | — | — | — | — | — | — | — | 10 | IV |
| 4 | Rubber goods | M | — | — | — | — | — | — | — | — | 9 | III M |
| 5 | Plastics goods | M | — | — | — | — | — | — | — | — | 10 | IV |
| 6 | Woodwork | M | — | — | — | — | — | — | — | — | 9 | III M |
| 7 | Inspectors, sorters in paper production, processing and printing | M | — | — | — | — | — | — | — | — | 9 | III M |
| 8 | Assemblers in paper production, processing and printing | M | — | — | 12 | III M | — | — | — | — | 9 | III M |
| 9 | Assemblers (plastics goods) | M | — | — | — | — | — | — | — | — | 10 | IV |
| 10 | Weighers | M | — | — | — | — | — | — | — | — | 10 | IV |
| 11 | Graders, sorters, selectors n.e.c. | M | — | — | — | — | — | — | — | — | 10 | IV |
| 12 | Painting, assembling and related occupations n.e.c. | M | 1.1, 2.1 | IV | 12 | IV | 2.2 | III M | 8 | III M | 10 | IV |
| 139 | Foremen—building and civil engineering n.e.c. | | | | | | | | | | | |
|  | Foremen— | | | | | | | | | | | |
| 1 | Bricklayers, tile setters | M | — | — | — | — | — | — | 8 | III M | — | — |
| 2 | Masons, stone cutters | M | — | — | — | — | — | — | 8 | III M | — | — |
| 3 | Plasterers | M | — | — | — | — | — | — | 8 | III M | — | — |
| 4 | Roofers, glaziers | M | — | — | — | — | — | — | 8 | III M | — | — |
| 5 | Handymen, general building workers | M | — | — | — | — | — | — | 8 | III M | — | — |
| 6 | Railway lengthmen | M | — | — | — | — | — | — | 8 | III M | — | — |
| 7 | Road surfacers, concreters | M | — | — | — | — | — | — | 8 | III M | — | — |
| 8 | Roadmen | M | — | — | — | — | — | — | 8 | III M | — | — |
| 9 | Paviors, kerb layers | M | — | — | — | — | — | — | 8 | III M | — | — |
| 10 | Sewage plant attendants | M | — | — | — | — | — | — | 8 | III M | — | — |
| 11 | Mains and service layers, pipe jointers | M | — | — | — | — | — | — | 8 | III M | — | — |
| 12 | Construction workers n.e.c. | M | — | — | — | — | — | — | 8 | III M | — | — |
| 140 | Building and construction workers | | | | | | | | | | | |
| 1 | Bricklayers, tile setters | M | 1.1, 2.1 | III M | 12 | III M | 2.2 | II | — | — | 9 | III M |
| 2 | Masons, stone cutters | M | 1.1, 2.1 | III M | 12 | III M | 2.2 | II | — | — | 9 | III M |
| 3 | Plasterers | M | 1.1, 2.1 | III M | 12 | III M | 2.2 | II | — | — | 9 | III M |
| 4 | Roofers, glaziers | M | 1.1, 2.1 | IV | 12 | IV | 2.2 | III M | — | — | 10 | IV |
| 5 | Handymen, general building workers | M | 1.1, 2.1 | IV | 12 | IV | 2.2 | III M | — | — | 10 | IV |
| 6 | Builders (so described) | M | 1.1, 2.1 | III M | 12 | III M | 2.2 | II | — | — | 9 | III M |
| 141 | Concreters, road surfacers, railway lengthmen | | | | | | | | | | | |
| 1 | Railway lengthmen | M | — | — | — | — | — | — | — | — | 10 | IV |
| 2 | Road surfacers, concreters | M | — | — | 12 | IV | — | — | — | — | 10 | IV |
| 3 | Roadmen | M | 2.1 | V | 12 | V | — | — | — | — | 11 | V |
| 4 | Paviors, kerb layers | M | 1.1, 2.1 | IV | 12 | IV | — | — | — | — | 10 | IV |
| 142 | Sewage plant attendants, sewermen (maintenance), mains and service layers, pipe jointers (gas, water, drainage, oil), inspectors (water supply), turncocks | | | | | | | | | | | |
| 1 | Sewage plant attendants | M | — | — | — | — | — | — | — | — | 11 | V |
| 2 | Mains and service layers, pipe jointers | M | 1.1, 2.1 | IV | 12 | IV | — | — | — | — | 10 | IV |

| Occupation | Manual Non-manual | Self-employed | | | | Managers | | Foremen | | Apprentices, etc., Employees n.e.c. | |
| | | with employees | | without employees | | | | | | | |
| | | S.E.G. | Social Class | S.E.G. | Social Class | S.E.G | Social Class | S.E.G. | Social Class | S.E.G. | Social Class |
|---|---|---|---|---|---|---|---|---|---|---|---|
| 143 Civil engineering labourers, craftsmen's mates and other builders' labourers n.e.c. | | | | | | | | | | | |
| 1 Craftsmen's mates | M | 2.1 | IV | 12 | IV | — | — | 8 | III M | 10 | IV |
| 2 Building and civil engineering labourers | M | 2.1 | V | 12 | V | — | — | 8 | III M | 11 | V |
| 144 Foremen/deputies—coalmining | | | | | | | | | | | |
| 0 Foremen/deputies—coalmining | M | — | — | — | — | — | — | 8 | III M | — | — |
| 145 Face-trained coalmining workers | | | | | | | | | | | |
| 0 Face-trained coalmining workers | M | 1.1, 2.1 | III M | 12 | III M | — | — | — | — | 9 | III M |
| 146 All other in construction, mining, quarrying, well drilling and related n.e.c. | | | | | | | | | | | |
| 1 Miners (not coal), quarrymen, well drillers | M | 1.1, 2.1 | IV | 12 | IV | 2.2 | III M | 8 | III M | 10 | IV |
| 2 Construction workers n.e.c. | M | 1.1, 2.1 | IV | 12 | IV | 2.2 | III M | — | — | 10 | IV |
| 147 Foremen—ships, lighters and others vessels | | | | | | | | | | | |
| 0 Foremen—ships, lighters and other vessels | M | — | — | — | — | — | — | 8 | III M | — | — |
| 148 Deck, engine-room hands, bargemen, lightermen, boatmen | | | | | | | | | | | |
| 0 Deck, engine-room hands, bargemen, lightermen, boatmen | M | 1.1, 2.1 | IV | 12 | IV | — | — | — | — | 10 | IV |
| 149 Foremen—rail transport operating | | | | | | | | | | | |
| Foremen— | | | | | | | | | | | |
| 1 Railway guards | M | — | — | — | — | — | — | 8 | III M | — | — |
| 2 Signalmen and crossing keepers, railway | M | — | — | — | — | — | — | 8 | III M | — | — |
| 3 Shunters, pointsmen | M | — | — | — | — | — | — | 8 | III M | — | — |
| 4 Other foremen rail transport | M | — | — | — | — | — | — | 8 | III M | — | — |
| 150 Rail transport operating staff | | | | | | | | | | | |
| 1 Drivers, motormen, secondmen, railway engines | M | — | — | — | — | — | — | — | — | 9 | III M |
| 2 Railway guards | M | — | — | — | — | — | — | — | — | 9 | III M |
| 3 Signalmen and crossing keepers, railway | M | — | — | — | — | — | — | — | — | 9 | III M |
| 4 Shunters, pointsmen | M | — | — | — | — | — | — | — | — | 9 | III M |
| 151 Foremen—road transport operating, bus inspectors | | | | | | | | | | | |
| 1 Bus inspectors | M | — | — | — | — | — | — | 8 | III M | — | — |
| Foremen— | | | | | | | | | | | |
| 2 Drivers of road goods vehicles | M | — | — | — | — | — | — | 8 | III M | — | — |
| 3 Other foremen road transport | M | — | — | — | — | — | — | 8 | III M | — | — |

| | | | | | | | | | | | |
|---|---|---|---|---|---|---|---|---|---|---|---|
| 152 | Bus, coach, lorry drivers, etc. | | | | | | | | | | |
| 1 | Bus and coach drivers ... | M | 1.1, 2.1 | III M | 12 | III M | 2.2 | II | — | — | 9 | III M |
| 2 | Drivers of road goods vehicles | M | 1.1, 2.1 | III M | 12 | III M | 2.2 | II | — | — | 9 | III M |
| 3 | Other motor drivers ... | M | 1.1, 2.1 | III M | 12 | III M | 2.2 | II | — | — | 9 | III M |
| 153 | Bus conductors, drivers' mates | | | | | | | | | | |
| 1 | Bus conductors | M | — | — | 12 | IV | — | — | — | — | 10 | IV |
| 2 | Drivers' mates ... | M | — | — | — | — | — | — | — | — | 11 | V |
| 154 | Foremen—civil engineering plant operating, materials handling equipment operating | | | | | | | | | | |
| | Foremen— | | | | | | | | | | |
| 1 | Mechanical plant drivers, operators (earth moving and civil engineering) ... | M | — | — | — | — | — | — | 8 | III M | — | — |
| 2 | Crane drivers, operators... | M | — | — | — | — | — | — | 8 | III M | — | — |
| 3 | Fork lift, mechanical truck drivers | M | — | — | — | — | — | — | 8 | III M | — | — |
| 4 | Slingers ... | M | — | — | — | — | — | — | 8 | III M | — | — |
| 155 | Mechanical plant, fork lift, mechanical truck drivers, crane drivers, operators | | | | | | | | | | |
| 1 | Mechanical plant drivers, operators (earth moving and civil engineering) ... | M | 1.1, 2.1 | III M | 12 | III M | 2.2 | II | — | — | 9 | III M |
| 2 | Crane drivers, operators | M | — | — | — | — | — | — | — | — | 9 | III M |
| 3 | Fork lift, mechanical truck drivers ... | M | — | — | 12 | III M | — | — | — | — | 9 | III M |
| 156 | Foremen—materials moving and storing | | | | | | | | | | |
| | Foremen— | | | | | | | | | | |
| 1 | Storekeepers, warehousemen | M | — | — | — | — | — | — | 8 | III M | — | — |
| 2 | Stevedores, dockers | M | — | — | — | — | — | — | 8 | III M | — | — |
| 3 | Goods porters ... | M | — | — | — | — | — | — | 8 | III M | — | — |
| 4 | Refuse collectors, dustmen | M | — | — | — | — | — | — | 8 | III M | — | — |
| 157 | Storekeepers, stevedores, warehouse, market and other goods porters | | | | | | | | | | |
| 1 | Storekeepers, warehousemen... | M | 1.1, 2.1 | IV | 12 | IV | 2.2 | III M | — | — | 10 | IV |
| 2 | Stevedores, dockers ... | M | 1.1, 2.1 | V | 12 | V | — | — | — | — | 11 | V |
| 3 | Goods porters ... | M | 1.1, 2.1 | V | 12 | V | 2.2 | III M | — | — | 11 | V |
| 4 | Refuse collectors, dustmen ... | M | — | — | — | — | — | — | — | — | 11 | V |
| 158 | All other in transport operating, materials moving and storing and related n.e.c. | | | | | | | | | | |
| 1 | Slingers... | M | — | — | — | — | — | — | — | — | 9 | III M |
| 2 | Workers in transport operating, materials moving and storing and related n.e.c. ... | M | 1.1, 2.1 | III M | 12 | III M | — | — | 8 | III M | 9 | III M |

| Occupation | Manual Non-manual | Self-employed | | | | Managers | | Foremen | | Apprentices, etc., Employees n.e.c. | |
| | | with employees | | without employees | | | | | | | |
| | | S.E.G. | Social Class | S.E.G. | Social Class | S.E.G. | Social Class | S.E.G. | Social Class | S.E.G. | Social Class |
|---|---|---|---|---|---|---|---|---|---|---|---|
| 159 Foremen—miscellaneous | | | | | | | | | | | |
|    Foremen— | | | | | | | | | | | |
|       Labourers and unskilled workers n.e.c.— | | | | | | | | | | | |
|   1    Textiles (not textile goods) | M | — | — | — | — | — | — | 8 | III M | — | — |
|   2    Chemicals and allied trades | M | — | — | — | — | — | — | 8 | III M | — | — |
|   3    Coke ovens and gas works | M | — | — | — | — | — | — | 8 | III M | — | — |
|   4    Glass and ceramics | M | — | — | — | — | — | — | 8 | III M | — | — |
|   5    Foundries in engineering and allied trades | M | — | — | — | — | — | — | 8 | III M | — | — |
|   6    Engineering and allied trades | M | — | — | — | — | — | — | 8 | III M | — | — |
|   7    Coal mines | M | — | — | — | — | — | — | 8 | III M | — | — |
|   8    Other | M | — | — | — | — | — | — | 8 | III M | — | — |
|   9   Boiler operators | M | — | — | — | — | — | — | 8 | III M | — | — |
| 160 General labourers | | | | | | | | | | | |
|       Labourers and unskilled workers n.e.c.— | | | | | | | | | | | |
|   1    Textiles (not textile goods) | M | — | — | — | — | — | — | — | — | 11 | V |
|   2    Chemicals and allied trades | M | — | — | — | — | — | — | — | — | 11 | V |
|   3    Coke ovens and gas works | M | — | — | — | — | — | — | — | — | 11 | V |
|   4    Glass and ceramics | M | — | — | — | — | — | — | — | — | 11 | V |
|   5    Foundries in engineering and allied trades | M | — | — | — | — | — | — | — | — | 11 | V |
|   6    Engineering and allied trades | M | — | — | — | — | — | — | — | — | 11 | V |
|   7    Coal mines | M | — | — | — | — | — | — | — | — | 10 | IV |
|   8    Other | M | 2.1 | V | 12 | V | — | — | — | — | 11 | V |
| 161 All other in miscellaneous occupations n.e.c. | | | | | | | | | | | |
|   1   Boiler operators | M | — | — | — | — | — | — | — | — | 10 | IV |
|   2   All other in miscellaneous occupations n.e.c. | M | 1.1, 2.1 | III M | 12 | III M | — | — | 8 | III M | 9 | III M |
| — | | | | | | | | | | | |
|   1   Inadequately described occupations | — | 17 | — | 17 | — | 17 | — | 17 | — | 17 | — |
|   2   Occupations not stated | — | — | — | — | — | — | — | — | — | 17 | — |

## Details of Socio-economic groups and Social Classes in terms of Occupation and Employment Status groups

# S.E.G. 1.1   Employers in industry, commerce, etc.—large establishments

### (a) Social Class II   Intermediate occupations

**Employment status**—*Self-employed with employees*

| | | | |
|---|---|---|---|
| 002.6 | Underwriters, brokers, investment analysts | 021.2 | Musicians |
| 005.1 | Marketing and sales managers and executives | 032.1 | Aircraft flight deck officers |
| 005.2 | Advertising and PR executives | 032.3 | Deck, engineering and radio officers and pilots, ship |
| 013.1 | Matrons, houseparents | 037.2 | Office managers n.e.c. |
| 019.0 | Authors, writers, journalists | 038.1 | Garage proprietors |
| 020.1 | Artists, commercial artists | 038.4 | Other proprietors and managers (sales) |
| 020.2 | Industrial designers (not clothing) | 039.1 | Hotel and residential club managers |
| 020.3 | Clothing designers | 039.2 | Publicans |
| 020.4 | Window dressers | 044.4 | Managers n.e.c. |
| 021.1 | Actors, entertainers, singers, stage managers | 057.1 | Importers, exporters, commodity brokers |

### (b) Social Class III (N)   Skilled occupations—Non-manual

**Employment status**—*Self-employed with employees*

| | | | |
|---|---|---|---|
| 022.1 | Photographers, cameramen | 044.1 | Proprietors and managers, service flats, holiday flats, caravan sites, etc. |
| 022.2 | Sound and vision equipment operators | 044.3 | Hairdressers' and barbers' managers and proprietors |
| 023.1 | Professional sportsmen, sports officials | 046.3 | Other clerks and cashiers (not retail) |
| 023.2 | Literary, artistic and sports workers n.e.c. | 049.2 | Typists, shorthand writers, secretaries |
| 029.0 | Draughtsmen | 050.0 | Office machine operators |
| 038.2 | Butchers (managers and proprietors) | 057.3 | Scrap dealers, general dealers, rag and bone merchants |
| 038.3 | Fishmongers (managers and proprietors) | 057.5 | Sales representatives |
| 039.3 | Restaurateurs | 057.6 | Sales representatives (property and services), other agents |
| 039.5 | Entertainment and sports managers | | |

### (c) Social Class III (M)   Skilled occupations—Manual

**Employment status**—*Self-employed with employees*

| | | | |
|---|---|---|---|
| 056.0 | Roundsmen, van salesmen | 106.0 | Sawyers, veneer cutters, woodworking machinists |
| 064.0 | Chefs, cooks | 107.2 | Dental technicians |
| 068.2 | Nursery nurses | 107.3 | Carpet fitters |
| 075.4 | Undertakers | 107.4 | Musical instrument makers, piano tuners |
| 075.5 | Bookmakers, betting shop managers | | Other making and repairing— |
| 085.1 | Tannery production workers | 107.5 | Glass and ceramics |
| 085.2 | Shoe repairers | 107.6 | Wood |
| 085.3 | Leather cutters and sewers, footwear lasters, makers, finishers | 107.7 | Leather |
| 087.4 | Warp preparers | 107.8 | Clothing and related products |
| 087.5 | Weavers | 107.9 | Paper goods and printing |
| 087.6 | Knitters | 107.10 | Rubber |
| 087.7 | Bleachers, dyers, finishers | 109.1 | Furnace operating occupations (metal) |
| 087.8 | Menders, darners | 109.2 | Rollermen |
| 091.0 | Bakers, flour confectioners | 109.3 | Smiths, forgemen |
| 094.1 | Paper, paperboard and leatherboard workers | 110.1 | Metal drawers |
| 094.2 | Bookbinders and finishers | 110.2 | Moulders, coremakers, die casters |
| 096.2 | Glass formers and shapers, finishers, decorators | 110.3 | Electroplaters |
| 096.3 | Casters and other pottery makers | 112.1 | Press and machine tool setters |
| 097.1 | Rubber process workers, moulding machine operators, tyre builders | 112.2 | Centre lathe turners |
| 098.2 | Brewery and vinery process workers | 112.3 | Machine tool setter operators |
| | Other material processing— | 113.2 | Metal polishers |
| 098.5 | Bakery and confectionery workers | 115.0 | Tool makers, tool fitters, markers-out |
| 098.8 | Wood and paper | 116.1 | Precision instrument makers and repairers |
| 100.1 | Compositors | 116.2 | Watch and chronometer makers and repairers |
| 100.2 | Electrotypers, stereotypers, printing plate and cylinder preparers | 117.0 | Metal working production fitters and fitter/machinists |
| 100.3 | Printing machine minders and assistants | 118.1 | Motor mechanics, auto engineers |
| 100.4 | Screen and block printers | 119.0 | Office machinery mechanics |
| 100.5 | Printers (so described) | 121.1 | Production fitters (electrical, electronic) |
| 102.1 | Tailors, tailoresses, dressmakers | 121.2 | Electricians, electrical maintenance fitters |
| 102.2 | Clothing cutters, milliners, furriers | 121.3 | Electrical engineers (so described) |
| 103.0 | Coach trimmers, upholsterers, mattress makers | 123.1 | Radio and TV mechanics |
| 105.1 | Carpenters, joiners | 123.2 | Other electronic maintenance engineers |
| 105.2 | Cabinet makers | 125.0 | Plumbers, heating and ventilating fitters, gas fitters |
| 105.3 | Case and box makers | 126.1 | Sheet metal workers |
| 105.4 | Pattern makers (moulds) | 126.2 | Metal plate workers, shipwrights, riveters |
| | | 127.1 | Steel erectors, benders, fixers |
| | | 128.0 | Welders |
| | | 130.1 | Goldsmiths, silversmiths, precious stone workers |

| 130.2 | Engravers, etchers (printing) | 140.3 | Plasterers |
|---|---|---|---|
| 131.1 | Coach and vehicle body builders | 140.6 | Builders (so described) |
| 131.2 | Galvanizers, tin platers, dip platers | 145.0 | Face-trained coalmining workers |
| 131.3 | Metal making and treating workers n.e.c. | 152.1 | Bus and coach drivers |
| 131.5 | Riggers | 152.2 | Drivers of road goods vehicles |
| 131.7 | Coil winders | 152.3 | Other motor drivers |
| 133.1 | Pottery decorators | 155.1 | Mechanical plant drivers, operators (earth moving and civil engineering) |
| 133.2 | Coach painters (so described) | | |
| 133.4 | Painters and decorators n.e.c., french polishers | 158.2 | Workers in transport operating, materials moving and storing and related n.e.c. |
| 140.1 | Bricklayers, tile setters | | |
| 140.2 | Masons, stone cutters | 161.2 | All other in miscellaneous occupations n.e.c. |

<h3 align="center">(c) Social Class IV   Partly skilled occupations</h3>

Employment status—Self-employed with employees

| 057.2 | Market and street traders and assistants | 110.4 | Annealers, hardeners, temperers (metal) |
|---|---|---|---|
| 057.4 | Credit agents, collector salesmen | 112.4 | Machine tool operators |
| 062.1 | Security guards and officers, patrolmen, watchmen | 113.1 | Press, stamping and automatic machine operators |
| 062.3 | Security and protective service workers n.e.c. | 113.3 | Fettlers, dressers |
| 075.6 | Service workers n.e.c. | 127.2 | Scaffolders, stagers |
| 078.2 | Gardeners, groundsmen | 131.9 | Other metal, jewellery, electrical production workers |
| 087.1 | Preparatory fibre processors | 133.3 | Other spray painters |
| 087.2 | Spinners, doublers, twisters | 135.1 | Assemblers, (electrical, electronic) |
| 087.3 | Winders, reelers | 137.2 | Packers, bottlers, canners, fillers |
| 089.0 | Chemical, gas and petroleum process plant operators | 138.12 | Painting, assembling and related occupations n.e.c. |
| 097.2 | Calender and extruding machine operators, moulders (plastics) | 140.4 | Roofers, glaziers |
| | Other material processing— | 140.5 | Handymen, general building workers |
| 098.4 | Textiles | 141.4 | Paviors, kerb layers |
| 098.7 | Food and drink n.e.c. | 142.2 | Mains and service layers, pipe jointers |
| 098.9 | All other (excluding metal) n.e.c. | 146.1 | Miners (not coal), quarrymen, well drillers |
| 102.3 | Sewers, embroiderers | 146.2 | Construction workers n.e.c. |
| | Other making and repairing— | 148.0 | Deck, engine-room hands, bargemen, lightermen, boatmen |
| 107.11 | Plastics | 157.1 | Storekeepers, warehousemen |
| 107.12 | All other (excluding metal and electrical) n.e.c. | | |

<h3 align="center">(c) Social Class V   Unskilled occupations—Manual</h3>

Employment status—Self-employed with employees

| 072.2 | Cleaners, window cleaners, chimney sweeps, road sweepers | 157.3 | Goods porters |
|---|---|---|---|
| 157.2 | Stevedores, dockers | | |

# S.E.G. 1.2  Managers in central and local government, industry, commerce, etc.—large establishments

<h3 align="center">(d) Social Class I   Professional, etc. occupations</h3>

Employment status—Managers

| 007.1 | General administrators—national government (Assistant Secretary level and above) |
|---|---|

<h3 align="center">(e) Social Class II   Intermediate occupations</h3>

Employment status—Managers

| 002.3 | Estimators | 009.8 | Professional workers and related supporting management and administration n.e.c. |
|---|---|---|---|
| 002.4 | Valuers, claims assessors | | |
| 002.5 | Financial managers | 010.2 | Teachers in establishments for further and higher education |
| 002.6 | Underwriters, brokers, investment analysts | | |
| 002.7 | Taxation experts | 011.0 | Teachers n.e.c. |
| 003.1 | Personnel and industrial relations officers | 012.1 | Vocational and industrial trainers |
| 003.2 | O and M, work study and OR officers | 013.1 | Matrons, houseparents |
| 004.2 | Systems analysts, computer programmers | 013.3 | Welfare occupations n.e.c. |
| 005.1 | Marketing and sales managers and executives | 016.0 | Nurse administrators, nurses |
| 005.2 | Advertising and PR executives | 017.2 | Medical radiographers |
| 005.3 | Buyers (retail trade) | 017.4 | Physiotherapists |
| 005.4 | Buyers and purchasing officers (not retail) | 017.5 | Chiropodists |
| 007.2 | General administrators—national government (HEO to Senior Principal level) | 017.6 | Therapists n.e.c. |
| | | 018.1 | Medical technicians, dental auxiliaries |
| 008.0 | Local government officers (administrative and executive functions) | 018.4 | Professional and related in education, welfare and health n.e.c. |
| 009.1 | Company secretaries | 019.0 | Authors, writers, journalists |
| 009.2 | Officials of trade associations, trade unions, professional bodies and charities | 020.1 | Artists, commercial artists |
| | | 020.2 | Industrial designers (not clothing) |
| 009.3 | Property and estate managers | 020.3 | Clothing designers |
| 009.4 | Librarians, information officers | 020.4 | Window dressers |
| 009.5 | Legal service and related occupations | 021.1 | Actors, entertainers, singers, stage managers |

cvi

| 021.2 | Musicians | 038.4 | Other proprietors and managers (sales) |
|---|---|---|---|
| 022.1 | Photographers, cameramen | 039.1 | Hotel and residential club managers |
| 022.2 | Sound and vision equipment operators | 039.2 | Publicans |
| 023.1 | Professional sportsmen, sports officials | 039.3 | Restaurateurs |
| 023.2 | Literary, artistic and sports workers n.e.c. | 039.5 | Entertainment and sports managers |
| 029.0 | Draughtsmen | 043.1 | Prison officers (chief officers and above) |
| 030.2 | Engineering technicians, technician engineers | 043.2 | Police officers (inspectors and above) |
| 032.1 | Aircraft flight deck officers | 043.3 | Fire service officers |
| 032.3 | Deck, engineering and radio officers and pilots, ship | 044.1 | Proprietors and managers, service flats, holiday flats, caravan sites, etc. |
| 033.3 | Technical and related workers n.e.c. | 044.3 | Hairdressers' and barbers' managers and proprietors |
| 034.0 | Production, works and maintenance managers, works foremen | 044.4 | Managers n.e.c. |
| 035.1 | Managers in building and contracting | 056.0 | Roundsmen, van salesmen |
| 036.1 | Managers in mining and public utilities | 057.1 | Importers, exporters, commodity brokers |
| 036.2 | Transport managers | 057.6 | Sales representatives (property and services), other agents |
| 036.3 | Stores controllers | 064.0 | Chefs, cooks |
| 036.4 | Managers in warehousing and materials handling n.e.c. | 075.4 | Undertakers |
| 037.1 | Credit controllers | 075.5 | Bookmakers, betting shop managers |
| 037.2 | Office managers n.e.c. | | |

### (f) Social Class III (N)   Skilled occupations—Non-manual

**Employment status—*Managers***

057.3   Scrap dealers, general dealers, rag and bone merchants

### (g) Social Class III (M)   Skilled occupations—Manual

**Employment status—*Managers***

| 075.3 | Launderers, dry cleaners, pressers | 078.2 | Gardeners, groundsmen |
|---|---|---|---|
| 075.6 | Service workers n.e.c. | | |

# S.E.G. 2.1   Employers in industry, commerce, etc.—small establishments

### (h) Social Class II   Intermediate occupations

**Employment status—*Self-employed with employees***

| 002.6 | Underwriters, brokers, investment analysts | 021.1 | Actors, entertainers, singers, stage managers |
|---|---|---|---|
| 005.1 | Marketing and sales managers and executives | 021.2 | Musicians |
| 005.2 | Advertising and PR executives | 037.2 | Office managers n.e.c. |
| 013.1 | Matrons, houseparents | 038.1 | Garage proprietors |
| 019.0 | Authors, writers, journalists | 038.4 | Other proprietors and managers (sales) |
| 020.1 | Artists, commercial artists | 039.1 | Hotel and residential club managers |
| 020.2 | Industrial designers (not clothing) | 039.2 | Publicans |
| 020.3 | Clothing designers | 044.4 | Managers n.e.c. |
| 020.4 | Window dressers | 057.1 | Importers, exporters, commodity brokers |

### (j) Social Class III (N)   Skilled occupations—Non-manual

**Employment status—*Self-employed with employees***

| 013.2 | Playgroup leaders | 039.5 | Entertainment and sports managers |
|---|---|---|---|
| 018.3 | Driving instructors (not HGV) | 044.1 | Proprietors and managers, service flats, holiday flats, caravan sites, etc. |
| 022.1 | Photographers, cameramen | 044.3 | Hairdressers' and barbers' managers and proprietors |
| 022.2 | Sound and vision equipment operators | 046.3 | Other clerks and cashiers (not retail) |
| 023.1 | Professional sportsmen, sports officials | 049.2 | Typists, shorthand writers, secretaries |
| 023.2 | Literary, artistic and sports workers n.e.c. | 050.0 | Office machine operators |
| 029.0 | Draughtsmen | 057.3 | Scrap dealers, general dealers, rag and bone merchants |
| 038.2 | Butchers (managers and proprietors) | 057.5 | Sales representatives |
| 038.3 | Fishmongers (managers and proprietors) | 057.6 | Sales representatives (property and services), other agents |
| 039.3 | Restaurateurs | | |

## (k) Social Class III (M)   Skilled occupations—Manual

**Employment status**—*Self-employed with employees*

| | |
|---|---|
| 056.0 | Roundsmen, van salesmen |
| 064.0 | Chefs, cooks |
| 068.2 | Nursery nurses |
| 075.4 | Undertakers |
| 075.5 | Bookmakers, betting shop managers |
| 085.1 | Tannery production workers |
| 085.2 | Shoe repairers |
| 085.3 | Leather cutters and sewers, footwear lasters, makers, finishers |
| 087.4 | Warp preparers |
| 087.5 | Weavers |
| 087.6 | Knitters |
| 087.7 | Bleachers, dyers, finishers |
| 087.8 | Menders, darners |
| 091.0 | Bakers, flour confectioners |
| 094.1 | Paper, paperboard and leatherboard workers |
| 094.2 | Bookbinders and finishers |
| 096.2 | Glass formers and shapers, finishers, decorators |
| 096.3 | Casters and other pottery makers |
| 097.1 | Rubber process workers, moulding machine operators, tyre builders |
| 098.2 | Brewery and vinery process workers |
| | Other material processing— |
| 098.5 | Bakery and confectionery workers |
| 098.8 | Wood and paper |
| 100.1 | Compositors |
| 100.2 | Electrotypers, stereotypers, printing plate and cylinder preparers |
| 100.3 | Printing machine minders and assistants |
| 100.4 | Screen and block printers |
| 100.5 | Printers (so described) |
| 102.1 | Tailors, tailoresses, dressmakers |
| 102.2 | Clothing cutters, milliners, furriers |
| 103.0 | Coach trimmers, upholsterers, mattress makers |
| 105.1 | Carpenters, joiners |
| 105.2 | Cabinet makers |
| 105.3 | Case and box makers |
| 105.4 | Pattern makers (moulds) |
| 106.0 | Sawyers, veneer cutters, woodworking machinists |
| 107.2 | Dental technicians |
| 107.3 | Carpet fitters |
| 107.4 | Musical instrument makers, piano tuners |
| | Other making and repairing— |
| 107.5 | Glass and ceramics |
| 107.6 | Wood |
| 107.7 | Leather |
| 107.8 | Clothing and related products |
| 107.9 | Paper goods and printing |
| 107.10 | Rubber |
| 109.1 | Furnace operating occupations (metal) |
| 109.2 | Rollermen |
| 109.3 | Smiths, forgemen |
| 110.1 | Metal drawers |
| 110.2 | Moulders, coremakers, die casters |
| 110.3 | Electroplaters |
| 112.1 | Press and machine tool setters |
| 112.2 | Centre lathe turners |
| 112.3 | Machine tool setter operators |
| 113.2 | Metal polishers |
| 115.0 | Tool makers, tool fitters, markers-out |
| 116.1 | Precision instrument makers and repairers |
| 116.2 | Watch and chronometer makers and repairers |
| 117.0 | Metal working production fitters and fitter/machinists |
| 118.1 | Motor mechanics, auto engineers |
| 119.0 | Office machinery mechanics |
| 121.1 | Production fitters (electrical, electronic) |
| 121.2 | Electricians, electrical maintenance fitters |
| 121.3 | Electrical engineers (so described) |
| 123.1 | Radio and TV mechanics |
| 123.2 | Other electronic maintenance engineers |
| 125.0 | Plumbers, heating and ventilating fitters, gas fitters |
| 126.1 | Sheet metal workers |
| 126.2 | Metal plate workers, shipwrights, riveters |
| 127.1 | Steel erectors, benders, fixers |
| 128.0 | Welders |
| 130.1 | Goldsmiths, silversmiths, precious stone workers |
| 130.2 | Engravers, etchers (printing) |
| 131.1 | Coach and vehicle body builders |
| 131.2 | Galvanizers, tin platers, dip platers |
| 131.3 | Metal making and treating workers n.e.c. |
| 131.5 | Riggers |
| 131.7 | Coil winders |
| 133.1 | Pottery decorators |
| 133.2 | Coach painters (so described) |
| 133.4 | Painters and decorators n.e.c., french polishers |
| 140.1 | Bricklayers, tile setters |
| 140.2 | Masons, stone cutters |
| 140.3 | Plasterers |
| 140.6 | Builders (so described) |
| 145.0 | Face-trained coalmining workers |
| 152.1 | Bus and coach drivers |
| 152.2 | Drivers of road goods vehicles |
| 152.3 | Other motor drivers |
| 155.1 | Mechanical plant drivers, operators (earth moving and civil engineering) |
| 158.2 | Workers in transport operating, materials moving and storing and related n.e.c. |
| 161.2 | All other in miscellaneous occupations n.e.c. |

## (l) Social Class IV   Partly skilled occupations

**Employment status**—*Self-employed with employees*

| | |
|---|---|
| 044.2 | Managers of laundry and dry cleaning receiving shops |
| 057.2 | Market and street traders and assistants |
| 057.4 | Credit agents, collector salesmen |
| 062.1 | Security guards and officers, patrolmen, watchmen |
| 062.3 | Security and protective service workers n.e.c. |
| 075.6 | Service workers n.e.c. |
| 078.2 | Gardeners, groundsmen |
| 082.0 | Fishermen |
| 087.1 | Preparatory fibre processors |
| 087.2 | Spinners, doublers, twisters |
| 087.3 | Winders, reelers |
| 089.0 | Chemical, gas and petroleum process plant operators |
| 097.2 | Calender and extruding machine operators, moulders (plastics) |
| | Other material processing— |
| 098.4 | Textiles |
| 098.7 | Food and drink n.e.c. |
| 098.9 | All other (excluding metal) n.e.c. |
| 102.3 | Sewers, embroiderers |
| | Other making and repairing— |
| 107.11 | Plastics |
| 107.12 | All other (excluding metal and electrical) n.e.c. |
| 110.4 | Annealers, hardeners, temperers (metal) |
| 112.4 | Machine tool operators |
| 113.1 | Press, stamping and automatic machine operators |
| 113.3 | Fettlers, dressers |
| 127.2 | Scaffolders, stagers |
| 131.9 | Other metal, jewellery, electrical production workers |
| 133.3 | Other spray painters |
| 135.1 | Assemblers (electrical, electronic) |
| 137.2 | Packers, bottlers, canners, fillers |
| 138.12 | Painting, assembling and related occupations n.e.c. |
| 140.4 | Roofers, glaziers |
| 140.5 | Handymen, general building workers |
| 141.4 | Paviors, kerb layers |
| 142.2 | Mains and service layers, pipe jointers |
| 143.1 | Craftsmen's mates |
| 146.1 | Miners (not coal), quarrymen, well drillers |
| 146.2 | Construction workers n.e.c. |
| 148.0 | Deck, engine-room hands, bargemen, lightermen, boatmen |
| 157.1 | Storekeepers, warehousemen |

## (m) Social Class V   Unskilled occupations

**Employment status**—*Self-employed with employees*

| | |
|---|---|
| 072.2 | Cleaners, window cleaners, chimney sweeps, road sweepers |
| 141.3 | Roadmen |
| 143.2 | Building and civil engineering labourers |
| 157.2 | Stevedores, dockers |
| 157.3 | Goods porters |
| | Labourers and unskilled workers n.e.c.— |
| 160.8 | Other |

cviii

# S.E.G. 2.2  Managers in industry, commerce, etc.—small establishments

## (n) Social Class II  Intermediate occupations

*Employment status—Managers*

| | | | |
|---|---|---|---|
| 002.3 | Estimators | 075.5 | Bookmakers, betting shop managers |
| 002.4 | Valuers, claims assessors | 085.1 | Tannery production workers |
| 002.5 | Financial managers | 085.2 | Shoe repairers |
| 002.6 | Underwriters, brokers, investment analysts | 085.3 | Leather cutters and sewers, footwear lasters, makers, finishers |
| 002.7 | Taxation experts | 087.4 | Warp preparers |
| 003.1 | Personnel and industrial relations officers | 087.5 | Weavers |
| 003.2 | O and M, work study and OR officers | 087.6 | Knitters |
| 004.2 | Systems analysts, computer programmers | 087.7 | Bleachers, dyers, finishers |
| 005.1 | Marketing and sales managers and executives | 087.8 | Menders, darners |
| 005.2 | Advertising and PR executives | 091.0 | Bakers, flour confectioners |
| 005.3 | Buyers (retail trade) | 094.2 | Bookbinders and finishers |
| 005.4 | Buyers and purchasing officers (not retail) | 096.2 | Glass formers and shapers, finishers, decorators |
| 009.1 | Company secretaries | 096.3 | Casters and other pottery makers |
| 009.2 | Officials of trade associations, trade unions, professional bodies and charities | 097.1 | Rubber process workers, moulding machine operators, tyre builders |
| 009.3 | Property and estate managers | 098.2 | Brewery and vinery process workers |
| 009.4 | Librarians, information officers | 100.1 | Compositors |
| 009.5 | Legal service and related occupations | 100.2 | Electrotypers, stereotypers, printing plate and cylinder preparers |
| 009.8 | Professional workers and related supporting management and administration n.e.c. | 100.4 | Screen and block printers |
| 010.2 | Teachers in establishments for further and higher education | 100.5 | Printers (so described) |
| 011.0 | Teachers n.e.c. | 102.1 | Tailors, tailoresses, dressmakers |
| 012.1 | Vocational and industrial trainers | 102.2 | Clothing cutters, milliners, furriers |
| 013.1 | Matrons, houseparents | 103.0 | Coach trimmers, upholsterers, mattress makers |
| 013.3 | Welfare occupations n.e.c. | 105.1 | Carpenters, joiners |
| 016.0 | Nurse administrators, nurses | 105.2 | Cabinet makers |
| 017.2 | Medical radiographers | 105.3 | Case and box makers |
| 017.4 | Physiotherapists | 105.4 | Pattern makers (moulds) |
| 017.5 | Chiropodists | 106.0 | Sawyers, veneer cutters, woodworking machinists |
| 017.6 | Therapists n.e.c. | 107.2 | Dental technicians |
| 018.1 | Medical technicians, dental auxiliaries | 107.4 | Musical instrument makers, piano tuners |
| 018.3 | Driving instructors (not HGV) | | Other making and repairing— |
| 018.4 | Professional and related in education, welfare and health n.e.c. | 107.6 | Wood |
| 019.0 | Authors, writers, journalists | 107.7 | Leather |
| 020.1 | Artists, commercial artists | 107.8 | Clothing and related products |
| 020.2 | Industrial designers (not clothing) | 107.9 | Paper goods and printing |
| 020.3 | Clothing designers | 107.10 | Rubber |
| 020.4 | Window dressers | 109.2 | Rollermen |
| 021.1 | Actors, entertainers, singers, stage managers | 109.3 | Smiths, forgemen |
| 021.2 | Musicians | 110.3 | Electroplaters |
| 022.1 | Photographers, cameramen | 112.1 | Press and machine tool setters |
| 022.2 | Sound and vision equipment operators | 112.2 | Centre lathe turners |
| 023.1 | Professional sportsmen, sports officials | 112.3 | Machine tool setter operators |
| 023.2 | Literary, artistic and sports workers n.e.c. | 113.2 | Metal polishers |
| 029.0 | Draughtsmen | 115.0 | Tool makers, tool fitters, markers-out |
| 030.1 | Laboratory technicians | 116.1 | Precision instrument makers and repairers |
| 030.2 | Engineering technicians, technician engineers | 116.2 | Watch and chronometer makers and repairers |
| 033.3 | Technical and related workers n.e.c. | 117.0 | Metal working production fitters and fitter/machinists |
| 034.0 | Production, works and maintenance managers, works foremen | 118.1 | Motor mechanics, auto engineers |
| 035.1 | Managers in building and contracting | 119.0 | Office machinery mechanics |
| 036.1 | Managers in mining and public utilities | 121.1 | Production fitters (electrical, electronic) |
| 036.2 | Transport managers | 121.2 | Electricians, electrical maintenance fitters |
| 036.3 | Stores controllers | 121.3 | Electrical engineers (so described) |
| 036.4 | Managers in warehousing and materials handling n.e.c. | 123.1 | Radio and TV mechanics |
| 037.1 | Credit controllers | 123.2 | Other electronic maintenance engineers |
| 037.2 | Office managers n.e.c. | 125.0 | Plumbers, heating and ventilating fitters, gas fitters |
| 038.2 | Butchers (managers and proprietors) | 126.1 | Sheet metal workers |
| 038.3 | Fishmongers (managers and proprietors) | 126.2 | Metal plate workers, shipwrights, riveters |
| 038.4 | Other proprietors and managers (sales) | 127.1 | Steel erectors, benders, fixers |
| 039.1 | Hotel and residential club managers | 128.0 | Welders |
| 039.2 | Publicans | 130.1 | Goldsmiths, silversmiths, precious stone workers |
| 039.3 | Restaurateurs | 131.1 | Coach and vehicle body builders |
| 039.5 | Entertainment and sports managers | 131.5 | Riggers |
| 044.1 | Proprietors and managers, service flats, holiday flats, caravan sites, etc. | 131.7 | Coil winders |
| 044.3 | Hairdressers' and barbers' managers and proprietors | 133.2 | Coach painters (so described) |
| 044.4 | Managers n.e.c. | 133.4 | Painters and decorators n.e.c., french polishers |
| 056.0 | Roundsmen, van salesmen | 140.1 | Bricklayers, tile setters |
| 057.1 | Importers, exporters, commodity brokers | 140.2 | Masons, stone cutters |
| 057.5 | Sales representatives | 140.3 | Plasterers |
| 057.6 | Sales representatives (property and services), other agents | 140.6 | Builders (so described) |
| 064.0 | Chefs, cooks | 152.1 | Bus and coach drivers |
| 075.4 | Undertakers | 152.2 | Drivers of road goods vehicles |
| | | 152.3 | Other motor drivers |
| | | 155.1 | Mechanical plant drivers, operators (earth moving and civil engineering) |

## (o) Social Class III (N)  Skilled occupations—Non-manual

*Employment status—Managers*

| | | | |
|---|---|---|---|
| 039.4 | Club stewards | 057.3 | Scrap dealers, general dealers, rag and bone merchants |
| 044.2 | Managers of laundry and dry cleaning receiving shops | 057.4 | Credit agents, collector salesmen |
| 057.2 | Market and street traders and assistants | | |

## (p) Social Class III (M)   Skilled occupations—Manual

**Employment status**—*Managers*

| | | | | |
|---|---|---|---|---|
| 072.2 | Cleaners, window cleaners, chimney sweeps, road sweepers | | | Other making and repairing— |
| 075.3 | Launderers, dry cleaners, pressers | | 107.11 | Plastics |
| 075.6 | Service workers n.e.c. | | 107.12 | All other (excluding metal and electrical) n.e.c. |
| 078.2 | Gardeners, groundsmen | | 113.1 | Press, stamping and automatic machine operators |
| 082.0 | Fishermen | | 131.9 | Other metal, jewellery, electrical production workers |
| 087.1 | Preparatory fibre processors | | 133.3 | Other spray painters |
| 087.2 | Spinners, doublers, twisters | | 138.12 | Painting, assembling and related occupations n.e.c. |
| 087.3 | Winders, reelers | | 140.4 | Roofers, glaziers |
| 089.0 | Chemical, gas and petroleum process plant operators | | 140.5 | Handymen, general building workers |
| 097.2 | Calender and extruding machine operators, moulders (plastics) | | 146.1 | Miners (not coal), quarrymen, well drillers |
| | Other material processing— | | 146.2 | Construction workers n.e.c. |
| 098.7 | Food and drink n.e.c. | | 157.1 | Storekeepers, warehousemen |
| | | | 157.3 | Goods porters |

# S.E.G. 3   Professional workers—self-employed

### (q) Social Class I   Professional, etc. occupations

**Employment status**—*Self-employed with and without employees*

| | | | | |
|---|---|---|---|---|
| 001.0 | Judges, barristers, advocates, solicitors | | 025.0 | Civil, structural, municipal, mining and quarrying engineers |
| 002.1 | Chartered and certified accountants | | 026.1 | Mechanical and aeronautical engineers |
| 004.1 | Economists, statisticians, actuaries | | 026.2 | Design and development engineers (mechanical) |
| 009.6 | Management consultants | | 027.1 | Electrical engineers |
| 012.3 | Social and behavioural scientists | | 027.2 | Electronic engineers |
| 014.0 | Clergy, ministers of religion | | 028.1 | Chemical engineers |
| 015.1 | Medical practitioners | | 028.2 | Production engineers |
| 015.2 | Dental practitioners | | 028.3 | Planning and quality control engineers |
| 017.1 | Pharmacists | | 028.4 | Engineers n.e.c. |
| 017.3 | Ophthalmic and dispensing opticians | | 028.5 | Metallurgists |
| 018.2 | Veterinarians | | 028.6 | Technologists n.e.c. |
| 024.1 | Biological scientists, biochemists | | 031.1 | Architects, town planners |
| 024.2 | Chemical scientists | | 031.3 | Building, land and mining surveyors |
| 024.3 | Physical and geological scientists, mathematicians | | | |

# S.E.G. 4   Professional workers—employees

### (r) Social Class I   Professional, etc. occupations

**Employment status**—*Apprentices, etc., Employees n.e.c.*

| | | | | |
|---|---|---|---|---|
| 001.0 | Judges, barristers, advocates, solicitors | | 024.3 | Physical and geological scientists, mathematicians |
| 002.1 | Chartered and certified accountants | | 025.0 | Civil, structural, municipal, mining and quarrying engineers |
| 004.1 | Economists, statisticians, actuaries | | 026.1 | Mechanical and aeronautical engineers |
| 009.6 | Management consultants | | 026.2 | Design and development engineers (mechanical) |
| 010.1 | University academic staff | | 027.1 | Electrical engineers |
| 012.2 | Education officers, school inspectors | | 027.2 | Electronic engineers |
| 012.3 | Social and behavioural scientists | | 028.1 | Chemical engineers |
| 014.0 | Clergy, ministers of religion | | 028.2 | Production engineers |
| 015.1 | Medical practitioners | | 028.3 | Planning and quality control engineers |
| 015.2 | Dental practitioners | | 028.4 | Engineers n.e.c. |
| 017.1 | Pharmacists | | 028.5 | Metallurgists |
| 017.3 | Ophthalmic and dispensing opticians | | 028.6 | Technologists n.e.c. |
| 018.2 | Veterinarians | | 031.1 | Architects, town planners |
| 024.1 | Biological scientists, biochemists | | 031.3 | Building, land and mining surveyors |
| 024.2 | Chemical scientists | | | |

# S.E.G. 5.1   Ancillary workers and artists

### (s) Social Class II   Intermediate occupations

**Employment status**—*Foreman and Supervisors*

| | | | | |
|---|---|---|---|---|
| 016.0 | Nurse administrators, nurses | | 020.1 | Artists, commercial artists |
| 017.2 | Medical radiographers | | 030.1 | Laboratory technicians |
| 017.4 | Physiotherapists | | 030.2 | Engineering technicians, technician engineers |
| 017.6 | Therapists n.e.c. | | 033.3 | Technical and related workers n.e.c. |
| 018.1 | Medical technicians, dental auxiliaries | | 045.1 | Civil service executive officers |

cx

Employment status—Apprentices, etc., Employees n.e.c.

| | | | | |
|---|---|---|---|---|
| 002.2 | Cost and works accountants | | 017.5 | Chiropodists |
| 002.3 | Estimators | | 017.6 | Therapists n.e.c. |
| 002.4 | Valuers, claims assessors | | 018.1 | Medical technicians, dental auxiliaries |
| 003.2 | O and M, work study and OR officers | | 018.4 | Professional and related in education, welfare and health n.e.c. |
| 004.2 | Systems analysts, computer programmers | | | |
| 006.1 | Environmental health officers | | 019.0 | Authors, writers, journalists |
| 006.2 | Building inspectors | | 020.1 | Artists, commercial artists |
| 006.3 | Inspectors (statutory and similar) | | 020.2 | Industrial designers (not clothing) |
| 009.2 | Officials of trade associations, trade unions, professional bodies and charities | | 020.3 | Clothing designers |
| | | | 020.4 | Window dressers |
| 009.4 | Librarians, information officers | | 021.1 | Actors, entertainers, singers, stage managers |
| 009.5 | Legal service and related occupations | | 021.2 | Musicians |
| 009.8 | Professional workers and related supporting management and administration n.e.c. | | 030.1 | Laboratory technicians |
| | | | 030.2 | Engineering technicians, technician engineers |
| 010.2 | Teachers in establishments for further and higher education | | 031.2 | Quantity surveyors |
| 011.0 | Teachers n.e.c. | | 032.1 | Aircraft flight deck officers |
| 012.1 | Vocational and industrial trainers | | 032.2 | Air traffic planners and controllers |
| 013.3 | Welfare occupations n.e.c. | | 033.1 | Architectural and town planning technicians |
| 016.0 | Nurse administrators, nurses | | 033.2 | Building and civil engineering technicians |
| 017.2 | Medical radiographers | | 033.3 | Technical and related workers n.e.c. |
| 017.4 | Physiotherapists | | | |

Employment status—Self-employed with employees

| | | | | |
|---|---|---|---|---|
| 002.2 | Cost and works accountants | | 012.1 | Vocational and industrial trainers |
| 002.3 | Estimators | | 016.0 | Nurse administrators, nurses |
| 002.4 | Valuers, claims assessors | | 017.2 | Medical radiographers |
| 002.7 | Taxation experts | | 017.4 | Physiotherapists |
| 003.1 | Personnel and industrial relations officers | | 017.5 | Chiropodists |
| 003.2 | O and M, work study and OR officers | | 017.6 | Therapists n.e.c. |
| 004.2 | Systems analysts, computer programmers | | 018.1 | Medical technicians, dental auxiliaries |
| 009.1 | Company secretaries | | 018.4 | Professional and related in education, welfare and health n.e.c. |
| 009.3 | Property and estate managers | | | |
| 009.5 | Legal service and related occupations | | 030.1 | Laboratory technicians |
| 009.8 | Professional workers and related supporting management and administration n.e.c. | | 030.2 | Engineering technicians, technician engineers |
| | | | 031.2 | Quantity surveyors |
| 010.2 | Teachers in establishments for further and higher education | | 033.3 | Technical and related workers n.e.c. |
| 011.0 | Teachers n.e.c. | | | |

Employment status—Self-employed without employees

| | | | | |
|---|---|---|---|---|
| 002.2 | Cost and works accountants | | 017.2 | Medical radiographers |
| 002.3 | Estimators | | 017.4 | Physiotherapists |
| 002.4 | Valuers, claims assessors | | 017.5 | Chiropodists |
| 002.6 | Underwriters, brokers, investment analysts | | 017.6 | Therapists n.e.c. |
| 002.7 | Taxation experts | | 018.1 | Medical technicians, dental auxiliaries |
| 003.1 | Personnel and industrial relations officers | | 018.4 | Professional and related in education, welfare and health n.e.c. |
| 003.2 | O and M, work study and OR officers | | | |
| 004.2 | Systems analysts, computer programmers | | 019.0 | Authors, writers, journalists |
| 005.1 | Marketing and sales managers and executives | | 020.1 | Artists, commercial artists |
| 005.2 | Advertising and PR executives | | 020.2 | Industrial designers (not clothing) |
| 009.1 | Company secretaries | | 020.3 | Clothing designers |
| 009.3 | Property and estate managers | | 020.4 | Window dressers |
| 009.5 | Legal service and related occupations | | 021.1 | Actors, entertainers, singers, stage managers |
| 009.8 | Professional workers and related supporting management and administration n.e.c. | | 021.2 | Musicians |
| | | | 030.1 | Laboratory technicians |
| 010.2 | Teachers in establishments for further and higher education | | 030.2 | Engineering technicians, technician engineers |
| 011.0 | Teachers n.e.c. | | 031.2 | Quantity surveyors |
| 012.1 | Vocational and industrial trainers | | 033.1 | Architectural and town planning technicians |
| 016.0 | Nurse administrators, nurses | | 033.3 | Technical and related workers n.e.c. |

---

# S.E.G. 5.2   Foreman and supervisors—Non-manual

## (t) Social Class III (N)   Skilled occupations—Non-manual

Employment status—Foremen and Supervisors

| | | | | |
|---|---|---|---|---|
| 022.1 | Photographers, cameramen | | | Supervisors of— |
| 022.2 | Sound and vision equipment operators | | 048.3 | Telephone operators |
| 029.0 | Draughtsmen | | 048.4 | Radio and telegraph operators |
| 034.0 | Production, works and maintenance managers, works foremen | | 054.1 | Shop salesmen and assistants |
| | Supervisors of— | | 054.2 | Petrol pump, forecourt attendants |
| 045.2 | Stores and despatch clerks | | 054.3 | Roundsmen, van salesmen |
| 045.3 | Tracers, drawing office assistants | | 060.1 | Police sergeants |
| 045.4 | Other clerks and cashiers (not retail) | | 060.2 | Fire service supervisors |
| 045.5 | Retail shop cashiers, check-out and cash and wrap operators | | 060.3 | Prison service principal officers |
| | | | | Supervisors of— |
| 048.1 | Typists, shorthand writers, secretaries | | 060.4 | Security guards and officers, patrolmen, watchmen |
| 048.2 | Office machine operators | | 060.5 | Traffic wardens |
| | | | 060.6 | Security and protective service workers n.e.c. |

# S.E.G. 6    Junior non-manual workers

## (u) Social Class III (N)    Skilled occupations—Non-manual

**Employment status**—*Apprentices, etc., Employees n.e.c.*

| | | | |
|---|---|---|---|
| 009.7 | Managers' personal assistants | 047.0 | Retail shop cashiers, check-out and cash and wrap operators |
| 013.2 | Playgroup leaders | 049.1 | Receptionists |
| 018.3 | Driving instructors (not HGV) | 049.2 | Typists, shorthand writers, secretaries |
| 022.1 | Photographers, cameramen | 050.0 | Office machine operators |
| 022.2 | Sound and vision equipment operators | 051.1 | Telephonist receptionists |
| 023.1 | Professional sportsmen, sports officials | 051.3 | Radio and telegraph operators |
| 023.2 | Literary, artistic and sports workers n.e.c. | 055.1 | Shop salesmen and assistants |
| 029.0 | Draughtsmen | 055.3 | Petrol pump, forecourt attendants |
| 035.2 | Clerks of works | 057.5 | Sales representatives |
| 046.1 | Stores and despatch clerks | 057.6 | Sales representatives (property and services), other agents |
| 046.2 | Tracers, drawing office assistants | 061.1 | Policemen (below sergeant) |
| 046.3 | Other clerks and cashiers (not retail) | 061.2 | Firemen |

## (v) Social Class IV    Partly skilled occupations

**Employment status**—*Employees n.e.c.*

| | | | |
|---|---|---|---|
| 051.2 | Telephone operators | 057.4 | Credit agents, collector salesmen |
| 055.2 | Shelf fillers | 061.3 | Prison officers (below principal officer) |
| 057.2 | Market and street traders and assistants | | |

# S.E.G. 7    Personal service workers

## (w) Social Class II    Intermediate occupations

**Employment status**—*Employees n.e.c.*

| | |
|---|---|
| 013.1 | Matrons, houseparents |

## (x) Social Class III (M)    Skilled occupations—Manual

**Employment status**—*Foremen and Supervisors*

| | | | |
|---|---|---|---|
| | Supervisors of— | 067.1 | Housekeepers (non-domestic) |
| 063.1 | Chefs, cooks | | Supervisors of— |
| 063.2 | Waiters, waitresses | 067.2 | Other domestic and school helpers |
| 063.3 | Barmen, barmaids | 067.3 | Travel stewards and attendants |
| 063.4 | Counter hands, assistants | 073.0 | Hairdressing supervisors |

**Employment status**—*Apprentices, etc., Employees n.e.c.*

| | | | |
|---|---|---|---|
| 064.0 | Chefs, cooks | 069.1 | Travel stewards and attendants |
| 068.1 | Domestic housekeepers | 074.0 | Hairdressers, barbers |
| 068.2 | Nursery nurses | | |

## (y) Social Class IV    Partly skilled occupations

**Employment status**—*Employees n.e.c.*

| | | | |
|---|---|---|---|
| 065.1 | Waiters, waitresses | 066.1 | Counter hands, assistants |
| 065.2 | Barmen, barmaids | 068.3 | Other domestic and school helpers |

## (z) Social Class III (M)   Skilled occupations—Manual

*Employment status—Foremen and Supervisors*

Supervisors of—
052.1   Postmen, mail sorters
052.2   Messengers
066.2   Kitchen porters, hands
Supervisors of—
067.4   Hospital porters
067.5   Hotel porters
067.6   Ambulancemen
067.7   Hospital, ward orderlies
071.1   Caretakers
071.2   Cleaners, window cleaners, chimney sweeps, road sweepers
071.3   Railway stationmen
071.4   Lift and car park attendants
075.3   Launderers, dry cleaners, pressers
075.6   Service workers n.e.c.
076.3   Foremen gardeners and groundsmen
081.0   Supervisors, mates—fishing
Foremen—
084.1   Tannery production workers
084.2   Shoe repairers
084.3   Leather cutters and sewers, footwear lasters, makers, finishers
084.4   Other making and repairing, leather
086.1   Preparatory fibre processors
086.2   Spinners, doublers, twisters
086.3   Winders, reelers
086.4   Warp preparers
086.5   Weavers
086.6   Knitters
086.7   Bleachers, dyers, finishers
086.8   Menders, darners
086.9   Other material processing, textiles
088.0   Chemical processing
090.1   Bakers, flour confectioners
090.2   Butchers, meat cutters
090.3   Fishmongers, poultry dressers
090.4   Brewery and vinery process workers
Other material processing—
090.5   Bakery and confectionery workers
090.6   Food and drink n.e.c.
093.1   Paper, paperboard and leatherboard workers
093.2   Bookbinders and finishers
093.3   Cutting and slitting machine operators (paper and paper products making)
093.4   Other material processing, wood and paper
093.5   Other making and repairing, paper goods and printing
095.1   Glass and ceramics furnacemen, kilnsetters
095.2   Glass formers and shapers, finishers, decorators
095.3   Casters and other pottery makers
095.4   Rubber process workers, moulding machine operators, tyre builders
095.5   Calender and extruding machine operators, moulders (plastics)
095.6   Man-made fibre makers
095.7   Washers, screeners and crushers in mines and quarries
Other making and repairing—
095.8   Glass and ceramics
095.9   Rubber
095.10  Plastics
Other material processing—
098.6   Tobacco
098.9   All other (excluding metal) n.e.c.
Foremen—
099.1   Compositors
099.2   Electrotypers, stereotypers, printing plate and cylinder preparers
099.3   Printing machine minders and assistants
099.4   Screen and block printers
099.5   Printers (so described)
101.1   Tailors, tailoresses, dressmakers
101.2   Clothing cutters, milliners, furriers
101.3   Sewers, embroiderers
101.4   Coach trimmers, upholsterers, mattress makers
101.5   Carpet fitters
101.6   Other making and repairing, clothing and related products
104.1   Carpenters, joiners
104.2   Cabinet makers
104.3   Case and box makers
104.4   Pattern makers (moulds)
104.5   Sawyers, veneer cutters, woodworking machinists
104.6   Other making and repairing, wood
107.2   Dental technicians
107.4   Musical instrument makers, piano tuners
Other making and repairing—
107.12  All other (excluding metal and electrical) n.e.c.
Foremen—
108.1   Furnace operating occupations (metal)
108.2   Rollermen
108.3   Smiths, forgemen
108.4   Metal drawers
108.5   Moulders, coremakers, die casters
108.6   Electroplaters

Foremen—(contd)
108.7   Annealers, hardeners, temperers (metal)
108.8   Galvanizers, tin platers, dip platers
108.9   Metal making and treating workers n.e.c.
111.1   Press and machine tool setters
111.2   Centre lathe turners
111.3   Machine tool setter operators
111.4   Machine tool operators
111.5   Press, stamping and automatic machine operators
111.6   Metal polishers
111.7   Fettlers, dressers
111.8   Shot blasters
114.1   Tool makers, tool fitters, markers-out
114.2   Precision instrument makers and repairers
114.3   Watch and chronometer makers and repairers
114.4   Metal working production fitters and fitter/machinists
114.5   Motor mechanics, auto engineers
114.6   Maintenance fitters (aircraft engines)
114.7   Office machinery mechanics
120.1   Production fitters (electrical, electronic)
120.2   Electricians, electrical maintenance fitters
120.3   Plant operators and attendants n.e.c.
120.4   Telephone fitters
120.5   Cable jointers, linesmen
120.6   Radio and TV mechanics
120.7   Other electronic maintenance engineers
124.1   Plumbers, heating and ventilating fitters, gas fitters
124.2   Sheet metal workers
124.3   Metal plate workers, shipwrights, riveters
124.4   Steel erectors, benders, fixers
124.5   Scaffolders, stagers
124.6   Welders
124.7   Riggers
129.1   Goldsmiths, silversmiths, precious stone workers
129.2   Engravers, etchers (printing)
129.3   Coach and vehicle body builders
129.4   Oilers, greasers, lubricators
129.5   Electronics wiremen
129.6   Coil winders
131.9   Other metal, jewellery, electrical production workers
—.1   Foremen (engineering and allied trades)
Foremen—
132.1   Pottery decorators
132.2   Coach painters (so described)
132.3   Other spray painters
132.4   Painters and decorators n.e.c., french polishers
Foremen assemblers—
134.1   Electrical, electronic
134.2   Instruments
134.3   Vehicles and other metal goods
134.4   Paper production, processing and printing
134.5   Plastics goods
Foremen inspectors, viewers, examiners—
136.1   Metal, electrical goods
136.2   Textiles
136.3   Food
136.4   Rubber goods
136.5   Plastics goods
136.6   Woodwork
Foremen—
136.7   Packers, bottlers, canners, fillers
136.8   Laboratory assistants
136.9   Inspectors, sorters in paper production, processing and printing
136.10  Weighers
136.11  Graders, sorters, selectors n.e.c.
138.12  Painting, assembling and related occupations n.e.c.
Foremen—
139.1   Bricklayers, tile setters
139.2   Masons, stone cutters
139.3   Plasterers
139.4   Roofers, glaziers
139.5   Handymen, general building workers
139.6   Railway lengthmen
139.7   Road surfacers, concreters
139.8   Roadmen
139.9   Paviors, kerb layers
139.10  Sewage plant attendants
139.11  Mains and service layers, pipe jointers
139.12  Construction workers n.e.c.
143.1   Craftsmen's mates
143.2   Building and civil engineering labourers
144.0   Foremen/deputies—coalmining
146.1   Miners (not coal), quarrymen, well drillers
147.0   Foremen—ships, lighters and other vessels
Foremen—
149.1   Railway guards
149.2   Signalmen and crossing keepers, railway
149.3   Shunters, pointsmen
149.4   Other foremen rail transport
151.1   Bus inspectors
Foremen—
151.2   Drivers of road goods vehicles
151.3   Other foremen road transport

Foremen—

| | |
|---|---|
| 154.1 | Mechanical plant drivers, operators (earth moving and civil engineering) |
| 154.2 | Crane drivers, operators |
| 154.3 | Fork lift, mechanical truck drivers |
| 154.4 | Slingers |
| 156.1 | Storekeepers, warehousemen |
| 156.2 | Stevedores, dockers |
| 156.3 | Goods porters |
| 156.4 | Refuse collectors, dustmen |
| 158.2 | Workers in transport operating, materials moving and storing and related n.e.c. |

Foremen—
Labourers and unskilled workers n.e.c.—

| | |
|---|---|
| 159.1 | Textiles (not textile goods) |
| 159.2 | Chemicals and allied trades |
| 159.3 | Coke ovens and gas works |
| 159.4 | Glass and ceramics |
| 159.5 | Foundries in engineering and allied trades |
| 159.6 | Engineering and allied trades |
| 159.7 | Coal mines |
| 159.8 | Other |
| 159.9 | Boiler operators |
| 161.2 | All other in miscellaneous occupations n.e.c. |

# S.E.G. 9   Skilled manual workers

## (aa) Social Class III (M)   Skilled occupations—Manual

**Employment status**—*Apprentices, etc., Employees n.e.c.*

| | |
|---|---|
| 056.0 | Roundsmen, van salesmen |
| 070.1 | Ambulancemen |
| 085.1 | Tannery production workers |
| 085.2 | Shoe repairers |
| 085.3 | Leather cutters and sewers, footwear lasters, makers, finishers |
| 087.4 | Warp preparers |
| 087.5 | Weavers |
| 087.6 | Knitters |
| 087.7 | Bleachers, dyers, finishers |
| 087.8 | Menders, darners |
| 091.0 | Bakers, flour confectioners |
| 092.1 | Butchers, meat cutters |
| 092.2 | Fishmongers, poultry dressers |
| 094.1 | Paper, paperboard and leatherboard workers |
| 094.2 | Bookbinders and finishers |
| 094.3 | Cutting and slitting machine operators (paper and paper products making) |
| 096.1 | Glass and ceramics furnacemen, kilnsetters |
| 096.2 | Glass formers and shapers, finishers, decorators |
| 096.3 | Casters and other pottery makers |
| 097.1 | Rubber process workers, moulding machine operators, tyre builders |
| 098.2 | Brewery and vinery process workers |
| | Other material processing— |
| 098.5 | Bakery and confectionery workers |
| 098.8 | Wood and paper |
| 100.1 | Compositors |
| 100.2 | Electrotypers, stereotypers, printing plate and cylinder preparers |
| 100.3 | Printing machine minders and assistants |
| 100.4 | Screen and block printers |
| 100.5 | Printers (so described) |
| 102.1 | Tailors, tailoresses, dressmakers |
| 102.2 | Clothing cutters, milliners, furriers |
| 103.0 | Coach trimmers, upholsterers, mattress makers |
| 105.1 | Carpenters, joiners |
| 105.2 | Cabinet makers |
| 105.3 | Case and box makers |
| 105.4 | Pattern makers (moulds) |
| 106.0 | Sawyers, veneer cutters, woodworking machinists |
| 107.1 | Labourers and mates to woodworking craftsmen |
| 107.2 | Dental technicians |
| 107.3 | Carpet fitters |
| 107.4 | Musical instrument makers, piano tuners |
| | Other making and repairing— |
| 107.5 | Glass and ceramics |
| 107.6 | Wood |
| 107.7 | Leather |
| 107.8 | Clothing and related products |
| 107.9 | Paper goods and printing |
| 107.10 | Rubber |
| 109.1 | Furnace operating occupations (metal) |
| 109.2 | Rollermen |
| 109.3 | Smiths, forgemen |
| 110.1 | Metal drawers |
| 110.2 | Moulders, coremakers, die casters |
| 110.3 | Electroplaters |
| 112.1 | Press and machine tool setters |
| 112.2 | Centre lathe turners |
| 112.3 | Machine tool setter operators |
| 113.2 | Metal polishers |

| | |
|---|---|
| 115.0 | Tool makers, tool fitters, markers-out |
| 116.1 | Precision instrument makers and repairers |
| 116.2 | Watch and chronometer makers and repairers |
| 117.0 | Metal working production fitters and fitter/machinists |
| 118.1 | Motor mechanics, auto engineers |
| 118.2 | Maintenance fitters (aircraft engines) |
| 119.0 | Office machinery mechanics |
| 121.1 | Production fitters (electrical, electronic) |
| 121.2 | Electricians, electrical maintenance fitters |
| 121.3 | Electrical engineers (so described) |
| 121.4 | Plant operators and attendants n.e.c. |
| 122.1 | Telephone fitters |
| 122.2 | Cable jointers, linesmen |
| 123.1 | Radio and TV mechanics |
| 123.2 | Other electronic maintenance engineers |
| 125.0 | Plumbers, heating and ventilating fitters, gas fitters |
| 126.1 | Sheet metal workers |
| 126.2 | Metal plate workers, shipwrights, riveters |
| 127.1 | Steel erectors, benders, fixers |
| 128.0 | Welders |
| 130.1 | Goldsmiths, silversmiths, precious stone workers |
| 130.2 | Engravers, etchers (printing) |
| 131.1 | Coach and vehicle body builders |
| 131.2 | Galvanizers, tin platers, dip platers |
| 131.3 | Metal making and treating workers n.e.c. |
| 131.4 | Oilers, greasers, lubricators |
| 131.5 | Riggers |
| 131.6 | Electronics wiremen |
| 131.7 | Coil winders |
| —.2 | Trainee craftsmen (engineering and allied trades) |
| 133.1 | Pottery decorators |
| 133.2 | Coach painters (so described) |
| 133.4 | Painters and decorators n.e.c., french polishers |
| 135.2 | Instrument assemblers |
| 138.1 | Laboratory assistants |
| | Inspectors, viewers, examiners— |
| 138.2 | Textiles |
| 138.4 | Rubber goods |
| 138.6 | Woodwork |
| 138.7 | Inspectors, sorters in paper production, processing and printing |
| 138.8 | Assemblers in paper production, processing and printing |
| 140.1 | Bricklayers, tile setters |
| 140.2 | Masons, stone cutters |
| 140.3 | Plasterers |
| 140.6 | Builders (so described) |
| 145.0 | Face-trained coalmining workers |
| 150.1 | Drivers, motormen, secondmen, railway engines |
| 150.2 | Railway guards |
| 150.3 | Signalmen and crossing keepers, railway |
| 150.4 | Shunters, pointsmen |
| 152.1 | Bus and coach drivers |
| 152.2 | Drivers of road goods vehicles |
| 152.3 | Other motor drivers |
| 155.1 | Mechanical plant drivers, operators (earth moving and civil engineering) |
| 155.2 | Crane drivers, operators |
| 155.3 | Fork lift, mechanical truck drivers |
| 158.1 | Slingers |
| 158.2 | Workers in transport operating, materials moving and storing and related n.e.c. |
| 161.2 | All other in miscellaneous occupations n.e.c. |

# S.E.G. 10   Semi-skilled manual workers

## (ab) Social Class IV   Partly skilled occupations

*Employment status—Apprentices, etc., Employees n.e.c.*

| | | | |
|---|---|---|---|
| 053.1 | Postmen, mail sorters | 113.3 | Fettlers, dressers |
| 062.1 | Security guards and officers, patrolmen, watchmen | 127.2 | Scaffolders, stagers |
| 062.2 | Traffic wardens | 131.8 | Shot blasters |
| 062.3 | Security and protective service workers n.e.c. | 131.9 | Other metal, jewellery, electrical production workers |
| 069.2 | Hospital porters | 133.3 | Other spray painters |
| 069.3 | Hotel porters | 135.1 | Assemblers (electrical, electronic) |
| 070.2 | Hospital, ward orderlies | 135.3 | Assemblers (vehicles and other metal goods) |
| 072.1 | Caretakers | 137.1 | Inspectors, viewers (metal, electrical goods) |
| 075.3 | Launderers, dry cleaners, pressers | 137.2 | Packers, bottlers, canners, fillers |

053.1 Postmen, mail sorters
062.1 Security guards and officers, patrolmen, watchmen
062.2 Traffic wardens
062.3 Security and protective service workers n.e.c.
069.2 Hospital porters
069.3 Hotel porters
070.2 Hospital, ward orderlies
072.1 Caretakers
075.3 Launderers, dry cleaners, pressers
075.6 Service workers n.e.c.
078.2 Gardeners, groundsmen
082.0 Fishermen
087.1 Preparatory fibre processors
087.2 Spinners, doublers, twisters
087.3 Winders, reelers
089.0 Chemical, gas and petroleum process plant operators
097.2 Calender and extruding machine operators, moulders (plastics)
098.1 Man-made fibre makers
098.3 Washers, screeners and crushers in mines and quarries
    Other material processing—
098.4     Textiles
098.6     Tobacco
098.7     Food and drink n.e.c.
098.9     All other (excluding metal) n.e.c.
102.3 Sewers, embroiderers
    Other making and repairing—
107.11     Plastics
107.12     All other (excluding metal and electrical) n.e.c.
110.4 Annealers, hardeners, temperers (metal)
112.4 Machine tool operators
113.1 Press, stamping and automatic machine operators

113.3 Fettlers, dressers
127.2 Scaffolders, stagers
131.8 Shot blasters
131.9 Other metal, jewellery, electrical production workers
133.3 Other spray painters
135.1 Assemblers (electrical, electronic)
135.3 Assemblers (vehicles and other metal goods)
137.1 Inspectors, viewers (metal, electrical goods)
137.2 Packers, bottlers, canners, fillers
    Inspectors, viewers, examiners—
138.3     Food
138.5     Plastics goods
138.9 Assemblers (plastics goods)
138.10 Weighers
138.11 Graders, sorters, selectors n.e.c.
138.12 Painting, assembling and related occupations n.e.c.
140.4 Roofers, glaziers
140.5 Handymen, general building workers
141.1 Railway lengthmen
141.2 Road surfacers, concreters
141.4 Paviors, kerb layers
142.2 Mains and service layers, pipe jointers
143.1 Craftsmen's mates
146.1 Miners (not coal), quarrymen, well drillers
146.2 Construction workers n.e.c.
148.0 Deck, engine-room hands, bargemen, lightermen, boatmen
153.1 Bus conductors
157.1 Storekeepers, warehousemen
    Labourers and unskilled workers n.e.c.—
160.7     Coal mines
161.1 Boiler operators

# S.E.G. 11   Unskilled manual workers

## (ac) Social Class V   Unskilled occupations

*Employment status—Employees n.e.c.*

053.2 Messengers
066.2 Kitchen porters, hands
072.2 Cleaners, window cleaners, chimney sweeps, road sweepers
075.1 Railway stationmen
075.2 Lift and car park attendants
141.3 Roadmen
142.1 Sewage plant attendants
143.2 Building and civil engineering labourers
153.2 Drivers' mates
157.2 Stevedores, dockers

157.3 Goods porters
157.4 Refuse collectors, dustmen
    Labourers and unskilled workers n.e.c.—
160.1     Textiles (not textile goods)
160.2     Chemicals and allied trades
160.3     Coke ovens and gas works
160.4     Glass and ceramics
160.5     Foundries in engineering and allied trades
160.6     Engineering and allied trades
160.8     Other

# S.E.G. 12   Own account workers (other than professional)

## (ad) Social Class II   Intermediate occupations

*Employment status—Self-employed without employees*

013.1 Matrons, houseparents
032.1 Aircraft flight deck officers
032.3 Deck, engineering and radio officers and pilots, ships
037.2 Office managers n.e.c.
038.1 Garage proprietors

038.4 Other proprietors and managers (sales)
039.1 Hotel and residential club managers
039.2 Publicans
044.4 Managers n.e.c.
057.1 Importers, exporters, commodity brokers

## (ae) Social Class III (N)   Skilled occupations—Non-manual

*Employment status—Self-employed without employees*

013.2 Playgroup leaders
018.3 Driving instructors (not HGV)
022.1 Photographers, cameramen
022.2 Sound and vision equipment operators
023.1 Professional sportsmen, sports officials
023.2 Literary, artistic and sports workers n.e.c.
029.0 Draughtsmen
038.2 Butchers (managers and proprietors)
038.3 Fishmongers (managers and proprietors)
039.3 Restaurateurs
039.5 Entertainment and sports managers

044.1 Proprietors and managers, service flats, holiday flats, caravan sites, etc.
044.3 Hairdressers' and barbers' managers and proprietors
046.2 Tracers, drawing office assistants
046.3 Other clerks and cashiers (not retail)
049.2 Typists, shorthand writers, secretaries
050.0 Office machine operators
057.3 Scrap dealers, general dealers, rag and bone merchants
057.5 Sales representatives
057.6 Sales representatives (property and services), other agents

## (af) Social Class III (M)   Skilled occupations—Manual

**Employment status**—*Self-employed without employees*

| | | | |
|---|---|---|---|
| 056.0 | Roundsmen, van salesmen | 110.1 | Metal drawers |
| 064.0 | Chefs, cooks | 110.2 | Moulders, coremakers, die casters |
| 068.2 | Nursery nurses | 110.3 | Electroplaters |
| 069.1 | Travel stewards and attendants | 112.1 | Press and machine tool setters |
| 075.4 | Undertakers | 112.2 | Centre lathe turners |
| 075.5 | Bookmakers, betting shop managers | 112.3 | Machine tool setter operators |
| 085.1 | Tannery production workers | 113.2 | Metal polishers |
| 085.2 | Shoe repairers | 115.0 | Tool makers, tool fitters, markers-out |
| 085.3 | Leather cutters and sewers, footwear lasters, makers, finishers | 116.1 | Precision instrument makers and repairers |
| 087.4 | Warp preparers | 116.2 | Watch and chronometer makers and repairers |
| 087.5 | Weavers | 117.0 | Metal working production fitters and fitter/machinists |
| 087.6 | Knitters | 118.1 | Motor mechanics, auto engineers |
| 087.7 | Bleachers, dyers, finishers | 118.2 | Maintenance fitters (aircraft engines) |
| 087.8 | Menders, darners | 119.0 | Office machinery mechanics |
| 091.0 | Bakers, flour confectioners | 121.1 | Production fitters (electrical, electronic) |
| 094.1 | Paper, paperboard and leatherboard workers | 121.2 | Electricians, electrical maintenance fitters |
| 094.2 | Bookbinders and finishers | 121.3 | Electrical engineers (so described) |
| 096.2 | Glass formers and shapers, finishers, decorators | 122.1 | Telephone fitters |
| 096.3 | Casters and other pottery makers | 122.2 | Cable jointers, linesmen |
| 097.1 | Rubber process workers, moulding machine operators, tyre builders | 123.1 | Radio and TV mechanics |
| 098.2 | ·Brewery and vinery process workers | 123.2 | Other electronic maintenance engineers |
| | Other material processing— | 125.0 | Plumbers, heating and ventilating fitters, gas fitters |
| 098.5 | Bakery and confectionery workers | 126.1 | Sheet metal workers |
| 098.8 | Wood and paper | 126.2 | Metal plate workers, shipwrights, riveters |
| 100.1 | Compositors | 127.1 | Steel erectors, benders, fixers |
| 100.2 | Electrotypers, stereotypers, printing plate and cylinder preparers | 128.0 | Welders |
| | | 130.1 | Goldsmiths, silversmiths, precious stone workers |
| 100.3 | Printing machine minders and assistants | 130.2 | Engravers, etchers (printing) |
| 100.4 | Screen and block printers | 131.1 | Coach and vehicle body builders |
| 100.5 | Printers (so described) | 131.2 | Galvanizers, tin platers, dip platers |
| 102.1 | Tailors, tailoresses, dressmakers | 131.3 | Metal making and treating workers n.e.c. |
| 102.2 | Clothing cutters, milliners, furriers | 131.5 | Riggers |
| 103.0 | Coach trimmers, upholsterers, mattress makers | 131.6 | Electronics wiremen |
| 105.1 | Carpenters, joiners | 131.7 | Coil winders |
| 105.2 | Cabinet makers | 133.1 | Pottery decorators |
| 105.3 | Case and box makers | 133.2 | Coach painters (so described) |
| 105.4 | Pattern makers (moulds) | 133.4 | Painters and decorators n.e.c., french polishers |
| 106.0 | Sawyers, veneer cutters, woodworking machinists | 135.2 | Instrument assemblers |
| 107.2 | Dental technicians | 138.8 | Assemblers in paper production, processing and printing |
| 107.3 | Carpet fitters | 140.1 | Bricklayers, tile setters |
| 107.4 | Musical instrument makers, piano tuners | 140.2 | Masons, stone cutters |
| | Other making and repairing— | 140.3 | Plasterers |
| 107.5 | Glass and ceramics | 140.6 | Builders (so described) |
| 107.6 | Wood | 145.0 | Face-trained coalmining workers |
| 107.7 | Leather | 152.1 | Bus and coach drivers |
| 107.8 | Clothing and related products | 152.2 | Drivers of road goods vehicles |
| 107.9 | Paper goods and printing | 152.3 | Other motor drivers |
| 107.10 | Rubber | 155.1 | Mechanical plant drivers, operators (earth moving and civil engineering) |
| 109.1 | Furnace operating occupations (metal) | | |
| 109.2 | Rollermen | 155.3 | Fork lift, mechanical truck drivers |
| 109.3 | Smiths, forgemen | 158.2 | Workers in transport operating, materials moving and storing and related n.e.c. |
| | | 161.2 | All other in miscellaneous occupations n.e.c. |

## (ag) Social Class IV   Partly skilled occupations

**Employment status**—*Self-employed without employees*

| | | | |
|---|---|---|---|
| 044.2 | Managers of laundry and dry cleaning receiving shops | 110.4 | Annealers, hardeners, temperers (metal) |
| 057.2 | Market and street traders and assistants | 112.4 | Machine tool operators |
| 057.4 | Credit agents, collector salesmen | 113.1 | Press, stamping and automatic machine operators |
| 062.1 | Security guards and officers, patrolmen, watchmen | 113.3 | Fettlers, dressers |
| 062.3 | Security and protective service workers n.e.c. | 127.2 | Scaffolders, stagers |
| 065.1 | Waiters, waitresses | 131.9 | Other metal, jewellery, electrical production workers |
| 065.2 | Barmen, barmaids | 133.3 | Other spray painters |
| 068.3 | Other domestic and school helpers | 135.1 | Assemblers (electrical, electronic) |
| 075.6 | Service workers n.e.c. | 135.3 | Assemblers (vehicles and other metal goods) |
| 078.2 | Gardeners, groundsmen | 137.1 | Inspectors, viewers (metal, electrical goods) |
| 082.0 | Fishermen | 137.2 | Packers, bottlers, canners, fillers |
| 087.1 | Preparatory fibre processors | 138.12 | Painting, assembling and related occupations n.e.c. |
| 087.2 | Spinners, doublers, twisters | 140.4 | Roofers, glaziers |
| 087.3 | Winders, reelers | 140.5 | Handymen, general building workers |
| 089.0 | Chemical, gas and petroleum process plant operators | 141.2 | Road surfacers, concreters |
| 097.2 | Calender and extruding machine operators, moulders (plastics) | 141.4 | Paviors, kerb layers |
| | | 142.2 | Mains and service layers, pipe jointers |
| | Other material processing— | 143.1 | Craftsmen's mates |
| 098.4 | Textiles | 146.1 | Miners (not coal), quarrymen, well drillers |
| 098.7 | Food and drink n.e.c. | 146.2 | Construction workers n.e.c. |
| 098.9 | All other (excluding metal) n.e.c. | 148.0 | Deck, engine-room hands, bargemen, lightermen, boatmen |
| 102.3 | Sewers, embroiderers | 153.1 | Bus conductors |
| | Other making and repairing— | 157.1 | Storekeepers, warehousemen |
| 107.11 | Plastics | | |
| 107.12 | All other (excluding metal and electrical) n.e.c. | | |

### (ah) Social Class V   Unskilled occupations

**Employment status—*Self-employed without employees***

| | | | |
|---|---|---|---|
| 053.2 | Messengers | 157.2 | Stevedores, dockers |
| 072.2 | Cleaners, window cleaners, chimney sweeps, road sweepers | 157.3 | Goods porters |
| 141.3 | Roadmen | | Labourers and unskilled workers n.e.c.— |
| 143.2 | Building and civil engineering labourers | 160.8 | Other |

# S.E.G. 13   Farmers—employers and managers

### (aj) Social Class II   Intermediate occupations

**Employment status—*Managers, Self-employed with employees***

040.0   Farmers, horticulturists, farm managers

# S.E.G. 14   Farmers—own account

### (ak) Social Class II   Intermediate occupations

**Employment status—*Self-employed without employees***

040.0   Farmers, horticulturists, farm managers

# S.E.G. 15   Agricultural workers

### (al) Social Class III (M)   Skilled occupations—Manual

**Employment status—*Foremen and Supervisors***

| | | | |
|---|---|---|---|
| 076.1 | Farm foremen | 076.5 | Forestry foremen |
| 076.2 | Horticultural foremen | 076.6 | Other foremen in farming and related |
| 076.4 | Agricultural machinery foremen | | |

### (am) Social Class IV   Partly skilled occupations

**Employment status—*Employees n.e.c.***

| | | | |
|---|---|---|---|
| 077.0 | Farm workers | 080.0 | Forestry workers |
| 078.1 | Horticultural workers | 083.0 | All other in farming and related |
| 079.0 | Agricultural machinery drivers, operators | | |

**Employment status—*Self-employed with and without employees***

| | | | |
|---|---|---|---|
| 077.0 | Farm workers | 080.0 | Forestry workers |
| 078.1 | Horticultural workers | 083.0 | All other in farming and related |
| 079.0 | Agricultural machinery drivers, operators | | |

# S.E.G. 16   Members of armed forces

**Employment status—*Managers***

| | | | |
|---|---|---|---|
| 041.0 | Officers, UK armed forces | 042.0 | Officers, foreign and Commonwealth armed forces |

**Employment status—*Employees n.e.c.***

| | | | |
|---|---|---|---|
| 058.0 | NCOs and other ranks, UK armed forces | 059.0 | NCOs and other ranks, foreign and Commonwealth armed forces |

# S.E.G. 17   Inadequately described and not stated occupations

**Employment status—*Managers, Foremen and Supervisors, Self-employed with and without employees***

—.1   Inadequately described occupations

**Employment status—*Apprentices, etc., Employees n.e.c.***

| | | | |
|---|---|---|---|
| —.1 | Inadequately described occupations | —.2 | Occupations not stated |

cxvii

# Appendix C

## Summary of Socio-economic Classes

**S.E.G. 1.1   Employers in industry, commerce, etc.—large establishments**

    (a)   Social Class II      Intermediate occupations
    (b)   Social Class III(N)   Skilled occupations—Non-manual
    (c)   Social Class III(M)   Skilled occupations—Manual*

**S.E.G. 1.2   Managers in central and local government, industry, commerce, etc.—large establishments**

    (d)   Social Class I      Professional, etc. occupations
    (e)   Social Class II      Intermediate occupations
    (f)   Social Class III(N)   Skilled occupations—Non-manual
    (g)   Social Class III(M)   Skilled occupations—Manual

**S.E.G. 2.1   Employers in industry, commerce, etc.—small establishments**

    (h)   Social Class II      Intermediate occupations
    (j)   Social Class III(N)   Skilled occupations—Non-manual
    (k)   Social Class III(M)   Skilled occupations—Manual
    (l)   Social Class IV     Partly skilled occupations
    (m)   Social Class V     Unskilled occupations

**S.E.G. 2.2   Managers in industry, commerce, etc.—small establishments**

    (n)   Social Class II      Intermediate occupations
    (o)   Social Class III(N)   Skilled occupations—Non-manual
    (p)   Social Class III(M)   Skilled occupations—Manual

**S.E.G. 3   Professional workers—self-employed**

    (q)   Social Class I      Professional, etc. occupations

**S.E.G. 4   Professional workers—employees**

    (r)   Social Class I      Professional, etc. occupations

**S.E.G. 5.1   Ancillary workers and artists**

    (s)   Social Class II      Intermediate occupations

**S.E.G. 5.2   Foremen and supervisors—Non-manual**

    (t)   Social Class III(N)   Skilled occupations—Non-manual

**S.E.G. 6   Junior non-manual workers**

    (u)   Social Class III(N)   Skilled occupations—Non-manual
    (v)   Social Class IV     Partly skilled occupations

**S.E.G. 7   Personal service workers**

    (w)   Social Class II      Intermediate occupations
    (x)   Social Class III(M)   Skilled occupations—Manual
    (y)   Social Class IV     Partly skilled occupations

---

* Including very small numbers of persons in Social Classes IV and V

**S.E.G. 8**    **Foremen and supervisors—Manual**

(z)    Social Class III(M)    Skilled occupations—Manual

**S.E.G. 9**    **Skilled manual workers**

(aa)    Social Class III(M)    Skilled occupations—Manual

**S.E.G. 10**    **Semi-skilled manual workers**

(ab)    Social Class IV    Partly skilled occupations

**S.E.G. 11**    **Unskilled manual workers**

(ac)    Social Class V    Unskilled Occupations

**S.E.G. 12**    **Own account workers (other than professional)**

(ad)    Social Class II    Intermediate occupations
(ae)    Social Class III(N)    Skilled occupations—Non-manual
(af)    Social Class III(M)    Skilled occupations—Manual
(ag)    Social Class IV    Partly skilled occupations
(ah)    Social Class V    Unskilled occupations

**S.E.G. 13**    **Farmers—employers and managers**

(aj)    Social Class II    Intermediate occupations

**S.E.G. 14**    **Farmers—own account**

(ak)    Social Class II    Intermediate occupations

**S.E.G. 15**    **Agricultural workers**

(al)    Social Class III(M)    Skilled occupations—Manual
(am)    Social Class IV    Partly skilled occupations

**S.E.G. 16**    **Members of armed forces**

**S.E.G. 17**    **Inadequately described and not stated occupations**

# Appendix D

## Industrial Classification for the 1981 Census
### Summary of Classes, Activity Headings and Subdivisions where applicable

| Class | Activity | |
|---|---|---|
| | | **DIVISION 0   AGRICULTURE, FORESTRY AND FISHING** |
| 01 | | Agriculture and horticulture |
| 02 | | Forestry |
| 03 | | Fishing |

| Class | Activity | |
|---|---|---|
| | | **DIVISION 1   ENERGY AND WATER SUPPLY INDUSTRIES** |
| 11 | | Coal extraction and manufacture of solid fuels |
| | 1113 | Deep coal mines |
| | 1114 | Opencast coal working |
| | 1115 | Manufacture of solid fuels |
| 12 | | Coke ovens |
| 13 | | Extraction of mineral oil and natural gas |
| 14 | | Mineral oil processing |
| | 1401 | Mineral oil refining |
| | 1402 | Other treatment of petroleum products (excluding petrochemicals manufacture) |
| 15 | | Nuclear fuel production |
| 16 | | Production and distribution of electricity, gas and other forms of energy |
| | 1610 | Production and distribution of electricity |
| | 1620 | Public gas supply |
| | 1630 | Production and distribution of other forms of energy |
| 17 | | Water supply industry |

| Class | Activity | |
|---|---|---|
| | | **DIVISION 2   EXTRACTION OF MINERALS AND ORES OTHER THAN FUELS; MANUFACTURE OF METALS, MINERAL PRODUCTS AND CHEMICALS** |
| 21 | | Extraction and preparation of metalliferous ores |
| 22 | | Metal manufacturing |
| | 2210 | Iron and steel industry (as defined in the European Coal and Steel Community Treaty of Paris 1951) |
| | 2220 | Steel tubes |
| | 2234 | Drawing and manufacture of steel wire and steel wire products |
| | 2235 | Other drawing, cold rolling and cold forming of steel |
| | 2245 | Aluminium and aluminium alloys |
| | 2246 | Copper, brass and other copper alloys |
| | 2247 | Other non-ferrous metals and their alloys |
| 23 | | Extraction of minerals not elsewhere specified |
| | 2310 | Extraction of stone, clay, sand and gravel |
| | 2330 | Salt extraction and refining |
| | 2396 | Extraction of other minerals not elsewhere specified |
| 24 | | Manufacture of non-metallic mineral products |
| | 2410 | Structural clay products |
| | 2420 | Cement, lime and plaster |
| | 2436 | Ready mixed concrete |
| | 2437 | Other building products of concrete, cement or plaster |
| | 2440 | Asbestos goods |
| | 2450 | Working of stone and other non-metallic minerals not elsewhere specified |
| | 2460 | Abrasive products |
| | 2471 | Flat glass |
| | 2478 | Glass containers |
| | 2479 | Other glass products |
| | 2481 | Refractory goods |
| | 2489 | Ceramic goods |

<table>
<tr><td>Class</td><td>Activity</td><td></td></tr>
</table>

**DIVISION 2** *(continued)*

| Class | Activity | |
|---|---|---|
| 25 | | Chemical industry |
| | 2511 | Inorganic chemicals except industrial gases |
| | 2512 | Basic organic chemicals except specialised pharmaceutical chemicals |
| | 2513 | Fertilisers |
| | 2514 | Synthetic resins and plastics materials |
| | 2515 | Synthetic rubber |
| | 2516 | Dyestuffs and pigments |
| | 2551 | Paints, varnishes and painters' fillings |
| | 2552 | Printing ink |
| | 2562 | Formulated adhesives and sealants |
| | 2563 | Chemical treatment of oils and fats |
| | 2564 | Essential oils and flavouring materials |
| | 2565 | Explosives |
| | 2567 | Miscellaneous chemical products for industrial use |
| | 2568 | Formulated pesticides |
| | 2569 | Adhesive film, cloth and foil |
| | 2570 | Pharmaceutical products |
| | 2581 | Soap and synthetic detergents |
| | 2582 | Perfumes, cosmetics and toilet preparations |
| | 2591 | Photographic materials and chemicals |
| | 2599 | Chemical products not elsewhere specified |
| 26 | | Production of man-made fibres |

**DIVISION 3   METAL GOODS, ENGINEERING AND VEHICLES INDUSTRIES**

| Class | Activity | |
|---|---|---|
| 31 | | Manufacture of metal goods not elsewhere specified |
| | 3111 | Ferrous metal foundries |
| | 3112 | Non-ferrous metal foundries |
| | 3120 | Forging, pressing and stamping |
| | 3137 | Bolts, nuts, washers, rivets, springs and non-precision chains |
| | 3138 | Heat and surface treatment of metals, including sintering |
| | 3142 | Metal doors, windows, etc. |
| | 3161 | Hand tools and implements |
| | 3162 | Cutlery, spoons, forks and similar tableware; razors |
| | 3163 | Metal storage vessels (mainly non-industrial) |
| | 3164 | Packaging products of metal |
| | 3165 | Domestic heating and cooking appliances (non-electrical) |
| | 3166 | Metal furniture and safes |
| | 3167 | Domestic and similar utensils of metal |
| | 3169 | Finished metal products not elsewhere specified |
| 32 | | Mechanical engineering |
| | 3204 | Fabricated constructional steelwork |
| | 3205 | Boilers and process plant fabrications |
| | 3211 | Agricultural machinery |
| | 3212 | Wheeled tractors |
| | 3221 | Metal-working machine tools |
| | 3222 | Engineers' small tools |
| | 3230 | Textile machinery |
| | 3244 | Food, drink and tobacco processing machinery; packaging and bottling machinery |
| | 3245 | Chemical industry machinery; furnaces and kilns; gas, water and waste treatment plant |
| | 3246 | Process engineering contractors |
| | 3251 | Mining machinery |
| | 3254 | Construction and earth moving equipment |
| | 3255 | Mechanical lifting and handling equipment |
| | 3261 | Precision chains and other mechanical power transmission equipment |
| | 3262 | Ball, needle and roller bearings |
| | 3275 | Machinery for working wood, rubber, plastics, leather and making paper, glass, bricks and similar materials; laundry and dry cleaning machinery |
| | 3276 | Printing, bookbinding and paper goods machinery |
| | 3281 | Internal combustion engines (except for road vehicles, wheeled tractors primarily for agricultural purposes and aircraft) and other prime movers |
| | 3283 | Compressors and fluid power equipment |
| | 3284 | Refrigerating machinery, space heating, ventilating and air conditioning equipment |
| | 3285 | Scales, weighing machinery and portable power tools |
| | 3286 | Other industrial and commercial machinery |
| | 3287 | Pumps |
| | 3288 | Industrial valves |
| | 3289 | Mechanical, marine and precision engineering not elsewhere specified |
| | 3290 | Ordnance, small arms and ammunition |

| Class | Activity | |
|---|---|---|

# Appendix E

## European Economic Community Status Groups

1  Farmers
2  Other agricultural workers
3  Employers in industry, construction, trade, transport and services
4  Own-account workers in industry, construction, trade, transport and services
5  Employers and own-account workers in liberal and related professions
6  Managers, legislative officials and government administrators
7  Employees with liberal and related professions
8  Foremen and supervisors of manual workers (employees)
9  Skilled and semi-skilled manual workers (employees)
10  Labourers (employees)
11  Supervisors of clerical workers, sales workers and service staff; government executive officials
12  Clerical, sales and service workers
13  Armed forces (regular members and persons on compulsory military service)
14  Economically active persons not elsewhere classified

## European Economic Community Socio-economic Status Group allocations of Occupation and Employment Status Groups

| Occupation | Self-employed | | Managers | Foremen | Apprentices, etc., Employees n.e.c. |
|---|---|---|---|---|---|
| | with employees | without employees | | | |
| **001 Judges, barristers, advocates, solicitors** | | | | | |
| 0  Judges, barristers, advocates, solicitors | 5 | 5 | — | — | 7 |
| **002 Accountants, valuers, finance specialists** | | | | | |
| 1  Chartered and certified accountants | 5 | 5 | — | — | 7 |
| 2  Cost and works accountants | 5 | 5 | — | — | 7 |
| 3  Estimators | 5 | 5 | 7 | — | 7 |
| 4  Valuers, claims assessors | 3 | 4 | 12 | — | 12 |
| 5  Financial managers | — | — | 6 | — | — |
| 6  Underwriters, brokers, investment analysts | 3 | 4 | 12 | — | — |
| 7  Taxation experts | 5 | 5 | 7 | — | — |
| **003 Personnel and industrial relations managers; O and M, work study and operational research officers** | | | | | |
| 1  Personnel and industrial relations officers | 3 | 4 | 6 | — | — |
| 2  O and M, work study and OR officers | 5 | 5 | 7 | — | 7 |
| **004 Economists, statisticians, systems analysts, computer programmers** | | | | | |
| 1  Economists, statisticians, actuaries | 5 | 5 | — | — | 7 |
| 2  Systems analysts, computer programmers | 5 | 5 | 7 | — | 7 |
| **005 Marketing, sales, advertising, public relations and purchasing managers** | | | | | |
| 1  Marketing and sales managers and executives | 3 | 4 | 6 | — | — |
| 2  Advertising and PR executives | 3 | 4 | 6 | — | — |
| 3  Buyers (retail trade) | — | — | 11 | — | — |
| 4  Buyers and purchasing officers (not retail) | — | — | 11 | — | — |
| **006 Statutory and other inspectors** | | | | | |
| 1  Environmental health officers | — | — | — | — | 11 |
| 2  Building inspectors | — | — | — | — | 11 |
| 3  Inspectors (statutory and similar) | — | — | — | — | 11 |
| **007 General administrators—national government** | | | | | |
| 1  General administrators—national government (Assistant Secretary level and above) | — | — | 6 | — | — |
| 2  General administrators—national government (HEO to Senior Principal level) | — | — | 6 | — | — |
| **008 Local government officers (administrative and executive functions)** | | | | | |
| 0  Local government officers (administrative and executive functions) | — | — | 6 | — | — |

| Occupation | Self-employed | | Managers | Foremen | Apprentices, etc., Employees n.e.c. |
|---|---|---|---|---|---|
| | with employees | without employees | | | |
| **009** All other professional and related supporting management and administration | | | | | |
| 1 Company secretaries | 3 | 4 | 6 | — | — |
| 2 Officials of trade associations, trade unions, professional bodies and charities | — | — | 6 | — | 6 |
| 3 Property and estate managers | 3 | 4 | 12 | — | — |
| 4 Librarians, information officers | — | — | 7 | — | 7 |
| 5 Legal service and related occupations | 5 | 5 | 7 | — | 7 |
| 6 Management consultants | 5 | 5 | — | — | 7 |
| 7 Managers' personal assistants | — | — | — | — | 12 |
| 8 Professional workers and related supporting management and administration n.e.c. | 3 | 4 | 6 | — | 6 |
| **010** Teachers in higher education | | | | | |
| 1 University academic staff | — | — | — | — | 7 |
| 2 Teachers in establishments for further and higher education | 5 | 5 | 7 | — | 7 |
| **011** Teachers n.e.c. | | | | | |
| 0 Teachers n.e.c. | 5 | 5 | 7 | — | 7 |
| **012** Vocational and industrial trainers, education officers, social and behavioural scientists | | | | | |
| 1 Vocational and industrial trainers | 5 | 5 | 7 | — | 7 |
| 2 Education officers, school inspectors | — | — | — | — | 6 |
| 3 Social and behavioural scientists | 5 | 5 | — | — | 7 |
| **013** Welfare workers | | | | | |
| 1 Matrons, houseparents | 5 | 5 | 7 | — | 7 |
| 2 Playgroup leaders | 5 | 5 | — | — | 7 |
| 3 Welfare occupations n.e.c. | — | — | 7 | — | 7 |
| **014** Clergy, ministers of religion | | | | | |
| 0 Clergy, ministers of religion | 5 | 5 | — | — | 7 |
| **015** Medical and dental practitioners | | | | | |
| 1 Medical practitioners | 5 | 5 | — | — | 7 |
| 2 Dental practitioners | 5 | 5 | — | — | 7 |
| **016** Nurse administrators, nurses | | | | | |
| 0 Nurse administrators, nurses | 5 | 5 | 7 | 7 | 7 |
| **017** Pharmacists, radiographers, therapists n.e.c. | | | | | |
| 1 Pharmacists | 5 | 5 | — | — | 7 |
| 2 Medical radiographers | 5 | 5 | 7 | 7 | 7 |
| 3 Ophthalmic and dispensing opticians | 5 | 5 | — | — | 7 |
| 4 Physiotherapists | 5 | 5 | 7 | 7 | 7 |
| 5 Chiropodists | 5 | 5 | 7 | — | 7 |
| 6 Therapists n.e.c. | 5 | 5 | 7 | 7 | 7 |
| **018** All other professional and related in education, welfare and health | | | | | |
| 1 Medical technicians, dental auxiliaries | 5 | 5 | 7 | 7 | 7 |
| 2 Veterinarians | 5 | 5 | — | — | 7 |
| 3 Driving instructors (not HGV) | 3 | 4 | 9 | — | 9 |
| 4 Professional and related in education, welfare and health n.e.c. | 5 | 5 | 7 | — | 7 |
| **019** Authors, writers, journalists | | | | | |
| 0 Authors, writers, journalists | 5 | 5 | 7 | — | 7 |
| **020** Artists, designers, window dressers | | | | | |
| 1 Artists, commercial artists | 5 | 5 | 7 | 7 | 7 |
| 2 Industrial designers (not clothing) | 5 | 5 | 7 | — | 7 |
| 3 Clothing designers | 5 | 5 | 7 | — | 7 |
| 4 Window dressers | 5 | 5 | 7 | — | 7 |
| **021** Actors, musicians, entertainers, stage managers | | | | | |
| 1 Actors, entertainers, singers, stage managers | 3 | 4 | 11 | — | 11 |
| 2 Musicians | 3 | 4 | 11 | — | 11 |
| **022** Photographers, cameramen, sound and vision equipment operators | | | | | |
| 1 Photographers, cameramen | 5 | 5 | 7 | 7 | 7 |
| 2 Sound and vision equipment operators | 3 | 4 | 9 | 9 | 9 |
| **023** All other literary, artistic and sports | | | | | |
| 1 Professional sportsmen, sports officials | 3 | 4 | 11 | — | 11 |
| 2 Literary, artistic and sports workers n.e.c. | 5 | 5 | 7 | — | 7 |
| **024** Scientists, physicists, mathematicians | | | | | |
| 1 Biological scientists, biochemists | 5 | 5 | — | — | 7 |
| 2 Chemical scientists | 5 | 5 | — | — | 7 |
| 3 Physical and geological scientists, mathematicians | 5 | 5 | — | — | 7 |
| **025** Civil, structural, municipal, mining and quarrying engineers | | | | | |
| 0 Civil, structural, municipal, mining and quarrying engineers | 5 | 5 | — | — | 7 |
| **026** Mechanical and aeronautical engineers | | | | | |
| 1 Mechanical and aeronautical engineers | 5 | 5 | — | — | 7 |
| 2 Design and development engineers (mechanical) | 5 | 5 | — | — | 7 |
| **027** Electrical and electronic engineers | | | | | |
| 1 Electrical engineers | 5 | 5 | — | — | 7 |
| 2 Electronic engineers | 5 | 5 | — | — | 7 |

| Occupation | Self-employed with employees | Self-employed without employees | Managers | Foremen | Apprentices, etc., Employees n.e.c. |
|---|---|---|---|---|---|
| **028 Engineers and technologists n.e.c.** | | | | | |
| 1  Chemical engineers | 5 | 5 | — | — | 7 |
| 2  Production engineers | 5 | 5 | — | — | 7 |
| 3  Planning and quality control engineers | 5 | 5 | — | — | 7 |
| 4  Engineers n.e.c. | 5 | 5 | — | — | 7 |
| 5  Metallurgists | 5 | 5 | — | — | 7 |
| 6  Technologists n.e.c. | 5 | 5 | — | — | 7 |
| **029 Draughtsmen** | | | | | |
| 0  Draughtsmen | 5 | 5 | 7 | 7 | 7 |
| **030 Laboratory and engineering technicians, technician engineers** | | | | | |
| 1  Laboratory technicians | 5 | 5 | 7 | 7 | 7 |
| 2  Engineering technicians, technician engineers | 5 | 5 | 7 | 7 | 7 |
| **031 Architects, town planners, quantity, building and land surveyors** | | | | | |
| 1  Architects, town planners | 5 | 5 | — | — | 7 |
| 2  Quantity surveyors | 5 | 5 | — | — | 7 |
| 3  Building, land and mining surveyors | 5 | 5 | — | — | 7 |
| **032 Officers (ships and aircraft), air traffic planners and controllers** | | | | | |
| 1  Aircraft flight deck officers | 5 | 5 | 7 | — | 7 |
| 2  Air traffic planners and controllers | — | — | — | — | 11 |
| 3  Deck, engineering and radio officers and pilots, ship | 5 | 5 | 7 | — | — |
| **033 Professional and related in science, engineering and other technologies and similar fields n.e.c.** | | | | | |
| 1  Architectural and town planning technicians | — | 5 | — | — | 7 |
| 2  Building and civil engineering technicians | — | — | — | — | 7 |
| 3  Technical and related workers n.e.c. | 5 | 5 | 7 | 7 | 7 |
| **034 Production, works and maintenance managers, works foremen** | | | | | |
| 0  Production, works and maintenance managers, works foremen | — | — | 6 | 8 | — |
| **035 Site and other managers, agents and clerks of works, general foremen (building and civil engineering)** | | | | | |
| 1  Managers in building and contracting | — | — | 6 | — | — |
| 2  Clerks of works | — | — | — | — | 6 |
| **036 Managers in transport, warehousing, public utilities and mining** | | | | | |
| 1  Managers in mining and public utilities | — | — | 6 | — | — |
| 2  Transport managers | — | — | 6 | — | — |
| 3  Stores controllers | — | — | 6 | — | — |
| 4  Managers in warehousing and materials handling n.e.c. | — | — | 6 | — | — |
| **037 Office managers** | | | | | |
| 1  Credit controllers | — | — | 6 | — | — |
| 2  Office managers n.e.c. | 3 | 4 | 6 | — | — |
| **038 Managers in wholesale and retail distribution** | | | | | |
| 1  Garage proprietors | 3 | 4 | — | — | — |
| 2  Butchers (managers and proprietors) | 3 | 4 | 6 | — | — |
| 3  Fishmongers (managers and proprietors) | 3 | 4 | 6 | — | — |
| 4  Other proprietors and managers (sales) | 3 | 4 | 6 | — | — |
| **039 Managers of hotels, clubs, etc., and in entertainment and sport** | | | | | |
| 1  Hotel and residential club managers | 3 | 4 | 6 | — | — |
| 2  Publicans | 3 | 4 | 6 | — | — |
| 3  Restaurateurs | 3 | 4 | 6 | — | — |
| 4  Club stewards | — | — | 6 | — | — |
| 5  Entertainment and sports managers | 3 | 4 | 6 | — | — |
| **040 Farmers, horticulturists, farm managers** | | | | | |
| 0  Farmers, horticulturists, farm managers | 1 | 1 | 2 | — | — |
| **041 Officers, UK armed forces** | | | | | |
| 0  Officers, UK armed forces | — | — | 13 | — | — |
| **042 Officers, foreign and Commonwealth armed forces** | | | | | |
| 0  Officers, foreign and Commonwealth armed forces | — | — | 13 | — | — |
| **043 Senior police, prison and fire service officers** | | | | | |
| 1  Prison officers (chief officers and above) | — | — | 6 | — | — |
| 2  Police officers (inspectors and above) | — | — | 6 | — | — |
| 3  Fire service officers | — | — | 6 | — | — |
| **044 All other managers** | | | | | |
| 1  Proprietors and managers, service flats, holiday flats, caravan sites, etc. | 3 | 4 | 6 | — | — |
| 2  Managers of laundry and dry cleaning receiving shops | 3 | 4 | 6 | — | — |
| 3  Hairdressers' and barbers' managers and proprietors | 3 | 4 | 12 | — | — |
| 4  Managers n.e.c. | 3 | 4 | 6 | — | — |
| **045 Supervisors of clerks, civil service executive officers** | | | | | |
| 1  Civil service executive officers | — | — | — | 11 | — |
|     Supervisors of— | | | | | |
| 2  Stores and despatch clerks | — | — | — | 11 | — |
| 3  Tracers, drawing office assistants | — | — | — | 11 | — |
| 4  Other clerks and cashiers (not retail) | — | — | — | 11 | — |
| 5  Retail shop cashiers, check-out and cash and wrap operators | — | — | — | 11 | — |

| Occupation | Self-employed | | Managers | Foremen | Apprentices, etc., Employees n.e.c. |
|---|---|---|---|---|---|
| | with employees | without employees | | | |
| **046 Clerks** | | | | | |
| 1 Stores and despatch clerks | — | — | — | — | 12 |
| 2 Tracers, drawing office assistants | — | 4 | — | — | 12 |
| 3 Other clerks and cashiers (not retail) | 3 | 4 | — | — | 12 |
| **047 Retail shop cashiers, check-out and cash and wrap operators** | | | | | |
| 0 Retail shop cashiers, check-out and cash and wrap operators | — | — | — | — | 12 |
| **048 Supervisors of typists, office machine operators, telephonists, etc.** | | | | | |
| Supervisors of— | | | | | |
| 1 Typists, shorthand writers, secretaries | — | — | — | 11 | — |
| 2 Office machine operators | — | — | — | 11 | — |
| 3 Telephone operators | — | — | — | 11 | — |
| 4 Radio and telegraph operators | — | — | — | 11 | — |
| **049 Secretaries, shorthand typists, receptionists** | | | | | |
| 1 Receptionists | — | — | — | — | 12 |
| 2 Typists, shorthand writers, secretaries | 3 | 4 | — | — | 12 |
| **050 Office machine operators** | | | | | |
| 0 Office machine operators | 3 | 4 | — | — | 12 |
| **051 Telephonists, radio and telegraph operators** | | | | | |
| 1 Telephonist receptionists | — | — | — | — | 12 |
| 2 Telephone operators | — | — | — | — | 12 |
| 3 Radio and telegraph operators | — | — | — | — | 12 |
| **052 Supervisors of postmen, mail sorters, messengers** | | | | | |
| Supervisors of— | | | | | |
| 1 Postmen, mail sorters | — | — | — | 11 | — |
| 2 Messengers | — | — | — | 11 | — |
| **053 Postmen, mail sorters, messengers** | | | | | |
| 1 Postmen, mail sorters | — | — | — | — | 12 |
| 2 Messengers | — | 4 | — | — | 12 |
| **054 Sales supervisors** | | | | | |
| Supervisors of— | | | | | |
| 1 Shop salesmen and assistants | — | — | — | 11 | — |
| 2 Petrol pump, forecourt attendants | — | — | — | 11 | — |
| 3 Roundsmen, van salesmen | — | — | — | 11 | — |
| **055 Salesmen, sales assistants, shop assistants, shelf fillers, petrol pump, forecourt attendants** | | | | | |
| 1 Shop salesmen and assistants | — | — | — | — | 12 |
| 2 Shelf fillers | — | — | — | — | 12 |
| 3 Petrol pump, forecourt attendants | — | — | — | — | 12 |
| **056 Roundsmen, van salesmen** | | | | | |
| 0 Roundsmen, van salesmen | 3 | 4 | 12 | — | 12 |
| **057 Sales representatives and agents** | | | | | |
| 1 Importers, exporters, commodity brokers | 3 | 4 | 6 | — | — |
| 2 Market and street traders and assistants | 3 | 4 | 12 | — | 12 |
| 3 Scrap dealers, general dealers, rag and bone merchants | 3 | 4 | 6 | — | — |
| 4 Credit agents, collector salesmen | 3 | 4 | 12 | — | 12 |
| 5 Sales representatives | 3 | 4 | 12 | — | 12 |
| 6 Sales representatives (property and services), other agents | 3 | 4 | 12 | — | 12 |
| **058 NCOs and other ranks, UK armed forces** | | | | | |
| 0 NCOs and other ranks, UK armed forces | — | — | — | — | 13 |
| **059 NCOs and other ranks, foreign and Commonwealth armed forces** | | | | | |
| 0 NCOs and other ranks, foreign and Commonwealth armed forces | — | — | — | — | 13 |
| **060 Supervisors (police sergeants, fire fighting and related)** | | | | | |
| 1 Police sergeants | — | — | — | 12 | — |
| 2 Fire service supervisors | — | — | — | 12 | — |
| 3 Prison service principal officers | — | — | — | 12 | — |
| Supervisors of— | | | | | |
| 4 Security guards and officers, patrolmen, watchmen | — | — | — | 12 | — |
| 5 Traffic wardens | — | — | — | 12 | — |
| 6 Security and protective service workers n.e.c. | — | — | — | 12 | — |
| **061 Policemen, firemen, prison officers** | | | | | |
| 1 Policemen (below sergeant) | — | — | — | — | 12 |
| 2 Firemen | — | — | — | — | 12 |
| 3 Prison officers (below principal officer) | — | — | — | — | 12 |
| **062 Other security and protective service workers** | | | | | |
| 1 Security guards and officers, patrolmen, watchmen | 3 | 4 | — | — | 12 |
| 2 Traffic wardens | — | — | — | — | 12 |
| 3 Security and protective service workers n.e.c. | 3 | 4 | — | — | 12 |
| **063 Catering supervisors** | | | | | |
| Supervisors of— | | | | | |
| 1 Chefs, cooks | — | — | — | 12 | — |
| 2 Waiters, waitresses | — | — | — | 12 | — |
| 3 Barmen, barmaids | — | — | — | 12 | — |
| 4 Counter hands, assistants | — | — | — | 12 | — |

| Occupation | Self-employed | | Managers | Foremen | Apprentices, etc., Employees n.e.c. |
| --- | --- | --- | --- | --- | --- |
| | with employees | without employees | | | |
| **064 Chefs, cooks** | | | | | |
| 0   Chefs, cooks … … … … … … … | 3 | 4 | 12 | — | 12 |
| **065 Waiters and bar staff** | | | | | |
| 1   Waiters, waitresses … … … … … | — | 4 | — | — | 12 |
| 2   Barmen, barmaids … … … … … | — | 4 | — | — | 12 |
| **066 Counter hands, assistants, kitchen porters, hands** | | | | | |
| 1   Counter hands, assistants … … … … | — | — | — | — | 12 |
| 2   Kitchen porters, hands … … … … | — | — | — | 10 | 10 |
| **067 Supervisors—housekeeping and related** | | | | | |
| 1   Housekeepers (non-domestic)… … … … | — | — | — | 11 | — |
|     Supervisors of— | | | | | |
| 2     Other domestic and school helpers … … | — | — | — | 12 | — |
| 3     Travel stewards and attendants … … | — | — | — | 11 | — |
| 4     Hospital porters … … … … … | — | — | — | 10 | — |
| 5     Hotel porters … … … … … | — | — | — | 12 | — |
| 6     Ambulancemen … … … … | — | — | — | 12 | — |
| 7     Hospital, ward orderlies … … … | — | — | — | 12 | — |
| **068 Domestic staff and school helpers** | | | | | |
| 1   Domestic housekeepers … … … … | — | — | — | — | 11 |
| 2   Nursery nurses … … … … … | 3 | 4 | — | — | 12 |
| 3   Other domestic and school helpers … … | — | 4 | — | — | 12 |
| **069 Travel stewards and attendants, hospital and hotel porters** | | | | | |
| 1   Travel stewards and attendants … … | — | 4 | — | — | 12 |
| 2   Hospital porters … … … … … | — | — | — | — | 10 |
| 3   Hotel porters … … … … … | — | — | — | — | 12 |
| **070 Ambulancemen, hospital orderlies** | | | | | |
| 1   Ambulancemen… … … … … | — | — | — | — | 12 |
| 2   Hospital, ward orderlies … … … | — | — | — | — | 12 |
| **071 Supervisors, foremen—caretaking, cleaning and related** | | | | | |
|     Supervisors of— | | | | | |
| 1   Caretakers … … … … … | — | — | — | 12 | — |
| 2   Cleaners, window cleaners, chimney sweeps, road sweepers | — | — | — | 12 | — |
| 3   Railway stationmen … … … … | — | — | — | 9 | — |
| 4   Lift and car park attendants … … … | — | — | — | 12 | — |
| **072 Caretakers, road sweepers and other cleaners** | | | | | |
| 1   Caretakers … … … … … | — | — | — | — | 12 |
| 2   Cleaners, window cleaners, chimney sweeps, road sweepers | 3 | 4 | 12 | — | 12 |
| **073 Hairdressing supervisors** | | | | | |
| 0   Hairdressing supervisors … … … | — | — | — | 12 | — |
| **074 Hairdressers, barbers** | | | | | |
| 0   Hairdressers, barbers … … … | — | — | — | — | 12 |
| **075 All other in catering, cleaning and other personal service** | | | | | |
| 1   Railway stationmen … … … … | — | — | — | — | 9 |
| 2   Lift and car park attendants … … … | — | — | — | — | 12 |
| 3   Launderers, dry cleaners, pressers … … … | — | — | 12 | 12 | 12 |
| 4   Undertakers … … … … … | 3 | 4 | 12 | — | — |
| 5   Bookmakers, betting shop managers … … … | 3 | 4 | 12 | — | — |
| 6   Service workers n.e.c. … … … … | 3 | 4 | 12 | 12 | 12 |
| **076 Foremen—farming, horticulture, forestry** | | | | | |
| 1   Farm foremen … … … … … | — | — | — | 2 | — |
| 2   Horticultural foremen … … … … | — | — | — | 2 | — |
| 3   Foremen gardeners and groundsmen … … | — | — | — | 2 | — |
| 4   Agricultural machinery foremen … … | — | — | — | 2 | — |
| 5   Forestry foremen … … … … | — | — | — | 2 | — |
| 6   Other foremen in farming and related … … | — | — | — | 2 | — |
| **077 Farm workers** | | | | | |
| 0   Farm workers … … … … … … | 1 | 1 | — | — | 2 |
| **078 Horticultural workers, gardeners, groundsmen** | | | | | |
| 1   Horticultural workers … … … … … | 1 | 1 | — | — | 2 |
| 2   Gardeners, groundsmen … … … … | 1 | 1 | 2 | — | 2 |
| **079 Agricultural machinery drivers, operators** | | | | | |
| 0   Agricultural machinery drivers, operators … … | 1 | 1 | — | — | 2 |
| **080 Forestry workers** | | | | | |
| 0   Forestry workers … … … … … | 1 | 1 | — | — | 2 |
| **081 Supervisors, mates—fishing** | | | | | |
| 0   Supervisors, mates—fishing … … … … | — | — | — | 2 | — |
| **082 Fishermen** | | | | | |
| 0   Fishermen … … … … … … | 1 | 1 | 2 | — | 2 |
| **083 All other in farming and related** | | | | | |
| 0   All other in farming and related … … … | 1 | 1 | — | — | 2 |

| Occupation | Self-employed | | Managers | Foremen | Apprentices, etc., Employees n.e.c. |
| --- | --- | --- | --- | --- | --- |
| | with employees | without employees | | | |
| 084 Foremen—tannery and leather (including leather substitutes) working | | | | | |
| Foremen— | | | | | |
| 1  Tannery production workers ... ... ... ... | — | — | — | 9 | — |
| 2  Shoe repairers ... ... ... ... | — | — | — | 9 | — |
| 3  Leather cutters and sewers, footwear lasters, makers, finishers ... ... ... ... ... ... | — | — | — | 9 | — |
| 4  Other making and repairing, leather ... ... ... | — | — | — | 9 | — |
| 085 Tannery and leather (including leather substitutes) workers | | | | | |
| 1  Tannery production workers ... ... ... ... | 3 | 4 | 9 | — | 9 |
| 2  Shoe repairers ... ... ... ... | 3 | 4 | 9 | — | 9 |
| 3  Leather cutters and sewers, footwear lasters, makers, finishers ... ... ... ... ... ... | 3 | 4 | 9 | — | 9 |
| 086 Foremen—textile processing | | | | | |
| Foremen— | | | | | |
| 1  Preparatory fibre processors ... ... ... | — | — | — | 9 | — |
| 2  Spinners, doublers, twisters... ... ... ... ... | — | — | — | 9 | — |
| 3  Winders, reelers ... ... ... ... ... | — | — | — | 9 | — |
| 4  Warp preparers ... ... ... ... ... | — | — | — | 9 | — |
| 5  Weavers ... ... ... ... ... | — | — | — | 9 | — |
| 6  Knitters ... ... ... ... ... | — | — | — | 9 | — |
| 7  Bleachers, dyers, finishers ... ... ... ... | — | — | — | 9 | — |
| 8  Menders, darners ... ... ... ... ... | — | — | — | 9 | — |
| 9  Other material processing, textiles ... ... ... | — | — | — | 9 | — |
| 087 Textile workers | | | | | |
| 1  Preparatory fibre processors ... ... ... ... | 3 | 4 | 9 | — | 9 |
| 2  Spinners, doublers, twisters ... ... ... ... | 3 | 4 | 9 | — | 9 |
| 3  Winders, reelers ... ... ... ... ... | 3 | 4 | 9 | — | 9 |
| 4  Warp preparers... ... ... ... ... ... | 3 | 4 | 9 | — | 9 |
| 5  Weavers ... ... ... ... ... ... | 3 | 4 | 9 | — | 9 |
| 6  Knitters ... ... ... ... ... ... | 3 | 4 | 9 | — | 9 |
| 7  Bleachers, dyers, finishers ... ... ... | 3 | 4 | 9 | — | 9 |
| 8  Menders, darners ... ... ... ... ... | 3 | 4 | 9 | — | 9 |
| 088 Foremen—chemical processing | | | | | |
| 0  Foremen—chemical processing ... ... ... | — | — | — | 9 | — |
| 089 Chemical, gas and petroleum process plant operators | | | | | |
| 0  Chemical, gas and petroleum process plant operators ... | 3 | 4 | 9 | — | 9 |
| 090 Foremen—food and drink processing | | | | | |
| Foremen— | | | | | |
| 1  Bakers, flour confectioners ... ... ... ... | — | — | — | 9 | — |
| 2  Butchers, meat cutters ... ... ... ... | — | — | — | 9 | — |
| 3  Fishmongers, poultry dressers ... ... ... ... | — | — | — | 9 | — |
| 4  Brewery and vinery process workers ... ... ... | — | — | — | 9 | — |
| Other material processing— | | | | | |
| 5  Bakery and confectionery workers ... ... ... | — | — | — | 9 | — |
| 6  Food and drink n.e.c. ... ... ... ... | — | — | — | 9 | — |
| 091 Bakers, flour confectioners | | | | | |
| 0  Bakers, flour confectioners ... ... ... ... | 3 | 4 | 9 | — | 9 |
| 092 Butchers | | | | | |
| 1  Butchers, meat cutters ... ... ... ... ... | — | — | — | — | 9 |
| 2  Fishmongers, poultry dressers... ... ... ... ... | — | — | — | — | 9 |
| 093 Foremen—paper and board making and paper products | | | | | |
| Foremen— | | | | | |
| 1  Paper, paperboard and leatherboard workers ... ... | — | — | — | 9 | — |
| 2  Bookbinders and finishers ... ... ... | — | — | — | 9 | — |
| 3  Cutting and slitting machine operators (paper and paper products making) ... ... ... ... ... | — | — | — | 9 | — |
| 4  Other material processing, wood and paper ... | — | — | — | 9 | — |
| 5  Other making and repairing, paper goods and printing ... | — | — | — | 9 | — |
| 094 Paper, board and paper product makers, bookbinders | | | | | |
| 1  Paper, paperboard and leatherboard workers ... ... | 3 | 4 | — | — | 9 |
| 2  Bookbinders and finishers ... ... ... ... | 3 | 4 | 9 | — | 9 |
| 3  Cutting and slitting machine operators (paper and paper products making) ... ... ... ... ... ... | — | — | — | — | 9 |
| 095 Foremen—glass, ceramics, rubber, plastics, etc. | | | | | |
| Foremen— | | | | | |
| 1  Glass and ceramics furnacemen, kilnsetters ... ... | — | — | — | 9 | — |
| 2  Glass formers and shapers, finishers, decorators ... | — | — | — | 9 | — |
| 3  Casters and other pottery makers ... ... ... | — | — | — | 9 | — |
| 4  Rubber process workers, moulding machine operators, tyre builders ... | — | — | — | 9 | — |
| 5  Calender and extruding machine operators, moulders (plastics) ... ... ... ... ... ... | — | — | — | 9 | — |
| 6  Man-made fibre makers ... ... ... ... | — | — | — | 9 | — |
| 7  Washers, screeners and crushers in mines and quarries ... | — | — | — | 9 | — |
| Other making and repairing— | | | | | |
| 8  Glass and ceramics ... ... ... ... ... | — | — | — | 9 | — |
| 9  Rubber ... ... ... ... ... ... | — | — | — | 9 | — |
| 10  Plastics ... ... ... ... ... ... | — | — | — | 9 | — |
| 096 Glass and ceramics furnacemen and workers | | | | | |
| 1  Glass and ceramics furnacemen, kilnsetters ... ... | — | — | — | — | 9 |
| 2  Glass formers and shapers, finishers, decorators ... ... | 3 | 4 | 9 | — | 9 |
| 3  Casters and other pottery makers ... ... ... ... | 3 | 4 | 9 | — | 9 |

| Occupation | Self-employed | | Managers | Foremen | Apprentices, etc., Employees n.e.c. |
| --- | --- | --- | --- | --- | --- |
| | with employees | without employees | | | |
| **097 Rubber and plastics workers** | | | | | |
| 1 Rubber process workers, moulding machine operators, tyre builders | 3 | 4 | 9 | — | 9 |
| 2 Calender and extruding machine operators, moulders (plastics) | 3 | 4 | 9 | — | 9 |
| **098 All other in processing materials (other than metal)** | | | | | |
| 1 Man-made fibre makers | — | — | — | — | 9 |
| 2 Brewery and vinery process workers | 3 | 4 | 9 | — | 9 |
| 3 Washers, screeners and crushers in mines and quarries | — | — | — | — | 9 |
| Other material processing— | | | | | |
| 4 Textiles | 3 | 4 | — | — | 9 |
| 5 Bakery and confectionery workers | 3 | 4 | — | — | 9 |
| 6 Tobacco | — | — | — | 9 | 9 |
| 7 Food and drink n.e.c. | 3 | 4 | 9 | — | 9 |
| 8 Wood and paper | 3 | 4 | — | — | 9 |
| 9 All other (excluding metal) n.e.c. | 3 | 4 | — | 9 | 9 |
| **099 Foremen—printing** | | | | | |
| Foremen— | | | | | |
| 1 Compositors | — | — | — | 9 | — |
| 2 Electrotypers, stereotypers, printing plate and cylinder preparers | — | — | — | 9 | — |
| 3 Printing machine minders and assistants | — | — | — | 9 | — |
| 4 Screen and block printers | — | — | — | 9 | — |
| 5 Printers (so described) | — | — | — | 9 | — |
| **100 Printing workers, screen and block printers** | | | | | |
| 1 Compositors | 3 | 4 | 9 | — | 9 |
| 2 Electrotypers, stereotypers, printing plate and cylinder preparers | 3 | 4 | 9 | — | 9 |
| 3 Printing machine minders and assistants | 3 | 4 | — | — | 9 |
| 4 Screen and block printers | 3 | 4 | 9 | — | 9 |
| 5 Printers (so described) | 3 | 4 | 9 | — | 9 |
| **101 Foremen—textile materials working** | | | | | |
| Foremen— | | | | | |
| 1 Tailors, tailoresses, dressmakers | — | — | — | 9 | — |
| 2 Clothing cutters, milliners, furriers | — | — | — | 9 | — |
| 3 Sewers, embroiderers | — | — | — | 9 | — |
| 4 Coach trimmers, upholsterers, mattress makers | — | — | — | 9 | — |
| 5 Carpet fitters | — | — | — | 9 | — |
| 6 Other making and repairing, clothing and related products | — | — | — | 9 | — |
| **102 Tailors, dressmakers and other clothing workers** | | | | | |
| 1 Tailors, tailoresses, dressmakers | 3 | 4 | 9 | — | 9 |
| 2 Clothing cutters, milliners, furriers | 3 | 4 | 9 | — | 9 |
| 3 Sewers, embroiderers | 3 | 4 | — | — | 9 |
| **103 Coach trimmers, upholsterers, mattress makers** | | | | | |
| 0 Coach trimmers, upholsterers, mattress makers | 3 | 4 | 9 | — | 9 |
| **104 Foremen—woodworking** | | | | | |
| Foremen— | | | | | |
| 1 Carpenters, joiners | — | — | — | 9 | — |
| 2 Cabinet makers | — | — | — | 9 | — |
| 3 Case and box makers | — | — | — | 9 | — |
| 4 Pattern makers (moulds) | — | — | — | 9 | — |
| 5 Sawyers, veneer cutters, woodworking machinists | — | — | — | 9 | — |
| 6 Other making and repairing, wood | — | — | — | 9 | — |
| **105 Woodworkers, pattern makers** | | | | | |
| 1 Carpenters, joiners | 3 | 4 | 9 | — | 9 |
| 2 Cabinet makers | 3 | 4 | 9 | — | 9 |
| 3 Case and box makers | 3 | 4 | 9 | — | 9 |
| 4 Pattern makers (moulds) | 3 | 4 | 9 | — | 9 |
| **106 Sawyers, veneer cutters, woodworking machinists** | | | | | |
| 0 Sawyers, veneer cutters, woodworking machinists | 3 | 4 | 9 | — | 9 |
| **107 All other in making and repairing (excluding metal and electrical)** | | | | | |
| 1 Labourers and mates to woodworking craftsmen | — | — | — | — | 10 |
| 2 Dental technicians | 3 | 4 | 9 | 9 | 9 |
| 3 Carpet fitters | 3 | 4 | — | 9 | 9 |
| 4 Musical instrument makers, piano tuners | 3 | 4 | 9 | 9 | 9 |
| Other making and repairing— | | | | | |
| 5 Glass and ceramics | 3 | 4 | — | — | 9 |
| 6 Wood | 3 | 4 | 9 | — | 9 |
| 7 Leather | 3 | 4 | 9 | — | 9 |
| 8 Clothing and related products | 3 | 4 | 9 | — | 9 |
| 9 Paper goods and printing | 3 | 4 | 9 | — | 9 |
| 10 Rubber | 3 | 4 | 9 | — | 9 |
| 11 Plastics | 3 | 4 | 9 | — | 9 |
| 12 All other (excluding metal and electrical) n.e.c. | 3 | 4 | 9 | 9 | 9 |
| **108 Foremen—metal making and treating** | | | | | |
| Foremen— | | | | | |
| 1 Furnace operating occupations (metal) | — | — | — | 9 | — |
| 2 Rollermen | — | — | — | 9 | — |
| 3 Smiths, forgemen | — | — | — | 9 | — |
| 4 Metal drawers | — | — | — | 9 | — |
| 5 Moulders, coremakers, die casters | — | — | — | 9 | — |
| 6 Electroplaters | — | — | — | 9 | — |
| 7 Annealers, hardeners, temperers (metal) | — | — | — | 9 | — |
| 8 Galvanizers, tin platers, dip platers | — | — | — | 9 | — |
| 9 Metal making and treating workers n.e.c. | — | — | — | 9 | — |

| Occupation | Self-employed | | Managers | Foremen | Apprentices, etc., Employees n.e.c. |
| --- | --- | --- | --- | --- | --- |
| | with employees | without employees | | | |
| **109 Furnacemen (metal), rollermen, smiths, forgemen** | | | | | |
| 1 Furnace operating occupations (metal) | 3 | 4 | — | — | 9 |
| 2 Rollermen | 3 | 4 | 9 | — | 9 |
| 3 Smiths, forgemen | 3 | 4 | 9 | — | 9 |
| **110 Metal drawers, moulders, die casters, electroplaters, annealers** | | | | | |
| 1 Metal drawers | 3 | 4 | — | — | 9 |
| 2 Moulders, coremakers, die casters | 3 | 4 | — | — | 9 |
| 3 Electroplaters | 3 | 4 | 9 | — | 9 |
| 4 Annealers, hardeners, temperers (metal) | 3 | 4 | — | — | 9 |
| **111 Foremen—engineering machining** | | | | | |
| Foremen— | | | | | |
| 1 Press and machine tool setters | — | — | — | 9 | — |
| 2 Centre lathe turners | — | — | — | 9 | — |
| 3 Machine tool setter operators | — | — | — | 9 | — |
| 4 Machine tool operators | — | — | — | 9 | — |
| 5 Press, stamping and automatic machine operators | — | — | — | 9 | — |
| 6 Metal polishers | — | — | — | 9 | — |
| 7 Fettlers, dressers | — | — | — | 9 | — |
| 8 Shot blasters | — | — | — | 9 | — |
| **112 Press and machine tool setter operators and operators, turners** | | | | | |
| 1 Press and machine tool setters | 3 | 4 | 9 | — | 9 |
| 2 Centre lathe turners | 3 | 4 | 9 | — | 9 |
| 3 Machine tool setter operators | 3 | 4 | 9 | — | 9 |
| 4 Machine tool operators | 3 | 4 | — | — | 9 |
| **113 Machine attendants, minders, press and stamping machine operators, metal polishers, fettlers, dressers** | | | | | |
| 1 Press, stamping and automatic machine operators | 3 | 4 | 9 | — | 9 |
| 2 Metal polishers | 3 | 4 | 9 | — | 9 |
| 3 Fettlers, dressers | 3 | 4 | — | — | 9 |
| **114 Foremen—production fitting (metal)** | | | | | |
| Foremen— | | | | | |
| 1 Tool makers, tool fitters, markers-out | — | — | — | 9 | — |
| 2 Precision instrument makers and repairers | — | — | — | 9 | — |
| 3 Watch and chronometer makers and repairers | — | — | — | 9 | — |
| 4 Metal working production fitters and fitter/machinists | — | — | — | 9 | — |
| 5 Motor mechanics, auto engineers | — | — | — | 9 | — |
| 6 Maintenance fitters (aircraft engines) | — | — | — | 9 | — |
| 7 Office machinery mechanics | — | — | — | 9 | — |
| **115 Tool makers, tool fitters, markers-out** | | | | | |
| 0 Tool makers, tool fitters, markers-out | 3 | 4 | 9 | — | 9 |
| **116 Instrument and watch and clock makers and repairers** | | | | | |
| 1 Precision instrument makers and repairers | 3 | 4 | 9 | — | 9 |
| 2 Watch and chronometer makers and repairers | 3 | 4 | 9 | — | 9 |
| **117 Metal working production fitters and fitter/machinists** | | | | | |
| 0 Metal working production fitters and fitter/machinists | 3 | 4 | 9 | — | 9 |
| **118 Motor vehicle and aircraft mechanics** | | | | | |
| 1 Motor mechanics, auto engineers | 3 | 4 | 9 | — | 9 |
| 2 Maintenance fitters (aircraft engines) | — | 4 | — | — | 9 |
| **119 Office machinery mechanics** | | | | | |
| 0 Office machinery mechanics | 3 | 4 | 9 | — | 9 |
| **120 Foremen—production fitting and wiring (electrical)** | | | | | |
| Foremen— | | | | | |
| 1 Production fitters (electrical, electronic) | — | — | — | 9 | — |
| 2 Electricians, electrical maintenance fitters | — | — | — | 9 | — |
| 3 Plant operators and attendants n.e.c. | — | — | — | 9 | — |
| 4 Telephone fitters | — | — | — | 9 | — |
| 5 Cable jointers, linesmen | — | — | — | 9 | — |
| 6 Radio and TV mechanics | — | — | — | 9 | — |
| 7 Other electronic maintenance engineers | — | — | — | 9 | — |
| **121 Production fitters, electricians, electricity power plant operators, switchboard attendants** | | | | | |
| 1 Production fitters (electrical, electronic) | 3 | 4 | 9 | — | 9 |
| 2 Electricians, electrical maintenance fitters | 3 | 4 | 9 | — | 9 |
| 3 Electrical engineers (so described) | 3 | 4 | 9 | — | 9 |
| 4 Plant operators and attendants n.e.c. | — | — | — | — | 9 |
| **122 Telephone fitters, cable jointers, linesmen** | | | | | |
| 1 Telephone fitters | — | 4 | — | — | 9 |
| 2 Cable jointers, linesmen | — | 4 | — | — | 9 |
| **123 Radio, TV and other electronic maintenance fitters and mechanics** | | | | | |
| 1 Radio and TV mechanics | 3 | 4 | 9 | — | 9 |
| 2 Other electronic maintenance engineers | 3 | 4 | 9 | — | 9 |
| **124 Foremen—metal working, pipes, sheets, structures** | | | | | |
| Foremen— | | | | | |
| 1 Plumbers, heating and ventilating fitters, gas fitters | — | — | — | 9 | — |
| 2 Sheet metal workers | — | — | — | 9 | — |
| 3 Metal plate workers, shipwrights, riveters | — | — | — | 9 | — |
| 4 Steel erectors, benders, fixers | — | — | — | 9 | — |
| 5 Scaffolders, stagers | — | — | — | 9 | — |
| 6 Welders | — | — | — | 9 | — |
| 7 Riggers | — | — | — | 9 | — |

| Occupation | Self-employed | | Managers | Foremen | Apprentices, etc., Employees n.e.c. |
| --- | --- | --- | --- | --- | --- |
| | with employees | without employees | | | |
| **125** Plumbers, heating and ventilating fitters, gas fitters | | | | | |
|   0 Plumbers, heating and ventilating fitters, gas fitters... ... | 3 | 4 | 9 | — | 9 |
| **126** Sheet metal workers, platers, shipwrights, riveters, etc. | | | | | |
|   1 Sheet metal workers ... ... ... ... ... | 3 | 4 | 9 | — | 9 |
|   2 Metal plate workers, shipwrights, riveters ... ... ... | 3 | 4 | 9 | | 9 |
| **127** Steel erectors, scaffolders, steel benders, fixers | | | | | |
|   1 Steel erectors, benders, fixers ... ... ... ... | 3 | 4 | 9 | — | 9 |
|   2 Scaffolders, stagers ... ... ... ... ... | 3 | 4 | — | — | 9 |
| **128** Welders | | | | | |
|   0 Welders ... ... ... ... ... ... | 3 | 4 | 9 | — | 9 |
| **129** Foremen—other processing, making and repairing (metal and electrical) | | | | | |
|   Foremen— | | | | | |
|   1 Goldsmiths, silversmiths, precious stone workers... ... | — | — | — | 9 | — |
|   2 Engravers, etchers (printing) ... ... ... ... | — | — | — | 9 | — |
|   3 Coach and vehicle body builders ... ... ... ... | — | — | — | 9 | — |
|   4 Oilers, greasers, lubricators ... ... ... ... | — | — | — | 9 | — |
|   5 Electronics wiremen ... ... ... ... ... | — | — | — | 9 | — |
|   6 Coil winders ... ... ... ... ... ... | — | — | — | 9 | — |
| **130** Goldsmiths, silversmiths, etc., engravers, etchers | | | | | |
|   1 Goldsmiths, silversmiths, precious stone workers ... | 3 | 4 | 9 | — | 9 |
|   2 Engravers, etchers (printing) ... ... ... ... | 3 | 4 | — | — | 9 |
| **131** All other in processing, making and repairing (metal and electrical) | | | | | |
|   1 Coach and vehicle body builders ... ... ... ... | 3 | 4 | 9 | — | 9 |
|   2 Galvanizers, tin platers, dip platers ... ... ... | 3 | 4 | — | — | 9 |
|   3 Metal making and treating workers n.e.c. ... ... | 3 | 4 | — | — | 9 |
|   4 Oilers, greasers, lubricators ... ... ... ... | — | — | — | — | 9 |
|   5 Riggers ... ... ... ... ... ... | 3 | 4 | 9 | — | 9 |
|   6 Electronics wiremen ... ... ... ... ... | — | 4 | — | — | 9 |
|   7 Coil winders ... ... ... ... ... ... | 3 | 4 | 9 | — | 9 |
|   8 Shot blasters ... ... ... ... ... ... | — | — | — | — | 9 |
|   9 Other metal, jewellery, electrical production workers ... | 3 | 4 | 9 | 9 | 9 |
|   — | | | | | |
|   1 Foremen (engineering and allied trades) ... ... | — | — | — | 9 | — |
|   2 Trainee craftsmen (engineering and allied trades) ... ... | — | — | — | — | 9 |
| **132** Foremen—painting and similar coating | | | | | |
|   Foremen— | | | | | |
|   1 Pottery decorators ... ... ... ... ... | — | — | — | 9 | — |
|   2 Coach painters (so described) ... ... ... ... | — | — | — | 9 | — |
|   3 Other spray painters... ... ... ... ... | — | — | — | 9 | — |
|   4 Painters and decorators n.e.c., french polishers ... ... | — | — | — | 9 | — |
| **133** Painters, decorators, french polishers | | | | | |
|   1 Pottery decorators ... ... ... ... ... | 3 | 4 | — | — | 9 |
|   2 Coach painters (so described) ... ... ... ... | 3 | 4 | 9 | — | 9 |
|   3 Other spray painters ... ... ... ... ... | 3 | 4 | 9 | — | 9 |
|   4 Painters and decorators n.e.c., french polishers ... ... | 3 | 4 | 9 | — | 9 |
| **134** Foremen—product assembling (repetitive) | | | | | |
|   Foremen assemblers— | | | | | |
|   1 Electrical, electronic... ... ... ... ... | — | — | — | 9 | — |
|   2 Instruments ... ... ... ... ... ... | — | — | — | 9 | — |
|   3 Vehicles and other metal goods ... ... ... ... | — | — | — | 9 | — |
|   4 Paper production, processing and printing ... ... | — | — | — | 9 | — |
|   5 Plastics goods ... ... ... ... ... | — | — | — | 9 | — |
| **135** Repetitive assemblers (metal and electrical goods) | | | | | |
|   1 Assemblers (electrical, electronic) ... ... ... ... | 3 | 4 | — | — | 9 |
|   2 Instrument assemblers ... ... ... ... ... | — | 4 | — | — | 9 |
|   3 Assemblers (vehicle and other metal goods) ... ... | — | 4 | — | — | 9 |
| **136** Foremen—product inspection and packaging | | | | | |
|   Foremen inspectors, viewers, examiners— | | | | | |
|   1 Metal, electrical goods ... ... ... ... | — | — | — | 9 | — |
|   2 Textiles ... ... ... ... ... ... | — | — | — | 9 | — |
|   3 Food ... ... ... ... ... ... | — | — | — | 9 | — |
|   4 Rubber goods ... ... ... ... ... | — | — | — | 9 | — |
|   5 Plastics goods ... ... ... ... ... | — | — | — | 9 | — |
|   6 Woodwork ... ... ... ... ... ... | — | — | — | 9 | — |
|   Foremen— | | | | | |
|   7 Packers, bottlers, canners, fillers ... ... ... | — | — | — | 9 | — |
|   8 Laboratory assistants ... ... ... ... ... | — | — | — | 9 | — |
|   9 Inspectors, sorters in paper production, processing and printing ... ... ... ... ... ... | — | — | — | 9 | — |
|   10 Weighers ... ... ... ... ... ... | — | — | — | 9 | — |
|   11 Graders, sorters, selectors n.e.c. ... ... ... | — | — | — | 9 | — |
| **137** Inspectors, viewers, testers, packers, bottlers, etc. | | | | | |
|   1 Inspectors, viewers (metal, electrical goods) ... ... ... | — | 4 | — | — | 9 |
|   2 Packers, bottlers, canners, fillers ... ... ... | 3 | 4 | — | — | 9 |

| Occupation | Self-employed | | Managers | Foremen | Apprentices, etc., Employees n.e.c. |
| --- | --- | --- | --- | --- | --- |
| | with employees | without employees | | | |
| **138** All other in painting, repetitive assembling, product inspection, packaging and related | | | | | |
| 1    Laboratory assistants ... ... ... ... ... ... | — | — | — | — | 9 |
|      Inspectors, viewers, examiners— | | | | | |
| 2    Textiles ... ... ... ... ... ... ... | — | — | — | — | 9 |
| 3    Food ... ... ... ... ... ... ... ... | — | — | — | — | 9 |
| 4    Rubber goods ... ... ... ... ... ... | — | — | — | — | 9 |
| 5    Plastics goods ... ... ... ... ... ... | — | — | — | — | 9 |
| 6    Woodwork ... ... ... ... ... ... | — | — | — | — | 9 |
| 7    Inspectors, sorters in paper production, processing and printing ... ... ... ... ... ... | — | — | — | — | 9 |
| 8    Assemblers in paper production, processing and printing | — | 4 | — | — | 9 |
| 9    Assemblers (plastics goods) ... ... ... ... ... | — | — | — | — | 9 |
| 10    Weighers ... ... ... ... ... ... ... | — | — | — | — | 9 |
| 11    Graders, sorters, selectors n.e.c. ... ... ... | — | — | — | — | 9 |
| 12    Painting, assembling and related occupations n.e.c. ... | 3 | 4 | 9 | 9 | 9 |
| **139** Foremen—building and civil engineering n.e.c. | | | | | |
|      Foremen— | | | | | |
| 1    Bricklayers, tile setters ... ... ... ... ... | — | — | — | 9 | — |
| 2    Masons, stone cutters ... ... ... ... ... | — | — | — | 9 | — |
| 3    Plasterers ... ... ... ... ... ... ... | — | — | — | 9 | — |
| 4    Roofers, glaziers ... ... ... ... ... | — | — | — | 9 | — |
| 5    Handymen, general building workers ... ... ... | — | — | — | 9 | — |
| 6    Railway lengthmen ... ... ... ... ... | — | — | — | 9 | — |
| 7    Road surfacers, concreters ... ... ... ... | — | — | — | 9 | — |
| 8    Roadmen ... ... ... ... ... ... ... | — | — | — | 9 | — |
| 9    Paviors, kerb layers ... ... ... ... ... | — | — | — | 9 | — |
| 10    Sewage plant attendants ... ... ... ... | — | — | — | 9 | — |
| 11    Mains and service layers, pipe jointers ... ... ... | — | — | — | 9 | — |
| 12    Construction workers n.e.c. ... ... ... ... | — | — | — | 9 | — |
| **140** Building and construction workers | | | | | |
| 1    Bricklayers, tile setters ... ... ... ... ... | 3 | 4 | 9 | — | 9 |
| 2    Masons, stone cutters ... ... ... ... ... | 3 | 4 | 9 | — | 9 |
| 3    Plasterers ... ... ... ... ... ... ... | 3 | 4 | 9 | — | 9 |
| 4    Roofers, glaziers ... ... ... ... ... | 3 | 4 | 9 | — | 9 |
| 5    Handymen, general building workers... ... ... ... | 3 | 4 | 9 | — | 9 |
| 6    Builders (so described) ... ... ... ... ... | 3 | 4 | 9 | — | 9 |
| **141** Concreters, road surfacers, railway lengthmen | | | | | |
| 1    Railway lengthmen ... ... ... ... ... | — | — | — | — | 10 |
| 2    Road surfacers, concreters ... ... ... ... ... | — | 4 | — | — | 9 |
| 3    Roadmen ... ... ... ... ... ... ... | 3 | 4 | — | — | 9 |
| 4    Paviors, kerb layers ... ... ... ... ... | 3 | 4 | — | — | 9 |
| **142** Sewage plant attendants, sewermen (maintenance), mains and service layers, pipe jointers (gas, water, drainage, oil), inspectors (water supply), turncocks | | | | | |
| 1    Sewage plant attendants ... ... ... ... | — | — | — | — | 9 |
| 2    Mains and service layers, pipe jointers ... ... ... | 3 | 4 | — | — | 9 |
| **143** Civil engineering labourers, craftsmen's mates and other builders' labourers n.e.c. | | | | | |
| 1    Craftsmen's mates ... ... ... ... ... | 3 | 4 | — | 9 | 9 |
| 2    Building and civil engineering labourers ... ... ... | 3 | 4 | — | 10 | 10 |
| **144** Foremen/deputies—coalmining | | | | | |
| 0    Foremen/deputies—coalmining ... ... ... ... | — | — | — | 9 | — |
| **145** Face-trained coalmining workers | | | | | |
| 0    Face-trained coalmining workers ... ... ... ... | 3 | 4 | — | — | 9 |
| **146** All other in construction, mining, quarrying, well drilling and related n.e.c. | | | | | |
| 1    Miners (not coal), quarrymen, well drillers ... ... ... | 3 | 4 | 9 | 9 | 9 |
| 2    Construction workers n.e.c. ... ... ... ... ... | 3 | 4 | 9 | — | 9 |
| **147** Foremen—ships, lighters and other vessels | | | | | |
| 0    Foremen—ships, lighters and other vessels ... ... ... | — | — | — | 11 | — |
| **148** Deck, engine-room hands, bargemen, lightermen, boatmen | | | | | |
| 0    Deck, engine-room hands, bargemen, lightermen, boatmen | 3 | 4 | — | — | 9 |
| **149** Foremen—rail transport operating | | | | | |
|      Foremen— | | | | | |
| 1    Railway guards ... ... ... ... ... ... | — | — | — | 11 | — |
| 2    Signalmen and crossing keepers, railway ... ... ... | — | — | — | 11 | — |
| 3    Shunters, pointsmen... ... ... ... ... | — | — | — | 11 | — |
| 4    Other foremen rail transport ... ... ... ... | — | — | — | 11 | — |
| **150** Rail transport operating staff | | | | | |
| 1    Drivers, motormen, secondmen, railway engines ... ... | — | — | — | — | 9 |
| 2    Railway guards ... ... ... ... ... ... | — | — | — | — | 12 |
| 3    Signalmen and crossing keepers, railway ... ... ... | — | — | — | — | 9 |
| 4    Shunters, pointsmen ... ... ... ... ... | — | — | — | — | 9 |
| **151** Foremen—road transport operating, bus inspectors | | | | | |
| 1    Bus inspectors ... ... ... ... ... ... | — | — | — | 11 | — |
|      Foremen— | | | | | |
| 2    Drivers of road goods vehicles ... ... ... ... | — | — | — | 11 | — |
| 3    Other foremen road transport ... ... ... ... | — | — | — | 11 | — |
| **152** Bus, coach, lorry drivers, etc. | | | | | |
| 1    Bus and coach drivers ... ... ... ... ... | 3 | 4 | 9 | — | 9 |
| 2    Drivers of road goods vehicles... ... ... ... ... | 3 | 4 | 9 | — | 9 |
| 3    Other motor drivers ... ... ... ... ... | 3 | 4 | 9 | — | 9 |

| Occupation | Self-employed | | Managers | Foremen | Apprentices, etc., Employees n.e.c. |
| --- | --- | --- | --- | --- | --- |
| | with employees | without employees | | | |
| **153** Bus conductors, drivers' mates | | | | | |
| 1    Bus conductors ... ... ... ... ... ... ... | — | 4 | — | — | 12 |
| 2    Drivers' mates ... ... ... ... ... ... ... | — | — | — | — | 10 |
| **154** Foremen—civil engineering plant operating, materials handling equipment operating | | | | | |
|    Foremen— | | | | | |
| 1    Mechanical plant drivers, operators (earth moving and civil engineering) ... ... ... ... ... ... ... | — | — | — | 9 | — |
| 2    Crane drivers, operators ... ... ... ... ... | — | — | — | 9 | — |
| 3    Fork lift, mechanical truck drivers ... ... ... | — | — | — | 9 | — |
| 4    Slingers ... ... ... ... ... ... ... | — | — | — | 9 | — |
| **155** Mechanical plant, fork lift, mechanical truck drivers, crane drivers, operators | | | | | |
| 1    Mechanical plant drivers, operators (earth moving and civil engineering) ... ... ... ... ... ... ... | 3 | 4 | 9 | — | 9 |
| 2    Crane divers, operators ... ... ... ... ... | — | — | — | — | 9 |
| 3    Fork lift, mechanical truck drivers ... ... ... | — | 4 | — | — | 9 |
| **156** Foremen—materials moving and storing | | | | | |
|    Foremen— | | | | | |
| 1    Storekeepers, warehousemen ... ... ... ... | — | — | — | 11 | — |
| 2    Stevedores, dockers ... ... ... ... ... ... | — | — | — | 9 | — |
| 3    Goods porters ... ... ... ... ... ... | — | — | — | 9 | — |
| 4    Refuse collectors, dustmen ... ... ... ... | — | — | — | 10 | — |
| **157** Storekeepers, stevedores, warehouse, market and other goods porters | | | | | |
| 1    Storekeepers, warehousemen ... ... ... ... ... | 3 | 4 | 12 | — | 12 |
| 2    Stevedores, dockers ... ... ... ... ... ... | 3 | 4 | — | — | 9 |
| 3    Goods porters ... ... ... ... ... ... | 3 | 4 | 9 | — | 9 |
| 4    Refuse collectors, dustmen ... ... ... ... ... | — | — | — | — | 10 |
| **158** All other in transport operating, materials moving and storing and related n.e.c. | | | | | |
| 1    Slingers ... ... ... ... ... ... ... | — | — | — | — | 9 |
| 2    Workers in transport operating, materials moving and storing and related n.e.c. ... ... ... ... ... ... | 3 | 4 | — | 9 | 9 |
| **159** Foremen—miscellaneous | | | | | |
|    Foremen— | | | | | |
|    Labourers and unskilled workers n.e.c.— | | | | | |
| 1    Textiles (not textile goods) ... ... ... ... | — | — | — | 10 | — |
| 2    Chemicals and allied trades ... ... ... ... | — | — | — | 10 | — |
| 3    Coke ovens and gas works ... ... ... ... | — | — | — | 10 | — |
| 4    Glass and ceramics ... ... ... ... ... | — | — | — | 10 | — |
| 5    Foundries in engineering and allied trades ... ... | — | — | — | 10 | — |
| 6    Engineering and allied trades ... ... ... ... | — | — | — | 10 | — |
| 7    Coal mines ... ... ... ... ... ... ... | — | — | — | 10 | — |
| 8    Other ... ... ... ... ... ... ... | — | — | — | 10 | — |
| 9    Boiler operators ... ... ... ... ... ... | — | — | — | 9 | — |
| **160** General labourers | | | | | |
|    Labourers and unskilled workers n.e.c.— | | | | | |
| 1    Textiles (not textile goods) ... ... ... ... | — | — | — | — | 10 |
| 2    Chemicals and allied trades ... ... ... ... | — | — | — | — | 10 |
| 3    Coke ovens and gas works ... ... ... ... | — | — | — | — | 10 |
| 4    Glass and ceramics ... ... ... ... ... | — | — | — | — | 10 |
| 5    Foundries in engineering and allied trades ... ... | — | — | — | — | 10 |
| 6    Engineering and allied trades ... ... ... ... | — | — | — | — | 10 |
| 7    Coal mines ... ... ... ... ... ... ... | — | — | — | — | 10 |
| 8    Other ... ... ... ... ... ... ... | 3 | 4 | — | — | 10 |
| **161** All other in miscellaneous occupations n.e.c. | | | | | |
| 1    Boiler operators ... ... ... ... ... ... | — | — | — | — | 9 |
| 2    All other in miscellaneous occupations n.e.c. ... ... | 3 | 4 | — | 9 | 9 |
| **—** | | | | | |
| 1    Inadequately described occupations ... ... ... ... | 14 | 14 | 14 | 14 | 14 |
| 2    Occupations not stated ... ... ... ... ... | — | — | — | — | 14 |

# CODING INDEX

## Notes on coding

The three digit codes used in the alphabetical index are an operational series of numbers only and must be used in combination with employment status to achieve allocation to the occupation groups. Four employment statuses, self-employed, manager, foremen and others are necessary. The derivation of the occupation group from the index number and employment status is shown in Appendix G.

## Description of the index

**General.** Occupation titles are arranged in this index under the word most nearly describing the operation performed,

> e.g. 'glass blower' is indexed under 'Blower'
>
> 'x-ray operator' is indexed under 'Operator'

For this purpose words such as 'assistant' and 'officer' are regarded as indexing words but the following terms are not:

| | | | | |
|---|---|---|---|---|
| Boy | Girl | Hand | Lad | Man |
| Operative | Woman | Workman | Worker | |

> e.g. 'errand boy' is indexed under 'Errand' but
>
> 'clerical officer' is indexed under 'Officer'

The index is arranged in alphabetical order of complete words. Words joined by a hyphen are treated as single words. Words joined by 'and' are indexed immediately following the single words. Occupational titles ending in any of the terms listed above are regarded for indexing purposes as two words, e.g. 'bagman' is indexed as though it were 'bag man' and therefore appears before 'bagger' in the index.

Compound words, such as 'postmaster', the final word of which may be used as an occupation title, are indexed under the final word, e.g. Master; post, Keeper; book. Some very common terms have also been indexed in their natural order.

The feminine form of an occupation title is not indexed unless it is very common or its coding differs from that of the masculine equivalent thus 'abbot' is indexed but not 'abbess'.

Three letters appear in the index against code numbers, of these 'M' and 'F' relate to employment status coding, see page 5. The letter 'L' indicates that the person is a labourer and that any of the codes 339–346 can be applied to this occupation depending on the industry of the establishment in which it is carried out. The quoted code should be used when the industry cannot be determined.

> e.g. *Index entry*      Ash man    ...    ...    ...    ...    L346
>
> *Occupation statement*    Ash man (cotton spinning mill)    code 339
>
> *Occupation statement*    Ash man (paint manufacturers)    code 340
>
> *Occupation statement*    Ash man    ...    ...    ...    ...code 346

### Qualifying terms

(*a*) The word used for indexing purposes is very rarely sufficient in itself to enable the occupation title to be correctly coded.

Frequently a term is made specific by the addition of a qualifying term, e.g. 'turner' may be specified by 'brass' and then becomes codable. These qualifying terms are entered in the index after the index word and separated from it by a semi-colon. The qualified terms may be used to code not only the specific term shown but also that term further qualified (unless the further qualification is itself indexed). Thus the index entry 'Controller; depot' could be used to code 'freight depot controller'.

An occupational title may be qualified by a clause following the word used for indexing purposes as, for example, 'Clerk in Holy Orders'. These terms are indexed at the end of the list of specifically qualified terms. As these terms are usually very specific, special care is necessary in coding any such term not actually in the index.

(*b*) An occupational title may depend for its coding on the branch of industry in which the person is employed. The industrial qualifications (which relate to the activity actually engaged in and not that of the establishment as a whole) appear in the index in italics. The term so qualified is followed by a dash, or alternatively, a single qualification may appear in brackets. These entries may be used to code occupational titles where the industry is part of the title, or may be inferred from it, unless an index entry as described in (*a*) or (*c*) is relevant, e.g. the index entry 'Furnacemen—*metal trades*' can be used to code 'furnaceman'—industry 'steelworks', 'blast furnace furnaceman' or 'steel furnaceman'.

(*c*) In a small number of cases the qualification for coding purposes is more easily stated in terms of materials worked on or dealt in, or the machinery used, or process involved and this enables a number of specific terms to be summarised by stating the specific qualification in a more general form. This type of qualification appears immediately preceding the industrial qualifications e.g. 'Turner—metal' (which would apply to titles 'aluminium turner' or 'lead turner', or in a limited number of cases indented below an industrial qualification e.g. 'Machinist—*hosiery mfr.*—sewing'.

(*d*) Where a code number appears against an index word that code applies to all occupation titles which include the index word unless they are listed specifically, generally or industrially as exceptions. Thus, referring to 'Smith' on page 95 of the index, all 'Smiths', e.g. blacksmith, hammersmith, are coded 233 except for those different codes in the list starting with boilersmith.

(*e*) Occupation titles qualified by terms such as 'assistant', 'head', 'deputy', 'apprentice' are normally coded as though the qualification did not exist. If, however, the coding is altered by the qualification the complete title is indexed but these entries only apply in the industry shown. If no industry is given in the index this means either that the particular term is only used in one industry or that this title is to be so coded in all industries.

(*f*) The letters n.o.s. stand for 'not otherwise specified'. When used in the index they mean that the particular index entry relates to that precise occupational term without further qualification.

**Industrial qualifications.** It must be noted, that it is the activity in which the person is actually engaged and not that of the establishment as a whole which is the determining factor. Thus a person in the cardboard box making department of a food factory must be referred in the index to 'cardboard box manufacture' and not 'food products manufacture'. N.B. This does not apply to persons coded as labourers to codes 339–346 for which see page 1.

The abbreviation 'mfr.' is used to cover manufacture, manufacturing, making, building and repairing.

The following Industrial terms are used in a special sense:

| Term | SIC Activity Heading |
|---|---|
| *Manufacturing* | 2210–2247, 2410–4959 |
| *Metal trades* | 2210–2247, 3111–3740 |
| *Clothing mfr.* | 4531–4536, 4539 |
| *Ceramic mfr.* | 2410, 2481, 2489 |
| *Paper goods mfr.* | 4721–4728 |
| *Engineering* | 3204–3740 |
| *Food products mfr.* | 4115, 4121–4180, 4213, 4221–4239 |
| *Glass mfr.* | 2471–2479 and the grinding of lenses and prisms from 3731–3733 |
| *Flour confectionery mfr.* | 4196, 4197 |
| *Sugar confectionery mfr.* | 4214 |
| *Mine, not coal* | 1300, 2100, 2310–2396 |

*Shipping* means service afloat other than in barges, small boats, fishing vessels, launches and dredgers.

*Fishing* means service afloat in a vessel actually engaged in fishing, not a factory ship or tender.

*Boat, barge* means service afloat in a boat, barge, launch, dredger or hopper and excludes service in a fishing vessel.

## Notes on coding occupations

### A. General

**Use of the index.** Occupational titles, unless consisting of an indexing word only, are coded by first referring to the list of specific terms and then using the generalised or industrially qualified entries in the sense indicated in sub-paragraphs (*b*) and (*c*) on page 2.

**Armed forces.** The more usual terms for forces personnel have been included because it is necessary to make a distinction between officers and other ranks. Officers will be given the employment status of manager. There are two codes to separate UK armed forces (135) from those of foreign and Commonwealth countries (136).

**Diplomatic personnel.** Members of foreign or Commonwealth diplomatic staffs are coded 020.

**Persons looking for work.** Persons looking for work without stated occupation are coded 350.

**Coal miners.** The correct coding of many occupational titles in the coal mining industry is dependent on whether the person is a face-trained coal miner. If sufficient information is given the occupation is coded according to the index; if the occupation title is vague but there is a statement indicating working at the coal face the occupation is coded to 314. Where this cannot be determined code 345 is used.

**Foreman**

(*a*) The following terms with certain listed exceptions may be regarded as synonymous with 'Foreman':

| | | |
|---|---|---|
| Boss | Gaffer | Overlooker |
| Charge hand | Ganger | Overseer |
| Charge man | Headman | Supervisor |

and also assistant foreman, assistant supervisor, etc.

(*b*) No index entries have been made for foreman over particular groups of workers, e.g. 'foreman of labourers', or for foremen whose title included a specific occupation, e.g. 'foreman carpenter', as these are coded to the group appropriate to the people supervised or the occupation stated, i.e. as labourer and carpenter respectively.

(*c*) If the entry to be coded is not for a foreman, supervisor, etc. over a particular occupation the index is first referred to under the particular term, e.g. supervisor, and if not found there, is referred to 'Foreman' in the index.

(*d*) Works foremen, general foremen and senior foremen in manufacturing although allocated to group 091 keep the employment status of foremen.

**Conventional codings.** Many terms frequently used for describing occupations cannot be coded without further information either as to materials worked with or the industry in which the occupation is followed. It is necessary, therefore, to assign arbitrary codes for these occupational statements on the basis of the most probable occupation. The most common cases and the codes assigned are listed separately. In any case not listed the most probable code is assigned so long as there is a reasonable chance of correct coding (a knowledge of local industries may be of assistance in this respect). Where no such chance of correct coding exists, as for example, with statements such as 'Foreman' or 'Manager', without industry information, or 'Workman', code 349 is used; but where no statement of occupation is given code 350 is used.

### B. Treatment of terms referred from the index

(1) **Apprentice**
**Articled clerk**
**Articled pupil**
**Graduate apprentice**
**Management trainee**
**Student apprentice**
**Learner**
**Trainee**
**Trainee craftsman**
**Trainee technician**

All persons in training for an occupation or profession are coded to the occupation or profession for which they are training. Where it is not possible to determine the precise occupation for which they are in training the following conventions are applied:

unspecified apprentices or trainee craftsmen (so described) generally coded 230 but in Industry 'metal trades' coded 278

3

$$\left.\begin{array}{l}\text{student apprentices} \quad \dots \quad \dots \quad \dots \\ \text{graduate apprentices} \quad \dots \quad \dots \end{array}\right\} \text{ coded } 076$$

management trainees ... ... coded 111

**Students** in educational establishments are coded to Economic position 'Student' and excluded from the classification by occupation. An apprenticeship training school is not regarded as an educational establishment for this purpose.

**Improver.** The term 'improver' is sometimes used as a synonym for apprentice, e.g. 'fitter's improver', for 'apprentice fitter', and is coded accordingly.

(2) **Chairman.** Apart from the industry of glass blowing a chairman is regarded as a 'company chairman' and coded as a 'Company Director' (see note (5)).

(3) **Checker.** A large number of checkers are listed in the index. Checkers not included in the index are coded as follows: if they appear to be checking articles they are coded to the 'not elsewhere classified' group, or, if metal goods, to code 286. Thus a checker of textiles is coded 289 and a checker of rubber goods 291. Unspecified checkers are coded as above in manufacturing industries and to code 299 otherwise.

(4) **Clerk.** It is not practicable to list all the various chief clerks such as 'chief accounts clerk', 'chief claims clerk'. Except as shown in the index, clerks coded 115 retain this code when qualified by 'chief' but take Employment status code 'Foreman' unless employed in central and local government, in which case codes 021 or 022 respectively apply.

(5) **Director/Company Director.** Directors with specific titles, e.g. sales director, are coded as shown in the index. Unspecified directors, company directors and company chairmen are coded as follows:

(*a*)   If another occupation is stated or professional qualifications are shown they are coded to the appropriate occupation or profession. If not then:

(*b*)   (i)   If a single company is shown they are coded as a 'manager' in the appropriate industry.

   (ii)   If no company or more than one company is shown they are coded to group 111.

(6) **Engineer.** The term engineer presents difficulty because it is commonly used in such a variety of circumstances. The index provides for the coding of various specific engineers but even with these terms doubt often exists as to whether the person is of professional status. If the specific title is prefixed by the terms professional, chartered, administrative, advisory, chief, commissioning, consultant, consulting, design, designing, development, research, senior, superintending, or if membership of a professional institution is stated, e.g. AMIEE, it is assumed that the person is a professional engineer. In cases of doubt the person is regarded as non-professional.

Persons returned simply as 'engineers' or 'mechanical engineers' without any indication of professional status (see preceding paragraph) are coded to group 241. There are, however, a few industries in which these terms are commonly used in a specific sense and these exceptions are listed in the index under 'Engineer; n.o.s.'. Similarly code 254 covers all electrical engineers with the exceptions listed in the index under 'Engineer; electrical; n.o.s.'.

(7) **Instructor/Lecturer/Teacher/Tutor.**

(*a*)   In educational establishments—are coded 031, 032, 033 depending on whether the establishment is a university, further education establishment, or primary or secondary school. The term further education establishment encompasses colleges of education, technical colleges and colleges of technology.

(*b*)   Elsewhere—are coded 033 unless considered vocational and industrial trainers, teaching occupational skills—who are coded 034.
Driving instructors giving tuition for driving private motor vehicles are coded 052.

(*c*)   Teachers of physical training and teachers of recreational subjects, at evening institutes and other similar establishments, also private tutors, including private music teachers and dancing teachers are coded 053.

(8) **Jeweller.** An attempt is made to distinguish between jewellers engaged in manufacture or repair, proper to code 266, and those wholesaling or retailing only, proper to code 101. If the distinction cannot be made code 101 is used.

(9) **Journeyman.** The term 'journeyman' is ignored in coding occupations except that, where doubt exists as to whether an occupation is in manufacture or distribution, as, for example, 'Confectioner', the term journeyman may be taken as implying manufacture. If no other occupation is stated persons so returned are coded 349.

(10) **Leading hand.** If another occupation is stated code to that occupation e.g. 'Plater; chrome' is used to code 'leading hand, chrome plater'. Where no other occupation is stated refer to index entries 'Leading hand—'.

(11) **Manager.** The general principles involved in coding managers are given on page vii. Persons managing a professional activity, such as the manager of a firm of consulting engineers or of the research department of a firm, are coded to their appropriate professions.

All managers are coded in accordance with the industry appropriate to the branch of the establishment in which they are employed and not necessarily the industry of the establishment as a whole. Thus all 'office managers' are coded to occupation group 099, 'sales managers' to group 013 and 'transport managers' to group 095 irrespective of the main activity of the establishment.

The following terms may be regarded as synonymous with 'Manager':

| | |
|---|---|
| Assistant Manager | Mill Manager |
| Under Manager | Works Manager |
| Departmental Manager | Factory Superintendent |
| Factory Manager | Works Superintendent |
| General Manager | Managing Director |
| Chairman | |
| Director | But see note (5) |
| Company Director | |

(12) **Quality controller.** Persons described as quality controller who hold professional qualifications are coded 075, otherwise they are coded to the groups 289–294, 299 as appropriate or, if metal or electrical goods, to code 286.

(13) **Farmer's wife.** Persons described as 'Farmer's wife' are coded 166 and are allocated the employment status of employees n.e.c. (which includes family workers) irrespective of any statement of employment status.


## Notes on coding employment status

(*a*) The status categories are listed on page vii. The division between the 'employed' and 'self-employed' and the recognition of apprentices depend on the information available. 'Self-employed' takes precedence over 'manager' and 'foreman'; 'apprentice' takes precedence over 'manager', (but see (13) above). With this exception the managerial and foremen codes are applied as follows:

(*b*) The managerial code is applied to

    (i) All persons coded to occupation groups 006, 015, 016, 020–022, 092, 094–098, 105, 108.

    (ii) All persons, not being self-employed, coded to occupation groups 007–009, 013, 014, 023, 025, 087, 099, 101–104, 106, 107, 109–111, 129, 131, 163, 164.

    (iii) All persons, not being self-employed, whose occupation code is preceded by an 'M' in the occupation index.

    (iv) All persons returned as directors of companies, except those coded to occupation groups 001, 002, 011, 028, 031, 035, 036, 040–042, 044, 046, 051, 065–078, 082.

    (v) All persons coded 091 unless preceded by an 'F' in the occupation index.

(*c*) The foreman code is applied to

    (i) All persons coded to occupation groups 112, 148, 277, 318, 323, 324.

    (ii) All persons returned as foremen or with one of the synonyms listed on page 3 but excluding assistant foreman, assistant supervisor, etc.

    (iii) All persons whose occupation code number is preceded by an 'F' in the occupation index.

## Alphabetical index for classifying occupations

Please note that the codes appearing in this index are intended for coding purposes only. For the relationship between these codes and the occupation groups see Appendix G.

Assistant; *continued*
administrative- *continued*

| | Code number |
|---|---|
|     *local government-* ... ... | 022 |
|         *town planning* ... | 088 |
|     *petroleum* ... ... | 099 |
| advertising ... ... ... | 134 |
| agent's; | |
|     coal ... ... ... | 125 |
|     commission ... ... | 115 |
|     estate ... ... ... | 134 |
|     patent ... ... ... | 090 |
| alteration ... ... ... | 210 |
| analyst's ... ... ... | 288 |
| anatomical ... ... ... | 288 |
| ancillary (education) ... ... | 151 |
| architect's ... ... ... | 088 |
| architectural ... ... | 088 |
| armouring ... ... ... | 230 |
| assay ... ... ... ... | 077 |
| assayer's ... ... ... | 077 |
| auctioneer's ... ... | 335 |
| audit ... ... ... ... | 115 |
| bakehouse ... ... ... | 200 |
| baker's ... ... ... | 185 |
| bakery ... ... ... | 200 |
| bank ... ... ... ... | 115 |
| banksman's (*coal mine*) ... | 338 |
| bar; snack ... ... | 146 |
| bar- ... ... ... | 145 |
|     non-alcoholic ... | 146 |
| barker's ... ... ... | L346 |
| barrow ... ... ... | 130 |
| beaterman's ... ... ... | 204 |
| beater's ... ... ... | 204 |
| binder's ... ... ... | 189 |
| bindery ... ... ... | 189 |
| bingo ... ... ... ... | 165 |
| blender's (margarine) ... | 202 |
| blower's; glass ... | 223 |
| boiler's, sugar ... ... | 202 |
| board; medical ... ... | 115 |
| bookbinder's ... ... | 189 |
| bookseller's ... ... | 125 |
| bookstall ... ... ... | 125 |
| borer's (*coal mine*) ... ... | 314 |
| bottling ... ... ... | 287 |
| brewer's- ... ... ... | 078 |
|     non-alcoholic ... | 202 |
| bricklayer's ... ... | 312 |
| broker's ... ... ... | 115 |
| budget ... ... ... | 115 |
| building ... ... ... | 089 |
| bundler's (metal) ... ... | 298 |
| bureau ... ... ... | 115 |
| burner's ... ... ... | 276 |
| bursar's ... ... ... | 115 |
| butcher's ... ... ... | 186 |
| buttery ... ... ... | 146 |
| buyer's ... ... ... | 115 |
| C.S.S.D. ... ... ... | 156 |
| cafe(teria) ... ... ... | 146 |
| calender- | |
|     *paper mfr.* ... ... | 203 |
|     *textile mfr.* ... ... | 182 |
| calenderman's (*paper mfr.*) ... | 203 |
| cameraman's ... ... | 061 |
| canteen ... ... ... | 146 |
| canvassing (*insurance*) ... | 134 |
| care; ... ... ... | 156 |
|     child ... ... ... | 165 |
| caretaker's ... ... | 157 |
| carpenter's ... ... | 219 |
| cartographic ... ... | 079 |
| cash and wrap ... ... | 116 |
| cashier's ... ... ... | 115 |
| caterer's ... ... ... | 146 |
| catering ... ... ... | 146 |
| centre; | |
|     play ... ... ... | 165 |
|     service ... ... ... | 125 |
| chairside ... ... ... | 165 |
| char house (sugar) ... ... | 202 |
| checker's (*metal trades*) ... | 299 |
| cheesemonger's ... ... | 125 |

Assistant; *continued*

| | Code number |
|---|---|
| chemical ... ... ... | 288 |
| chemist's- ... ... ... | 288 |
|     *retail trade* ... ... | 125 |
| chief- | |
|     *library* ... ... ... | 115 |
|     *local government* ... | 022 |
| churner's ... ... ... | 202 |
| circulation ... ... | 115 |
| civil ... ... ... | 115 |
| claims ... ... ... | 115 |
| class; nursery ... ... | 151 |
| clerical ... ... ... | 115 |
| clerk's; ... ... ... | 115 |
|     justices ... ... | 115 |
| clinic; ... ... ... | 156 |
|     animal ... ... | 151 |
| clinical ... ... ... | 156 |
| clothier's ... ... ... | 125 |
| collection ... ... ... | 115 |
| collector's; rate ... ... | 115 |
| collier('s) ... ... ... | 314 |
| commercial ... ... | 115 |
| computer ... ... ... | 119 |
| confectioner and tobacco- | |
|     nist's ... ... ... | 125 |
| confectioner's- ... ... | 125 |
|     *flour confectionery* ... | 185 |
|     *sugar confectionery mfr.* ... | 202 |
| conference ... ... ... | 115 |
| consular ... ... ... | 115 |
| contracts ... ... ... | 115 |
| control; | |
|     air traffic ... ... | 122 |
|     load (*aircraft*) ... | 115 |
|     passenger (*air transport*) ... | 152 |
|     production ... ... | 115 |
|     quality ... ... | 115 |
|     sensitometric ... | 227 |
| control (*L.T.E.*) ... ... | 095 |
| controller (*banking*) ... | 115 |
| conveyancing ... ... | 115 |
| cookery ... ... ... | 147 |
| cook's ... ... ... | 147 |
| correspondence ... ... | 115 |
| cost ... ... ... ... | 115 |
| costing ... ... ... | 115 |
| counter- ... ... ... | 125 |
|     *bookmaker's, turf* | |
|         *accountant's* ... | 115 |
|     *catering* ... ... | 146 |
|     *library* ... ... | 115 |
|     *P.O.* ... ... | 115 |
|     *take-away food shop* ... | 125 |
| craft (*railways*) ... ... | 276 |
| crematorium ... ... | 348 |
| curator's ... ... ... | 115 |
| cutter's; paper ... ... | 227 |
| cutter's- | |
|     *clothing mfr.* ... ... | 211 |
|     *paper mfr.* ... ... | 227 |
|     *paper pattern mfr.* ... | 227 |
| dairy (*retail trade*) ... ... | 125 |
| dairyman's- | |
|     *milk processing* ... | 202 |
|     *retail trade* ... ... | 125 |
| dealer's ... ... ... | 125 |
| dental ... ... ... | 156 |
| department; operating ... | 156 |
| depot; chart ... ... | 333 |
| depot- | |
|     *L.T.E.-* | |
|         rail ... ... | F318 |
|         road ... ... | F324 |
| design ... ... ... | 079 |
| designer's (*textile mfr.*) ... | 115 |
| despatch ... ... ... | 333 |
| dip; hot ... ... ... | 269 |
| dipper's (*ceramic mfr.*) ... | 299 |
| director's; funeral ... | 165 |
| dispensary ... ... | 050 |
| dispenser's ... ... | 050 |
| dispensing ... ... ... | 050 |

Assistant; *continued*
display-

| | Code number |
|---|---|
|     *retail trade-* ... ... | 055 |
|         shelf filling ... | 126 |
| distribution (*water board*) ... | 310 |
| diver's; sea ... ... | 316 |
| divisional (*insurance*) ... | 115 |
| domestic ... ... ... | 151 |
| draper's ... ... ... | 125 |
| draughtsman's ... ... | 114 |
| drayman's ... ... ... | 329 |
| driver's's; | |
|     crane ... ... ... | 337 |
|     dumper ... ... | 338 |
|     engine ... ... | 255 |
|     lorry ... ... ... | 329 |
|     motor wagon ... | 329 |
|     turbine ... ... | 255 |
|     van ... ... ... | 329 |
| driver's (*road transport*) ... | 329 |
| dryerman's (*paper*) ... | 188 |
| dyer's (*textile mfr.*) ... | 199 |
| editorial ... ... ... | 054 |
| editor's; newspaper ... | 115 |
| electrician's ... ... | 276 |
| electronics ... ... | 081 |
| electroplating ... ... | 270 |
| embosser's ... ... | 223 |
| employment ... ... | 115 |
| engineering; ... ... | 081 |
|     civil ... ... ... | 089 |
| engineer's- ... ... | 081 |
|     maintenance ... ... | 276 |
| establishment... ... | 115 |
| estates ... ... ... | 115 |
| estimating ... ... | 115 |
| estimator's ... ... | 115 |
| etcher's ... ... ... | 223 |
| ethical... ... ... | 115 |
| executive- ... ... | 111 |
|     *insurance* ... ... | 099 |
|     *L.T.E.* ... ... | 111 |
| experimental; ... ... | 090 |
|     senior ... ... | 090 |
| export ... ... ... | 115 |
| extrusion- | |
|     plastics ... ... | 229 |
|     rubber ... ... | 228 |
| factory ... ... ... | L346 |
| farm; ... ... ... | 166 |
|     mink ... ... ... | 172 |
| fashion (*printing*) ... | 115 |
| fashion artist and designer's | 115 |
| fatstock ... ... ... | 115 |
| film ... ... ... | 062 |
| financial ... ... ... | 115 |
| fingerprint ... ... | 115 |
| fireman's ... ... ... | 138 |
| first (millinery) ... ... | 211 |
| fishmonger's ... ... | 187 |
| fitter's... ... ... | 276 |
| flanger's ... ... ... | L344 |
| floor (*retail trade*) ... | 125 |
| florist's ... ... ... | 125 |
| foreman's ... ... | 115 |
| forge ... ... ... | 270 |
| frier's; fish ... ... | 146 |
| fruiterer's ... ... | 125 |
| funeral ... ... ... | 165 |
| furnace (*metal trades*) ... | 231 |
| furnisher's; | |
|     funeral ... ... | 165 |
|     house ... ... | 125 |
| furrier's ... ... ... | 125 |
| gallery; art ... ... | 142 |
| galvanizer's ... ... | L344 |
| garage ... ... ... | 249 |
| gardener's- ... ... | 168 |
|     *market gardening* ... | 167 |
|     *nursery* ... ... | 167 |
| gas regulator's ... ... | L341 |
| general- ... ... ... | 115 |
|     *catering* ... ... | 146 |
|     *home for the disabled* ... | 156 |

Assistant; *continued*
general- *continued*

| | Code number |
|---|---|
| *hotel* ... ... ... | 151 |
| *old people's home* ... ... | 156 |
| *retail trade* ... ... | 125 |
| *school meals* ... ... | 146 |
| gilder's (electro-gilding) ... | 270 |
| glazer's ... ... ... | 276 |
| glazier's ... ... ... | 312 |
| grade I, II (*electricity board*) | 115 |
| grinder's- ... ... ... | L344 |
| plate glass ... ... | 223 |
| grocer's- ... ... ... | 125 |
| mobile ... ... ... | 128 |
| group officer's (*ordnance factory*) ... ... | 115 |
| haberdashery ... ... ... | 125 |
| hairdresser's ... ... ... | 159 |
| hammer ... ... ... | 270 |
| hammerman's ... ... ... | 270 |
| hardener's ... ... ... | L344 |
| hatchery ... ... ... | 166 |
| heater's (*metal trades*) ... | 231 |
| horticultural ... ... ... | 167 |
| hotel ... ... ... | 115 |
| house; | |
| boarding ... ... ... | 151 |
| cook ... ... ... | 147 |
| dye ... ... ... | 199 |
| green- ... ... ... | 167 |
| *ceramic mfr.* ... | 299 |
| test (*steelworks*) ... | 288 |
| household ... ... ... | 151 |
| housing ... ... ... | 115 |
| hydropulper ... ... ... | 203 |
| income ... ... ... | 115 |
| information ... ... ... | 115 |
| inspector's- | |
| *banking* ... ... | 115 |
| *local government* ... | 115 |
| *metal trades* ... | 299 |
| insurance ... ... ... | 115 |
| iron checker's ... ... | L344 |
| jeweller's ... ... ... | 125 |
| joiner's ... ... ... | 219 |
| jointer's ... ... ... | 276 |
| keeper('s); | |
| hall (*local government*) ... | 157 |
| school ... ... ... | 157 |
| store ... ... ... | 333 |
| kiln ... ... ... | 204 |
| kitchen ... ... ... | 147 |
| laboratory ... ... ... | 288 |
| ladler's (glass) ... ... | 223 |
| laminating (*paper mfr.*) ... | 203 |
| land(s) ... ... ... | 115 |
| language ... ... ... | 053 |
| launderette ... ... ... | 162 |
| laundry ... ... ... | 162 |
| legal ... ... ... | 027 |
| letterpress ... ... ... | 207 |
| library ... ... ... | 115 |
| licensee's ... ... ... | 145 |
| lifter's ... ... ... | 276 |
| lighting; street ... ... | 165 |
| linesman's ... ... ... | 276 |
| linotype ... ... ... | L346 |
| lithographer's ... ... | 299 |
| lithographic ... ... ... | 206 |
| litigation ... ... ... | 115 |
| loader's ... ... ... | L341 |
| machine *see Machinist* | |
| machine man's (*paper mfr.*) | 203 |
| machinery; outdoor (*British Rail*) ... ... ... | 091 |
| magisterial ... ... ... | 115 |
| mains (*water company*) ... | L346 |
| maintenance- ... ... ... | 276 |
| machinery, plant ... | 271 |
| maker's; | |
| boiler ... ... ... | 276 |
| book ... ... ... | 165 |
| cheese ... ... ... | 202 |
| coach ... ... ... | 276 |

Assistant; *continued*
maker's; *continued*

| | Code number |
|---|---|
| crucible ... ... ... | 223 |
| dress ... ... ... | 226 |
| rope ... ... ... | 199 |
| shoe ... ... ... | 175 |
| taper ... ... ... | 230 |
| tool ... ... ... | L344 |
| management; housing ... | 115 |
| manager's ... ... ... | 115 |
| market ... ... ... | 130 |
| marketing ... ... ... | 115 |
| mason's ... ... ... | 312 |
| master's; harbour ... | 115 |
| matcher's; colour ... | 199 |
| mathematical ... ... | 067 |
| matron's ... ... ... | 151 |
| meals; school ... ... | 146 |
| measurement; work ... | 010 |
| mechanical ... ... ... | 081 |
| mechanic's ... ... ... | 276 |
| media ... ... ... | 115 |
| medical (*hospital*) ... | 156 |
| melting pot (electric cable) ... | 204 |
| mercantile ... ... ... | 115 |
| mercer's ... ... ... | 125 |
| merchant's coal ... ... | 113 |
| merchant's ... ... ... | 125 |
| metallurgical ... ... | 090 |
| meteorological ... ... | 067 |
| meter ... ... ... | 276 |
| methods ... ... ... | 010 |
| mid-day (*school*) ... | 151 |
| mill; ... ... ... | L346 |
| offal (*tobacco mfr.*) ... | 201 |
| rolling ... ... ... | 270 |
| miller's (*food*) ... ... | 202 |
| milliner's ... ... ... | 211 |
| millwright's ... ... ... | 276 |
| minder's; machine (*printing*) | 207 |
| minder's (*cotton mfr.*) ... | 199 |
| mixer's; colour ... ... | 204 |
| moulder's (*abrasive mfr.*) ... | 223 |
| museum ... ... ... | 030 |
| N.A.A.F.I. ... ... ... | 125 |
| news (*broadcasting*) ... | 115 |
| newsagent's ... ... ... | 125 |
| non-teaching (*schools*) ... | 151 |
| nursery- ... ... ... | 150 |
| *agriculture* ... ... | 167 |
| nursing ... ... ... | 043 |
| off-licence ... ... ... | 125 |
| office; ... ... ... | 115 |
| drawing ... ... ... | 114 |
| receiving ... ... ... | 125 |
| officer's; group ... ... | 115 |
| onsetter's ... ... ... | 338 |
| operating; railway ... | 095 |
| operation; programme ... | 059 |
| operator's; cinematograph ... | 062 |
| optician's ... ... ... | 230 |
| organisation and methods ... | 115 |
| outfitter's ... ... ... | 125 |
| output (*L.T.E.*) ... ... | 115 |
| oven (*bakery*) ... ... | 200 |
| painter's ... ... ... | 299 |
| passenger (*railways*) ... | 095 |
| pastry ... ... ... | 185 |
| pawnbroker's ... ... ... | 125 |
| perfumer's ... ... ... | 125 |
| personal; manager's ... | 029 |
| personal- ... ... ... | 118 |
| managerial ... ... | 029 |
| personnel ... ... ... | 009 |
| pharmacy ... ... ... | 125 |
| photographer's ... ... | 061 |
| photographic ... ... ... | 061 |
| physiotherapy ... ... | 047 |
| pickler's (galvanized sheet) ... | 270 |
| planning; town ... ... | 088 |
| planning- ... ... ... | 090 |
| *local government* ... | 088 |
| plans (*land registry*) ... | 115 |
| plant; pilot ... ... ... | 276 |

Assistant; *continued*

| | Code number |
|---|---|
| plasterer's ... ... ... | 312 |
| plater's ... ... ... | 276 |
| plating (*electroplating*) ... | 270 |
| play leader's ... ... | 165 |
| playgroup ... ... ... | 165 |
| plumber's ... ... ... | 276 |
| point; check ... ... | 116 |
| polisher's; glass ... ... | 223 |
| post-mortem ... ... ... | 165 |
| postal (*P.O.*) ... ... | 115 |
| post office- ... ... ... | 115 |
| sub-post office ... | 125 |
| potter's ... ... ... | 223 |
| poulterer's ... ... ... | 125 |
| poultry ... ... ... | 166 |
| prescription (optician's) ... | 192 |
| presentation (*printing*) ... | 227 |
| press; electric cable ... | 230 |
| press (*printing*) ... ... | 207 |
| principal- | |
| *building society* ... | 099 |
| *local government* ... | 022 |
| *public utilities* ... | 094 |
| printer's ... ... ... | 207 |
| printing ... ... ... | 207 |
| process (*printing*) ... | 227 |
| producer's (*entertainment*) ... | 059 |
| production- ... ... ... | 115 |
| *broadcasting* ... ... | 059 |
| professional (*local government-surveyor's dept.*) ... | 084 |
| programme (*broadcasting*) ... | 059 |
| progress ... ... ... | 115 |
| provision ... ... ... | 125 |
| publicity ... ... ... | 014 |
| publisher's ... ... ... | 333 |
| purchasing ... ... ... | 115 |
| rate fixing ... ... ... | 115 |
| rating ... ... ... | 115 |
| reader's ... ... ... | 115 |
| records ... ... ... | 115 |
| reelerman's (*paper mfr.*) ... | 203 |
| refectory ... ... ... | 146 |
| refiner's ... ... ... | 184 |
| registrar's ... ... ... | 115 |
| relations; | |
| customer ... ... ... | 115 |
| employee ... ... ... | 115 |
| public ... ... ... | 115 |
| remover's; furniture ... | 335 |
| repairer's; wagon ... | 276 |
| repairer's (*coal mine*) ... | 345 |
| reprographic ... ... ... | 119 |
| research; marketing ... | 115 |
| research- ... ... ... | 080 |
| *broadcasting* ... ... | 030 |
| *journalism* ... ... | 030 |
| *printing and publishing* ... | 030 |
| *university* ... ... | 031 |
| reservations ... ... ... | 115 |
| reshearer's ... ... ... | 276 |
| roller's ... ... ... | 270 |
| room; | |
| blowing ... ... ... | 176 |
| control- | |
| *L.T.E.* ... ... | 255 |
| *fire service* ... ... | 115 |
| cutting (*clothing mfr.*) ... | 211 |
| dark ... ... ... | 227 |
| dining ... ... ... | 146 |
| engine ... ... ... | 255 |
| grey ... ... ... | 333 |
| linen ... ... ... | 333 |
| pattern (*textile mfr.*) ... | 333 |
| print (*engineering*) ... | 119 |
| publishing ... ... ... | 115 |
| receiving (*tailoring*) ... | 338 |
| retort (*food products mfr.*) | 202 |
| sale- | |
| *auctioneer's* ... ... | 335 |
| *retail, wholesale trade* ... | 125 |
| sample ... ... ... | 333 |
| show ... ... ... | 125 |

## Attendant; *continued*

| | Code number |
|---|---|
| traffic (*coal mine*) | 321 |
| train- | 152 |
|    *coal mine* | 320 |
| transfer (*coal mine*) | 314 |
| transformer | 255 |
| travel | 152 |
| treatment; water | 184 |
| tumbler | 162 |
| turbine | 255 |
| turnstile | 115 |
| unit; cracker | 198 |
| valve | 348 |
| van | 329 |
| vat (*textile dyeing*) | 182 |
| ventilation | 348 |
| wagon | 338 |
| ward | 156 |
| washer; | 184 |
|   beet | 202 |
| washer's | 202 |
| washery (*coal mine*) | 198 |
| water | 348 |
| welfare | 039 |
| wharf; oil | 334 |
| winch | 331 |

## Attendant-

| | Code number |
|---|---|
| agricultural machinery | 169 |
| public conveniences | 165 |
| road goods vehicles | 329 |
| *ambulance service* | 155 |
| *art gallery* | 142 |
| *baths* | 165 |
| *catering* | 146 |
| *domestic service* | 151 |
| *entertainment* | 165 |
| *gas works* | 184 |
| *government* | 124 |
| *home for the disabled* | 156 |
| *hospital service* | 156 |
| *local government* | 165 |
| *museum* | 142 |
| *old people's home* | 156 |
| *racing stables* | 172 |
| *sewage farm* | 310 |
| *water works* | 310 |

| | Code number |
|---|---|
| Attender (*tinplate mfr.*) | 270 |
| Attorney | 001 |
| Au pair | 151 |
| Auctioneer | 134 |
| Audiologist | 050 |
| Audiometrician | 050 |
| Auditor; | |
|   chief (*N.C.B.*) | 002 |
|   internal | 115 |
| Auditor- | 115 |
|   qualified | 002 |
|   *government* | 002 |
|   *insurance* | 115 |
|   *local government* | 002 |
| Auditor of Court (Scotland) | 001 |
| Aurist- | 041 |
|   not registered | 050 |
| Author- | 054 |
|   technical | 054 |
| Autoclave worker (*aluminium refining*) | 184 |
| Autolysis man | 202 |
| Auto-setter (*metal trades*) | 238 |
| Auto-weigher | 297 |
| Auxiliary; | |
|   dental | 050 |
|   nursing; | 043 |
|     animal | 053 |
| Aviator | 085 |
| Axeman | 170 |
| Axle worker (*perambulator mfr.*) | 233 |

## B

| | Code number |
|---|---|
| B.Ch. | 041 |
| Babbitter | 270 |
| Back end man (*textile mfr.*) | 182 |
| Back girl | 226 |
| Back hand (*leather cloth mfr.*) | 199 |
| Back man (*textile mfr.*) | 182 |
| Back room man (*distillery*) | 197 |
| Back-bye man | 315 |
| Back-edger (corset) | 212 |
| Back-end man (*cement mfr.*) | 204 |
| Backer; | |
|   mirror | 269 |
|   professional | 165 |
|   saw | 276 |
|   spindle (*rolling mill*) | 270 |
|   stencil paper | 203 |
| Backer- | |
|   *bookbinding* | 189 |
|   *clothing mfr.* | 212 |
|   *fustian mfr.* | 182 |
|   *linoleum mfr.* | 204 |
|   *paper mfr.* | 203 |
|   *rolling mill* | 270 |
| Backer-up- | |
|   *printing* | 206 |
|   *sawmilling* | 219 |
|   *steelworks* | 270 |
| Backwasher | 199 |
| Bacon hand | 125 |
| Bacteriologist | 065 |
| Badge worker | 212 |
| Badger | 192 |
| Bag hand- | 226 |
|   *paper products mfr.* | 227 |
| Bagman (*cement mfr.*) | 287 |
| Bag woman | 226 |
| Baggage man | 235 |
| Bagger; | |
|   cake | 287 |
|   coal | 287 |
|   fibre (*asbestos mfr.*) | 287 |
| Bagger- | 287 |
|   *clothing mfr.* | 212 |
|   *footwear mfr.* | 175 |
|   *textile finishing* | 212 |
| Bagger-off (*starch mfr.*) | 287 |
| Bagger-out | 212 |
| Bagger-up | 287 |
| Bagging-off man | 287 |
| Bailer *see Baler* | |
| Bailiff; | |
|   broker's | 142 |
|   estate | 107 |
|   farm | 107 |
|   land | 107 |
|   landlord's | 142 |
|   rent | 142 |
|   reservoir | 316 |
|   river | 019 |
|   water | 019 |
| Bailiff- | |
|   certificated | 142 |
|   *county, high courts* | 142 |
|   *level, sewer commissioners* | F316 |
|   *local government* | 142 |
|   *property owning* | 142 |
| Baister-*see Baster* | |
| Baker; hand oven | 200 |
| Baker- | |
|   *bakery* | 185 |
|   *flour confectionery mfr.* | 185 |
|   *food products mfr.* | 202 |
|   *retail trade-* | 101 |
|     employee | 185 |
|   *shipping* | 185 |
|   *textile mfr.* | 182 |
| Baker and confectioner- | |
|   *bakery* | 185 |
|   *retail trade-* | 101 |
|     employee | 185 |
| Bakery hand | 200 |
| Bakery worker | 200 |

| | Code number |
|---|---|
| Baking powder operative | 202 |
| Balancer; | |
|   armature | 252 |
|   crank | 286 |
|   crank shaft | 286 |
|   dynamic(s) | 286 |
|   flyer | 248 |
|   sound | 062 |
|   wheel- | |
|     *abrasive mfr.* | 230 |
|     *railway workshops* | 286 |
| Balancer- | |
|   *abrasive mfr.* | 230 |
|   *engineering* | 286 |
| Balcony man | 192 |
| Baler; | |
|   hay | 169 |
|   paper | 287 |
|   salle | 287 |
|   scrap | 276 |
| Baler- | 287 |
|   *oil wells* | 348 |
| Ballast man | 334 |
| Baller; | |
|   cross | 178 |
|   wool | 178 |
| Baller- | |
|   twine | 178 |
|   yarn | 178 |
|   *ceramic mfr.* | 204 |
|   *iron works* | 231 |
|   *wool combing* | 176 |
| Ballistician | 067 |
| Band master | 060 |
| Bander; | |
|   armature | 283 |
|   cigar | 287 |
|   clay | 299 |
|   coil | 287 |
|   glass | 299 |
|   wash | 279 |
| Bander- | |
|   *boot polish mfr.* | 287 |
|   *cardboard box mfr.* | 227 |
|   *ceramic mfr.* | 279 |
|   *iron and steelworks* | 287 |
|   *rubber tyre mfr.* | 228 |
|   *textile mfr.-* | 271 |
|     *textile bleaching, dyeing* | 182 |
| Bandyman (*provender milling*) | 202 |
| Bank hand- | |
|   *coal mine* | 331 |
|   *rope mfr.* | 199 |
| Bankman; rail | 338 |
| Bankman (*rolling mill*) | L344 |
| Banker- | |
|   stone working | 301 |
|   *finance-* | 099 |
|     self-employed | 007 |
|     *merchant banking* | 006 |
|   *mine, not coal* | 331 |
|   *totalisator* | 115 |
|   *yarn warping* | 177 |
| Banker hand | 301 |
| Banksman; | |
|   crane | 337 |
|   staple pit | 331 |
| Banksman- | |
|   *blast furnace* | L344 |
|   *canal contractors* | 316 |
|   *civil engineers* | 337 |
|   *coal mine* | 331 |
|   *manufacturing* | 337 |
|   *mine, not coal* | 331 |
|   *opencast coal mining* | 297 |
|   *salt works* | 331 |
| Barber | 159 |
| Bargain man- | |
|   *coal mine* | 314 |
|   *mine, not coal-* | |
|     *above ground* | L346 |
|     *below ground* | 315 |
| Barge boy | 317 |
| Barge hand | 317 |

Blaster;
hot ... 175
sand- ... 275
  *briar pipe mfr.* ... 224
  *ceramic mfr.* ... 223
shot ... 275
vapour ... 275
Blaster-
  furnace ... 231
  *mine, not coal* ... 315
Bleach hand (*textile mfr.*) ... 182
Bleach worker (*textile mfr.*) ... 182
Bleacher; yarn ... 182
Bleacher-
  feather ... 182
  flour ... 202
  oil ... 184
  paper ... 188
  textiles ... 182
  wood pulp ... 188
Bleacher and dyer ... 182
Blender;
  batch ... 184
  butter ... 202
  coal-
    *coke ovens* ... 184
    *steel mfr.* ... 204
  cocoa ... 202
  coffee ... 202
  colour-
    *chemical mfr.* ... 184
    *textile spinning* ... 176
  flour ... 202
  grease (mineral oil) ... 184
  in-line ... 184
  liquor ... 204
  oil ... 184
  pigment (chemicals) ... 184
  rag ... 176
  shade (wool) ... 176
  spice ... 202
  tea ... 202
  varnish ... 184
  whisky ... 197
Blender- ... 184
  margarine ... 202
  spirits ... 197
  wines ... 197
  wool ... F176
  *arc welding electrode mfr.* ... 184
  *asbestos composition goods mfr.* ... 176
  *candle mfr.* ... 204
  *cast stone products mfr.* ... 204
  *chemical mfr.* ... 184
  *explosives mfr.* ... 184
  *food products mfr.* ... 202
  *fur fibre mfr.* ... 199
  *linoleum mfr.* ... 204
  *man-made fibre mfr.* ... 204
  *mineral oil refining* ... 184
  *mineral water mfr.* ... 202
  *oilskin mfr.* ... 199
  *petroleum storage and distribution* ... 184
  *plastics goods mfr.* ... 204
  *tobacco mfr.* ... 201
  *wool blending* ... F176
Blockman-
  *butchers* ... 186
  *fishmongers* ... 187
  *metal trades* ... L344
  *mine, not coal* ... 301
Block worker; concrete ... 230
Blocker;
  fur ... 211
  gold ... 227
  hat ... 226
  lens ... 223
  pan (*hat mfr.*) ... 226
  prism ... 223
  sole ... 225
Blocker-
  *bookbinding* ... 189

Blocker- *continued*
  *brick mfr.* ... 223
  *footwear mfr.* ... 225
  *hat mfr.* ... 226
  *laundry* ... 162
  *leather goods mfr.* ... 225
  *lens mfr.* ... 223
  *lifting tackle mfr.* ... 248
  *textile mfr.* ... 199
  *wood heel mfr.* ... 218
Blouse hand ... 210
Blower;
  bottle ... 192
  bulb (lamp, valve) ... 192
  core ... 235
  dry ... 182
  fur ... 199
  glass ... 192
  glaze ... 279
  sand ... 275
  shot ... 275
  soot (*power station*) ... 255
  steam ... 195
  thermometer ... 192
  tube (*glass mfr.*) ... 192
Blower-
  *ceramic mfr.* ... 279
  *chemical mfr.* ... 255
  *cotton mfr.* ... 182
  *glass mfr.* ... 192
  *plastics goods mfr.* ... 195
  *slag wool mfr.* ... 204
  *steelworks* ... 231
  *textile finishing* ... 182
Blower-up (*textile mfr.*) ... 176
Blowing room hand ... 176
Blowing room operative ... 176
Blowlamp worker (*shipbuilding*) ... 262
Blowpipe worker (quartz glass) ... 192
Blowroom operative ... 176
Blue coat (*holiday camp*) ... 165
Blue-button ... 115
Bluer; china ... 279
Bluer-
  *metal goods* ... 237
  *laundry* ... 162
  *textile mfr.* ... 182
Board boy (*bookmakers*) ... 124
Boardman-
  *bakery* ... 185
  *bookmakers* ... 165
Boarder (*hosiery mfr.*) ... 182
Boat boy ... 317
Boat hand ... 317
Boatman;
  ... 317
  foy ... 317
Boatswain- ... F317
  *fishing* ... F171
Boatswain's boy ... 317
Boatwright ... 262
Bobber;
  emery ... 243
  fish ... 334
Bobber-
  *metal goods* ... 243
  *wood products* ... 224
  *arc welding electrode mfr.* ... 243
  *embroidery mfr.* ... L346
  *fish dock* ... 334
Bobber and polisher; spur ... 243
Bobbin and carriage hand ... 248
Bobbin boy ... 338
Bobbin worker; bottle ... 178
Bobbiner ... 178
Bodier (*ceramic mfr.*) ... 279
Bodyer (*organ, piano mfr.*) ... 282
Bodyguard ... 140
Boiler;
  acid ... 204
  biscuit ... 200
  fat ... 204
  fruit ... 202
  glue ... 184
  grease ... 184

Boiler; *continued*
  gum-
    *sugar confectionery mfr.* ... 202
    *textile dyeing* ... 182
  jelly ... 202
  liquorice ... 202
  oil- ... 184
    *oilskin mfr.* ... 199
  pan (*sugar refinery*) ... 202
  rag ... 203
  salt ... 184
  sauce ... 202
  size ... 184
  sizing ... 184
  soap ... 184
  starch ... 184
  steam ... 347
  sugar ... 202
  tar-
    *building and contracting* ... 316
    *gas works* ... 184
  woodpulp ... 203
Boiler-
  chemicals ... 184
  flax ... 182
  food products ... 202
  sugar confectionery ... 202
  *paper mfr.* ... 203
  *textile finishing* ... 182
Boilerman- ... 347
  *food products mfr.* ... 202
  *gelatine, glue, size mfr.* ... 184
  *paper mfr.* ... 203
  *textile waste merchants* ... 199
Boiling hand; soap ... 184
Boiling man; tar (*cable mfr.*) ... 204
Boiling-off man ... 182
Bolter; roof (*coal mine*) ... 314
Bolter-
  *metal trades* ... 262
  *textile dyeing* ... 287
Bolter-down (*metal trades*) ... 270
Bolter-up (*metal trades*) ... 285
Bombadier-
  *armed forces-*
    *foreign and Commonwealth* ... 136
    *U.K.* ... 135
Bonder; garment; rainproof ... 226
Bonder (electrical) ... 283
Bonderiser ... 269
Boner-
  corsets ... 299
  fish ... 187
  meat ... 186
Book hand (*printing*) ... 205
Bookbinder ... 189
Booker ... 115
Bookman (*timber yard*) ... 115
Bookstall boy ... 125
Booster; gas (*steelworks*) ... 255
Boot and shoe operative ... 175
Boot and shoe worker ... 175
Boots (hotel) ... 165
Borer;
  artesian ... 315
  brush ... 230
  cylinder ... 241
  fine; barrel ... 241
  gas emission (*coal mine*) ... 314
  hole (*shipbuilding*) ... 262
  horizontal ... 241
  iron ... 241
  ironstone ... 315
  jig ... 241
  methane (*coal mine*) ... 314
  scissors ... 241
  shot ... 315
  spill (barrel, small arms) ... 241
  tong (tubes) ... 241
  tool room ... 240
  tunnel ... 304
  tyre ... 241
  universal ... 241
  vertical ... 241

| | Code number |
|---|---|
| **Brusher;** | |
| cloth (*textile finishing*) ... 182 | |
| dry ... 223 | |
| enamel ... 299 | |
| flannelette ... 182 | |
| flour ... 202 | |
| glaze ... 279 | |
| glove ... 173 | |
| paint ... 299 | |
| pigment ... 188 | |
| roller ... 182 | |
| sanitary ... 279 | |
| scratch ... 243 | |
| tube (*railways*) ... 276 | |
| ware (*ceramic mfr.*) ... 223 | |
| wire ... 243 | |
| **Brusher-** | |
| *carpet mfr.* ... 182 | |
| *ceramic mfr.* ... 223 | |
| *clothing mfr.* ... L346 | |
| *coal mine* ... 314 | |
| *dyeing and cleaning* ... 162 | |
| *file mfr.* ... L344 | |
| *footwear mfr.* ... 175 | |
| *foundry* ... 244 | |
| *hosiery mfr.* ... 182 | |
| *leather finishing* ... 173 | |
| *needle mfr.* ... 276 | |
| *paper mfr.* ... 188 | |
| *scissors mfr.* ... 243 | |
| *textile mfr.* ... 182 | |
| *wallpaper mfr.* ... 188 | |
| *wool spinning* ... 182 | |
| **Brusher-in; scratch** ... 243 | |
| **Brusher-off-** | |
| *clothing mfr.* ... L346 | |
| *metal trades* ... 299 | |
| **Brusher-up-** ... 223 | |
| *footwear mfr.* ... 175 | |
| **Buckler** ... 299 | |
| **Budder; rose** ... 167 | |
| **Buddler** ... 198 | |
| **Buffer;** | |
| band ... 228 | |
| blacksmith's ... 243 | |
| blade ... 243 | |
| bottom ... 175 | |
| brass ... 243 | |
| comb- ... 229 | |
| metal ... 243 | |
| cutlery ... 243 | |
| hollow-ware ... 243 | |
| lime ... 243 | |
| sand ... 243 | |
| spoon and fork ... 243 | |
| wheel; emery ... 173 | |
| **Buffer-** | |
| bone, etc. ... 230 | |
| *flax processing* ... 176 | |
| *footwear mfr.* ... 175 | |
| *furniture mfr.* ... 299 | |
| *glass mfr.* ... 192 | |
| *leather dressing* ... 173 | |
| *metal trades* ... 243 | |
| *rubber goods mfr.* ... 228 | |
| **Buffer and polisher** ... 243 | |
| **Builder;** | |
| ambulance ... 268 | |
| arch; brick ... 300 | |
| armature ... 252 | |
| barge ... 262 | |
| barrow ... 224 | |
| bead (tyre) ... 228 | |
| belt (*rubber goods mfr.*) ... 228 | |
| boat ... 214 | |
| body (vehicle) ... 268 | |
| box (*P.O.*) ... 300 | |
| caravan ... 268 | |
| carriage ... 268 | |
| cart ... 224 | |
| chassis ... 265 | |
| chimney ... 300 | |
| coach ... 268 | |
| commutator ... 252 | |

| | Code number |
|---|---|
| **Builder;** *continued* | |
| condenser ... 283 | |
| conveyor ... 248 | |
| core ... 283 | |
| cupola ... 300 | |
| cycle ... 248 | |
| drum (cables) ... 216 | |
| fireplace ... 300 | |
| float ... 224 | |
| fork (cycles) ... 248 | |
| frame- | |
| *cycle mfr.* ... 248 | |
| *vehicle mfr.* ... 268 | |
| furnace ... 300 | |
| garage ... 304 | |
| harness (*textile mfr.*) ... 199 | |
| heel ... 299 | |
| hoarding ... 214 | |
| horticultural ... 214 | |
| hose ... 228 | |
| house ... 305 | |
| jobbing ... 304 | |
| kiln; brick ... 300 | |
| lathe ... 248 | |
| loom ... 248 | |
| machine ... 248 | |
| maintenance ... 304 | |
| manhole ... 300 | |
| master ... 305 | |
| micanite ... 204 | |
| millstone ... 301 | |
| mop (*steelworks*) ... 270 | |
| motor ... 248 | |
| organ ... 222 | |
| oven ... 300 | |
| plate (mica, micanite) ... 204 | |
| pole ... 214 | |
| radiator; car ... 261 | |
| retort ... 300 | |
| roller ... 228 | |
| rolley ... 224 | |
| rubber ... 228 | |
| sewer ... 300 | |
| shed ... 214 | |
| ship ... 262 | |
| staircase ... 214 | |
| stove ... 300 | |
| table (sewing machine) ... 248 | |
| tank (rubber lining) ... 228 | |
| tool; machine ... 248 | |
| transformer ... 252 | |
| tyre ... 194 | |
| vat ... 216 | |
| vehicle ... 268 | |
| wagon ... 268 | |
| wheel- | |
| perambulators ... 285 | |
| rubber ... 228 | |
| vehicles ... 285 | |
| wood ... 224 | |
| wheelbarrow ... 224 | |
| **Builder-** | |
| *building and contracting* ... 305 | |
| *plastics goods mfr.* ... 229 | |
| *printing* ... 206 | |
| **Builder and contractor** ... 305 | |
| **Builder and decorator** ... 305 | |
| **Builder and repairer; boat** ... 214 | |
| **Builder-up; last** ... 225 | |
| **Building operative** ... 304 | |
| **Building worker** ... 304 | |
| **Bulb worker-** | |
| *glassware mfr.* ... 192 | |
| *horticulture* ... 167 | |
| **Bulker** (*tobacco mfr.*) ... 201 | |
| **Bummaree** ... 335 | |
| **Bumper-** | |
| *ceramic mfr.* ... 223 | |
| *coal mine* ... 338 | |
| *hat mfr.* ... 199 | |
| *textile mfr.* ... 199 | |
| *tin box mfr.* ... 242 | |
| **Buncher;** | |
| hank ... 199 | |

| | Code number |
|---|---|
| **Buncher;** *continued* | |
| watercress ... 287 | |
| **Buncher-** | |
| *cigar mfr.* ... 201 | |
| *textile mfr.* ... 199 | |
| **Bundler;** | |
| bag ... 287 | |
| flax ... 199 | |
| press ... 287 | |
| scrap ... 298 | |
| sheet (metal) ... 298 | |
| waste (*textile mfr.*) ... 287 | |
| **Bundler-** | |
| *brush mfr.* ... 298 | |
| *clothing mfr.* ... 299 | |
| *metal trades* ... 298 | |
| **Bundler and wrapper (cigarettes)** ... 287 | |
| **Bunker-** | |
| *coal mine* ... 338 | |
| *docks* ... 334 | |
| *footwear mfr.* ... 175 | |
| **Bunkerman; kiln-** | |
| *chemical mfr.* ... 184 | |
| *lime burning* ... 184 | |
| **Bunkerman-** | |
| *blast furnace* ... 338 | |
| *chemical mfr.* ... 184 | |
| *coal gas, coke ovens* ... 338 | |
| *coal mine* ... 338 | |
| *power station* ... L346 | |
| **Burden man** ... 182 | |
| **Burler** ... 183 | |
| **Burler and mender** ... 183 | |
| **Burner;** | |
| acetylene ... 265 | |
| brick ... 191 | |
| chalk ... 184 | |
| gas- | |
| *building and contracting* ... 265 | |
| *coal gas, coke ovens* ... 184 | |
| gypsum ... 184 | |
| head (*ceramic mfr.*) ... 191 | |
| kiln- | |
| *carbon goods mfr.* ... 204 | |
| *cement mfr.* ... 204 | |
| *ceramic mfr.* ... 191 | |
| *glass mfr.* ... 191 | |
| lead ... 265 | |
| lime ... 204 | |
| mould (*rubber tyre mfr.*) ... 204 | |
| oxy-acetylene ... 265 | |
| profile ... 265 | |
| rotary furnace (*aluminium refining*) ... 184 | |
| sand ... 191 | |
| scrap (*steelworks*) ... 265 | |
| tile ... 191 | |
| **Burner-** | |
| scrap metal ... 265 | |
| *cement mfr.* ... 204 | |
| *ceramic mfr.* ... 191 | |
| *charcoal mfr.* ... 204 | |
| *chemical mfr.* ... 184 | |
| *coal mine* ... 265 | |
| *demolition* ... 265 | |
| *glass mfr.* ... 191 | |
| *lime burning* ... 204 | |
| *metal trades-* ... 265 | |
| *sinter plant* ... 270 | |
| *railways* ... 265 | |
| **Burnerman; acid** ... 184 | |
| **Burnerman** ... 184 | |
| **Burner-off-** | |
| *incandescent mantles* ... 204 | |
| *glass mfr.* ... 192 | |
| **Burnisher;** | |
| gold (*ceramic mfr.*) ... 223 | |
| heel ... 175 | |
| **Burnisher-** | |
| *ceramic mfr.* ... 223 | |
| *footwear mfr.* ... 175 | |
| *metal trades* ... 243 | |
| **Burr man** ... 199 | |
| **Burrer** ... 173 | |

**Carrier;**
- bag- ... 338
  - *docks* ... 335
- bar ... 270
- barley ... 338
- batch (rubber) ... 338
- beam (carpets) ... 338
- board ... 338
- bobbin ... 338
- brick ... 338
- clay ... 338
- cloth ... 338
- coal ... 326
- colour (*textile printing*) ... 338
- cop ... 338
- cotton; hosiery ... 338
- deal- ... 338
  - *docks* ... 334
- dust ... 338
- fillet; card ... 338
- fish box ... 334
- general ... 326
- glass (*glass mfr.*) ... 338
- hod ... 312
- lap ... 338
- liquor ... 338
- metal ... 338
- piece ... 338
- pitwood ... 334
- pole (linoleum) ... 338
- prop ... 334
- rag ... 338
- railway ... 326
- rivet ... 276
- roller ... L346
- rover ... 338
- roving ... 338
- sack (cement) ... 338
- sample ... 338
- sanitary pipe ... 338
- set ... 333
- sheet (paper) ... 338
- skip ... 338
- sliver (flax, hemp) ... 338
- timber- ... 338
  - *docks* ... 334
- tool ... 338
- top (*textile printing*) ... 338
- tow ... 338
- ware ... 338
- weft ... 338
- wool ... 338
- yarn ... 338

**Carrier-** ... 338
- *docks* ... 334
- *mine, not coal-* ... 326
  - *below ground* ... 338
- *n.o.s.* ... 326
- *transport* ... 326

Carrier-away ... 338
Carrier-in (*glass mfr.*) ... 191
Carrier-off ... 338
Carrotter ... 173
Cart boy; top (*rope mfr.*) ... 199
Cart boy (*textile mfr.*) ... 338
Cartman ... 338
Carter; coal ... 326

**Carter-**
- *farming* ... 172
- *mine, not coal* ... 338
- *transport* ... 338

**Carter's boy-**
- *farming* ... 172
- *transport* ... 329

Cartographer ... 079
Cartographer-draughtsman ... 079
Cartoner ... 287
Cartoonist ... 055
Cartridger ... 230

**Carver;**
- architectural ... 301
- frame ... 224
- gold ... 276
- ivory ... 230

**Carver;** *continued*
- letter-
  - brass ... 276
  - wood ... 224
- monumental ... 301
- stock (gun) ... 224
- stone ... 301
- wood ... 224

**Carver-**
- food ... 165
- furniture ... 224
- wood ... 224

Case hand (*printing*) ... 205
Case worker; family ... 039

**Case worker-**
- *piano organ mfr.* ... 215
- *welfare services* ... 039

**Casein worker-**
- *chemical mfr.* ... 184
- *food products mfr.* ... 202

**Caser;**
- bone ... 212
- die ... 276

**Caser-**
- metal ... 237
- packing ... 287
- *corset mfr.* ... 212

**Cashier;**
- chief- ... F115
  - *government* ... F112

**Cashier-**
- café ... 116
- canteen ... 116
- restaurant ... 116
- *garage* ... 116
- *local government* ... 115
- *retail trade* ... 116

Cast off; fishing boat ... 171

**Caster;**
- brass ... 270
- china ... 193
- cold (rubber) ... 228
- concrete ... 230
- die ... 235
- furnace; blast ... 270
- hollow-ware (*ceramic mfr.*) ... 193
- ingot ... 270
- iron ... 270
- lead (*battery mfr.*) ... 270
- metal ... 270
- monotype ... 205
- needle ... 270
- parchester ... 303
- roller (printer's) ... 228
- sanitary ... 193
- shot ... 270
- slab ... 230
- statue ... 223
- stone ... 230
- strip ... 270
- tile ... 230
- type ... 270
- at machine ... 235

**Caster-**
- *cast stone products mfr.* ... 230
- *ceramic mfr.* ... 193
- *footwear mfr.* ... 228
- *glassware mfr.* ... 223
- *metal trades* ... 270
- *printing* ... 206

Caster-off; fishing boat ... 171
Casting man (*blast furnace*) ... 270

**Castrator-**
- *farm livestock* ... 166

Cataloguer ... 115
Catalyst man ... 184

**Catcher;**
- bar ... 270
- bird ... 172
- chicken ... 172
- cigarette ... 299
- eel ... 171
- finishing ... 270
- machine ... 299

**Catcher;** *continued*
- mole ... 165
- pole (linoleum) ... 204
- rabbit ... 172
- rat ... 165
- rivet ... 276
- roll; cold ... 270
- sheet (paper) ... 203
- sheet mill ... 270

**Catcher-**
- *laundry* ... 162
- *paper mfr.* ... 203
- *steelworks* ... 270

Catcher and sticker (wire) ... 270
Caterer; ... 104
- amusement ... 106
Catering boy (*shipping*) ... 152
Catering worker ... 147
Catsmeat man ... 130
Cattleman ... 166
Caulker ... 262
Caulker-burner ... 262
Causticizer ... 184
Caver (*coal mine*) ... 314
Cellar boy *see Cellarman*
Cellarer ... 197

**Cellarman;**
- bar ... 333
- oil ... 333

**Cellarman-**
- *bacon, meat curing* ... L346
- *brewery* ... 197
- *catering* ... 333
- *hotel* ... 333
- *rubber mfr.* ... 204
- *steelworks* ... 231
- *textile mfr.* ... 333
- *wine mfr.* ... 333
- *wine merchants* ... 333

Cellarman-waiter ... 144
Cellist ... 060
Cellophaner ... 287
Cellroom man ... 184
Cement worker ... 204

**Cementer;**
- envelope ... 295
- outsole ... 299
- paper ... 203
- rubber ... 299
- ship ... 316
- upper ... 299
- waterproof (*clothing mfr.*) ... 226

**Cementer-**
- *ceramic mfr.-* ... 223
- *electrical insulator mfr.* ... 283
- *footwear mfr.* ... 299
- *lens mfr.* ... 299
- *metal capsule mfr.* ... 285
- *plastics goods mfr.* ... 296
- *rubber goods mfr.* ... 299

Cemetery worker ... L346
Centerer (*lens mfr.*) ... 223
Centerer and edger (*lens mfr.*) ... 192
Centrer *see Centerer*
Ceramist ... 078
Certifier; money order ... 294
Chain boy ... 316
Chainman- ... 316
- *docks* ... 333
- *mine, not coal* ... 338

**Chairman-** *see also notes p.4*
- appeals tribunal, inquiry, etc. M027
- *glass mfr.* ... 192

Chalkman ... 182
Chamberman; cotton ... 176

**Chamberman-**
- *acids* ... 184
- *chemical mfr.* ... 184
- *cold storage* ... 333

Chamberlain ... 157
Chambermaid ... 151
Chambermaster ... 091
Chamferer ... 242
Chandler ... 101

| | Code number |
|---|---|
| Chocolate man | 202 |
| Chocolate worker | 202 |
| Chocolatier | 202 |
| Chopper; | |
| firewood | L346 |
| sugar | 202 |
| wood (*sawmilling*) | 218 |
| Chopper (*clothing mfr.*) | 211 |
| Chopperman (*paper mfr.*) | 176 |
| Choreographer | 059 |
| Chorister | 059 |
| Chorus girl | 059 |
| Chromer- | |
| *metal trades* | 236 |
| Chummer-in (*ceramic mfr.*) | 223 |
| Church Army worker | 040 |
| Church worker | 040 |
| Cider worker | 197 |
| Cinema worker | 165 |
| Cinematographer | 062 |
| Circuit man; electric light | 253 |
| Circular hand | 181 |
| Circus hand | L346 |
| Civil servant (n.o.s.) | 115 |
| Clammer (*roller engraving*) | 267 |
| Clampman (*fire brick mfr.*) | 204 |
| Clamper- | |
| *pencil mfr.* | 299 |
| *roller engraving* | 267 |
| *textile finishing* | 182 |
| Clapper boy | 062 |
| Clapper-loader | 061 |
| Clarifier man | 202 |
| Clarinettist | 060 |
| Classer | 298 |
| Classifier; | |
| livestock | 172 |
| Clatter (*celluloid*) | 229 |
| Clay boy (*metal mfr.*) | L344 |
| Clay man- | |
| *ceramic mfr.* | 204 |
| *clay pit* | 315 |
| Clay worker- | |
| *ceramic mfr.* | 223 |
| *clay pit* | 315 |
| Cleaner; | |
| aircraft | 158 |
| bag | 348 |
| bank | 158 |
| bar (*catering*) | 158 |
| barrel | 348 |
| bedding | 162 |
| belt (*coal mine*) | 338 |
| berth | 158 |
| blende | 198 |
| boat | 158 |
| bobbin | 199 |
| bogie | L346 |
| boiler | 276 |
| bone | 204 |
| book | L346 |
| boot | 175 |
| bottle | 348 |
| box (*textile printing*) | L339 |
| brass | L346 |
| bristle | 176 |
| buddle | L346 |
| building | 316 |
| bus | 158 |
| button | 229 |
| cab | 158 |
| cabinet; office; call | 158 |
| canteen | 158 |
| car | 158 |
| card | 276 |
| cardroom | 199 |
| carpet | 162 |
| carriage | 158 |
| casings; sausage | 202 |
| cask | 348 |
| casting | 244 |
| chimney | 158 |
| church | 158 |
| clock | 247 |

| Cleaner; *continued* | Code number |
|---|---|
| closet | 158 |
| cloth | 182 |
| clothes | 162 |
| coal | 198 |
| core | 270 |
| crane | 271 |
| cycle | L344 |
| decomposer (*nickel mfr.*) | L344 |
| domestic | 158 |
| drain | 158 |
| drum | L340 |
| dry | 162 |
| dye vat (straw plait) | L346 |
| economiser; boiler | 276 |
| engine; carding | 276 |
| engine- | |
| *coal mine* | 271 |
| *railways* | 271 |
| *shipping* | 317 |
| *waterworks* | 271 |
| equipment | L346 |
| factory | 158 |
| feather | 199 |
| fish | 187 |
| floor | 158 |
| flue | 158 |
| frame (cycles, motors) | L344 |
| french | 162 |
| fruit | 202 |
| fur | 162 |
| garment | 162 |
| general | 158 |
| glass (dry plates) | 227 |
| glove | 162 |
| gulley | L346 |
| gut | 204 |
| hat | 226 |
| heald | 276 |
| heddle | 276 |
| hide | 173 |
| hospital | 158 |
| house; | 158 |
| boiler | 276 |
| power | 158 |
| hydraulic | 271 |
| hygiene | 165 |
| iron | 244 |
| jet | L346 |
| kernel | 202 |
| key (locks) | 276 |
| kiosk; telephone | 158 |
| kitchen | 158 |
| laboratory | 158 |
| lace | 199 |
| lamp- | L346 |
| *coal mine* | 345 |
| lens | L342 |
| library | 158 |
| line | 338 |
| loco | 271 |
| locomotive | 271 |
| loom | 199 |
| machine- | L346 |
| *textile mfr.* | 199 |
| maintenance | L346 |
| meat | 186 |
| metal | 244 |
| meter | 246 |
| motor (*garage*) | 158 |
| mould | L346 |
| night | 158 |
| office | 158 |
| omnibus | 158 |
| picture | 055 |
| piece | 182 |
| pipe | 276 |
| pirn | 199 |
| pit (*railways*) | L346 |
| plant | L346 |
| plaster | 223 |
| plate- | |
| *catering* | 147 |
| *printing* | 227 |

| Cleaner; *continued* | Code number |
|---|---|
| potato | 165 |
| press (*rolling mill*) | 270 |
| printer's | 338 |
| rag | 176 |
| ramie | 182 |
| rice | 202 |
| ring | 244 |
| river | 316 |
| road- | 158 |
| *mine, not coal* | L346 |
| road and yard (*railways*) | 158 |
| roller | 199 |
| room; | |
| mess | 158 |
| show | 158 |
| sack | 348 |
| school | 158 |
| scrap- | L344 |
| *tobacco mfr.* | 201 |
| seed | 202 |
| sheet (*plastics mfr.*) | L340 |
| ship's | 158 |
| shop | 158 |
| silver- | 276 |
| *catering, hotels, etc.* | 147 |
| *domestic service* | 147 |
| skin; sausage | 202 |
| spillage | 345 |
| sponge | 204 |
| station (*railways*) | 158 |
| steam (*building and contracting*) | 316 |
| steel (*foundry*) | 244 |
| still | L340 |
| stone- | 316 |
| *iron* | 198 |
| street | 158 |
| table (*textile mfr.*) | 199 |
| tank | L346 |
| tape; magnetic | 348 |
| telephone | 158 |
| tin- | |
| bakery | L346 |
| *food canning* | L346 |
| *mine, not coal* | 198 |
| toilet | 165 |
| tongue | 186 |
| tramcar | 158 |
| tray (*bakery*) | L346 |
| tripe | 202 |
| tube; boiler | 276 |
| tube- | |
| *blast furnace* | L344 |
| *lamp, valve mfr.* | 348 |
| *railways* | 276 |
| upholstery | 158 |
| upper (*footwear mfr.*) | 175 |
| vacuum | 162 |
| vat | L346 |
| wagon (*coal mine*) | 345 |
| ware | 299 |
| warehouse | 158 |
| warp (*textile mfr.*) | 199 |
| waste | 176 |
| watch | 247 |
| wet | 162 |
| window | 158 |
| wire (*wire mfr.*) | 270 |
| wood | 203 |
| works | 158 |
| workshop | 158 |
| yard | 158 |
| Cleaner- | 158 |
| educational establishments | 158 |
| food products | 202 |
| institutional premises | 158 |
| machinery- | L346 |
| *textile machinery* | 199 |
| metal goods | 276 |
| office premises | 158 |
| residential premises | 158 |
| vehicles | 158 |
| *asbestos-cement mfr.* | 230 |

Code number

**Designer;** *continued*

| | Code number |
|---|---|
| display ... ... ... ... | 055 |
| dress ... ... ... ... | 057 |
| electric ... ... ... | 071 |
| electrical (control systems) ... | 071 |
| electronics ... ... ... | 072 |
| embroidery ... ... ... | 056 |
| exhibition ... ... ... | 055 |
| formwork ... ... ... | 082 |
| furniture ... ... ... | 056 |
| garden ... ... ... | 168 |
| gem ... ... ... ... | 056 |
| graphic ... ... ... | 079 |
| handbag ... ... ... | 056 |
| industrial ... ... ... | 056 |
| interior ... ... ... | 055 |
| jewellery ... ... ... | 056 |
| lace ... ... ... ... | 056 |
| lithographic ... ... ... | 056 |
| machinery; electrical ... ... | 071 |
| mechanical ... ... ... | 079 |
| nautical ... ... ... | 069 |
| naval ... ... ... ... | 069 |
| packaging ... ... ... | 056 |
| pattern (*textile printing*) ... | 056 |
| pottery ... ... ... | 056 |
| printer's ... ... ... | 056 |
| project *see Engineer-prof.-* | |
| roll (*steelworks*) ... ... | 079 |
| set ... ... ... ... | 055 |
| shopfitting ... ... ... | 056 |
| stage ... ... ... ... | 055 |
| stamp ... ... ... | 056 |
| structural ... ... ... | 082 |
| systems (*railway signalling*) ... | 071 |
| textile ... ... ... | 056 |
| textile print ... ... ... | 056 |
| tool ... ... ... ... | 079 |
| toy ... ... ... ... | 056 |
| trade mark ... ... ... | 055 |
| typographical ... ... | 205 |

**Designer-**

| | |
|---|---|
| ceramics ... ... ... | 056 |
| clothing ... ... ... | 057 |
| footwear ... ... ... | 056 |
| glassware ... ... ... | 056 |
| leather goods ... ... ... | 056 |
| plastics goods ... ... ... | 056 |
| scenery ... ... ... | 055 |
| wallpaper ... ... ... | 056 |
| wood products ... ... ... | 056 |
| *advertising* ... ... ... | 055 |
| *artificial flower mfr.* ... | 056 |
| *flour confectionery mfr.* ... | 185 |
| *fur goods mfr.* ... ... | 057 |
| *metal trades* ... ... ... | 056 |
| *millinery mfr.* ... ... | 057 |
| *rubber goods mfr.* ... ... | 056 |
| *soft toy mfr.* ... ... | 056 |
| *textile mfr.* ... ... ... | 056 |

**Designer and transferer** (*linoleum mfr.*) ... ... 115

**Designer-cutter-**

| | |
|---|---|
| *clothing mfr.* ... ... | 226 |
| *paper products mfr.* ... | 227 |

| | |
|---|---|
| **Designer-detailer** ... ... | 079 |
| **Designer-draughtsman** ... ... | 079 |
| **Desilveriser** ... ... | 231 |
| **Desizer** ... ... ... | 199 |
| **Despatch hand** ... ... | 333 |
| ,, man ... ... | 333 |
| ,, worker ... ... | 333 |

**Despatcher;**

| | |
|---|---|
| flight ... ... ... | 086 |
| goods ... ... ... | 333 |
| radio ... ... ... | 122 |
| traffic (*aircraft*) ... ... | 115 |
| train ... ... ... | 297 |

| | |
|---|---|
| **Destroyer** (pest) ... ... | 165 |
| **Destructor man; refuse** ... | 348 |

**Detective;**

| | |
|---|---|
| hotel ... ... ... | 140 |
| private ... ... ... | 140 |
| store ... ... ... | 140 |

Code number

**Detective-**

| | |
|---|---|
| *airport* ... ... ... | 137 |
| *docks* ... ... ... | 137 |
| *government* ... ... ... | 137 |
| *police service* ... ... | 137 |
| *private detective agency* | 140 |
| *railways* ... ... ... | 137 |
| *retail trade* ... ... | 140 |

| | |
|---|---|
| **Detector; crack** (*metal mfr.*) ... | 286 |
| **Detonator worker** (*chemical mfr.*) ... ... | 230 |

**Developer;**

| | |
|---|---|
| estate ... ... ... | 134 |
| film ... ... ... | 227 |
| property ... ... ... | 134 |

**Developer-**

| | |
|---|---|
| *coal mine* ... ... ... | 314 |
| *photographic processing* ... | 227 |
| *textile mfr.* ... ... | 182 |

| | |
|---|---|
| **Development worker** (*coal mine*) | 314 |
| **Devil** (*printing*) ... ... | L.346 |
| **Devilman** (*paper mfr.*) ... | 176 |
| **Deviller** ... ... ... | 176 |
| **Devulcaniser man** (*rubber reclamation*) ... ... | 204 |
| **Dewer** ... ... ... | 182 |

**Diagnostician-**
*H.M. Dockyard-*

| | |
|---|---|
| electrical ... ... ... | 259 |
| mechanical ... ... | 248 |

| | |
|---|---|
| **Diarist** ... ... ... | 054 |
| **Die man** (*plastics goods mfr.*) ... | 195 |
| **Dietician** ... ... ... | 053 |
| **Digester** ... ... ... | 184 |
| ,, man ... ... ... | 184 |
| ,, worker ... ... | 184 |

**Digger;**

| | |
|---|---|
| bait ... ... ... | 171 |
| coal (*coal mine*) ... ... | 314 |
| grave ... ... ... | 316 |
| peat ... ... ... | 172 |
| trench ... ... ... | 313 |
| turf ... ... ... | 168 |

| | |
|---|---|
| **Digger** (*mine, not coal*) ... | 315 |
| **Digger man** ... ... | 330 |
| **Dingman** ... ... ... | 261 |
| **Dinker** (*coal mine*) ... ... | 314 |
| **Diplomat** ... ... ... | 020 |

**Dipper;**

| | |
|---|---|
| acid ... ... ... | 270 |
| automatic (*ceramic mfr.*) ... | 279 |
| brass ... ... ... | 270 |
| cellulose ... ... ... | 299 |
| chocolate ... ... ... | 202 |
| core ... ... ... | 270 |
| enamel ... ... ... | 299 |
| fondant ... ... ... | 202 |
| galvanizing ... ... ... | 269 |
| glove ... ... ... | 228 |
| hand (*sugar confectionery mfr.*) ... ... | 202 |
| machine (*ceramic mfr.*) ... | 279 |
| metal ... ... ... | 269 |
| paint ... ... ... | 299 |
| rubber ... ... ... | 228 |
| tank (*petroleum distribution*) | 297 |
| toffee ... ... ... | 202 |
| wire ... ... ... | 269 |

**Dipper-**

| | |
|---|---|
| *ceramic mfr.* ... ... | 279 |
| *leather dressing* ... ... | 173 |
| *match mfr.* ... ... | 230 |
| *metal trades-* ... ... | 299 |
| *arc welding electrode mfr.* | 269 |
| *galvanizing* ... ... | 269 |
| *precious metal, plate mfr.* | 236 |
| *oil refining* ... ... | 297 |
| *paper mfr.* ... ... | 203 |
| *rubber mfr.* ... ... | 228 |
| *sugar confectionery mfr.* ... | 202 |
| *textile mfr.* ... ... | 182 |

| | |
|---|---|
| **Dipper and stripper** ... ... | 270 |

**Director;** *see also notes p.4*

| | |
|---|---|
| art ... ... ... | 055 |

Code number

**Director;** *continued*

| | |
|---|---|
| casting (*entertainment*) ... | M059 |
| commercial ... ... | 013 |
| divisional (*Red Cross*) ... | M039 |
| film ... ... ... | M059 |
| financial ... ... ... | 006 |
| funeral ... ... ... | 163 |
| housing ... ... ... | M039 |
| managing *see Manager* | |
| media ... ... ... | 014 |
| museum ... ... ... | 030 |
| musical ... ... ... | 060 |
| regional- | |
| *government* ... ... | 021 |
| *P.O.* ... ... ... | 099 |
| sales ... ... ... | 013 |
| sales and export ... ... | 013 |
| stage ... ... ... | M059 |
| technical ... ... ... | 078 |
| of contracts (*government*) ... | 016 |
| of education ... ... | 035 |
| of music (*entertainment*) ... | M060 |
| of photography ... ... | M059 |
| of production (*entertainment*) | M059 |
| of programmes ... ... | M059 |
| of research- | |
| biological science ... | 065 |
| chemistry ... ... | 066 |
| physical science ... | 067 |
| of social services ... ... | M039 |

| | |
|---|---|
| **Director** (*W.R.N.S.*) ... ... | M135 |
| **Director and Secretary** ... ... | 023 |
| **Dis hand** ... ... ... | 227 |
| **Disc man** ... ... ... | 192 |

**Discharger-**

| | |
|---|---|
| *coal gas, coke ovens* ... | 338 |
| *docks* ... ... ... | 334 |

| | |
|---|---|
| **Disinfector;** ... ... | 165 |
| fitter ... ... ... | 276 |

**Disintegrator-**

| | |
|---|---|
| *asbestos composition goods mfr.* ... ... | 176 |
| *food products mfr.* ... | 202 |

**Dismantler;**

| | |
|---|---|
| engine; aircraft ... ... | 250 |
| furnace ... ... ... | 312 |
| machinery ... ... | 276 |
| ship ... ... ... | 276 |

**Dismantler-**

| | |
|---|---|
| *building and contracting* ... | 316 |
| *coal mine* ... ... | 314 |
| *scrap merchant, breakers* ... | 276 |

| | |
|---|---|
| **Dispatch hand** ... ... | 333 |

**Dispatch man-**

| | |
|---|---|
| *bakery* ... ... | 333 |
| *catering* ... ... | 146 |

| | |
|---|---|
| **Dispense hand** (*catering*) ... | 146 |
| **Dispenser; drink** ... ... | 145 |

**Dispenser-**

| | |
|---|---|
| food and beverages ... ... | 050 |
| *bakery* ... ... | 146 |
| *licensed trade* ... ... | 297 |

**Display hand-**

| | |
|---|---|
| *firework mfr.* ... ... | 064 |
| *retail trade-* ... ... | 055 |
| shelf filling ... ... | 126 |

| | |
|---|---|
| **Displayman; window** ... ... | 058 |

**Displayman-**

| | |
|---|---|
| *printing* ... ... | 205 |
| *retail trade-* ... ... | 055 |
| shelf filling ... ... | 126 |

| | |
|---|---|
| **Dissector** (*clothing mfr.*) ... | 211 |

**Distiller-** ... ... ... 184

| | |
|---|---|
| *lead, zinc refining* ... | 231 |

**Distributor;**

| | |
|---|---|
| bill ... ... ... | 124 |
| circular ... ... ... | 124 |
| coal ... ... ... | 101 |
| film ... ... ... | 134 |
| food ... ... ... | 101 |
| freight (*railways*) ... ... | 097 |
| leaflet ... ... ... | 124 |
| paste (*aluminium*) ... ... | 270 |
| tract ... ... ... | 124 |

| | Code number |
|---|---|
| **Distributor;** *continued* | |
| weft ... ... ... ... | 338 |
| work ... ... ... ... | 338 |
| **Distributor-** | |
| *manufacturing* ... | 338 |
| *wholesale, retail trade* ... | 101 |
| **Ditcher;** ... ... ... | 316 |
| stone ... ... ... | 301 |
| **Diver** ... ... ... | 316 |
| **Divider;** | |
| hand- ... ... ... | 246 |
| *bakery* ... ... ... | 200 |
| mathematical instrument | 246 |
| thermometer ... ... | 246 |
| **Divider-** | |
| *clothing mfr.* ... ... | 299 |
| *type foundry* ... ... | 298 |
| **Divider hand** (*bakery*) ... | 200 |
| **Divider man** (*bakery*) ... | 200 |
| **Diviner; water** ... ... | 165 |
| **Dock crew** ... ... | 334 |
| **Dock man-** ... ... | 334 |
| *ship repairing* ... ... | L344 |
| **Dock worker-** ... ... | 334 |
| dry dock ... ... | L344 |
| **Docker; cork** ... ... | 230 |
| **Docker** (*docks*) ... ... | 334 |
| **Dockside worker** ... ... | 334 |
| **Dockyard worker** ... ... | L344 |
| **Doctor;** ... ... ... | 041 |
| saw ... ... ... | 276 |
| **Dodger; can** ... ... | 176 |
| **Dodger** (*textile finishing*) ... | 176 |
| **Doffer;** ... ... ... | 199 |
| ring ... ... ... | 177 |
| **Doffer and setter** ... ... | 199 |
| **Dogger** ... ... ... | 270 |
| **Dogger-on** ... ... | 270 |
| **Dogger-up** (tubes) ... | 270 |
| **Dollier-** | |
| *silversmiths* ... ... | 243 |
| *textile mfr.* ... ... | 179 |
| **Dolly hand** ... ... | 182 |
| **Dollyer** ... ... ... | 179 |
| **Dolomite man** (*iron, steelworks*) | 204 |
| **Domestic** ... ... | 151 |
| **Domestic worker** ... ... | 151 |
| **Donkeyman-** ... ... | 331 |
| *shipping* ... ... | F317 |
| **Door boy-** | |
| *catering, hotels, etc.* ... | 165 |
| *iron, steelworks* ... | L344 |
| **Doorman; furnace** ... | 270 |
| **Doorman-** ... ... | 165 |
| *coke ovens* ... ... | L341 |
| *forging* ... ... | 270 |
| **Doper-** | |
| *aircraft mfr.* ... ... | 299 |
| *leather dressing* ... | 173 |
| **Doubler;** | |
| asbestos ... ... | 177 |
| cloth ... ... ... | 199 |
| derby ... ... ... | 177 |
| ring ... ... ... | 177 |
| warp ... ... ... | 199 |
| **Doubler-** | |
| *metal rolling* ... ... | 270 |
| *textile mfr.-* ... ... | 177 |
| *textile bleaching* ... | 199 |
| *textile dyeing* ... | 199 |
| **Dough man** ... ... | 200 |
| **Draffman** (*whisky*) ... | 197 |
| **Drafter;** | |
| fibre ... ... ... | 176 |
| policy (*insurance*) ... | 115 |
| slipper ... ... ... | 176 |
| stone ... ... ... | 301 |
| **Drafter** (*brush mfr.*) ... | 176 |
| **Draftsman; parliamentary** ... | 001 |
| **Dragger;** | |
| bar ... ... ... | 231 |
| pipe (*brickworks*) ... | 338 |
| set ... ... ... | 338 |
| skip ... ... ... | 338 |

| | Code number |
|---|---|
| **Dragger-down** ... ... ... | 270 |
| **Drainman** ... ... ... | L346 |
| **Drainage worker** ... ... | 316 |
| **Drainer-** ... ... ... | 316 |
| *brewery* ... ... | L346 |
| **Dramatist** ... ... ... | 054 |
| **Draper;** ... ... ... | 101 |
| armhole ... ... | 162 |
| credit ... ... ... | 132 |
| market ... ... ... | 130 |
| travelling ... ... | 130 |
| **Draughter** *see Drafter* | |
| **Draughtsman;** ... ... | 079 |
| cartographical ... | 079 |
| chief ... ... ... | F079 |
| embroidery ... ... | 115 |
| geographical ... ... | 079 |
| lace ... ... ... | 115 |
| lithographic ... ... | 205 |
| photographic (chart) ... | 079 |
| printer's ... ... | 205 |
| **Draughtsman-engineer** ... | 079 |
| **Draughtsman-surveyor** ... | 079 |
| **Drawer;** | |
| bar ... ... ... | 234 |
| brick ... ... ... | 338 |
| brush ... ... ... | 230 |
| card ... ... ... | 176 |
| chock (*coal mine*) ... | 314 |
| cloth- ... ... ... | 289 |
| *textile finishing* ... | 182 |
| coke (*coke ovens*) ... | 338 |
| cotton ... ... ... | 176 |
| fine- | |
| *clothes repairing* ... | 183 |
| *textile mfr.* ... | 183 |
| fork ... ... ... | 270 |
| french ... ... ... | 183 |
| gear ... ... ... | 179 |
| hair ... ... ... | 176 |
| kiln- | |
| *ceramic mfr.* ... | 338 |
| *chemical mfr.* ... | 184 |
| lime- | |
| *lime burning* ... | 204 |
| *mine, not coal* ... | 338 |
| oven (*ceramic mfr.*) ... | 338 |
| pick ... ... ... | 233 |
| plate (wire) ... ... | 270 |
| prop- ... ... ... | 315 |
| *coal mine* ... ... | 314 |
| rod- | |
| glass ... ... ... | 192 |
| metal ... ... ... | 234 |
| salvage (*coal mine*) ... | 314 |
| steel- ... ... ... | 234 |
| *coal mine* ... ... | 314 |
| strip (metal) ... ... | 234 |
| tape (metal) ... ... | 234 |
| timber- | |
| *coal mine* ... ... | 314 |
| *mine, not coal* ... | 315 |
| tube- | |
| glass ... ... ... | 192 |
| metal ... ... ... | 234 |
| waste (*coal mine*) ... | 314 |
| wire ... ... ... | 234 |
| wool ... ... ... | 176 |
| worsted ... ... ... | 176 |
| yarn ... ... ... | 176 |
| **Drawer-** | |
| glass ... ... ... | 192 |
| metal ... ... ... | 234 |
| *brush mfr.* ... ... | 230 |
| *ceramic mfr.* ... ... | 338 |
| *coal mine* ... ... | 338 |
| *glass mfr.* ... ... | 192 |
| *metal trades-* ... ... | 234 |
| *forging* ... ... | 233 |
| *puddling* ... ... | 231 |
| *zinc refining* ... | 231 |
| *mine, not coal* ... | 338 |
| *paper mfr.* ... ... | 338 |

| | Code number |
|---|---|
| **Drawer-** *continued* | |
| *textile mfr.-* ... ... | 176 |
| *jute mfr.* ... ... | 179 |
| *lace mfr.* ... ... | 289 |
| *textile finishing* ... | 182 |
| *textile weaving* ... | 179 |
| **Drawer and marker** | |
| (*assay office*) ... | 270 |
| **Drawer and setter** | |
| (*brick mfr.*) ... ... | 191 |
| **Drawer-in** (*textile mfr.*) ... | 179 |
| **Drawer-off-** | |
| *coal mine* ... ... | 338 |
| *textile mfr.* ... ... | 199 |
| **Drawing hand-** | |
| *brush, broom mfr.* ... | 230 |
| *textile mfr.* ... ... | 176 |
| **Drawtwist operative; nylon** ... | 177 |
| **Dray boy** ... ... | 329 |
| **Drayman** ... ... ... | 326 |
| **Dredgeman-** ... ... | 330 |
| shell fish ... ... | 171 |
| **Dredger-** ... ... ... | 330 |
| shell fish ... ... | 171 |
| **Dredgerman** ... ... | 330 |
| **Dredgermaster** ... ... | F330 |
| **Dreep man** | |
| (*by-products mfr.*) ... | 184 |
| **Drencher** ... ... ... | 173 |
| **Dresser;** | |
| bag ... ... ... | 182 |
| bass ... ... ... | 176 |
| bow ... ... ... | 276 |
| box; ... ... ... | 287 |
| axle ... ... ... | 244 |
| brick (*brick mfr.*) ... | 223 |
| bristle ... ... ... | 176 |
| card ... ... ... | 276 |
| casings; sausage ... | 202 |
| casting ... ... ... | 244 |
| cloth ... ... ... | 182 |
| coloured ... ... | 179 |
| concrete ... ... | 230 |
| core ... ... ... | 244 |
| cork ... ... ... | 230 |
| diamond ... ... | 266 |
| doll ... ... ... | 230 |
| fibre ... ... ... | 176 |
| flour ... ... ... | 202 |
| fly ... ... ... | 230 |
| fowl ... ... ... | 187 |
| frame (*rolling mill*) ... | 265 |
| fur ... ... ... | 173 |
| game ... ... ... | 187 |
| gypsum ... ... ... | 204 |
| hair; horse ... ... | 176 |
| hair- | |
| *broom, brush mfr.* ... | 176 |
| *hairdressing* ... | 159 |
| heald ... ... ... | 276 |
| iron ... ... ... | 244 |
| kerb ... ... ... | 301 |
| leather ... ... ... | 173 |
| lime ... ... ... | 204 |
| meat ... ... ... | 186 |
| metal ... ... ... | 244 |
| pipe ... ... ... | 244 |
| plate ... ... ... | 244 |
| potato ... ... ... | 172 |
| poultry ... ... ... | 187 |
| sack ... ... ... | 182 |
| scissors ... ... | 276 |
| seed ... ... ... | 202 |
| sett ... ... ... | 301 |
| shirt (*shirt mfr.*) ... | 162 |
| silk ... ... ... | 176 |
| skin- ... ... ... | 173 |
| *sausage mfr.* ... | 202 |
| slate ... ... ... | 301 |
| steel ... ... ... | 244 |
| stick ... ... ... | 224 |
| stone- ... ... ... | 301 |
| *concrete products mfr.* ... | 230 |
| tin ... ... ... | 198 |

Fitter; *continued*

| | Code number |
|---|---|
| jig and tool | 245 |
| keg | 248 |
| knife | 248 |
| laboratory | 248 |
| lamp; arc | 252 |
| last; bespoke | 175 |
| lift (electric) | 248 |
| light (electric) | 253 |
| limb | 050 |
| lining; brake | 249 |
| lino- | 316 |
| linotype machine | 248 |
| linoleum | 316 |
| linotype | 248 |
| locking (signals) | 248 |
| locomotive | 248 |
| loom | 248 |
| machine- | 248 |
| electrical machines | 252 |
| mains- | |
| *electricity board* | 253 |
| *water board* | 311 |
| maintenance; | |
| computer | 259 |
| electrical | 253 |
| maintenance- | 248 |
| aircraft engines | 250 |
| office machinery servicing | 251 |
| radio, television servicing | 258 |
| vehicle servicing | 249 |
| *gas board-* | 260 |
| *gas works* | 248 |
| *P.O.* | 256 |
| marine | 248 |
| mattress (wire) | 248 |
| mechanical- | 248 |
| vehicle- | 249 |
| *vehicle mfr.* | 248 |
| metal | 248 |
| meter | 246 |
| mirror (*furniture mfr.*) | 224 |
| motor; gramophone | 285 |
| motor- | 249 |
| electric | 252 |
| *vehicle mfr.* | 248 |
| mould; | 270 |
| bottle | 248 |
| mount; boiler | 248 |
| mouthpiece (pipes) | 299 |
| mule | 248 |
| net | 199 |
| nicker and turner's | 248 |
| n.o.s. | 248 |
| office | 214 |
| optical | 246 |
| ordnance | 248 |
| organ | 222 |
| oven | 248 |
| overmantel | 215 |
| palisade | 233 |
| paragon (umbrellas) | 285 |
| paste | 299 |
| pattern (*engineering*) | 245 |
| pen; fountain | 299 |
| piano | 222 |
| pillar | 253 |
| pipe; | 260 |
| boiler | 248 |
| briar | 299 |
| drain | 311 |
| plant | 248 |
| plate; | 262 |
| boot | 299 |
| potter's | 248 |
| precision- | 248 |
| *instrument mfr.* | 246 |
| printing | 248 |
| pump | 248 |
| radar | 259 |
| radio | 258 |
| rail (bedstead) | 248 |
| range | 248 |
| rectification | 248 |

Fitter; *continued*

| | Code number |
|---|---|
| repair; engine | 248 |
| research | 248 |
| retort | 248 |
| rheostat | 252 |
| room; tool | 245 |
| rope and belt | 272 |
| ropery; wire | 272 |
| rough | 248 |
| saddle (cycles) | 285 |
| safe | 248 |
| sanitary | 260 |
| scale | 246 |
| scissors | 248 |
| screen- | |
| *coal mine* | 248 |
| *vehicle mfr.* | 299 |
| scythe | 276 |
| semi-skilled | 285 |
| service- | 248 |
| aircraft | 250 |
| instruments | 246 |
| office machines | 251 |
| ship | 248 |
| shoe (*retail trade*) | 125 |
| shop; machine | 248 |
| shop- | 214 |
| *metal trades* | 248 |
| shop and office | 214 |
| sign- | 316 |
| *electric signs* | 253 |
| signal; railway | 259 |
| skilled | 248 |
| skip (*coal mine*) | 248 |
| soundbox | 285 |
| speed | 248 |
| speedometer | 246 |
| spring; | 248 |
| elastic | 175 |
| hat; opera | 212 |
| spring (*forging*) | 233 |
| sprinkler | 260 |
| stand- | |
| exhibition stand | 214 |
| sewing machine stand | 248 |
| starter; motor | 252 |
| steam | 260 |
| steam and hot water | 260 |
| steel | 248 |
| steelyard | 248 |
| stock- | |
| *bedstead mfr.* | 248 |
| *footwear mfr.* | 298 |
| stove- | |
| *building and contracting* | 260 |
| *stove mfr.* | 285 |
| structural | 248 |
| sun-blind | 316 |
| superintendent | F248 |
| surface | 248 |
| switch | 252 |
| switchboard | 252 |
| switchgear | 252 |
| table; billiard | 230 |
| tailor's | 210 |
| tank | 248 |
| taximeter | 246 |
| telegraph; | 259 |
| ship's | 246 |
| telephone | 256 |
| television | 258 |
| tender | 248 |
| textile | 248 |
| tool; | 245 |
| edge | 245 |
| machine | 248 |
| press | 248 |
| torpedo | 248 |
| tractor | 248 |
| transformer | 252 |
| transport | 249 |
| tread; tyre | 194 |
| trolleybus | 248 |
| truck (electric) | 252 |

Fitter; *continued*

| | Code number |
|---|---|
| try-out | 248 |
| tube- | 260 |
| *boiler mfr.* | 262 |
| *locomotive mfr.* | 262 |
| turbine | 248 |
| turning | 248 |
| tyre | 276 |
| umbrella | 299 |
| upholsterer's | 213 |
| valve- | |
| *engineering* | 248 |
| *tyre mfr.* | 299 |
| vehicles- | 249 |
| *vehicle mfr.* | 248 |
| ventilation | 260 |
| wagon (*railway workshops*) | 248 |
| water | 260 |
| weighbridge | 248 |
| wheel | 248 |
| window (metal) | 248 |
| windscreen | 299 |
| work; smith's | 248 |
| Fitter- | |
| machinery- | 248 |
| electrical machines | 252 |
| vehicles- | 249 |
| *vehicle mfr.* | 248 |
| *bag frame mfr.* | 285 |
| *cabinet making* | 215 |
| *cardboard container mfr.* | 295 |
| *clothing mfr.* | 210 |
| *electricity board* | 253 |
| *fishing rod mfr.* | 230 |
| *footwear mfr.* | 175 |
| *garage* | 249 |
| *gas board-* | 260 |
| *gas works* | 248 |
| *heating contracting* | 260 |
| *leather goods mfr.* | 225 |
| *loose leaf book mfr.* | 285 |
| *metal trades-* | 248 |
| *instrument mfr.* | 246 |
| *jewellery, plate mfr.* | 266 |
| *mining* | 248 |
| *musical instrument mfr.* | 222 |
| *net mfr.* | 199 |
| *railways* | 248 |
| *shipbuilding* | 248 |
| *shop blind mfr.* | 316 |
| *tobacco pipe mfr.* | 299 |
| Fitter and assembler | 248 |
| Fitter and erector- | 248 |
| public lighting | 312 |
| *constructional engineering* | 263 |
| Fitter and examiner | 248 |
| Fitter and marker-off | 245 |
| Fitter and tester | 248 |
| Fitter and trimmer | 210 |
| Fitter and turner | 248 |
| Fitter-assembler | 248 |
| Fitter-driver | 248 |
| Fitter-engineer | 248 |
| Fitter-erector | 248 |
| Fitter-in-charge | F248 |
| Fitter-inspector | 248 |
| Fitter-machinist | 248 |
| Fitter-mechanic- | 248 |
| *garage* | 249 |
| Fitter-on | 210 |
| Fitter-operator; | |
| capstan | 248 |
| machine tool | 248 |
| Fitter-tester | 248 |
| Fitter-turner | 248 |
| Fitter-up; | |
| frame; picture | 299 |
| table; billiard | 230 |
| Fitter-up- | |
| *clothing mfr.* | 211 |
| *footwear mfr.* | 299 |
| *foundry* | 248 |
| *musical instrument mfr.-* | 222 |
| *piano case mfr.* | 215 |

**Foreman-** *continued* — Code number

| | |
|---|---|
| *auctioneering* | F335 |
| *bakery* | F185 |
| *baths* | F165 |
| *bedding mfr.* | F213 |
| *blue and starch mfr.* | F184 |
| *bookcloth mfr.* | F180 |
| *brake linings mfr.* | F230 |
| *brewery* | F197 |
| *brush mfr.* | F230 |
| *building and contracting* | F316 |
| *calico printers* | F227 |
| *canvas goods mfr.* | F226 |
| *cardboard box mfr.* | F227 |
| *cast concrete products mfr.* | F230 |
| *catering* | F146 |
| *cattle food mfr.* | F202 |
| *cement mfr.* | F204 |
| *cemetery* | F165 |
| *ceramic mfr.* | F193 |
| *chemical mfr.* | F184 |
| *chocolate mfr.* | F202 |
| *cigarette mfr.* | F201 |
| *cinema* | F165 |
| *civil engineering* | F316 |
| *clothing mfr.* | F226 |
| *coal merchants* | F324 |
| *coke ovens* | F184 |
| *construction* | F316 |
| *cork mfr.* | F230 |
| *cotton waste merchants* | F176 |
| *D.O.E.* | F316 |
| *dairy-* | F202 |
|    *retail trade* | F128 |
| *denture mfr.* | F220 |
| *docks* | F334 |
| *dry cleaning* | F162 |
| *dyeing and cleaning* | F162 |
| *dyeworks* | F182 |
| *electrical contracting* | F253 |
| *electricity board* | F253 |
| *enamelling* | F299 |
| *entertainment* | F165 |
| *fancy goods mfr.* | F230 |
| *flooring contracting* | F316 |
| *flour confectionery mfr.* | F185 |
| *food canning* | F287 |
| *food products mfr.* | F202 |
| *footwear mfr.* | F175 |
| *forestry* | F170 |
| *furniture mfr.* | F215 |
| *garage* | F249 |
| *gas board-* | F260 |
|    *by-product plant* | F184 |
|    *gas works* | F184 |
| *gelatine mfr.* | F184 |
| *glass mfr.* | F192 |
| *grain milling* | F202 |
| *grinding wheel mfr.* | F230 |
| *heating engineering* | F260 |
| *horticulture* | F167 |
| *joinery mfr.* | F214 |
| *lairage* | F172 |
| *laundry* | F162 |
| *leather cloth mfr.* | F199 |
| *leather dressing* | F173 |
| *leather goods mfr.* | F225 |
| *linoleum mfr.* | F204 |
| *local government-* | F316 |
|    *baths dept.* | F165 |
|    *cleansing dept.* | F336 |
|    *council depot* | F338 |
|    *engineer's dept.* | F316 |
|    *highways dept.* | F308 |
|    *housing dept.* | F316 |
|    *parks dept.* | F168 |
|    *public works* | F316 |
|    *refuse tip* | FL346 |
|    *sanitary dept.* | F336 |
|    *sewage works* | F310 |
|    *surveyor's dept.* | F316 |
|    *transport dept.* | F324 |
|    *treasurer's dept.* | F115 |
| *match mfr.* | F230 |

**Foreman-** *continued* — Code number

| | |
|---|---|
| *metal trades-* | F277 |
|    *annealing* | F237 |
|    *assembling* | F285 |
|    *blast furnace* | F231 |
|    *cable mfr.* | F276 |
|    *coach building* | F268 |
|    *constructional engineering* | F263 |
|    *electronic equipment mfr.* | F252 |
|    *electroplating* | F236 |
|    *forging* | F233 |
|    *foundry* | F235 |
|    *heat treatment* | F237 |
|    *instrument mfr.* | F246 |
|    *jewellery mfr.* | F266 |
|    *lamp, valve mfr.* | F238 |
|    *machine shop* | F241 |
|    *metal extrusion* | F270 |
|    *metal pressing* | F242 |
|    *metal refining* | F231 |
|    *metal tube mfr.* | F270 |
|    *press tool mfr.* | F245 |
|    *radio, television mfr.* | F252 |
|    *rolling mill* | F232 |
|    *sheet metal working* | F261 |
|    *shipbuilding* | F262 |
|    *stamping and piercing* | F242 |
|    *tinplate mfr.* | F232 |
|    *tool room* | F245 |
|    *welding* | F265 |
|    *wire mfr.* | F234 |
| *mine, not coal* | F315 |
| *mineral water mfr.* | F202 |
| *nursery* | F167 |
| *oil refining* | F184 |
| *oil seed crushing* | F202 |
| *opencast coal mining* | F315 |
| *ordnance depot* | F333 |
| *ordnance factory-* | F277 |
|    *explosive mfr.* | F184 |
|    *shell filling* | F230 |
| *P.L.A.* | F334 |
| *P.O.-* | F256 |
|    *post office railway* | F123 |
| *packing* | F287 |
| *paint mfr.* | F184 |
| *paper mfr.* | F188 |
| *paper goods mfr.* | F227 |
| *patent fuel mfr.* | F184 |
| *pen mfr.* | F230 |
| *pencil, crayon mfr.* | F230 |
| *petrol station* | F127 |
| *petroleum distribution* | F338 |
| *plasterboard mfr.* | F204 |
| *plastics goods mfr.-* | F229 |
|    *calendering* | F195 |
|    *extruding* | F195 |
|    *moulding* | F195 |
| *power station* | F255 |
| *printing* | F207 |
| *provision merchants* | F125 |
| *publishing* | F207 |
| *railways-* | F318 |
|    *carriage and wagon dept.* | F277 |
|    *district engineer's dept.* | F306 |
|    *locomotive shop* | F248 |
|    *motive power dept.* | F248 |
|    *signal and telegraph dept.* | F259 |
| *removal contracting* | F335 |
| *repository* | F333 |
| *retail trade* | F125 |
| *river board* | F316 |
| *road transport* | F324 |
| *rubber goods mfr.-* | F228 |
|    *calendering* | F194 |
|    *extruding* | F194 |
|    *moulding* | F194 |
| *sawmilling* | F218 |
| *scrap merchants* | F338 |
| *security services* | F140 |
| *sewage disposal* | F310 |
| *slag wool mfr.* | F184 |
| *soap mfr.* | F184 |
| *spirit distilling* | F184 |

**Foreman-** *continued* — Code number

| | |
|---|---|
| *sports goods mfr.* | F230 |
| *sugar confectionery mfr.* | F202 |
| *sugar refining* | F202 |
| *surgical dressing mfr.* | F199 |
| *tailoring* | F210 |
| *tannery* | F173 |
| *textile mfr.-* | F199 |
|    *combing dept.* | F176 |
|    *doubling, twisting dept.* | F177 |
|    *dyeing dept.* | F182 |
|    *finishing dept.* | F182 |
|    *hosiery mfr.* | F181 |
|    *man-made fibre mfr.* | F196 |
|    *opening, carding dept.* | F176 |
|    *printing dept.* | F227 |
|    *spinning dept.* | F177 |
|    *weaving dept.* | F180 |
|    *winding dept.* | F178 |
| *timber merchants* | F333 |
| *tobacco mfr.* | F201 |
| *tobacco pipe mfr.* | F224 |
| *toilet preparation mfr.* | F184 |
| *toy mfr.* | F230 |
| *typewriter ribbon mfr.* | F199 |
| *upholstering* | F213 |
| *wallpaper mfr.* | FL346 |
| *warehousing* | F333 |
| *water works* | F310 |
| *waterways* | F316 |
| *woodware mfr.* | F214 |
| *wreck raising* | FL346 |
| *zoo* | F172 |
| **Foreman-ganger-** *see also Fore-* | |
|    *man-* | |
|    *maintenance* | F316 |
| *agriculture* | F166 |
| *building and contracting* | F316 |
| *cable laying* | F311 |
| *docks* | F334 |
| *electricity board* | F311 |
| *gas board* | F311 |
| *local government* | F316 |
| *P.O.* | F257 |
| *railways* | F306 |
| *water works* | F311 |
| **Forewoman; factory (***P.O.***)** | F283 |
| **Forewoman-** *see also Foreman-* | |
|    *government* | F158 |
|    *P.O.* | F227 |
| **Forest workman** | 170 |
| **Forest worker** | 170 |
| **Forester** | F170 |
| **Forestry worker** | 170 |
| **Forge hand** | 270 |
| **Forgeman** | 270 |
| **Forge worker** | 270 |
| **Forger** | 233 |
| **Forker-** | 338 |
|    *glass mfr.* | 204 |
|    *wrought iron mfr.* | 231 |
| **Former;** | |
|    *accumulator* | 276 |
|    *battery* | 276 |
|    *cable* | 274 |
|    *cell (battery)* | 276 |
|    *coil* | 274 |
|    *copper (generators)* | 274 |
|    *filament* | 276 |
|    *glass* | 192 |
|    *hat* | 199 |
|    *lap* | 176 |
|    *loom* | 274 |
|    *plate; tungsten* | 276 |
|    *rope* | 199 |
|    *strand* | 199 |
|    *toe; veldtschoen* | 175 |
|    *tube* | 270 |
|    *wire (spring mfr.)* | 276 |
| **Former-** | |
|    *felt hat mfr.* | 199 |
|    *plastics mfr.* | 229 |
|    *tube mfr.* | 270 |
| **Fortune teller** | 165 |

| | Code number |
|---|---|
| Forwarder ... ... ... | 189 |
| Founder; type ... ... | 270 |
| Founder- | |
| *glass mfr.* ... ... | 191 |
| *metal trades-* | 270 |
| *blast furnace* | 231 |
| *copper refining* | 231 |
| *type foundry* | 270 |
| Foundry hand ... | L343 |
| Foundry man ... ... | 270 |
| Foundry worker ... | L343 |
| Fourth hand (*rolling mill*) ... | 270 |
| Fractionator (*chemical mfr.*) | 184 |
| Fraiser ... ... ... | 244 |
| Frame hand; mustard ... | 202 |
| Frame hand- | |
| *hosiery mfr.* ... ... | 181 |
| *sugar confectionery mfr.* ... | 202 |
| Frame man (*rope mfr.*) ... | 199 |
| Frame worker; | |
| hand ... ... ... | 181 |
| knitting ... ... | 181 |
| Frame worker (*rope mfr.*) ... | 199 |
| Framer; | |
| bag ... ... ... | 299 |
| binocular ... ... | 246 |
| calico ... ... ... | 226 |
| curtain (*laundry*) ... | 162 |
| picture ... ... | 224 |
| ring ... ... ... | 177 |
| rule ... ... ... | 218 |
| seat ... ... ... | 215 |
| Framer- | |
| *chair mfr.* ... ... | 215 |
| *laundry* ... ... | 162 |
| *leather goods mfr.* ... | 299 |
| *shipbuilding* ... | 262 |
| *textile mfr.-* | 176 |
| *hosiery mfr.* ... | 182 |
| *wool spinning* ... | 177 |
| Frazer- | |
| *metal trades* ... | 244 |
| *tobacco pipe mfr.* ... | 218 |
| Freeman (River Thames) ... | 317 |
| Freezer ... ... ... | 202 |
| Friar ... ... ... | 040 |
| Fridgeman (*ice cream mfr.*) | 202 |
| Frier *see Fryer* | |
| Friller ... ... ... | 212 |
| Fringer ... ... ... | 181 |
| Fritter ... ... ... | 204 |
| Frogman ... ... | 316 |
| Front boy (*clothing mfr.*) ... | 226 |
| ,, girl (*clothing mfr.*) | 226 |
| ,, hand (*clothing mfr.*) | 226 |
| Frontsman (*retail trade*) ... | 125 |
| Froster- | |
| *electric lamp mfr.* ... | 192 |
| *glass mfr.* ... ... | 192 |
| Fruitman; ... ... | 167 |
| head ... ... ... | F167 |
| Fruiterer- | 101 |
| *market trading* ... | 130 |
| Fryer; fish- ... ... | 143 |
| self-employed ... | 104 |
| Fryer- | |
| *catering* ... ... | 143 |
| *food products mfr.* ... | 202 |
| Fuelman (ship) ... ... | 317 |
| Fuller ... ... ... | 199 |
| Fumigator ... ... | 165 |
| Furnace hand; blast ... | 231 |
| Furnace hand- | |
| *charcoal mfr.* ... ... | 204 |
| *metal mfr.* ... ... | 231 |
| *mine, not coal* ... | 204 |
| Furnaceman; | |
| annealing ... ... | 237 |
| barium ... ... | 184 |
| blast ... ... ... | 231 |
| boiler ... ... ... | 347 |
| brass ... ... ... | 231 |
| calcining- ... ... | 184 |
| flint ... ... ... | 204 |

| | Code number |
|---|---|
| Furnaceman; *continued* | |
| chrome ... ... ... | 231 |
| cupola ... ... ... | 231 |
| electric ... ... ... | 231 |
| graphitising ... ... | 204 |
| hardening; case ... | 237 |
| hearth; open ... ... | 231 |
| spring; coach ... ... | 237 |
| treatment; heat ... | 237 |
| Furnaceman- | |
| *ceramic mfr.* ... ... | 191 |
| *chemical mfr.* ... ... | 184 |
| *crematorium* ... ... | 348 |
| *electric bulb mfr.* ... | 191 |
| *gas works* ... ... | 184 |
| *glass mfr.* ... ... | 191 |
| *lead pencil mfr.* ... | 204 |
| *metal trades-* ... | 231 |
| *annealing* ... | 237 |
| *oil refining* ... | 184 |
| *red lead mfr.* ... | 184 |
| Furnace worker; | |
| blast ... ... ... | 231 |
| talbot ... ... ... | 270 |
| Furnace worker (*metal trades*) | 231 |
| Furnisher; | |
| ball ... ... ... | 104 |
| coffin ... ... ... | 224 |
| house ... ... ... | 101 |
| funeral ... ... ... | 163 |
| Furnisher (*retail trade*) ... | 101 |
| Furrier- | |
| *fur products mfr.* ... | 211 |
| *retail trade* ... ... | 101 |
| Fuser; enamel ... ... | 204 |
| Fuser- | |
| *glass mfr.* ... ... | 204 |
| *metal trades* ... ... | 204 |
| *textile products mfr.* ... | 299 |
| Fuseroom worker (*chemical mfr.*) ... ... ... | 184 |
| Fusilier- | |
| *armed forces-* | |
| *foreign and Commonwealth* | 136 |
| *U.K.* ... ... ... | 135 |

### G

| | Code number |
|---|---|
| G.I. (*armed forces-foreign*) ... | 136 |
| Gabler and corder (net) ... | 199 |
| Gaffer-*see also Foreman-* | |
| *glass mfr.* ... ... | 192 |
| Gaiter; | |
| beam ... ... ... | 179 |
| harness ... ... ... | 248 |
| loom ... ... ... | F180 |
| warp ... ... ... | 179 |
| Gaiter- | |
| *textile spinning* ... | 178 |
| *textile weaving* ... | 248 |
| Galenical worker ... | 184 |
| Galley boy ... ... | 147 |
| Galley hand ... ... | 147 |
| Galvanizer ... ... | 269 |
| Gambler; professional ... | 165 |
| Gang man; shore (*shipbuilding*) | L344 |
| Gang man (*agriculture*) ... | 166 |
| Ganger; | |
| electrification ... | F306 |
| filtration (*water works*) ... | F184 |
| highways ... ... | F308 |
| mains ... ... ... | F311 |
| navvy ... ... ... | F308 |
| Ganger- *see also Foreman-* | |
| *canal* ... ... ... | F316 |
| *coal mine* ... ... | 338 |
| *docks* ... ... ... | F334 |
| *electricity board* ... | F311 |
| *gas board* ... ... | F311 |
| *local government* ... | F316 |

| | Code number |
|---|---|
| Ganger- *continued* | |
| *railways* ... ... | F306 |
| *water works* ... ... | F311 |
| Gangwayman ... ... | 334 |
| Gantry man; forge (*steelworks*) | 331 |
| Gantry man ... ... | 331 |
| Garage hand ... ... | 249 |
| Garage worker (*P.O.*) ... | L346 |
| Garde-manger ... ... | F143 |
| Gardener; | |
| fruit- ... ... ... | 107 |
| employee ... ... | 167 |
| landscape ... ... | 168 |
| market- ... ... | 107 |
| employee ... ... | 167 |
| nursery- ... ... | 107 |
| employee ... ... | 167 |
| Gardener- | |
| *fruit growing-* | 168 |
| *employee* ... | 107 |
| *market gardening-* ... | 107 |
| *employee* ... | 167 |
| *nursery-* ... | 107 |
| *employee* ... | 167 |
| Gardener-caretaker ... | 168 |
| Gardener-chauffeur ... | 327 |
| Gardener-groundsman ... | 168 |
| Gardener-handyman ... | 168 |
| Gardener's boy ... ... | 168 |
| Garnet worker ... ... | 176 |
| Garnetter ... ... ... | 176 |
| Garterer ... ... ... | 299 |
| Garthman ... ... | 166 |
| Gas man; assistant (*iron and steelworks*) ... ... | 255 |
| Gasman- | |
| coal gas ... ... | 184 |
| water gas ... ... | 184 |
| *blast furnace* ... | 348 |
| *cider mfr.* ... ... | 197 |
| *gas works* ... ... | 184 |
| *railways* ... ... | 338 |
| Gas worker; | |
| chlorine ... ... ... | 184 |
| maintenance ... ... | 260 |
| Gas worker- ... ... | L341 |
| *industrial gas* ... | 184 |
| Gasser ... ... ... | 182 |
| Gateman; | |
| bridge ... ... ... | 338 |
| dock ... ... ... | 338 |
| flood ... ... ... | 338 |
| lock ... ... ... | 338 |
| Gateman- | |
| *coal mine* ... ... | 321 |
| *docks* ... ... | 338 |
| *entertainment* ... | 165 |
| *railways* ... ... | 321 |
| *waterways* ... ... | 338 |
| Gatekeeper- ... ... | 140 |
| *coal mine* ... ... | 321 |
| Gatekeeper and pointsman ... | 321 |
| Gatherer; | |
| coal; sea ... ... | L346 |
| mussel .. ... ... | 171 |
| quill ... ... ... | 338 |
| rag- ... ... ... | 131 |
| *woollen mfr.* ... | 338 |
| seaweed ... ... | 171 |
| watercress ... ... | 172 |
| Gatherer- | |
| *agricultural products* ... | 172 |
| *bookbinding* ... ... | 189 |
| *ceramic mfr.* ... ... | 338 |
| *glass mfr.* ... ... | 223 |
| Gauger; | |
| bullet ... ... ... | 286 |
| cement ... ... ... | 297 |
| furnace ... ... ... | 231 |
| gut ... ... ... | 204 |
| mica ... ... ... | 204 |
| tank- | |
| *oil refining* ... ... | 297 |
| *petroleum distribution* ... | 297 |

| | Code number |
|---|---|
| **Grinder;** *continued* | |
| cutter- | |
|   cemented carbide goods | |
|     mfr. ... ... ... | 230 |
|   metal trades ... ... | 241 |
| cylinder- | |
|   *metal trades* ... ... | 241 |
|   *textile mfr.* ... ... | 176 |
| cylindrical ... ... ... | 241 |
| disc- | |
|   *abrasive wheel mfr.* ... | 230 |
|   *metal trades* ... ... | 241 |
| drill ... ... ... ... | 241 |
| dry (metal) ... ... ... | 276 |
| dust ... ... ... ... | 204 |
| ebonite ... ... ... | 228 |
| edge- | |
|   *abrasive wheel mfr.* ... | 230 |
|   *gramophone record mfr.* | 229 |
| emery (*steelworks*) ... ... | 244 |
| enamel ... ... ... | 204 |
| face ... ... ... ... | 241 |
| file ... ... ... ... | 241 |
| flat- ... ... ... ... | 176 |
|   glass ... ... ... | 192 |
|   textiles ... ... | 176 |
| flint (*ceramic mfr.*) ... ... | 204 |
| flock ... ... ... ... | 176 |
| ganister ... ... ... | 198 |
| gear ... ... ... ... | 241 |
| gelatine ... ... ... | 184 |
| glass ... ... ... ... | 192 |
| glaze (*ceramic mfr.*) ... | 204 |
| hob ... ... ... ... | 241 |
| ink ... ... ... ... | 184 |
| instrument ... ... ... | 241 |
| internal ... ... ... | 241 |
| jig ... ... ... ... | 241 |
| jobbing ... ... ... | 276 |
| jute ... ... ... ... | 176 |
| knife ... ... ... ... | 241 |
| lens ... ... ... ... | 192 |
| logwood ... ... ... | 203 |
| machine (*metal trades*) ... | 241 |
| mower; lawn ... ... | 241 |
| needle ... ... ... | 276 |
| optical ... ... ... | 192 |
| organ ... ... ... ... | 060 |
| paint ... ... ... ... | 204 |
| paper ... ... ... ... | 188 |
| precision ... ... ... | 241 |
| profile; optical ... ... | 241 |
| race ... ... ... ... | 241 |
| rag ... ... ... ... | 176 |
| razor ... ... ... ... | 241 |
| resin ... ... ... ... | 184 |
| roll ... ... ... ... | 241 |
| roller ... ... ... ... | 241 |
| rough cast ... ... ... | 244 |
| rubber ... ... ... ... | 204 |
| sand ... ... ... ... | 204 |
| saw ... ... ... ... | 241 |
| scissors ... ... ... | 276 |
| segmental ... ... ... | 241 |
| shaft ... ... ... ... | 241 |
| shears ... ... ... ... | 241 |
| shoddy ... ... ... | 176 |
| silica ... ... ... ... | 204 |
| slab; optical ... ... | 192 |
| slag ... ... ... ... | 204 |
| snuff ... ... ... ... | 201 |
| soap; dry ... ... ... | 184 |
| spindle ... ... ... | 241 |
| spline ... ... ... ... | 241 |
| spring ... ... ... ... | 241 |
| steel ... ... ... ... | 276 |
| stone; ... ... ... | 301 |
|   lime (*quarry*) ... | 198 |
|   lithographic ... ... | 301 |
|   wet ... ... ... | 276 |
| stopper; glass ... ... | 192 |
| straight ... ... ... | 276 |
| sugar ... ... ... ... | 202 |

| | Code number |
|---|---|
| **Grinder;** *continued* | |
| surface- ... ... ... | 241 |
|   carbon goods mfr. ... | 230 |
|   glass mfr. ... ... | 192 |
| sweep ... ... ... | L344 |
| swing ... ... ... | 276 |
| tool; ... ... ... | 241 |
|   universal ... ... | 240 |
| tool and cutter ... ... | 240 |
| tool room ... ... ... | 240 |
| universal ... ... ... | 241 |
| valve ... ... ... | 241 |
| wet- ... ... ... | 276 |
|   chemicals ... ... | 184 |
| wheel; emery- ... ... | 276 |
|   glass mfr. ... ... | 192 |
| **Grinder-** | |
|   *abrasive paper, etc. mfr.* | 230 |
|   *brake lining mfr.* ... | 230 |
|   *carbon goods mfr.* ... | 230 |
|   *cast concrete products mfr.* | 230 |
|   *ceramic mfr.* ... ... | 223 |
|   *chemical mfr.* ... ... | 184 |
|   *food products mfr.* ... | 202 |
|   *glass mfr.* ... ... | 192 |
|   *metal trades-* ... ... | 241 |
|     *foundry* ... ... | 244 |
|     *precious metal, plate mfr.* | 244 |
|   *mine, not coal* ... ... | 198 |
|   *paper mfr.* ... ... | 203 |
|   *patent fuel mfr.* ... | 204 |
|   *plastics goods mfr.* ... | 229 |
|   *printing* ... ... | 227 |
|   *textile mfr.-* ... ... | 176 |
|     *textile finishing* ... | 182 |
| **Grinder and finisher; spring** | 241 |
| **Grinder and polisher-** | |
|   *metal trades* ... ... | 276 |
|   *optical goods mfr.* ... | 192 |
| **Grinderman-** | |
|   *grain milling* ... ... | 202 |
|   *paper mfr.* ... ... | 203 |
| **Grinder-setter** (*metal trades*) ... | 238 |
| **Gristman** (*brewery*) ... | 197 |
| **Griswold hand** ... ... | 181 |
| **Grocer-** ... ... ... | 101 |
|   travelling ... ... | 128 |
| **Grommeter** ... ... ... | 299 |
| **Groom** ... ... ... | 172 |
| **Groom-gardener** ... ... | 172 |
| **Groomsman** ... ... ... | 172 |
| **Groover; pencil** ... ... | 218 |
| **Groover** (*metal trades*) ... | 241 |
| **Grosser** (*textile making-up*) | 287 |
| **Groundman; hard** ... ... | 314 |
| **Groundman** (*water works*) | 316 |
| **Ground worker**(*building and contracting*) ... | 313 |
| **Grounder; fur** ... ... | 299 |
| **Grounder** (*wallpaper printing*) | 299 |
| **Groundsman; excavator** ... | 330 |
| **Groundsman-** ... ... | 168 |
|   market ... ... | L346 |
| **Grouter; mould** (*steelworks*) | 270 |
| **Grower-** ... ... ... | 107 |
|   bulb- ... ... ... | 107 |
|     employee ... ... | 167 |
|   crystal ... ... ... | 080 |
|   fruit- ... ... ... | 107 |
|     employee ... ... | 167 |
|   mushroom- ... ... | 107 |
|     employee ... ... | 167 |
|   osier ... ... ... | 170 |
|   rose- ... ... ... | 107 |
|     employee ... ... | 167 |
|   tomato- ... ... ... | 107 |
|     employee ... ... | 167 |
|   watercress- ... ... | 107 |
|     employee ... ... | 167 |
|   willow ... ... ... | 170 |
|   withy ... ... ... | 170 |
|   wood ... ... ... | 170 |
| **Guard;** | |
|   ballast ... ... ... | 320 |

| | Code number |
|---|---|
| **Guard;** *continued* | |
| bank ... ... ... ... | 140 |
| body ... ... ... ... | 140 |
| bus ... ... ... ... | 328 |
| coast ... ... ... ... | 142 |
| custody ... ... ... | 140 |
| fire ... ... ... ... | 138 |
| forest ... ... ... | 170 |
| goods ... ... ... | 320 |
| life ... ... ... ... | 142 |
| loco ... ... ... ... | 320 |
| motor ... ... ... | 140 |
| night ... ... ... ... | 140 |
| passenger ... ... | 320 |
| security ... ... ... | 140 |
| train- ... ... ... | 320 |
|   ropes ... ... | 338 |
| van ... ... ... ... | 140 |
| water (*Customs and Excise*) | 019 |
| works ... ... ... | 140 |
| **Guard-** | |
|   *L.T.E.* ... ... ... | 320 |
|   *manufacturing* ... ... | 140 |
|   *railways* ... ... | 320 |
|   *road goods transport* ... | 140 |
|   *road passenger transport* | 328 |
| **Guarder** (*net mfr.*) ... | 199 |
| **Guardsman; coast** ... | 142 |
| **Guardsman** (*armed forces-U.K.*) | 135 |
| **Guide;** ... ... ... | 152 |
|   store ... ... ... | 165 |
| **Guide man; coke** ... | 338 |
| **Guider-** | |
|   *textile printing* ... ... | 227 |
|   *tube mfr.* ... ... | 270 |
| **Guider-in** ... ... ... | 199 |
| **Guillotine hand-** | |
|   *asbestos-cement products mfr.* | 230 |
|   *metal trades* ... ... | 276 |
|   *paper products mfr.* ... | 190 |
| **Guillotine man** *see Guillotine hand* | |
| **Guillotine worker** *see Guillotine hand* | |
| **Guitarist** ... ... ... | 060 |
| **Gulley man** ... ... ... | L346 |
| **Gummer-** | |
|   *coal mine* ... ... ... | 314 |
|   *paper products mfr.* ... | 295 |
| **Gunner;** | |
|   civilian (*Min. of Defence*) | 348 |
| **Gunner-** | |
|   *armed forces-* | |
|     *foreign and Commonwealth* | 136 |
|     *U.K.* ... ... ... | 135 |
|   *steelworks* ... ... ... | 276 |
| **Gunsmith** ... ... ... | 248 |
| **Gutman** ... ... ... | 186 |
| **Gutta percha worker** ... | 228 |
| **Gutter; fish** ... ... | 187 |
| **Gymnast;** ... ... ... | 063 |
|   remedial ... ... ... | 049 |
| **Gynaecologist** ... ... | 041 |

# H

| | Code number |
|---|---|
| **H.M.F.I.** ... ... ... | 019 |
| **H.M.I.S.** ... ... ... | 035 |
| **Haberdasher-** ... ... ... | 101 |
|   *market trading* ... ... | 130 |
| **Hackler** ... ... ... | 176 |
| **Haematologist** ... ... | 080 |
| **Hafter** ... ... ... | 276 |
| **Hair hand** (*brush, etc. mfr.*) ... | 298 |
| **Hair worker** ... ... ... | 176 |
| **Hairdresser** ... ... ... | 159 |
| **Hall boy** (*hotel*) ... ... | 154 |
| **Hall man** (*hotel*) ... ... | 154 |
| **Halsher** (*wool*) ... ... | 178 |
| **Hammer lad** ... ... ... | 270 |
| **Hammer worker; power** ... | 270 |

# (Ma)

## (Ma)

# (Ma)

Code number

**Manager;** *continued*
  sales; *continued*
    district ... ... ...M133
    field ... ... ...M133
    regional ... ... ...M133
  sales- ... ... 013
    *retail trade* ... ... 101
  sales and advertising ... ... 013
  sales and commercial ... 013
  sales and service ... ... 013
  section *see Manager-*
  security ... ... ... 111
  service; ... ... ... 091
    rental ... ... ... 111
  shed (*textile mfr.*) ... ... 091
  shift ... ... ... 091
  shipping ... ... ... 099
  shop;
    betting ... ... 164
    butcher's ... ... ...M186
    fishmonger's ... ...M187
    mobile ... ... ...M128
  shop-
    *dyeing and cleaning* ... 110
    *hairdressing* ... ...M159
    *laundry receiving shop* ... 110
    *metal trades* ... ... 091
    *retail trade* ... ... 101
      *butchers* ... ...M186
      *fishmongers* ... ...M187
      *mobile shop* ... ...M128
      *pharmacists* ... 044
  showroom ... ... 101
  site; ... ... ... 092
    caravan ... ... ... 109
  society;
    bible ... ... ... 101
    building ... ... ... 099
    friendly ... ... ... 099
  solicitor's ... ... ...M027
  spares ... ... ... 096
  sports ... ... ... 106
  stable ... ... ... 111
  staff ... ... ... 009
  stage (*entertainment*) ...M059
  stall; book ... ... 101
  stall (*retail trade*) ...M130
  stand (*entertainment*) ... 106
  station;
    airline ... ... ... 095
    petrol ... ... ... 101
  stock ... ... ... 096
  stores; ship's ... ... 096
  store(s)-
    *retail trade* ... ... 101
  studio- ...M055
    *entertainment* ...M059
  study; works ... ...M010
  systems ...M012
  tailor's ... ... 101
  taxation (*accountancy*) ... 008
  team (sports) ... ...M063
  technical- ... ... 078
    lighting ... ...M059
  telephone ... ... 099
  terminal (*oil distribution*) ... 097
  theatre ... ... ... 106
  touring (*entertainment*) ...M059
  trade ... ... ... 101
  traffic ... ... ... 095
  training ... ... ...M034
  transport ... ... 095
  travel ... ... ... 099
  underground (*mine, not coal*) 094
  valuation ... ...M005
  wages ... ... ... 099
  warehouse ... ... 097
  wharf ... ... ... 097
  works; sewage ... ... 111
  works- ... ... ... 091
    *building and contracting* ... 092
  workshop(s) ... ... 091
  yard; ... ... ... 097
    ship ... ... ... 091

**Manager;** *continued*
  of field trials (*N.I.A.B.*) ... 065
**Manager-**
  catering ... ... 104
  accountancy ... ... 099
  advertising ... ... 014
  agricultural contracting ... 107
  agriculture ... ... 107
  auctioneering ... ...M134
  average adjusting ... ...M008
  banking and finance-
    merchant banking ... ... 006
  betting and gambling- ... 164
    casino, gaming club ... 106
  building and contracting ... 092
  building society ... ... 099
  car hire ... ... 111
  caravan site ... ... 109
  cinema ... ... 106
  circulating library ... ... 101
  coal mine- ... ... 094
    open cast ... ... 092
  coke ovens ... ... 091
  credit company ... ... 098
  education- ... ... 111
    driving school ...M052
    training centre ...M034
  employment agency (*private*) 099
  estate agency ... ... 025
  export agency ... ... 129
  fishing company ... ... 111
  football club ... ...M063
  forestry ... ... 111
  funeral direction ... ... 163
  gardening/grounds keeping
    services ... ... 111
  hairdressing ... ...M159
  holiday camp ... ... 109
  horticulture ... ... 107
  hostel ... ... ... 111
  hotel, etc. ... ... 102
  import agency ... ... 129
  insurance ... ... 099
  insurance brokers ... 007
  Job Centre (*Dept. of Emp.*) 021
  laundry, dry cleaners-
    launderette ... ... 110
    receiving office, shop ... 110
  manufacturing- ... ... 091
    mine (*not coal*), quarry ... 094
  market gardening ... ... 107
  market research ... ... 013
  mineral oil processing ... 091
  money lending ... ... 098
  *N.A.A.F.I.-*
    canteen ... ... 104
    shop ... ... ... 101
  night club ... ... 106
  nuclear fuel production ... 091
  nursing home ... ...M043
  off-licence ... ... 101
  park ... ... ... 106
  pawn brokers ... ... 101
  photographic studios ... 111
  plant hire ... ... 111
  postal, telecommunications
    services ... ... 099
  property investment company 025
  public baths ... ... 106
  public house ... ... 103
  public utilities ... ... 094
  quarry ... ... 094
  refuse disposal, sanitation,
    etc. ... ... ... 111
  religious organisation ... 111
  repairing-
    motor vehicles ... 091
    consumer goods ... 111
  residential club ... ... 102
  retail trade- ... ... 101
    butchers ... ...M186
    fishmongers ... ...M187
    market stall ... ...M130
    mobile shop ... ...M128

Code number

**Manager-** *continued*
  *retail trade-* continued
    opticians ... ... ... 046
    *party plan sales* ... ...M132
    *pharmacists* ... ... 044
  safe deposit ... ... 111
  ship broker's ... ... 129
  *Social Security Office* ... 021
  solid fuel mfr. ... ... 091
  sports activities ... ... 106
  stock jobbers ... ... 007
  storage ... ... ... 097
  theatre ... ... ... 106
  trade association ... ...M024
  trade union ... ...M024
  trading stamp redemption
    office ... ... ... 101
  transport- ... ... 095
    loading, unloading ... 097
  travel agency ... ... 099
  typewriting agency ... ... 111
  warehousing ... ... 097
  welfare services ...M039
  well drilling ... ... 094
  wholesale trade- ... ... 101
    butchers ... ...M186
    fishmongers ... ...M187
**Manciple** ... ... ... 016
**Mangle hand** *see Mangler*
**Mangle man** *see Mangler*
**Mangler; plate** ... ... ... 270
**Mangler-**
  steelworks ... ... ... 270
  textile mfr. ... ... 182
**Manicurist** ... ... ... 165
**Manipulator;**
  glass ... ... ... 192
  tub (*coal mine*) ... ... 338
  tube-
    metal ... ... ... 276
    rubber ... ... ... 228
**Manipulator-**
  *metal mfr.* ... ... ... 270
  *plastics goods mfr.* ... ... 229
**Mannequin** ... ... ... 064
**Manual worker** ... ...L346
**Manufacturer-**
  badges ... ... ... 212
  bags ... ... ... 225
  basketry ... ... ... 230
  bedding ... ... ... 213
  brushes, brooms ... ... 230
  buttons ... ... ... 230
  canvas goods ... ... 226
  cast concrete goods ... 230
  ceramics ... ... ... 223
  chemicals ... ... ... 184
  clothing ... ... ... 226
  fancy goods ... ... 230
  firelighters ... ... 299
  fireplaces ... ... 300
  food products- ... ... 202
    flour confectionery ... 185
    sugar confectionery ... 202
  footwear ... ... ... 175
  furniture- ... ... 215
    cane furniture ... 230
    metal furniture ... 276
  gas ... ... ... 184
  glass ... ... ... 192
  gloves ... ... ... 212
  hats ... ... ... 226
  instruments ... ... 246
  jewellery, plate ... 266
  joinery ... ... ... 214
  leather ... ... ... 173
  leather goods ... ... 225
  machinery ... ... 248
  metal goods- ... ... 276
    sheet metal goods ... 261
  metals ... ... ... 231
  models ... ... ... 214
  musical instruments ... 222
  packing cases ... ... 216

| | Code number |
|---|---|
| **Mender;** *continued* | |
| cloth (*textile mfr.*) ... ... | 183 |
| comb ... ... ... ... | 248 |
| crate ... ... ... ... | 216 |
| curtain; lace ... ... ... | 183 |
| dress (hosiery) ... ... | 183 |
| dressed (lace) ... ... | 183 |
| embroidery ... ... | 226 |
| finish (hosiery) ... ... | 183 |
| finished ... ... ... | 183 |
| hosiery ... ... ... | 183 |
| invisible ... ... ... | 183 |
| lace ... ... ... ... | 183 |
| net ... ... ... ... | 183 |
| piece ... ... ... ... | 183 |
| road ... ... ... ... | 308 |
| rough (hosiery) ... ... | 183 |
| sack ... ... ... ... | 212 |
| sheet (wool bales) ... ... | 212 |
| shoe ... ... ... ... | 174 |
| stocking ... ... ... | 183 |
| strap ... ... ... ... | 225 |
| tank ... ... ... ... | 261 |
| trawl ... ... ... ... | 183 |
| tub (*coal mine*) ... ... | 276 |
| **Mender—** | |
| *embroidery mfr.* ... ... | 226 |
| *hotel, catering, etc.* ... | 226 |
| *institution* ... ... ... | 226 |
| *laundry* ... ... ... | 226 |
| *textile mfr.* ... ... | 183 |
| **Mercer** ... ... ... | 101 |
| **Merceriser** ... ... | 182 |
| **Merchandiser** ... ... | 064 |
| **Merchant;** *see also Agent* | |
| agricultural ... ... | 101 |
| builders' ... ... ... | 101 |
| coal ... ... ... ... | 101 |
| firewood ... ... ... | 130 |
| fish- ... ... ... ... | 187 |
| wholesale ... ... | 101 |
| log ... ... ... ... | 130 |
| paper; waste ... ... | 131 |
| rag and bone ... ... | 131 |
| scrap ... ... ... ... | 131 |
| wine ... ... ... ... | 101 |
| **Mess boy** ... ... ... | 146 |
| **Messman** ... ... ... | 146 |
| **Messenger;** ... ... | 124 |
| chief ... ... ... ... | F124 |
| head ... ... ... ... | F124 |
| Queen's ... ... ... | 124 |
| **Messenger at arms** ... | 142 |
| **Messenger-clerk** ... ... | 115 |
| **Messroom boy** ... ... | 146 |
| **Metal man** (*coal mine*) ... | 314 |
| **Metal worker;** | |
| architectural ... ... | 276 |
| art ... ... ... ... | 276 |
| ornamental ... ... | 276 |
| precious ... ... ... | 266 |
| sheet ... ... ... ... | 261 |
| white ... ... ... ... | 266 |
| **Metal worker-** ... ... | L344 |
| *hospital service* ... ... | 248 |
| *linoleum mfr.* ... ... | 276 |
| **Metaler** (glass) ... ... | 191 |
| **Metaller;** ... ... ... | 270 |
| bronzing ... ... ... | 227 |
| **Metalliser; spray** ... ... | 269 |
| **Metalliser** (*lamp, valve mfr.*) ... | 269 |
| **Metallographer** ... ... | 077 |
| **Metallurgist** ... ... | 077 |
| **Meteorologist** ... ... | 067 |
| **Meter;** sworn ... ... | 297 |
| **Meter hand** ... ... | 246 |
| **Meterman;** coal ... ... | 115 |
| **Methylator** ... ... | 184 |
| **Metrologist** ... ... | 080 |
| **Mica man** (*mine, not coal*) | 315 |
| **Mica worker** ... ... | 204 |
| **Micanite worker** ... ... | 204 |
| **Microbiologist** ... ... | 065 |
| **Microscopist;** electron ... | 080 |

| | Code number |
|---|---|
| **Middleman** (*slaughterhouse*) ... | 186 |
| **Middler** (*rolling mill*) ... ... | 270 |
| **Midshipman-** | |
| *armed forces-* | |
| *foreign and Commonwealth* | M136 |
| *U.K.* ... ... ... | M135 |
| *shipping* ... ... ... | 087 |
| **Midwife;** ... ... ... | 043 |
| superintendent ... ... | F043 |
| **Milk boy** (*farming*) ... | 172 |
| **Milkman-** | |
| *farming* ... ... ... | 172 |
| *milk retailing* ... ... | 128 |
| **Milker** ... ... ... | 172 |
| **Milkmaid** ... ... ... | 172 |
| **Mill hand;** | |
| finishing ... ... ... | 184 |
| flour ... ... ... ... | 202 |
| grain ... ... ... ... | 202 |
| grinding ... ... ... | 184 |
| ink ... ... ... ... | 184 |
| nitrate ... ... ... | L340 |
| provender ... ... ... | 202 |
| roller (gramophone records) | 195 |
| rolling ... ... ... ... | 270 |
| rubber ... ... ... ... | 194 |
| saw ... ... ... ... | 218 |
| tints ... ... ... ... | 184 |
| wash (cement) ... ... | 204 |
| **Mill hand-** | 204 |
| *cattle food mfr.* ... ... | 202 |
| *chemical mfr.* ... ... | 184 |
| *food processing* ... ... | 202 |
| *galvanized sheet mfr.* ... | 270 |
| *hair, fibre dressing* ... | 176 |
| *mine, not coal* ... ... | 198 |
| *rubber goods mfr.* ... ... | 194 |
| *tinplate mfr.* ... ... | 270 |
| **Mill man;** | |
| lead ... ... ... ... | 204 |
| malt ... ... ... ... | 197 |
| paint ... ... ... ... | 204 |
| potter's ... ... ... | 204 |
| pug ... ... ... ... | 204 |
| rubber ... ... ... ... | 194 |
| **Mill man-** | |
| *carbon goods mfr.* ... | 204 |
| *ceramic mfr.* ... ... | 204 |
| *chemical mfr.* ... ... | 184 |
| *leather dressing* ... ... | 173 |
| *metal mfr.* ... ... ... | 270 |
| *mine, not coal* ... ... | 198 |
| *plastics goods mfr.* ... | 204 |
| *rubber goods mfr.* ... | 194 |
| *salt mfr.* ... ... ... | 202 |
| *textile finishing* ... ... | 182 |
| *whiting mfr.* ... ... | 204 |
| **Mill operative** ... ... | L346 |
| **Mill worker;** | |
| asbestos ... ... ... | 176 |
| corn ... ... ... ... | L346 |
| cotton ... ... ... ... | L339 |
| flour ... ... ... ... | L346 |
| grog ... ... ... ... | 204 |
| paper ... ... ... ... | 203 |
| rolling ... ... ... ... | 270 |
| rubber ... ... ... ... | 194 |
| saw ... ... ... ... | 218 |
| sheet ... ... ... ... | 270 |
| slate ... ... ... ... | 301 |
| woollen ... ... ... | L339 |
| **Mill worker-** ... ... | L346 |
| *animal foods mfr.* ... | 202 |
| *metal mfr.* ... ... | 270 |
| **Miller;** | |
| bayonet ... ... ... | 241 |
| blanket ... ... ... | 182 |
| broaching ... ... ... | 241 |
| cement ... ... ... | 204 |
| cloth ... ... ... ... | 182 |
| coal (*cement mfr.*) ... ... | 204 |
| concave (needles) ... ... | 241 |
| corn ... ... ... ... | 202 |
| die ... ... ... ... | 241 |

| | Code number |
|---|---|
| **Miller;** *continued* | |
| dry (*textile mfr.*) ... ... | 182 |
| dust (*ceramic mfr.*) ... ... | 204 |
| dyewood ... ... ... | 204 |
| engineer's ... ... ... | 241 |
| felt ... ... ... ... | 182 |
| flint (*ceramic mfr.*) ... ... | 204 |
| flour; ... ... ... ... | 202 |
| wood ... ... ... | 203 |
| glaze (*ceramic mfr.*) ... | 204 |
| grain ... ... ... ... | 202 |
| grist ... ... ... ... | 202 |
| gypsum ... ... ... | 204 |
| horizontal ... ... ... | 241 |
| lime ... ... ... ... | 204 |
| logwood ... ... ... | 203 |
| machine; ... ... ... | 241 |
| knife ... ... ... | 241 |
| madder ... ... ... | 204 |
| malt ... ... ... ... | 197 |
| metal ... ... ... ... | 241 |
| mustard ... ... ... | 202 |
| oil ... ... ... ... | 202 |
| optical ... ... ... | 192 |
| paint ... ... ... ... | 204 |
| profile ... ... ... | 241 |
| provender ... ... ... | 202 |
| rice ... ... ... ... | 202 |
| rubber ... ... ... ... | 194 |
| saw ... ... ... ... | 218 |
| soap ... ... ... ... | 184 |
| solvent ... ... ... | 182 |
| space band ... ... | 241 |
| spice ... ... ... ... | 202 |
| stone (*mine, not coal*) ... | 198 |
| tool ... ... ... ... | 240 |
| tool room ... ... ... | 240 |
| universal ... ... ... | 241 |
| vertical ... ... ... | 241 |
| wash (*cement mfr.*) ... ... | 204 |
| wet (*cement mfr.*) ... ... | 204 |
| woollen ... ... ... | 182 |
| **Miller-** | |
| *animal foods mfr.* ... ... | 202 |
| *brewery* ... ... ... | 197 |
| *cement mfr.* ... ... | 204 |
| *ceramic mfr.* ... ... | 204 |
| *chemical mfr.* ... ... | 184 |
| *grain milling* ... ... | 202 |
| *hair, fibre dressing* ... | 176 |
| *metal trades* ... ... | 241 |
| *mine, not coal* ... ... | 198 |
| *paper mfr.* ... ... | 203 |
| *plastics goods mfr.* ... | 195 |
| *sugar refining* ... ... | 202 |
| *textile mfr.* ... ... | 182 |
| *whisky distilling* ... ... | 197 |
| **Milliner;** hosiery ... ... | 181 |
| **Milliner-** ... ... ... | 211 |
| *retail trade* ... ... | 101 |
| **Milling hand** (*soap mfr.*) ... | 184 |
| **Millwright** ... ... ... | 248 |
| **Milner** (*textile finishing*) ... | 182 |
| **Mincer;** sausage meat ... | 186 |
| **Minder;** | |
| back (*textile mfr.*) ... ... | 199 |
| backwash ... ... ... | 199 |
| backwasher ... ... ... | 199 |
| belt (*coal mine*)- ... ... | 338 |
| *above ground* ... ... | 338 |
| block (*wire mfr.*) ... ... | L344 |
| boiler ... ... ... ... | 347 |
| bowl; | |
| scouring ... ... ... | 199 |
| wash (*textile mfr.*) ... | 199 |
| bowl (*worsted mfr.*) ... ... | 199 |
| box (*textile mfr.*) ... ... | 176 |
| can ... ... ... ... | 176 |
| card ... ... ... ... | 176 |
| carding ... ... ... | 176 |
| cart ... ... ... ... | 329 |
| cell ... ... ... ... | 269 |
| chain ... ... ... ... | 338 |
| child ... ... ... ... | 151 |

<table>
<thead>
<tr><th></th><th>Code number</th></tr>
</thead>
<tbody>
<tr><td colspan="2">Officer; continued</td></tr>
<tr><td>executive;</td><td></td></tr>
<tr><td>chief-</td><td></td></tr>
<tr><td>government ... ...</td><td>021</td></tr>
<tr><td>P.O. ... ... ...</td><td>099</td></tr>
<tr><td>higher-</td><td></td></tr>
<tr><td>government ... ...</td><td>021</td></tr>
<tr><td>P.O. ... ... ...</td><td>099</td></tr>
<tr><td>senior-</td><td></td></tr>
<tr><td>government ... ...</td><td>021</td></tr>
<tr><td>P.O. ... ... ...</td><td>099</td></tr>
<tr><td>executive- see also Manager</td><td></td></tr>
<tr><td>government ... ...</td><td>F112</td></tr>
<tr><td>insurance ...</td><td>F115</td></tr>
<tr><td>local government ...</td><td>022</td></tr>
<tr><td>P.L.A. ... ...</td><td>095</td></tr>
<tr><td>P.O. ... ... ...</td><td>F115</td></tr>
<tr><td>expenditure (N.C.B.) ...</td><td>003</td></tr>
<tr><td>experimental; ... ...</td><td>080</td></tr>
<tr><td>chief- ... ...</td><td>067</td></tr>
<tr><td>biologist ... ...</td><td>065</td></tr>
<tr><td>chemist ... ...</td><td>066</td></tr>
<tr><td>senior- ... ...</td><td>067</td></tr>
<tr><td>biologist ...</td><td>065</td></tr>
<tr><td>chemist ...</td><td>066</td></tr>
<tr><td>fatstock (Min. of A.F.F.) ...</td><td>065</td></tr>
<tr><td>field-</td><td></td></tr>
<tr><td>advisory ... ...</td><td>065</td></tr>
<tr><td>professional ...</td><td>065</td></tr>
<tr><td>food products mfr. ...</td><td>290</td></tr>
<tr><td>Min. of A.F.F. ...</td><td>090</td></tr>
<tr><td>finance;</td><td></td></tr>
<tr><td>deputy ... ...</td><td>115</td></tr>
<tr><td>regional- ... ...</td><td>021</td></tr>
<tr><td>P.O. ... ...</td><td>099</td></tr>
<tr><td>finance- ... ...</td><td>115</td></tr>
<tr><td>hospital service ...</td><td>099</td></tr>
<tr><td>local government ...</td><td>022</td></tr>
<tr><td>N.C.B. ... ...</td><td>099</td></tr>
<tr><td>P.O. ... ...</td><td>099</td></tr>
<tr><td>financial (local government)</td><td>022</td></tr>
<tr><td>fingerprint; ... ...</td><td>137</td></tr>
<tr><td>civilian ... ...</td><td>115</td></tr>
<tr><td>fire;</td><td></td></tr>
<tr><td>chief ... ...</td><td>M138</td></tr>
<tr><td>divisional ...</td><td>M138</td></tr>
<tr><td>fire- ... ...</td><td>M138</td></tr>
<tr><td>coal mine ...</td><td>138</td></tr>
<tr><td>fire brigade ... ...</td><td>M138</td></tr>
<tr><td>first-</td><td></td></tr>
<tr><td>hovercraft ... ...</td><td>090</td></tr>
<tr><td>aircraft ...</td><td>085</td></tr>
<tr><td>fire service ...</td><td>M138</td></tr>
<tr><td>shipping ...</td><td>087</td></tr>
<tr><td>fishery- ... ...</td><td>019</td></tr>
<tr><td>Min. of A.F.F. ...</td><td>090</td></tr>
<tr><td>food (local government) ...</td><td>017</td></tr>
<tr><td>forestry ... ...</td><td>111</td></tr>
<tr><td>freight (air transport) ...</td><td>115</td></tr>
<tr><td>fuel ... ... ...</td><td>333</td></tr>
<tr><td>government;</td><td></td></tr>
<tr><td>local; n.o.s. ...</td><td>115</td></tr>
<tr><td>n.o.s. ... ...</td><td>115</td></tr>
<tr><td>grade I—IV (Dept. of Emp.)</td><td>021</td></tr>
<tr><td>V (Dept. of Emp.) ...</td><td>F112</td></tr>
<tr><td>VI (Dept. of Emp.) ...</td><td>115</td></tr>
<tr><td>graphics ... ...</td><td>079</td></tr>
<tr><td>group (Min. of Defence) ...</td><td>115</td></tr>
<tr><td>chief (Min. of Defence) ...</td><td>021</td></tr>
<tr><td>senior (Min. of Defence) ...</td><td>021</td></tr>
<tr><td>health;</td><td></td></tr>
<tr><td>environmental ...</td><td>017</td></tr>
<tr><td>mental ... ...</td><td>039</td></tr>
<tr><td>public ... ...</td><td>017</td></tr>
<tr><td>horticultural ... ...</td><td>065</td></tr>
<tr><td>hospital- ... ...</td><td>115</td></tr>
<tr><td>prison service ...</td><td>156</td></tr>
<tr><td>house ... ...</td><td>041</td></tr>
<tr><td>House; Trinity ...</td><td>087</td></tr>
<tr><td>housing ... ...</td><td>M039</td></tr>
<tr><td>husbandry; stock; live ...</td><td>065</td></tr>
<tr><td>hydrographic ... ...</td><td>090</td></tr>
<tr><td>hygiene ... ...</td><td>043</td></tr>
</tbody>
</table>

<table>
<thead>
<tr><th></th><th>Code number</th></tr>
</thead>
<tbody>
<tr><td colspan="2">Officer; continued</td></tr>
<tr><td>immigration; ... ... ...</td><td>019</td></tr>
<tr><td>chief ... ... ...</td><td>021</td></tr>
<tr><td>indoor ... ... ...</td><td>F112</td></tr>
<tr><td>information; research ...</td><td>026</td></tr>
<tr><td>information- ... ...</td><td>026</td></tr>
<tr><td>public relations ...</td><td>014</td></tr>
<tr><td>Inland Revenue ...</td><td>115</td></tr>
<tr><td>inspecting (Dept. of Transport)</td><td>019</td></tr>
<tr><td>inspection (Dept. of Energy)</td><td>069</td></tr>
<tr><td>instructional ... ...</td><td>034</td></tr>
<tr><td>insurance ... ...</td><td>115</td></tr>
<tr><td>intelligence;</td><td></td></tr>
<tr><td>grade II (Min. of Defence)</td><td>026</td></tr>
<tr><td>trade ... ...</td><td>011</td></tr>
<tr><td>intelligence-</td><td></td></tr>
<tr><td>government ... ...</td><td>026</td></tr>
<tr><td>investigating (Dept. of Transport) ...</td><td>019</td></tr>
<tr><td>investigation;</td><td></td></tr>
<tr><td>chief (Customs and Excise)</td><td>019</td></tr>
<tr><td>sales (P.O.) ... ...</td><td>115</td></tr>
<tr><td>veterinary ... ...</td><td>051</td></tr>
<tr><td>investigation-</td><td></td></tr>
<tr><td>D.H.S.S. ... ...</td><td>115</td></tr>
<tr><td>local government ...</td><td>039</td></tr>
<tr><td>P.O. ... ...</td><td>140</td></tr>
<tr><td>J.I.B. (Joint Intelligence Bureau) ... ...</td><td>026</td></tr>
<tr><td>labour ... ... ...</td><td>009</td></tr>
<tr><td>land and minerals (N.C.B.) ...</td><td>084</td></tr>
<tr><td>lands ... ... ...</td><td>025</td></tr>
<tr><td>legal ... ... ...</td><td>001</td></tr>
<tr><td>lettings (local government) ...</td><td>115</td></tr>
<tr><td>liaison; ... ...</td><td>115</td></tr>
<tr><td>customer ... ...</td><td>101</td></tr>
<tr><td>labour ... ...</td><td>009</td></tr>
<tr><td>medical ... ...</td><td>133</td></tr>
<tr><td>press ... ...</td><td>014</td></tr>
<tr><td>sales ... ...</td><td>101</td></tr>
<tr><td>technical ... ...</td><td>090</td></tr>
<tr><td>liaison-</td><td></td></tr>
<tr><td>government ... ...</td><td>021</td></tr>
<tr><td>manufacturing ...</td><td>090</td></tr>
<tr><td>railways ... ...</td><td>014</td></tr>
<tr><td>licensing (local government)</td><td>022</td></tr>
<tr><td>local I (D.H.S.S.) ...</td><td>F112</td></tr>
<tr><td>local II (D.H.S.S.) ...</td><td>115</td></tr>
<tr><td>local authority ...</td><td>115</td></tr>
<tr><td>magisterial ... ...</td><td>115</td></tr>
<tr><td>maintenance- ... ...</td><td>316</td></tr>
<tr><td>local government ...</td><td>F316</td></tr>
<tr><td>P.O. ... ...</td><td>256</td></tr>
<tr><td>printing ...</td><td>248</td></tr>
<tr><td>management; labour ...</td><td>009</td></tr>
<tr><td>manpower (N.C.B.) ...</td><td>009</td></tr>
<tr><td>marketing ... ...</td><td>013</td></tr>
<tr><td>markets (Min. of A.F.F.) ...</td><td>015</td></tr>
<tr><td>measurement; work ...</td><td>010</td></tr>
<tr><td>mechanisation ...</td><td>081</td></tr>
<tr><td>medical- ... ...</td><td>041</td></tr>
<tr><td>armed forces-</td><td></td></tr>
<tr><td>foreign and Commonwealth ...</td><td>M136</td></tr>
<tr><td>U.K. ... ...</td><td>M135</td></tr>
<tr><td>membership; district (motoring association) ... ...</td><td>115</td></tr>
<tr><td>merchant navy ...</td><td>087</td></tr>
<tr><td>meteorological ...</td><td>067</td></tr>
<tr><td>methods ... ...</td><td>010</td></tr>
<tr><td>Milk Marketing Board ...</td><td>115</td></tr>
<tr><td>mining ... ...</td><td>094</td></tr>
<tr><td>municipal ... ...</td><td>115</td></tr>
<tr><td>navigating-</td><td></td></tr>
<tr><td>aircraft ... ...</td><td>085</td></tr>
<tr><td>shipping ... ...</td><td>087</td></tr>
<tr><td>non-commissioned-</td><td></td></tr>
<tr><td>armed forces-</td><td></td></tr>
<tr><td>foreign and Commonwealth ... ...</td><td>136</td></tr>
<tr><td>U.K. ... ...</td><td>135</td></tr>
<tr><td>nursing ... ...</td><td>M043</td></tr>
<tr><td>o & m- ... ... ...</td><td>010</td></tr>
<tr><td>government ... ...</td><td>M010</td></tr>
</tbody>
</table>

<table>
<thead>
<tr><th></th><th>Code number</th></tr>
</thead>
<tbody>
<tr><td colspan="2">Officer; continued</td></tr>
<tr><td>o & m- continued</td><td></td></tr>
<tr><td>local government ...</td><td>M010</td></tr>
<tr><td>occupational ... ...</td><td>049</td></tr>
<tr><td>occupations ... ...</td><td>049</td></tr>
<tr><td>operations; ... ...</td><td>111</td></tr>
<tr><td>flight ... ...</td><td>086</td></tr>
<tr><td>organisation (government) ...</td><td>M010</td></tr>
<tr><td>outdoor ... ...</td><td>124</td></tr>
<tr><td>p. & c. (N.C.B.) ...</td><td>111</td></tr>
<tr><td>passenger-</td><td></td></tr>
<tr><td>hovercraft ... ...</td><td>F152</td></tr>
<tr><td>air transport ...</td><td>115</td></tr>
<tr><td>patent(s) (government) ...</td><td>090</td></tr>
<tr><td>patrol ... ...</td><td>140</td></tr>
<tr><td>pensions ... ...</td><td>115</td></tr>
<tr><td>personnel ... ...</td><td>009</td></tr>
<tr><td>pest ... ... ...</td><td>165</td></tr>
<tr><td>petty-</td><td></td></tr>
<tr><td>armed forces-</td><td></td></tr>
<tr><td>foreign and Commonwealth ... ...</td><td>136</td></tr>
<tr><td>U.K. ... ...</td><td>135</td></tr>
<tr><td>planning-</td><td></td></tr>
<tr><td>building and contracting ...</td><td>082</td></tr>
<tr><td>local government ...</td><td>082</td></tr>
<tr><td>manufacturing ...</td><td>075</td></tr>
<tr><td>police- ... ...</td><td>137</td></tr>
<tr><td>non-statutory ...</td><td>140</td></tr>
<tr><td>port ... ... ...</td><td>095</td></tr>
<tr><td>postal (P.O.) ...</td><td>115</td></tr>
<tr><td>postal and telegraph ...</td><td>115</td></tr>
<tr><td>power; motive ...</td><td>091</td></tr>
<tr><td>press ... ...</td><td>054</td></tr>
<tr><td>press and information ...</td><td>054</td></tr>
<tr><td>prevention;</td><td></td></tr>
<tr><td>accident ... ...</td><td>039</td></tr>
<tr><td>fire-</td><td></td></tr>
<tr><td>fire service ... ...</td><td>138</td></tr>
<tr><td>hospital service ...</td><td>138</td></tr>
<tr><td>preventive ... ...</td><td>019</td></tr>
<tr><td>pricing ... ...</td><td>115</td></tr>
<tr><td>principal-</td><td></td></tr>
<tr><td>government-</td><td>021</td></tr>
<tr><td>prison service</td><td>F139</td></tr>
<tr><td>printing and binding ...</td><td>F112</td></tr>
<tr><td>prison; ... ...</td><td>139</td></tr>
<tr><td>chief ... ...</td><td>108</td></tr>
<tr><td>probation ... ...</td><td>039</td></tr>
<tr><td>procurement;</td><td></td></tr>
<tr><td>facilities (T.V., etc.) ...</td><td>016</td></tr>
<tr><td>livestock; assistant ...</td><td>016</td></tr>
<tr><td>production;</td><td></td></tr>
<tr><td>milk ... ... ...</td><td>065</td></tr>
<tr><td>technical ... ...</td><td>090</td></tr>
<tr><td>productivity and costs (N.C.B.) ... ...</td><td>074</td></tr>
<tr><td>professional and technological (government)-</td><td></td></tr>
<tr><td>grade I, II see Engineer- prof.-</td><td></td></tr>
<tr><td>grade III, IV ... ...</td><td>081</td></tr>
<tr><td>progress ... ...</td><td>115</td></tr>
<tr><td>promotion; sales ...</td><td>013</td></tr>
<tr><td>protection;</td><td></td></tr>
<tr><td>consumer ... ...</td><td>019</td></tr>
<tr><td>fire ... ...</td><td>M138</td></tr>
<tr><td>publicity ... ...</td><td>014</td></tr>
<tr><td>purchasing ... ...</td><td>016</td></tr>
<tr><td>R.S.P.C.A. ... ...</td><td>019</td></tr>
<tr><td>radio- ... ...</td><td>087</td></tr>
<tr><td>aircraft ... ...</td><td>122</td></tr>
<tr><td>government ...</td><td>111</td></tr>
<tr><td>rates ... ... ...</td><td>115</td></tr>
<tr><td>rates and charges (transport)</td><td>004</td></tr>
<tr><td>rating ... ...</td><td>005</td></tr>
<tr><td>rating and valuation ...</td><td>005</td></tr>
<tr><td>rebate (local government) ...</td><td>022</td></tr>
<tr><td>reception ... ...</td><td>117</td></tr>
<tr><td>records ... ...</td><td>099</td></tr>
<tr><td>recruiting (P.O.) ...</td><td>009</td></tr>
<tr><td>recruitment ... ...</td><td>009</td></tr>
<tr><td>reference ... ...</td><td>115</td></tr>
</tbody>
</table>

| | Code number |
|---|---|
| **Owner-** | |
| agricultural machinery ... | 169 |
| amusement ... ... ... | 106 |
| art gallery ... ... ... | 106 |
| assembly rooms ... ... | 104 |
| automatic machines ... ... | 106 |
| betting shop ... ... | 164 |
| billiard room ... ... | 106 |
| boarding house ... ... | 102 |
| boat; ... ... ... | 317 |
| fishing ... ... ... | 111 |
| bowling green ... ... | 106 |
| bus service ... ... | 325 |
| butchers ... ... ... | 186 |
| cab ... ... ... ... | 327 |
| café ... ... ... ... | 104 |
| camp; holiday ... ... | 109 |
| car hire service ... ... | 134 |
| caravan ... ... ... | 109 |
| caravan site ... ... | 109 |
| carriage ... ... ... | 327 |
| chess room ... ... | 106 |
| cinema ... ... ... | 106 |
| circulating library ... | 101 |
| club- ... ... ... | 104 |
| sports club ... ... ... | 106 |
| coach service ... ... | 325 |
| coconut shy ... ... | 165 |
| contract cleaning services | 111 |
| convalescent home ... | 037 |
| dance hall ... ... ... | 106 |
| detective agency ... ... | 140 |
| drifter ... ... ... | 111 |
| drug store ... ... ... | 101 |
| dry cleaning service ... | 111 |
| employment agency ... | 099 |
| engineering works ... | 276 |
| fish hatchery ... ... | 111 |
| fishing vessel ... ... | 111 |
| fishmongers ... ... | 187 |
| flats; | |
| holiday ... ... | 109 |
| service ... ... | 109 |
| garage ... ... ... ... | 100 |
| general store ... ... | 101 |
| guest house ... ... | 102 |
| horse ... ... ... | 111 |
| hotel ... ... ... | 102 |
| kennels ... ... ... | 111 |
| launderette ... ... | 110 |
| laundry ... ... ... | 111 |
| loan office ... ... | 134 |
| newspaper ... ... | 054 |
| nursing home ... ... | 043 |
| old people's home ... | 037 |
| petrol pump ... ... | 100 |
| petrol station ... ... | 100 |
| photographic agency ... | 134 |
| pleasure pier ... ... | 106 |
| property ... ... | 025 |
| public house ... ... | 103 |
| quarry... ... ... | 315 |
| refreshment room ... | 104 |
| restaurant ... ... | 104 |
| sawmill ... ... ... | 218 |
| school- | |
| *driving school* ... | 052 |
| *educational establishments-* | 033 |
| *further education estab-* | |
| *lishment* ... ... | 032 |
| *riding school* ... | 106 |
| shop *see Shopkeeper* | |
| skating rink ... ... | 106 |
| skittle alley ... ... | 106 |
| stable ... ... ... | 111 |
| stall (street, market) ... | 130 |
| taxi ... ... ... | 327 |
| taxi and garage ... ... | 100 |
| tea gardens ... ... | 104 |
| textile mill ... ... | 199 |
| travel agency ... ... | 099 |
| typewriting bureau ... | 134 |
| **Owner-driver; taxi** ... | 327 |
| **Oxidiser** (*metal trades*) ... | 269 |

| | Code number |
|---|---|
| Oxidiser man ... ... ... | 184 |
| Oyster bed worker ... ... | 171 |

# P

| | Code number |
|---|---|
| P.O. n.o.s. (*local government*) | 022 |
| P. and T.O. (*government*)- | |
| grade I, II *see Engineer- prof.-* | |
| grade III, IV ... ... | 081 |
| Packman (*woollen carding*) ... | L339 |
| **Packer;** | |
| asbestos ... ... ... | 316 |
| cable ... ... ... | 287 |
| chlorine ... ... ... | 287 |
| cop ... ... ... | 287 |
| drum; furnace ... | 297 |
| flock (*bedding mfr.*) ... | 213 |
| gland ... ... ... | 271 |
| kiln ... ... ... | 191 |
| oven (*foundry*) ... | 270 |
| potter's ... ... ... | 191 |
| sagger ... ... ... | 204 |
| shoddy ... ... ... | 176 |
| wheel ... ... ... | 276 |
| wool ... ... ... | 287 |
| **Packer-** | 287 |
| *coal mine* ... ... | 314 |
| *furniture mfr.* ... | 287 |
| *mine, not coal* ... | 338 |
| *shipbuilding* ... | 262 |
| *steel mfr.* ... ... | 287 |
| Packer and sorter (*laundry*) ... | 287 |
| Packer and stacker ... ... | 287 |
| Packer-driver ... ... | 326 |
| Packer-hooper ... ... | 287 |
| Packer-labourer ... ... | 287 |
| Padder; colour ... ... | 299 |
| **Padder-** | |
| *clothing mfr.* ... ... | 212 |
| *leather dressing* ... | 173 |
| *textile mfr.* ... ... | 182 |
| Paediatrician ... ... | 041 |
| Page (*hotel*) ... ... | 154 |
| Page boy ... ... | 154 |
| **Pager-** | |
| *bookbinding* ... ... | 189 |
| *printing* ... ... | 227 |
| *type foundry* ... | 287 |
| Paint boy ... ... ... | L346 |
| Paint hand ... ... | 299 |
| **Paint worker-** | |
| *paint mfr.* ... ... | 184 |
| *vehicle mfr.* ... | 281 |
| **Painter;** | |
| aircraft ... ... ... | 281 |
| biscuit ... ... ... | 279 |
| bottom ... ... ... | 299 |
| car ... ... ... | 281 |
| coach ... ... ... | 280 |
| design ... ... ... | 079 |
| enamel ... ... ... | 279 |
| engraver's (*textile printing*) ... | 276 |
| flower ... ... ... | 279 |
| freehand ... ... ... | 279 |
| glaze ... ... ... | 279 |
| heraldic ... ... ... | 055 |
| hide (*tannery*) ... | 173 |
| house ... ... ... | 282 |
| landscape ... ... ... | 055 |
| marine ... ... ... | 055 |
| miniature ... ... ... | 055 |
| portrait ... ... ... | 055 |
| pottery ... ... ... | 279 |
| roller (*textile printing*) ... | 276 |
| rough (*glass mfr.*) ... | 299 |
| scenic ... ... ... | 282 |
| skin (*fellmongering*) ... | 173 |
| slide; lantern ... ... | 055 |
| slip ... ... ... | 279 |

| | Code number |
|---|---|
| **Painter;** *continued* | |
| spray- ... ... ... | 281 |
| *ceramic mfr.* ... | 279 |
| *painting and decorating* ... | 282 |
| tin ... ... ... | 281 |
| toy ... ... ... | 299 |
| underglaze ... ... | 279 |
| velvet ... ... ... | 227 |
| wagon ... ... ... | 281 |
| **Painter-** | 282 |
| *artificial flower mfr.* ... | 299 |
| *ceramic mfr.* ... | 279 |
| *garage* ... ... | 281 |
| *glass etching* ... | 299 |
| *roller engraving* ... | 276 |
| *tannery* ... ... | 173 |
| *textile designing* ... | 115 |
| *vehicle mfr.* ... | 281 |
| Painter and decorator ... | 282 |
| Painter and glazier ... | 282 |
| Painter hand ... ... | 299 |
| Painter-decorator ... | 282 |
| **Pairer-** | |
| *corset mfr.* ... ... | 299 |
| *hosiery mfr.* ... ... | 287 |
| Palaeographist ... ... | 036 |
| Palaeontologist ... ... | 067 |
| Palm and needle hand ... | 212 |
| Palmist ... ... ... | 165 |
| Pan hand; bass ... ... | 230 |
| Pan hand (*brush mfr.*) ... | 230 |
| **Pan man;** | |
| acid ... ... ... | 184 |
| boiling (foods) ... ... | 202 |
| vacuum (*food products mfr.*) | 202 |
| **Pan man-** | |
| *catering, hotels, etc.* ... | 147 |
| *ceramic mfr.* ... ... | 204 |
| *chemical mfr.* ... | 184 |
| *coal mine* ... ... | 314 |
| *food products mfr.* ... | 202 |
| *paper mfr.* ... ... | 203 |
| *sugar refining* ... | 202 |
| Pan worker; revolving (*sugar* | |
| *confectionery mfr.*) ... | 202 |
| Panelman (*oil refining*) ... | 184 |
| Paneller; veneer ... ... | 224 |
| Panner- ... ... ... | 201 |
| *coal mine* ... ... | 314 |
| Panner-out ... ... | L341 |
| Pansman (*sugar refining*) ... | 202 |
| **Pantographer-** | |
| *embroidery mfr.* ... | 212 |
| *glassware mfr.* ... | 192 |
| *lace mfr.* ... ... | 226 |
| *roller engraving* ... | 267 |
| Pantry boy ... ... | 147 |
| Pantry man ... ... | 147 |
| Paper boy (*newsagents*) ... | 124 |
| Paper hand (piano hammers) ... | 218 |
| Paper man (*plasterboard mfr.*) | 204 |
| **Paper worker-** | |
| *paper mfr.* ... ... | 188 |
| *printing* ... ... | L346 |
| **Paperer;** | |
| chair ... ... ... | 299 |
| sand- ... ... ... | 299 |
| *mask mfr.* ... ... | 230 |
| *tin (bakery)* ... | 200 |
| **Paperer-** | |
| *ceramic mfr.* ... ... | 287 |
| *lace mfr.* ... ... | 287 |
| *tobacco pipe mfr.* ... | 218 |
| Paperer-on (whips) ... | 299 |
| Paperhanger ... ... | 282 |
| Paperkeeper ... ... | 115 |
| Paraflow man (brewing) ... | 197 |
| Parasitologist ... ... | 065 |
| **Paratrooper-** | |
| *armed forces-* | |
| *foreign and Commonwealth* | 136 |
| *U.K.* ... ... | 135 |
| Parceller ... ... ... | 287 |
| Parchmentiser ... ... | 203 |

| | Code number |
|---|---|
| **Piecer;** *continued* | |
| silk ... ... ... ... | 177 |
| sole ... ... ... ... | 299 |
| twiner ... ... ... ... | 177 |
| waste ... ... ... ... | 176 |
| **Piecer-** | |
| *leather dressing* ... ... | 173 |
| *textile mfr.* ... ... | 177 |
| **Piecer-out** (*flax mfr.*) ... | 177 |
| **Piecer-up** (*clothing mfr.*) ... | 212 |
| **Pier head man** ... ... | 338 |
| **Pierman** ... ... ... | 338 |
| **Pierce worker** ... ... | 266 |
| **Piercer;** | |
| saw ... ... ... | 266 |
| strap ... ... ... | 175 |
| **Piercer-** | |
| *ceramic mfr.* ... ... | 223 |
| *jewellery and plate mfr.* | 266 |
| *pen nib mfr.* ... ... | 242 |
| *tube mfr.* ... ... | 270 |
| **Pigman** ... ... ... | 166 |
| **Piggeryman** ... ... ... | 166 |
| **Pikeman** (*coal mine*) ... | 314 |
| **Piler;** ... ... ... | 338 |
| bobbin ... ... ... | 199 |
| hot ... ... ... | 338 |
| roving ... ... ... | 176 |
| **Pilot;** | |
| canal ... ... ... | 087 |
| dock ... ... ... | 087 |
| helicopter ... ... | 085 |
| hovercraft ... ... | M090 |
| river ... ... ... | 087 |
| test ... ... ... | 085 |
| **Pilot-** | |
| *aircraft* ... ... ... | 085 |
| *shipping* ... ... ... | 087 |
| **Pinner;** woollen comb ... | 285 |
| **Pinner-** | |
| *ceramic mfr.* ... ... | 223 |
| *lamp, valve mfr.* ... | 283 |
| *metal trades* ... ... | 285 |
| *textile mfr.-* ... ... | 179 |
| *textile making-up* ... | 199 |
| **Pinner-on** (*textile mfr.*) ... | 199 |
| **Pipe man;** brine ... ... | 260 |
| **Pipe man** (*coal mine*) ... | 260 |
| **Piper;** sugar ... ... | 202 |
| **Piper** (*sugar confectionery mfr.*) | 202 |
| **Pisciculturist** ... ... | 171 |
| **Pit hand** (*tube mfr.*) ... | 231 |
| **Pit man;** soaking (*steelworks*) .. | 231 |
| **Pit man-** | |
| *coal mine-* ... ... | 314 |
| *above ground* ... | 345 |
| *mine, not coal* ... | 315 |
| *steelworks-* ... ... | 270 |
| *soaking pit* ... ... | 231 |
| **Pit worker;** siemens ... | 270 |
| **Pit worker** (*coal mine*) ... | 345 |
| **Pitch man** ... ... | L346 |
| **Pitcher;** | |
| flour ... ... ... | L346 |
| stone ... ... ... | 316 |
| **Pitcher-** | |
| *building and contracting* ... | 316 |
| *ceramic mfr.* ... ... | 204 |
| *meat market* ... ... | 335 |
| **Pitcher and malletter** ... | 223 |
| **Placer;** | |
| biscuit ... ... ... | 191 |
| glost ... ... ... | 191 |
| kiln ... ... ... | 191 |
| litho ... ... ... | 279 |
| sanitary ... ... ... | 191 |
| tile ... ... ... | 191 |
| **Placer** (*ceramic mfr.*) ... | 191 |
| **Plaiter;** grass ... ... | 230 |
| **Plaiter-** | |
| *cordage* ... ... ... | 199 |
| *textile mfr.* ... ... | 199 |
| **Plaiter and finisher** (whips) ... | 225 |
| **Planeman;** engine ... ... | 306 |

| | Code number |
|---|---|
| **Planer;** | |
| die ... ... ... | 241 |
| edge; plate ... ... | 276 |
| slate ... ... ... | 301 |
| stone ... ... ... | 301 |
| **Planer-** | |
| metal ... ... ... | 241 |
| plastics ... ... ... | 229 |
| stereotypes ... ... | 206 |
| wood ... ... ... | 218 |
| *coal mine* ... ... | 241 |
| *metal trades* ... ... | 241 |
| **Planer and slotter;** wall ... | 241 |
| **Planisher;** iron ... ... | 261 |
| **Planisher** (*sheet metal goods mfr.*) | 261 |
| **Planker** ... ... ... | 199 |
| **Planner;** | |
| carpet ... ... ... | 226 |
| clothier's ... ... | 226 |
| die (*footwear mfr.*) ... | 225 |
| footwear ... ... ... | 056 |
| gravure ... ... ... | 206 |
| group (*N.C.B.*) ... | 075 |
| kitchen ... ... ... | 055 |
| line ... ... ... | 010 |
| linoleum ... ... ... | 316 |
| load ... ... ... | 338 |
| materials ... ... ... | 090 |
| media ... ... ... | 014 |
| mine (*N.C.B.*) ... | 075 |
| production ... ... | 075 |
| progress ... ... ... | 115 |
| sales ... ... ... | 013 |
| scheme; pension ... | 011 |
| tool and jig ... ... | 075 |
| town ... ... ... | 082 |
| traffic; ... ... ... | 115 |
| air ... ... ... | 086 |
| transport ... ... | 115 |
| work ... ... ... | 115 |
| **Planner-** | |
| *clothing mfr.* ... ... | 226 |
| *engineering* ... ... | 075 |
| *printing* ... ... ... | 206 |
| **Plant hand;** | |
| acid ... ... ... | 184 |
| bakery ... ... ... | 200 |
| **Plant man;** | |
| benzol ... ... ... | 184 |
| dehydration (*food products mfr.*) | 202 |
| **Plant man** (*chemical mfr.*) ... | 184 |
| **Plant worker;** | |
| gas ... ... ... | 184 |
| hydrating; lime ... | 198 |
| screening ... ... | 198 |
| sinter ... ... ... | 270 |
| **Plant worker-** | |
| *bakery* ... ... ... | 200 |
| *chemical mfr.* ... ... | 184 |
| *coke ovens* ... ... | 184 |
| **Planter;** | |
| coffee ... ... ... | 107 |
| rubber ... ... ... | 107 |
| tea ... ... ... | 107 |
| tobacco ... ... ... | 107 |
| tree ... ... ... | 170 |
| **Plasterer;** fibrous ... ... | 302 |
| **Plasterer-** ... ... ... | 302 |
| *cast concrete products mfr.* ... | 230 |
| *coke ovens* ... ... | L341 |
| *plaster cast mfr.* ... | 223 |
| **Plasterer and decorator** ... | 304 |
| **Plastics worker** ... ... | 229 |
| **Plate hand-** | |
| *printing* ... ... ... | 206 |
| *rope mfr.* ... ... | 199 |
| **Plate man-** | |
| asphalt spreading ... | 330 |
| hotel, etc. ... ... | 147 |
| **Plate worker;** | |
| iron ... ... ... | 262 |
| metal ... ... ... | 262 |

| | Code number |
|---|---|
| **Plate worker;** *continued* | |
| tin- ... ... ... | 261 |
| *tinplate mfr.-* | |
| female ... ... | L344 |
| male ... ... | 270 |
| zinc ... ... ... | 261 |
| **Plater;** | |
| barrel ... ... ... | 269 |
| boiler ... ... ... | 262 |
| brass ... ... ... | 269 |
| bridge ... ... ... | 262 |
| cadmium ... ... | 236 |
| chrome ... ... ... | 236 |
| chromium ... ... | 236 |
| constructional ... | 262 |
| copper ... ... ... | 236 |
| dip ... ... ... | 269 |
| electro ... ... ... | 236 |
| engineers; gas ... | 262 |
| framing ... ... ... | 262 |
| gold ... ... ... | 236 |
| hand ... ... ... | 236 |
| heavy ... ... ... | 262 |
| hoe ... ... ... | 233 |
| hot ... ... ... | 182 |
| iron ... ... ... | 262 |
| last ... ... ... | 261 |
| light ... ... ... | 262 |
| lock ... ... ... | 269 |
| metal ... ... ... | 269 |
| needle ... ... ... | 269 |
| nickel ... ... ... | 236 |
| roof ... ... ... | 262 |
| shell ... ... ... | 262 |
| ship('s) ... ... ... | 262 |
| shovel ... ... ... | 233 |
| silver ... ... ... | 236 |
| steel ... ... ... | 262 |
| stem ... ... ... | 262 |
| structural ... ... | 262 |
| tank ... ... ... | 262 |
| tin- | |
| *tinplate mfr.* ... | 269 |
| *tinplate printing* | 207 |
| tool; edge- ... ... | 233 |
| *surgical instrument mfr.* ... | 236 |
| white metal ... ... | 236 |
| wire ... ... ... | 269 |
| **Plater-** | |
| *bookbinding* ... ... | 189 |
| *chemical mfr.* ... ... | 262 |
| *coal mine* ... ... | 262 |
| *construction* ... ... | 262 |
| *fertiliser mfr.* ... ... | 184 |
| *gas board* ... ... | 262 |
| *leather dressing* ... | 173 |
| *metal trades-* | |
| *boiler mfr.* ... ... | 262 |
| *boot last mfr.* ... | 261 |
| *constructional engineering* | 262 |
| *cutlery mfr.* ... ... | 233 |
| *edge tool mfr.* ... | 233 |
| *electroplating* ... | 236 |
| *iron tank mfr.* ... | 262 |
| *railway locomotive shop* ... | 262 |
| *shipbuilding* ... ... | 262 |
| *steelworks* ... ... | 262 |
| *paper mfr.* ... ... | 188 |
| *textile mfr.* ... ... | 182 |
| **Plater and gilder** ... ... | 236 |
| **Plater-down** (*textile making-up*) | 199 |
| **Plater-welder** ... ... | 262 |
| **Platform boy** (*steelworks*) ... | L344 |
| **Platform man;** | |
| milk reception ... | F338 |
| regulating ... ... | 338 |
| **Platform man** (*steelworks*) ... | 270 |
| **Player-** | |
| *musical instruments* ... | 060 |
| *sports* ... ... ... | 063 |
| **Playwright** ... ... ... | 054 |
| **Pleater;** | |
| accordion ... ... | 199 |
| cloth ... ... ... | 199 |

Code number

**Potter-** *continued*

| | |
|---|---|
| *ceramic mfr.* ... ... ... | 193 |
| *lead smelting* ... ... | 231 |
| *zinc refining* ... ... | 223 |
| Pottery worker ... ... | 223 |
| Poulterer- ... ... ... | 187 |
| *farming* ... ... ... | 166 |
| Poultry boy ... ... ... | 166 |
| Poultry hand (*food processing*) | 187 |
| Poultry man ... ... ... | 166 |
| Poultry worker ... ... | 166 |
| Pouncer ... ... ... | 226 |
| Pounder ... ... ... | 225 |
| Pourer (*foundry*) ... ... | 270 |
| Powder man; ... ... | 333 |
| bleaching ... ... | L340 |
| Powderer ... ... ... | 299 |
| Power house man ... ... | 255 |
| Practitioner; | |
| Christian Science ... | 040 |
| dental ... ... ... | 042 |
| general ... ... ... | 041 |
| homeopathic- ... | 050 |
| medically qualified | 041 |
| hydropathic ... ... | 049 |
| medical; ... ... | 041 |
| registered ... ... | 041 |
| study; works ... ... | 010 |
| veterinary ... ... | 051 |
| Prebendary ... ... ... | 040 |
| Pre-boarder (*hosiery mfr.*) ... | 182 |
| Precipitator ... ... ... | 184 |
| Pre-former ... ... ... | 195 |
| Premixer (chemicals) ... ... | 184 |
| Pre-packer *see Packer* | |
| Preparer; | |
| case ... ... ... ... | 225 |
| colour (*ceramic mfr.*) ... | 204 |
| cylinder ... ... ... | 348 |
| dough (artificial teeth) ... | 204 |
| fish ... ... ... ... | 187 |
| food ... ... ... ... | 143 |
| fruit; preserved ... ... | 202 |
| gelatine ... ... ... | 202 |
| glass; safety ... ... | 223 |
| glaze (*ceramic mfr.*) ... | 204 |
| hair- ... ... ... | 176 |
| *wig mfr.* ... ... | 230 |
| jute ... ... ... ... | 176 |
| litho (*ceramic mfr.*) ... | 299 |
| lithographic (*printing*) ... | 206 |
| paper ... ... ... | 227 |
| plate; lithographic ... | 276 |
| raw ingredient (*flour confec-* | |
| *tionery mfr.*) ... | 200 |
| starch ... ... ... | 182 |
| veneer ... ... ... | 224 |
| warp ... ... ... | 179 |
| welt ... ... ... | 225 |
| yarn ... ... ... | 177 |
| for dyeing ... ... | 199 |
| Preparer- | |
| *ceramic mfr.* ... ... | 223 |
| *clothing mfr.* ... ... | 211 |
| *embroidery mfr.* ... | 226 |
| *food preserving* ... ... | 202 |
| *footwear mfr.* ... ... | 175 |
| *glass mfr.* ... ... | 223 |
| *laundry* ... ... ... | 162 |
| *leather goods mfr.* ... | 225 |
| *lithography* ... ... | 206 |
| *metal trades* ... ... | 276 |
| *textile mfr.-* ... ... | 176 |
| *cotton doubling* ... | 182 |
| Preparer and sealer (*cable mfr.*) | 276 |
| Preserver; timber ... ... | 203 |
| Preserver (*food products mfr.*) | 202 |
| President (college) ... ... | 031 |
| Press hand *see Presser-* | |
| Press man *see Presser-* | |
| Press operator *see Presser-* | |
| Press worker *see Presser-* | |
| Presser; | |
| barm ... ... ... ... | 202 |

**Presser;** *continued*

| | |
|---|---|
| belt ... ... ... ... | 204 |
| bending ... ... ... | 270 |
| blanking ... ... ... | 175 |
| block (*plastics goods mfr.*) ... | 195 |
| blouse ... ... ... | 162 |
| brick ... ... ... | 223 |
| brush; carbon ... ... | 204 |
| cap ... ... ... ... | 162 |
| carbon ... ... ... | 204 |
| clicking ... ... ... | 175 |
| clipping ... ... ... | 270 |
| cloth ... ... ... | 182 |
| clothes ... ... ... | 162 |
| cocoa ... ... ... | 202 |
| coil ... ... ... ... | 274 |
| coining ... ... ... | 242 |
| collar ... ... ... | 162 |
| compo ... ... ... | 204 |
| component ... ... ... | 242 |
| die ... ... ... ... | 193 |
| draw ... ... ... | 242 |
| dust (*ceramic mfr.*) ... ... | 193 |
| electric; edge-setting ... | 162 |
| extruding (*metal trades*) ... | 270 |
| filter- | |
| *coal mine* ... ... | 198 |
| *food products mfr.* ... | 202 |
| final ... ... ... | 162 |
| fitter's ... ... ... | 270 |
| flat- | |
| *ceramic mfr.* ... | 193 |
| *pressed woollen felt mfr.* ... | 182 |
| fly- | |
| *cutlery mfr.* ... ... | 242 |
| *forging* ... ... | 233 |
| forge ... ... ... | 233 |
| fusing ... ... ... | 299 |
| garment ... ... ... | 162 |
| general ... ... ... | 162 |
| glass ... ... ... | 192 |
| gramophone record ... | 195 |
| hand- | |
| *metal trades* ... ... | 242 |
| *sports goods mfr.* ... | 230 |
| *tailoring* ... ... | 162 |
| *textile finishing* ... | 162 |
| heel- | |
| *footwear mfr.* ... ... | 299 |
| *rubber goods mfr.* ... | 194 |
| Hoffman ... ... ... | 162 |
| hollow-ware ... ... | 193 |
| hop ... ... ... ... | 197 |
| hosiery ... ... ... | 182 |
| hot- | |
| *cemented carbide goods mfr.* | 204 |
| *ceramic mfr.* ... ... | 193 |
| *metal trades* ... ... | 233 |
| *paper mfr.* ... ... | 203 |
| *printing* ... ... | 188 |
| *rubber goods mfr.* ... | 194 |
| *textile finishing* ... | 182 |
| hydraulic- | |
| *metal trades-* ... ... | 242 |
| *forging* ... ... | 233 |
| *packing* ... ... | 287 |
| *paper merchants* ... | 287 |
| *plastics goods mfr.* ... | 195 |
| *textile mfr.* ... ... | 182 |
| jobbing ... ... ... | 204 |
| lead (*cable mfr.*) ... ... | 270 |
| lining; brake ... ... | 204 |
| lining- ... ... ... | 162 |
| *footwear mfr.* ... ... | 299 |
| machine- | |
| *clothing mfr.* ... ... | 162 |
| *metal trades* ... ... | 242 |
| *textile mfr.* ... ... | 182 |
| mantle ... ... ... | 162 |
| mica ... ... ... | 204 |
| oil (*oil seed crushing*) ... | 202 |
| paper ... ... ... | 287 |
| pipe ... ... ... | 270 |
| plastics ... ... ... | 195 |

**Presser;** *continued*

| | |
|---|---|
| polishing ... ... ... | 229 |
| porcelain; electric ... | 193 |
| pottery ... ... ... | 193 |
| powder (*chemical mfr.*) ... | 184 |
| power- | |
| *carbon goods mfr.* ... | 230 |
| *metal trades* ... ... | 242 |
| revolution ... ... | 175 |
| ring ... ... ... | 242 |
| rotary- | |
| *printing* ... ... | 207 |
| *textile mfr.* ... ... | 182 |
| rubber ... ... ... | 194 |
| sagger ... ... ... | 223 |
| scale (*knife handle mfr.*) ... | 230 |
| seam ... ... ... | 162 |
| shirt ... ... ... | 162 |
| shoe ... ... ... | 299 |
| sleeve ... ... ... | 162 |
| stamping ... ... ... | 242 |
| steam- | |
| *clothing* ... ... | 162 |
| *metal* ... ... ... | 242 |
| *rubber* ... ... | 194 |
| steel- ... ... ... | 233 |
| stock ... ... ... | 162 |
| stone; artificial ... | 230 |
| stuff ... ... ... | 182 |
| sweetland ... ... ... | 202 |
| tailor's ... ... ... | 162 |
| terra cotta ... ... | 193 |
| tile (*ceramic mfr.*) ... ... | 193 |
| tool ... ... ... | 242 |
| top ... ... ... ... | 162 |
| trouser ... ... ... | 162 |
| tube ... ... ... | 242 |
| underclothing ... ... | 162 |
| veneer ... ... ... | 203 |
| washer ... ... ... | 204 |
| yarn ... ... ... | 182 |
| yeast ... ... ... | 197 |
| Presser- | |
| *asbestos-cement goods mfr.* | 230 |
| *bookbinding* ... ... | 189 |
| *cable mfr.* ... ... | 230 |
| *cast concrete products mfr.* ... | 230 |
| *cemented carbide goods mfr.* | 204 |
| *ceramic mfr.* ... ... | 193 |
| *chemical mfr.* ... ... | 184 |
| *cider mfr.* ... ... | 197 |
| *clothing mfr.* ... ... | 162 |
| *crayon, pencil mfr.* ... | 204 |
| *distillery* ... ... | 197 |
| *food products mfr.* ... | 202 |
| *footwear mfr.* ... ... | 299 |
| *glass mfr.* ... ... | 192 |
| *gramophone record mfr.* ... | 195 |
| *laundry* ... ... ... | 162 |
| *leather dressing* ... | 173 |
| *leather goods mfr.* ... | 299 |
| *metal trades-* ... ... | 242 |
| *electric battery mfr.* ... | 230 |
| *forging* ... ... | 233 |
| *rolling mill* ... ... | 233 |
| *tube mfr.* ... ... | 270 |
| *mica, micanite goods mfr.* ... | 204 |
| *mine, not coal* ... ... | 198 |
| *oil seed crushing* ... | 202 |
| *paper mfr.* ... ... | 203 |
| *patent fuel mfr.* ... | 204 |
| *plastics goods mfr.* ... | 195 |
| *plywood mfr.* ... ... | 203 |
| *printing* ... ... | 207 |
| *rubber goods mfr.* ... | 194 |
| *textile mfr.-* ... ... | 182 |
| *textile packing* ... | 137 |
| *tobacco mfr.* ... ... | 082 |
| *waste merchants* ... | 137 |
| *wood pulp mfr.* ... ... | 083 |
| Presser and threader ... ... | 073 |
| Presser-off (*clothing mfr.*) ... | 162 |
| Presser-out (*textile machinery* | |
| *mfr.*) ... ... ... | 242 |

| | Code number |
|---|---|
| Raker; asphalt ... ... ... | 307 |
| Raker-out (*asbestos mfr.*) | L339 |
| Ram man ... ... ... | 338 |
| **Rammer;** | |
|   chair ... ... ... | 235 |
|   plug ... ... ... | 231 |
| **Rammer-** | |
|   *foundry* ... ... | 235 |
|   *metal mfr.* ... | 231 |
| Rammerman ... ... | 313 |
| Rammer-up ... ... | 235 |
| Rander (*twine mfr.*) ... | 178 |
| Range worker ... ... | L346 |
| **Ranger;** | |
|   estate ... ... ... | 140 |
|   forest ... ... ... | 170 |
|   park ... ... ... | 140 |
|   wood ... ... ... | 170 |
| **Ranger-** ... | 140 |
|   *footwear mfr.* ... | 175 |
|   *glass mfr.* ... | 299 |
| Ransacker (*fishing net mfr.*) | 289 |
| Rasper (remould tyres) ... | 228 |
| Rating; engine-room (*shipping*) | 317 |
| **Rating-** | |
|   *armed forces-* | |
|     *foreign and Commonwealth* | 136 |
|     *U.K.* ... ... | 135 |
| Ratliner ... ... | 199 |
| Rayon worker ... ... | 196 |
| Reacher; drawer's ... | 179 |
| Reacher (*textile mfr.*) ... | 179 |
| Reacher-in (*textile mfr.*) ... | 179 |
| **Reader;** | |
|   design; textile ... | 115 |
|   film (*aircraft mfr.*) ... | 115 |
|   instrument ... ... | 115 |
|   lay ... ... ... | 040 |
|   literary ... ... | 054 |
|   manuscript ... ... | 115 |
|   meter ... ... ... | 115 |
|   news (*broadcasting*) ... | 059 |
|   newspaper ... ... | 115 |
|   press ... ... ... | 115 |
|   printer's ... ... | 115 |
|   proof ... ... ... | 115 |
|   publisher's ... ... | 054 |
| **Reader-** | |
|   dentistry ... ... | 042 |
|   medicine ... ... | 041 |
|   surgery ... ... | 041 |
|   *lace mfr.* ... ... | 199 |
|   *press cutting agency* ... | 115 |
|   *printing* ... ... | 115 |
|   *university* ... ... | 031 |
| Reader-compositor ... | 205 |
| Reader-in ... ... | 179 |
| Reader-off ... ... | 199 |
| Reamer (metal) ... ... | 241 |
| Reamerer; barrel ... | 241 |
| Reamerer (*metal trades*) ... | 241 |
| Rearer; poultry ... ... | 107 |
| Re-beamer ... ... | 179 |
| Recaster ... ... | 270 |
| **Receiver;** | |
|   goods ... ... ... | 333 |
|   grain ... ... ... | 333 |
|   official ... ... | 002 |
|   of arms ... ... | 333 |
| **Receiver-** ... | 333 |
|   *Board of Trade* ... | 002 |
|   *docks* ... ... | 115 |
|   *laundry* ... ... | 125 |
|   *leather cloth mfr.* ... | 182 |
|   *rolling mill* ... | 270 |
|   *tobacco mfr.* ... | 299 |
| **Receptionist;** | |
|   beet ... ... ... | 333 |
|   dental ... ... | 117 |
|   door ... ... ... | 165 |
|   vehicle (*garage*) ... | 249 |
| **Receptionist-** | |
|   television, radio hire ... | 115 |
|   *cinema, theatre* ... | 165 |

| | Code number |
|---|---|
| Receptionist- *continued* | |
|   garage ... ... ... | 249 |
| Reckoner (*tinplate mfr.*) ... | 297 |
| Reclaimer (rubber) ... | 204 |
| **Reconditioner;** | |
|   girder ... ... ... | 276 |
|   machine ... ... | 248 |
| **Recorder;** | |
|   furnace ... ... | 115 |
|   meter ... ... ... | 115 |
|   milk ... ... ... | 115 |
|   mould (*steel mfr.*) ... | 115 |
|   progress ... ... | 115 |
|   stock ... ... ... | 113 |
|   temperature ... ... | 115 |
|   time ... ... ... | 115 |
|   train ... ... ... | 115 |
|   wagon ... ... ... | 115 |
| **Recorder-** | |
|   laboratory ... ... | 288 |
|   *explosive mfr.* ... | 115 |
|   *H.M. dockyard* ... | 115 |
|   *legal services* ... | 001 |
|   *milk marketing board* ... | 115 |
|   *sound recording* ... | 062 |
|   *steelworks* ... | 115 |
| Recorder of work ... | 115 |
| **Recordist;** | |
|   electroencephalographic ... | 050 |
|   sound ... ... ... | 062 |
| **Recoverer;** | |
|   acetone ... ... | 184 |
|   solvent ... ... | 184 |
|   zinc ... ... ... | 231 |
| **Recoverer-** | |
|   *paper mfr.* ... ... | 203 |
|   *rubber reclamation* ... | 204 |
| Recovery hand *see Recoverer-* | |
| Recovery man *see Recoverer-* | |
| Recovery worker *see Recoverer-* | |
| **Rectifier;** | |
|   cycle; motor ... | 276 |
|   paint (*vehicle mfr.*) ... | 299 |
|   tube ... ... ... | 270 |
| **Rectifier-** ... | 184 |
|   *footwear mfr.* ... | 225 |
|   *metal trades* ... | 248 |
|   *textile mfr.* ... | 183 |
| **Rectifying man-** ... | 184 |
|   *metal trades* ... | 248 |
| **Rector-** | |
|   church ... ... | 040 |
|   college ... ... | 031 |
| Red-button ... ... | 115 |
| Red coat (*holiday camp*) ... | 165 |
| Re-drawer (silk) ... ... | 178 |
| Reducer; data; geophysical ... | 067 |
| **Reducer-** | |
|   *textile printing* ... | 182 |
|   *wool drawing* ... | 176 |
| Re-dyer ... ... ... | 182 |
| Reeder ... ... ... | 179 |
| Reel hand ... ... | 207 |
| Reelman ... ... | 188 |
| **Reeler;** | |
|   bar ... ... ... | 270 |
|   bobbin ... ... | 178 |
|   cop ... ... ... | 178 |
|   rope ... ... ... | 199 |
|   twine ... ... | 178 |
|   twist ... ... | 178 |
|   yarn ... ... ... | 178 |
| **Reeler-** | |
|   *paper mfr.* ... ... | 188 |
|   *photographic film mfr.* ... | 227 |
|   *plastics goods mfr.* ... | 229 |
|   *printing* ... ... | 207 |
|   *rolling mill* ... | 270 |
|   *textile mfr.-* ... | 178 |
|     *textile bleaching* ... | 182 |
|   *wallpaper mfr.* ... | 188 |
|   *wire rope, cable mfr.* ... | 276 |
| Reeler and lacer ... ... | 178 |
| Reeler boy ... ... | 299 |

| | Code number |
|---|---|
| **Reelerman-** | |
|   *paper mfr.* ... ... | 188 |
|   *rolling mill* ... | 270 |
|   *roofing felt mfr.* ... | 199 |
| Referee; official (*legal services*) | 001 |
| **Referee-** ... ... | 063 |
|   medical (*government*) ... | 041 |
| Reference man ... ... | 140 |
| Referencer ... ... | 115 |
| **Refiner;** | |
|   bullion ... ... | 231 |
|   clay; china ... ... | 198 |
|   dripping ... ... | 202 |
|   fat ... ... ... | 202 |
|   gold ... ... ... | 231 |
|   lard ... ... ... | 202 |
|   nickel ... ... | 231 |
|   oil; cotton ... ... | 202 |
|   paint ... ... ... | 184 |
|   silver ... ... ... | 231 |
| **Refiner-** | |
|   *candle mfr.* ... ... | 184 |
|   *chemical mfr.* ... | 184 |
|   *chocolate mfr.* ... | 202 |
|   *food products mfr.* ... | 202 |
|   *metal mfr.* ... | 231 |
|   *oil refining* ... | 184 |
|   *oil seed refining* ... | 202 |
|   *paper mfr.* ... | 188 |
|   *rubber reclamation* ... | 204 |
|   *sugar refining* ... | 202 |
| Refiner hand *see Refiner-* | |
| Refiner man *see Refiner-* | |
| Refinery worker; oil ... | 184 |
| Refinisher ... ... | 281 |
| Refooter (stockings) ... | 181 |
| Refractory worker ... | L342 |
| Refrigerator man (*brewery*) ... | 197 |
| **Refueller-** | |
|   vehicles ... ... | 127 |
|   *airport* ... ... | 338 |
| Regenerator; oil (*coal gas*) ... | 184 |
| Register boy; train ... | 115 |
| **Registrar;** | |
|   additional ... ... | 022 |
|   cemetery ... ... | 111 |
|   company ... ... | 030 |
|   land ... ... ... | 027 |
|   probate ... ... | 001 |
|   superintendent ... | 022 |
|   of births, deaths and marriages | 022 |
|   of deeds ... ... | 022 |
|   of marriages ... ... | 022 |
|   of stock ... ... | 030 |
|   of stocks and bonds ... | 030 |
| **Registrar-** ... ... | 030 |
|   *educational services* ... | 111 |
|   *government* ... | 021 |
|   *hospital service* ... | 041 |
|   *legal services* ... | 001 |
|   *local government* ... | 022 |
|   *Post Office* ... ... | 111 |
| Regulating platform man ... | 338 |
| **Regulator;** | |
|   gas (*coal gas, coke ovens*) ... | 348 |
|   steam ... ... | 347 |
|   traffic ... ... | F323 |
| **Regulator-** | |
|   *piano, organ mfr.* ... | 222 |
|   *transport* ... ... | F323 |
| Reheater ... ... | 231 |
| Re-laster ... ... | 175 |
| Relayer (*railways*) ... | 306 |
| **Reliner;** | |
|   bearing ... ... | 270 |
|   brake ... ... | 299 |
| Reliner (*steelworks*) ... | 300 |
| Remoistener (dextrin) ... | 202 |
| **Remoulder-** | |
|   *glass mfr.* ... ... | 192 |
|   *rubber goods mfr.* ... | 228 |
| Removal hand (*road transport*) | 335 |
| Removalman (*road transport*) ... | 335 |

Code number

Remover;
belt (*coal mine*) ... ... 276
cattle ... ... ... 326
conveyor (*coal mine*) ... 276
furniture ... ... 335
refuse ... ... ... 336
scrap ... ... ... 338
Renderer; lard ... ... 202
Renewer; tread ... ... 228
Renovator;
  antiques ... ... ... 215
  car ... ... ... 261
  figure; display ... ... 230
Renovator-
  clothing ... ... ... 226
  furniture ... ... ... 215
Renter; film ... ... ... 134
Repairman *see* Repairer-
Repair worker (*coal mine*)- ... 314
  *above ground* ... ... 262
Repairer;
  airway-
    *coal mine* ... ... 314
    *mine, not coal* ... ... 315
  antiques ... ... 215
  appliance; domestic ... 253
  bag-
    canvas goods ... ... 212
    hand bags ... ... ... 225
  bank (canal) ... ... ... 316
  barge ... ... ... 262
  battery ... ... ... 230
  beam (*textile mfr.*) ... 248
  belt ... ... ... 225
  belting ... ... ... 225
  blanket; electric ... ... 253
  blind ... ... ... 230
  boat ... ... ... 214
  bobbin ... ... 248
  body (vehicle) ... ... 261
  boiler ... ... ... 262
  book ... ... ... 189
  box; ... ... ... 216
    horse ... ... 268
  brake ... ... ... 248
  bridge ... ... ... 316
  builder's ... ... ... 304
  building ... ... 304
  cable (electric) ... ... 257
  canvas goods ... ... 212
  carpet ... ... ... 183
  carriage ... ... ... 248
  case-
    watch ... ... ... 266
    wood ... ... ... 216
  cask ... ... ... 216
  chain ... ... ... 233
  chair- ... ... ... 215
    cane furniture ... 230
  chimney ... ... ... 300
  china ... ... ... 223
  chronometer ... ... 247
  clock ... ... ... 247
  clockwork ... ... 247
  coach- ... ... ... 268
    *railways* ... ... 248
  coil ... ... ... 274
  controller ... ... 253
  conveyor ... ... 248
  cord (telephones) ... 256
  crate ... ... ... 216
  cupola ... ... ... 300
  cycle- ... ... 248
    motor ... ... 249
  die ... ... ... 245
  farm implements ... 248
  film ... ... ... 230
  furnace ... ... ... 300
  furniture ... ... 215
  glass ... ... ... 223
  hosiery ... ... ... 183
  house ... ... ... 304
  hydraulic ... ... 248

Code number

Repairer; *continued*
  instrument- ... ... ... 246
    dental and surgical
      instruments ... ... 276
    musical instruments ... 222
    precision ... ... 246
  jewellery and plate ... 266
  kiln ... ... ... 300
  lamp ... ... ... 248
  machine-
    office machinery ... 251
  magneto ... ... 253
  mangle ... ... 248
  meter ... ... ... 246
  motor ... ... ... 249
  net (fishing nets) ... 183
  oven ... ... ... 300
  paint-work (*vehicle mfr.*) 281
  pen; fountain ... ... 230
  pipe (tobacco pipes) ... 224
  propeller ... ... 233
  property ... ... 304
  purse ... ... ... 225
  radiator (vehicle) ... 261
  rail (*railways*) ... ... 306
  railway ... ... 306
  recorder; time ... ... 247
  reed ... ... ... 230
  revolver ... ... 248
  road- ... ... ... 308
    *coal mine* ... ... 314
    *mine, not coal* ... 306
  roof ... ... ... 303
  sack ... ... ... 212
  saw ... ... ... 276
  scale ... ... ... 246
  sheet ... ... ... 226
  ship ... ... ... 262
  shoe ... ... ... 174
  spring ... ... ... 233
  stove (gas stoves) ... 248
  syphon ... ... ... 248
  tarpaulin ... ... 212
  tent ... ... ... 212
  tool ... ... ... 245
  toy ... ... ... 230
  tractor ... ... 248
  tub ... ... ... 276
  tube-
    *boiler mfr.* ... ... 262
    *carpet mfr.* ... ... 248
  typewriter ... ... 251
  tyre ... ... ... 228
  umbrella ... ... 226
  van ... ... ... 261
  veneer ... ... ... 224
  wagon ... ... ... 248
  watch ... ... ... 247
  watch and clock ... 247
  wire ... ... ... 257
  wireless ... ... 258
  wringer ... ... 248
Repairer-
  clothing ... ... ... 226
  dental and surgical
    instruments ... ... 276
  domestic appliances-... ... 253
    gas appliances ... 248
  electrical machinery ... 253
  footwear ... ... ... 174
  instruments ... ... 246
  jewellery ... ... 266
  leather goods ... ... 225
  machinery ... ... 248
  motor vehicles ... ... 249
  musical instruments ... 222
  office machinery ... 251
  precious metal, plate ... 266
  radio, television ... 258
  sports goods ... ... 230
  telephone apparatus ... 256
  watches, clocks ... 247
  *ceramic mfr.* ... ... 223
  *coal mine* ... ... ... 314

Code number

Repairer- *continued*
  *embroidery mfr.* ... ... 226
  *L.T.E.* ... ... ... 276
Repairer and builder; boat ... 214
Repairer and jeweller; watch ... 247
Reporter;
  loading (*L.T.E.*) ... ... 115
  status (*finance*) ... ... 140
  train ... ... ... 115
  to children's panel ... 027
Reporter-
  *broadcasting* ... ... ... 054
  *newspaper* ... ... ... 054
Reporter and signalman;
  meteorological ... ... 122
Representative;
  accounts ... ... ... 115
  advertisement ... ... 134
  advertising ... ... 134
  agricultural ... ... 133
  architectural ... ... 133
  banker's ... ... ... 099
  catering ... ... ... 134
  circulation ... ... 134
  claims; insurance ... 005
  commercial ... ... 134
  company ... ... 133
  credit ... ... ... 132
  default ... ... ... 115
  display ... ... ... 134
  dock ... ... ... 115
  educational ... ... 133
  freight ... ... ... 134
  heating ... ... ... 133
  liaison ... ... ... 133
  medical ... ... ... 133
  newspaper ... ... 134
  press ... ... ... 054
  publicity ... ... ... 134
  publisher's ... ... 133
  sales- ... ... ... 133
    property ... ... 134
    services ... ... 134
    *mail order house* ... 132
    *P.O.* ... ... ... 134
    *retail trade-* ... ... 134
      *door to door sales* ... 132
      *party plan sales* ... 132
  service; railway ... ... 134
  shipping ... ... ... 134
  space (*printing*) ... ... 134
  technical ... ... 133
  traffic (*air transport*) ... 134
Representative-
  services ... ... ... 134
  *banking* ... ... ... 099
  *electricity board* ... 133
  *gas board* ... ... 133
  *insurance* ... ... 134
  *mail order house* ... 132
  *manufacturing* ... ... 133
  *motor factors*... ... 125
  *retail trade-* ... ... 134
    *credit trade*... ... 132
    *door to door sales* ... 132
    *party plan sales* ... 132
  *trade union* ... ... 024
  *transport* ... ... 134
  *water board* ... ... 134
  *wholesale trade* ... 133
Reproducer;
  design (*textile mfr.*) ... 115
  plan (*printer's*) ... ... 206
Re-roller (*wire mfr.*) ... 232
Rescue worker ... ... 039
Research worker-
  agricultural ... ... 065
  biology ... ... ... 065
  chemistry ... ... 066
  economic ... ... 011
  fire protection ... ... 090
  fuel ... ... ... 080
  medical ... ... ... 080
  mining ... ... ... 067

| | Code number |
|---|---|
| Rover; *continued* | |
| cone ... ... ... ... | 178 |
| dandy (*wool*) ... ... ... | 176 |
| Rover (*textile mfr.*) | 176 |
| Rubber- | |
| *textile finishing* ... ... | 182 |
| *vehicle mfr.* ... ... | 299 |
| Rubber and flatter (*coach building*) ... | 299 |
| Rubber and polisher (*vehicle mfr.*) ... ... ... | 299 |
| Rubber goods worker ... ... | 228 |
| Rubber worker ... ... ... | 194 |
| Rubber-down- ... ... ... | 299 |
| *footwear mfr.* ... ... | 175 |
| *jewellery, plate mfr.* ... | 244 |
| Rubberer; tyre ... ... | 194 |
| Rubberiser (*carpets*) ... ... | 199 |
| Rubber-off- | |
| *footwear mfr.* ... ... | 175 |
| *foundry* ... ... ... | 244 |
| Rucker (*blast furnace*) ... ... | L344 |
| Ruler; | |
| account book ... ... ... | 227 |
| machine (*printing*) ... ... | 227 |
| paper ... ... ... ... | 227 |
| printer's ... ... ... | 227 |
| Ruler- | |
| *printing* ... ... ... | 227 |
| *textile printing* ... ... | 267 |
| Ruller (*mine, not coal*) ... ... | 338 |
| Rullyman ... ... ... | 326 |
| Rumbler- | |
| ceramics ... ... ... | 223 |
| metal ... ... ... ... | 243 |
| Runner; | |
| beer (*brewery*) ... ... | 287 |
| belt (*coal mine*) ... ... | 338 |
| bobbin ... ... ... ... | 338 |
| clay ... ... ... ... | 338 |
| deal (*timber merchants*) ... | 335 |
| end ... ... ... ... | 270 |
| metal (*white*) ... ... | 270 |
| mould (*ceramic mfr.*) ... | 223 |
| rope ... ... ... ... | 338 |
| wagon- ... ... ... | 338 |
| *coal mine* ... ... | 338 |
| water ... ... ... ... | 338 |
| wool ... ... ... ... | 338 |
| wort ... ... ... ... | 197 |
| Runner- | |
| *bookmaking* ... ... ... | 115 |
| *ceramic mfr.* ... ... | 338 |
| *docks* ... ... ... ... | 334 |
| *shipping* ... ... ... | 317 |
| *steelworks* ... ... ... | 331 |
| *textile mfr.* ... ... ... | 338 |
| Runner man (*steelworks*) ... | 331 |
| Runner-off (*hosiery mfr.*) ... | 181 |
| Runner-on (*hosiery mfr.*) ... | 181 |
| Rusher; chair ... ... ... | 230 |
| Rustic worker ... ... ... | 224 |

## S

| | Code number |
|---|---|
| S.E.A.N. ... ... ... ... | 043 |
| S.O. n.o.s. (*local government*) | 022 |
| S.R.N. ... ... ... | 043 |
| Sackhand (*sack mfr.*) ... ... | 226 |
| Sacristan ... ... ... | 157 |
| Saddle worker ... ... ... | 225 |
| Saddler ... ... ... ... | 225 |
| Safe man (*sugar refining*) ... | 202 |
| Safety man- | |
| *coal mine* ... ... ... | 276 |
| *steel mfr.* ... ... ... | 039 |
| Safety worker (*U.K.A.E.A.*) ... | 039 |
| Sailor- | |
| *armed forces-* | |
| *foreign and Commonwealth* | 136 |
| *U.K.* ... ... ... | 135 |

| | Code number |
|---|---|
| Sailor- *continued* | |
| *shipbuilding* ... ... ... | 276 |
| *shipping* ... ... ... | 317 |
| Sailorman ... ... ... | 276 |
| Sale worker ... ... ... | 230 |
| Sales; first ... ... ... | 125 |
| Salesman; | |
| advertising ... ... ... | 134 |
| bread- | |
| *retail trade-* ... ... | 125 |
| *delivery round* ... | 128 |
| brush ... ... ... ... | 132 |
| butcher's ... ... ... | 125 |
| car ... ... ... ... | 125 |
| cattle ... ... ... ... | 133 |
| cleaner; vacuum ... ... | 132 |
| commercial ... ... ... | 133 |
| commission ... ... ... | 133 |
| counter ... ... ... | 125 |
| credit ... ... ... ... | 132 |
| delivery ... ... ... | 133 |
| drinks; soft ... ... ... | 128 |
| export ... ... ... ... | 133 |
| fish- ... ... ... ... | 125 |
| self-employed ... ... | 187 |
| *wholesale trade* ... | 133 |
| fish and fruit ... ... | 125 |
| fish and poultry ... ... | 125 |
| fishmonger's ... ... ... | 125 |
| forecourt (*garage*) ... ... | 127 |
| ice cream ... ... ... | 128 |
| indoor ... ... ... ... | 125 |
| insurance ... ... ... | 134 |
| land (*estate agents*) ... ... | 134 |
| laundry ... ... ... | 134 |
| market- ... ... ... | 130 |
| *wholesale trade* ... | 125 |
| meat- ... ... ... ... | 125 |
| *wholesale trade* ... | 133 |
| milk- | |
| *retail trade-* ... ... | 125 |
| *delivery round* ... | 128 |
| mineral water ... ... ... | 133 |
| motor ... ... ... ... | 125 |
| oil ... ... ... ... | 128 |
| outside ... ... ... ... | 133 |
| petrol (*garage*) ... ... | 127 |
| powder (*mining*) ... ... | 333 |
| property ... ... ... | 134 |
| retail ... ... ... ... | 125 |
| shop- ... ... ... ... | 125 |
| mobile shop ... ... | 128 |
| showroom ... ... ... | 125 |
| space; advertising ... ... | 134 |
| speciality ... ... ... | 133 |
| sundries ... ... ... | 133 |
| tea ... ... ... ... | 133 |
| technical ... ... ... | 133 |
| telephone ... ... ... | 115 |
| travelling- ... ... ... | 133 |
| *retail trade* ... ... | 132 |
| tyre ... ... ... ... | 133 |
| van ... ... ... ... | 128 |
| warehouse ... ... ... | 125 |
| wool (*scrap merchant*) ... | 133 |
| yeast ... ... ... ... | 133 |
| Salesman- | |
| hawking ... ... ... | 130 |
| ice cream ... ... ... | 128 |
| self-employed ... ... | 133 |
| services ... ... ... | 134 |
| *building and contracting* | 125 |
| *mail order house* ... | 132 |
| *manufacturers' agents* ... | 133 |
| *manufacturing* ... ... | 133 |
| *retail trade-* ... ... | 125 |
| *credit trade* ... ... | 132 |
| *door to door sales* ... | 132 |
| *mobile shop* ... ... | 128 |
| *party plan sales* ... | 132 |
| *wholesale trade* ... | 133 |
| Salesman-buyer ... ... | 015 |
| Salesman-collector ... ... | 132 |
| Salesman-driver ... ... | 128 |

| | Code number |
|---|---|
| Salesman-mechanic ... ... | 133 |
| Salle worker ... ... ... | 294 |
| Saloon boy ... ... ... | 144 |
| Salt cake man ... ... ... | 184 |
| Salt man ... ... ... ... | L340 |
| Salt worker ... ... ... | 184 |
| Salter; | |
| dry ... ... ... ... | 202 |
| fish ... ... ... ... | 202 |
| Salter- | |
| *bacon, meat curing* ... | 202 |
| *tannery* ... ... ... | 173 |
| Salvage corps man ... ... | 138 |
| Salvage hand- ... ... ... | L346 |
| *coal mine* ... ... ... | 314 |
| *mooring and wreck raising* | |
| *service* ... ... ... | 317 |
| Salvage man (*coal mine*) ... | 314 |
| Salvage worker- ... ... | L346 |
| *coal mine* ... ... ... | 314 |
| Sample hand- | |
| *clothing mfr.* ... ... | 212 |
| *footwear mfr.* ... ... | 225 |
| Sample man ... ... ... | 333 |
| Sampler; | |
| grain (*grain milling*) ... | 290 |
| milk ... ... ... ... | 290 |
| tea ... ... ... ... | 290 |
| Sampler- ... ... ... | 299 |
| *food processing* ... ... | 290 |
| *sugar refining* ... ... | 290 |
| Sandman- ... ... ... | L346 |
| *abrasive paper, etc. mfr.* | 203 |
| Sander; | |
| hand (*furniture mfr.*) ... | 299 |
| wet (*motor body mfr.*) ... | 299 |
| Sander- | |
| *metal trades* ... ... | 244 |
| *wood products mfr.* ... | 218 |
| Sandwichman ... ... ... | 165 |
| Sand worker (*quarry*) ... ... | 315 |
| Sapper- | |
| *armed forces-* | |
| *foreign and Commonwealth* | 136 |
| *U.K.* ... ... ... | 135 |
| Sanforizer ... ... ... | 182 |
| Saucier ... ... ... ... | F143 |
| Sausage room worker ... ... | 202 |
| Saw man- | |
| metal ... ... ... ... | 276 |
| stone ... ... ... ... | 301 |
| Saw worker; hot ... ... | 276 |
| Sawduster ... ... ... | 173 |
| Sawer; *see also Sawyer* | |
| leg (*bacon and meat curing*) | 186 |
| Sawyer; | |
| back- ... ... ... ... | 218 |
| metal ... ... ... | 276 |
| band- ... ... ... ... | 218 |
| metal ... ... ... | 276 |
| circular ... ... ... | 218 |
| cross cut ... ... ... | 218 |
| diamond ... ... ... | 266 |
| hot ... ... ... ... | 276 |
| ivory ... ... ... ... | 230 |
| mill ... ... ... ... | 218 |
| rack ... ... ... ... | 218 |
| rail ... ... ... ... | 276 |
| roller ... ... ... ... | 276 |
| slate ... ... ... ... | 301 |
| whip ... ... ... ... | 218 |
| wood pulp ... ... ... | 218 |
| Sawyer- | |
| bone, ivory, etc. ... ... | 230 |
| meat ... ... ... ... | 186 |
| metal ... ... ... ... | 276 |
| plastics ... ... ... | 229 |
| stone ... ... ... ... | 301 |
| wood ... ... ... ... | 218 |
| *asbestos-cement goods mfr.* | 230 |
| *coal mine* ... ... ... | 218 |
| *converting mill* ... ... | 218 |
| *steel tube mfr.* ... ... | 276 |
| Scabbler (*stone*) ... ... ... | 301 |

| | Code number |
|---|---|
| **Setter;** *continued* | |
| pin ... ... ... ... | 276 |
| pipe ... ... ... ... | 191 |
| press; power ... ... | 238 |
| press- | |
|    *metal trades* ... | 238 |
|    *textile finishing* ... | 182 |
| prop (*coal mine*) ... | 314 |
| rate ... ... ... ... | 010 |
| reed ... ... ... ... | 230 |
| retort ... ... ... ... | 300 |
| road ... ... ... ... | 306 |
| roll (*steelworks*) ... | 248 |
| saw ... ... ... ... | 276 |
| spindle ... ... ... | 248 |
| spool ... ... ... ... | 179 |
| spring ... ... ... | 237 |
| steel (*corset mfr.*) ... | 299 |
| stone (*jewellery*) ... | 266 |
| teasel ... ... ... | 182 |
| teazle ... ... ... | 182 |
| thermostat ... ... | 283 |
| tile- ... ... ... | 191 |
|    *building and contracting* ... | 300 |
| timber ... ... ... | 315 |
| tool; ... ... ... | 238 |
|    edge ... ... | 276 |
|    machine ... ... | 238 |
| tube (*textile mfr.*) ... | 199 |
| type ... ... ... | 205 |
| van (*railways*) ... | 326 |
| yarn ... ... ... | 182 |
| **Setter-** | |
| *arc welding electrode mfr.* ... | 230 |
| *brush, broom mfr.* ... | 230 |
| *carpet mfr.* ... ... | 179 |
| *ceramic mfr.* ... ... | 191 |
| *glass mfr.* ... ... | 192 |
| *metal trades-* ... ... | 238 |
|    *cutlery mfr.* ... | 233 |
|    *jewellery mfr.* ... | 266 |
|    *typefounding* ... | 270 |
|    *watch, clock mfr.* ... | 247 |
| *sugar confectionery mfr.* ... | 202 |
| *tannery* ... ... | 173 |
| *textile mfr.* ... ... | 182 |
| **Setter and drawer** (*ceramic mfr.*) | 191 |
| **Setter and turner; lathe** ... | 239 |
| **Setter-in** (*ceramic mfr.*) ... | 191 |
| **Setter-operator;** | |
| capstan ... ... | 240 |
| engraving; pantograph ... | 276 |
| lathe; ... ... ... | 239 |
|    capstan ... ... | 240 |
|    centre ... ... | 239 |
|    turret ... ... | 240 |
| machine; paper ... | 227 |
| tool ... ... ... | 240 |
| turret ... ... ... | 240 |
| **Setter-operator** (*metal trades*) | 240 |
| **Setter-out;** | |
| lead light ... ... | 303 |
| mill (*sawmilling*) ... | 276 |
| **Setter-out-** | |
| technical drawings ... | 079 |
| *metal trades* ... ... | 245 |
| *wood products mfr.* ... | F218 |
| **Setter-up-** | |
| *metal trades-* ... ... | 238 |
|    *diamond polishing* | 266 |
|    *typefounding* | 276 |
| *spectacle mfr.* ... | 229 |
| **Settlement worker** ... | 039 |
| **Settler; claims; insurance** ... | 005 |
| **Settler-** | |
| *betting* ... ... | 115 |
| *fish hook mfr.* ... | 242 |
| *hat mfr.* ... ... | 199 |
| **Sewage worker** ... ... | 310 |
| **Sewer;** | |
| bag ... ... ... | 212 |
| ball; tennis ... ... | 212 |
| belting ... ... ... | 175 |
| button ... ... ... | 212 |
| **Sewer;** *continued* | |
| carpet ... ... ... | 212 |
| cloth ... ... ... | 212 |
| felt ... ... ... | 212 |
| fine (*rubber shoe mfr.*) ... | 175 |
| fur ... ... ... | 212 |
| glove ... ... ... | 212 |
| hand ... ... ... | 212 |
| harness (*wool weaving*) ... | 199 |
| hat ... ... ... | 212 |
| mantle; gas ... ... | 212 |
| piece ... ... ... | 212 |
| seam ... ... ... | 212 |
| skin rug ... ... | 175 |
| sole ... ... ... | 175 |
| spangle ... ... ... | 212 |
| tape (*textile spinning*) ... | 271 |
| tent ... ... ... | 212 |
| top ... ... ... | 212 |
| vellum ... ... ... | 189 |
| welt ... ... ... | 175 |
| wire ... ... ... | 175 |
| **Sewer-** | |
| *bookbinding* ... ... | 189 |
| *canvas goods mfr.* ... | 212 |
| *carpet, rug mfr.* ... | 212 |
| *cloth mending* ... | 183 |
| *clothing mfr.* ... | 212 |
| *footwear mfr.-* ... | 175 |
|    *rubber footwear mfr.* ... | 175 |
| *glove mfr.* ... | 212 |
| *hat mfr.* ... ... | 212 |
| *leather goods mfr.* ... | 175 |
| *powder puff mfr.* ... | 226 |
| *textile goods mfr.* ... | 212 |
| **Sewerage man** (*local government*) ... | 310 |
| **Sewerman** ... ... | 310 |
| **Sewer-round** ... ... | 212 |
| **Sewing hand** ... ... | 212 |
| **Sew-round man** ... ... | 175 |
| **Sexer; chick** ... ... | 172 |
| **Sexton** ... ... ... | 157 |
| **Shackler** ... ... ... | 338 |
| **Shader-** | |
| *artificial flower mfr.* ... ... | 299 |
| *ceramic mfr.* ... ... | 204 |
| *textile mfr.* ... ... | 199 |
| **Shaft boy** (*coal mine*) ... | 338 |
| **Shaft lad** (*coal mine*) ... | 338 |
| **Shaftman** (*coal mine*) ... | 276 |
| **Shaftsman** (*coal mine*) ... | 276 |
| **Shaker;** | |
| bag ... ... ... | L346 |
| rag ... ... ... | 176 |
| waste ... ... ... | 176 |
| **Shaker** (*textile mfr.*) ... | 176 |
| **Shaker-out** (*laundry*) ... | 162 |
| **Shampooer** ... ... | 165 |
| **Shanker** (*footwear mfr.*) ... | 299 |
| **Shaper;** | |
| blades; airscrew- | |
|    metal ... ... | 241 |
|    wood ... ... | 218 |
| brim ... ... ... | 226 |
| chair ... ... ... | 224 |
| collar ... ... ... | 211 |
| die ... ... ... | 241 |
| filament ... ... | 276 |
| glass ... ... ... | 192 |
| tool; machine ... | 240 |
| tool room ... ... | 240 |
| **Shaper-** | |
| *clothing mfr.* ... ... | 211 |
| *glass mfr.* ... ... | 192 |
| *hosiery mfr.* ... ... | 182 |
| *incandescent mantle mfr.* ... | 230 |
| *metal trades-* ... ... | 241 |
|    *clog iron mfr.* ... | 233 |
|    *steel pen mfr.* ... | 276 |
| *millinery mfr.* ... ... | 226 |
| *wood products mfr.* ... | 218 |
| **Sharpener;** | |
| gear (*mining*) ... ... | 233 |
| **Sharpener;** *continued* | |
| pick ... ... ... | 241 |
| pit prop ... ... | 218 |
| saw ... ... ... | 276 |
| tool ... ... ... | 241 |
| **Sharpener** (*edge tool mfr.*) ... | 276 |
| **Sherper** *see* **Sharpener** | |
| **Shaver;** | |
| bate ... ... ... | 173 |
| gear ... ... ... | 241 |
| hood ... ... ... | 226 |
| **Shaver-** | |
| *hat mfr.* ... ... | 226 |
| *leather dressing* ... | 173 |
| **Shearman-** | |
| *clothing mfr.* ... ... | 226 |
| *metal trades* ... ... | 276 |
| **Shearer;** | |
| billet (*rolling mill*) ... | 276 |
| bloom ... ... ... | 276 |
| cloth ... ... ... | 182 |
| coil (*metal trades*) ... | 276 |
| mat ... ... ... | 182 |
| rotary ... ... ... | 276 |
| sheep ... ... ... | 172 |
| **Shearer-** | |
| *carpet, rug mfr.* ... | 182 |
| *coal mine-* ... ... | 276 |
|    *below ground* ... | 314 |
| *glove mfr.* ... ... | 226 |
| *leather dressing* ... | 173 |
| *metal trades* ... ... | 276 |
| *textile finishing* ... | 182 |
| **Shearsman; scrap** (*metal trades*) | 276 |
| **Sheather; cable** ... ... | 270 |
| **Sheavesman** (*coal mine*) ... | 271 |
| **Shecheta** ... ... ... | 186 |
| **Shed boy** (*railways*) ... | L346 |
| **Shedman-** | |
| *docks* ... ... ... | 334 |
| *leather dressing* ... | 173 |
| *transport* ... ... | L346 |
| **Shed worker-** | |
| *railways* ... ... | L346 |
| *tannery* ... ... | 173 |
| **Sheerer** (*metal*) ... ... | 262 |
| **Sheet woman** ... ... | 226 |
| **Sheet worker** (*metal*) ... | 261 |
| **Sheeter;** | |
| asbestos- | |
|    *asbestos-cement goods mfr.* | 230 |
|    *building and contracting* | 303 |
|    *n.o.s.* ... ... | 303 |
| cement; asbestos ... | 303 |
| constructional ... | 303 |
| iron; corrugated ... | 303 |
| roof ... ... ... | 303 |
| wagon ... ... ... | 160 |
| **Sheeter-** | |
| *building and contracting* ... | 303 |
| *chemical mfr.* ... ... | 303 |
| *docks* ... ... ... | 334 |
| *paper mfr.* ... ... | 203 |
| *plastics goods mfr.* ... | 195 |
| *railways* ... ... | 160 |
| *rubber goods mfr.* ... | 194 |
| *steel mfr.* ... ... | 262 |
| **Shellerman** ... ... | 202 |
| **Shepherd** ... ... | 166 |
| **Shepherd's boy** ... ... | 166 |
| **Sherardizer** ... ... | 231 |
| **Sheriff** (*Scottish Courts*) ... | 001 |
| **Sheriff-substitute** (*Scottish Courts*) ... ... | 001 |
| **Shifthand** (*coal mine*) ... | 345 |
| **Shiftman** (*mine, not coal*) ... | 315 |
| **Shift worker** (*coal mine*) ... | 345 |
| **Shifter;** | |
| coal ... ... ... | 314 |
| conveyor (*coal mine*) ... | 276 |
| iron ... ... ... | 338 |
| scene ... ... ... | 348 |
| **Shifter-** | |
| *coal mine* ... ... | 314 |

| | Code number |
|---|---|
| **Shifter-** *continued* | |
| *jute spinning* ... ... ... | 177 |
| *rolling mill* ... ... ... | 338 |
| Shingler (*iron works*) ... ... | 270 |
| Ship worker ... ... ... | 334 |
| **Shipper-** | |
| *docks* ... ... ... ... | 334 |
| *patent fuel mfr.* ... ... | 338 |
| *tinplate mfr.* ... ... | 338 |
| *wholesale trade* ... ... | 129 |
| Ship's boy ... ... ... | 317 |
| Shipsmith ... ... ... | 233 |
| Shipwright ... ... ... | 262 |
| Shipwright-liner ... ... | 262 |
| Shiver ... ... ... ... | 230 |
| Shocket ... ... ... ... | 186 |
| Shoddy man ... ... ... | 176 |
| Shoe hand ... ... ... | 225 |
| Shoe operative ... ... ... | 175 |
| Shoeblack ... ... ... | 165 |
| Shoer; horse ... ... ... | 233 |
| Shoeroom worker ... ... | 175 |
| Shoot lad (*food, starch mfr.*) ... | L346 |
| Shooter; trouble ... ... | 081 |
| Shooter (*gun mfr.*) ... ... | 286 |
| Shop boy (*printing*) ... ... | L346 |
| Shop girl; tailor's ... ... | 124 |
| **Shop worker;** | |
| *core (metal trades)* ... ... | 235 |
| *paint-* ... ... ... | L346 |
| *vehicle mfr.* ... ... | 281 |
| **Shop worker-** | |
| *fried fish* ... ... ... | 125 |
| *retail trade* ... ... | 125 |
| *take-away food shop* ... | 125 |
| **Shopkeeper;** | |
| *chip potato* ... ... ... | 104 |
| *cook* ... ... ... ... | 104 |
| *cooked meat* ... ... ... | 101 |
| *eel* ... ... ... ... | 104 |
| *fish* ... ... ... ... | 187 |
| *fish and chip* ... ... | 104 |
| *fried fish* ... ... ... | 104 |
| *ham and beef* ... ... | 101 |
| *ice cream* ... ... ... | 101 |
| *receiving (laundry, etc.)* ... | 110 |
| *sweet* ... ... ... ... | 101 |
| *tripe* ... ... ... ... | 101 |
| **Shopkeeper-** | |
| *butchers* ... ... ... | 186 |
| *fishmongers* ... ... | 187 |
| *mobile shop* ... ... | 128 |
| **Shopman;** | |
| *bottle (iron, steel tube mfr.)* | 270 |
| *butcher's* ... ... ... | 186 |
| *meat* ... ... ... ... | 186 |
| Shopman (*railway workshops*) | L344 |
| Shopman-cutter (butcher's) ... | 186 |
| Shotman (*mine, not coal*) ... | 315 |
| Shotsman (*coal mine*) ... | 314 |
| Show girl ... ... ... | 059 |
| Showman ... ... ... | 106 |
| **Shredder-** | |
| *chemical mfr.* ... ... | 184 |
| *food products mfr.* ... | 202 |
| Shreinerer ... ... ... | 182 |
| Shrimper ... ... ... | 171 |
| Shrinker; London ... ... | 182 |
| **Shrinker-** | |
| *rubber goods mfr.* ... | 228 |
| *textile mfr.* ... ... | 182 |
| Shuntman (*mine, not coal*) ... | 338 |
| Shunter- ... ... ... | 322 |
| *road transport* ... ... | 325 |
| Shutter; door (*coke ovens*) ... | L341 |
| Shutterer (*building and contracting*) ... ... ... | 214 |
| Shuttler ... ... ... | 226 |
| Side man (*brewery*) ... ... | 197 |
| Sider; glass ... ... ... | 192 |
| Sider (*glass mfr.*) ... ... | 192 |
| Sidesman; copper (*brewery*) ... | 197 |
| **Siever-** | |
| *abrasive paper, etc. mfr.* ... | 203 |

| | Code number |
|---|---|
| **Siever-** *continued* | |
| *chemical mfr.* ... ... | 184 |
| *food products mfr.* ... | 202 |
| **Sifter;** | |
| *dust (ceramic mfr.)* ... | 204 |
| *flour* ... ... ... | 202 |
| **Sifter-** | |
| *ceramic mfr.* ... ... | 204 |
| *chemical mfr.* ... ... | 184 |
| *food products mfr.* ... | 202 |
| Sighter; bottle (*brewery*) ... | 287 |
| Signal box lad ... ... | 321 |
| Signal lad (*railways*) ... | 321 |
| **Signalman;** | |
| *civilian (Min. of Defence)* ... | 122 |
| *diver's* ... ... ... | 316 |
| *Lloyd's* ... ... ... | 338 |
| *marine* ... ... ... | 122 |
| *port* ... ... ... | 122 |
| *relief* ... ... ... | 321 |
| **Signalman-** | |
| *mining* ... ... ... | 331 |
| *railways* ... ... ... | 321 |
| *steelworks* ... ... | 337 |
| *yacht club* ... ... | 063 |
| Signaller (*mine, not coal*) ... | 331 |
| **Silk worker-** ... ... | L339 |
| *greeting card mfr.* ... | 212 |
| Silker (*textile mfr.*) ... | 212 |
| Silksman ... ... ... | 202 |
| Siloman (*seed crushing*) ... | 202 |
| Silo worker ... ... ... | 333 |
| Silverman ... ... ... | 147 |
| Silver worker ... ... ... | 266 |
| **Silverer-** | |
| *electroplating* ... ... | 236 |
| *glass mfr.* ... ... | 269 |
| **Silviculturist-** ... ... | 170 |
| *professionally qualified* ... | 065 |
| **Singer-** | |
| *entertainment* ... ... | 059 |
| *textile mfr.* ... ... | 182 |
| **Sinker;** | |
| *counter* ... ... ... | 241 |
| *die-* | |
| *metal trades* ... ... | 245 |
| *printing* ... ... | 267 |
| *pit* ... ... ... | 304 |
| *seat* ... ... ... | 175 |
| *shaft* ... ... ... | 304 |
| *well* ... ... ... | 304 |
| Sinker (*mine sinking*) ... | 304 |
| **Sinterer-** | |
| *metal mfr.* ... ... | 270 |
| *mine, not coal* ... ... | 270 |
| **Sister-** ... ... ... | F043 |
| *religion* ... ... ... | 040 |
| Sister-tutor ... ... ... | F043 |
| Sitter; baby ... ... ... | 151 |
| **Sizeman-** ... ... ... | 173 |
| *paper mill* ... ... | 203 |
| **Sizer;** | |
| *bobbin* ... ... ... | 218 |
| *engine (paper mfr.)* ... | 203 |
| *hank* ... ... ... | 179 |
| *slasher* ... ... ... | 179 |
| *tape* ... ... ... | 179 |
| *warp* ... ... ... | 179 |
| *yarn* ... ... ... | 179 |
| **Sizer-** | |
| *paper mfr.* ... ... | 203 |
| *textile mfr.-* ... ... | 179 |
| *rope, twine mfr.* ... | 182 |
| Sizer and dryer; back ... | 182 |
| Skater; ice ... ... ... | 059 |
| Skeiner (*textile mfr.*) ... | 178 |
| Sketcher; design ... ... | 115 |
| Skewerer (*textile dyeing*) ... | 199 |
| Skid boy (*rolling mill*) ... | 270 |
| Skilled workman (*P.O.*) ... | 256 |
| **Skimmer-** | |
| *glass mfr.* ... ... | 204 |
| *metal mfr.* ... ... | 231 |

| | Code number |
|---|---|
| **Skinner-** | |
| *food products mfr.* ... | 186 |
| *slaughterhouse* ... ... | 186 |
| *tannery* ... ... ... | 173 |
| Skipman ... ... ... | 297 |
| Skipper; yacht ... ... | 087 |
| **Skipper-** | |
| *barge, boat* ... ... | 087 |
| *building and contracting* ... | F316 |
| *fishing* ... ... ... | 111 |
| *shipping* ... ... ... | 087 |
| Skirt hand ... ... ... | 210 |
| Skiver; belt (*abrasive paper, etc. mfr.*) ... ... ... | 230 |
| **Skiver-** | |
| *footwear mfr.* ... ... | 175 |
| *leather dressing* ... | 173 |
| Slab hand ... ... ... | 202 |
| Slab man ... ... ... | 301 |
| **Slabber;** | |
| *tile* ... ... ... | 300 |
| *toffee* ... ... ... | 202 |
| **Slabber-** | |
| *builder's merchant* ... | 300 |
| *fireplace mfr.* ... ... | 300 |
| *textile mfr.* ... ... | 199 |
| Slagman (*blast furnace*) ... | 231 |
| **Slagger-** | |
| *blast furnace* ... ... | 231 |
| *steel casting* ... ... | 270 |
| Slaker (*ceramic mfr.*) ... | 204 |
| Slaker man ... ... ... | 204 |
| Slasher (*textile mfr.*) ... | 179 |
| Slate worker; enamelled ... | 301 |
| Slater ... ... ... ... | 303 |
| Slater and tiler ... ... | 303 |
| Slaughterman ... ... ... | 186 |
| Slaughterer ... ... ... | 186 |
| **Sleever-** | |
| *cable mfr.* ... ... | 230 |
| *clothing mfr.* ... ... | 212 |
| *electrical goods mfr.* ... | 242 |
| *radio valve mfr.* ... | 283 |
| Slicer; veneer ... ... | 218 |
| **Slicer-** | |
| *bakery* ... ... ... | 200 |
| *celluloid sheet mfr.* ... | 229 |
| Slicker (*leather dressing*) ... | 173 |
| Slider (*metal trades*) ... | 239 |
| Slimer (*gut cleaning*) ... | 204 |
| Slingman ... ... ... | 192 |
| Slinger- ... ... ... | 337 |
| *textile mfr.* ... ... | 199 |
| Sliphouse hand ... ... | 204 |
| **Slipper;** | |
| *cushion* ... ... ... | 212 |
| *last* ... ... ... | 225 |
| *shoe* ... ... ... | 225 |
| *tie* ... ... ... | 212 |
| **Slipper-** | |
| *asbestos-cement mfr.* ... | 204 |
| *furniture mfr.* ... ... | 212 |
| Slipper operative ... ... | 175 |
| Slipper worker ... ... | 175 |
| **Slitter;** | |
| *fabrics* ... ... ... | 226 |
| *foil; tin* ... ... ... | 276 |
| *metal* ... ... ... | 276 |
| *optical glass* ... ... | 192 |
| *paper* ... ... ... | 190 |
| *steel* ... ... ... | 276 |
| **Slitter-** | |
| *abrasive paper mfr.* ... | 190 |
| *paper and printing* ... | 190 |
| *pen nib mfr.* ... ... | 276 |
| *plastics goods mfr.* ... | 229 |
| *steelworks* ... ... | 276 |
| *tobacco mfr.* ... ... | 201 |
| *transparent cellulose wrapping mfr.* ... ... ... | 190 |
| Slitterman (*paper mfr.*) ... | 190 |
| Sliverer ... ... ... | 176 |
| Slotter; frame ... ... | 241 |

| | Code number |
|---|---|
| Storeman; | 333 |
| chief | F333 |
| head | F333 |
| Storeman-clerk | 333 |
| Storeman-driver | 333 |
| Storewoman; superintendent (*P.O.*) | F333 |
| Storehouse boy | 335 |
| Storehouseman | 333 |
| Storer | 333 |
| Storeroom man | 333 |
| Storesman | 333 |
| Stove hand *see Stover-* | |
| Stoveman *see Stover-* | |
| Stover; seasoning | 204 |
| Stover- | 204 |
| *bacon, ham curing* | 202 |
| *blast furnace* | 231 |
| *food products mfr.* | 202 |
| *hat mfr.* | 182 |
| *iron foundry* | 270 |
| *leather dressing* | 173 |
| *starch mfr.* | 202 |
| *textile mfr.* | 182 |
| *tobacco mfr.* | 201 |
| Stower; | |
| cake | 338 |
| cement | 338 |
| coal | 338 |
| power | 314 |
| ship | 334 |
| Stower- | |
| *coal mine* | 314 |
| *grain milling* | 338 |
| *railways* | 160 |
| Straightener; | |
| axle | 233 |
| bar | 270 |
| barrel | 276 |
| carriage (*textile machinery mfr.*) | 248 |
| comb | 276 |
| drill | 270 |
| hard (*needle mfr.*) | 276 |
| iron | 270 |
| plate; | 270 |
| iron | 276 |
| saw | 276 |
| prop (*coal mine*) | 276 |
| rail | 270 |
| rod mills | 270 |
| roller | 270 |
| section | 270 |
| shaft; crank | 270 |
| steel- | 270 |
| *coal mine* | 276 |
| tube | 270 |
| wire | 276 |
| yarn | 289 |
| at machine | 270 |
| Straightener- | |
| *coal mine* | 276 |
| *metal mfr.* | 270 |
| *needle mfr.* | 276 |
| *sheet metal working* | 261 |
| *textile mfr.-* | 289 |
| *flax mfr.* | 176 |
| *hosiery mfr.* | 182 |
| *textile machinery mfr.* | 248 |
| *vehicle mfr.* | 261 |
| *wire mfr.* | 276 |
| Strainer; toggle | 173 |
| Strainer- | |
| *chemical mfr.* | 184 |
| *paint, etc. mfr.* | 204 |
| *tannery* | 173 |
| *textile printing* | 204 |
| Strainerman (*paper mfr.*) | 203 |
| Strander; wire | 276 |
| Strander- | |
| *cable mfr.* | 276 |
| *rope mfr.* | 199 |
| *wire rope mfr.* | 276 |
| Strap man | 225 |

| | Code number |
|---|---|
| Strapper- | |
| *corset mfr.* | 212 |
| *textile mfr.* | 338 |
| Stratigrapher | 067 |
| Straw worker (*hat mfr.*) | 226 |
| Stressman | 079 |
| Stretcher; | |
| clip (*textile mfr.*) | 182 |
| dry (*textile mfr.*) | 182 |
| tube | 270 |
| yarn | 182 |
| Stretcher- | |
| *metal mfr.* | 270 |
| *tannery* | 173 |
| *textile mfr.* | 182 |
| Stretcher hand (*aluminium mfr.*) | 270 |
| Striker; | |
| anvil | 270 |
| catch (*coal mine*) | 338 |
| chain | 270 |
| colour | 204 |
| forge | 270 |
| forger's | 270 |
| iron | 270 |
| smith's | 270 |
| wheel | 270 |
| Striker- | |
| *metal trades* | 270 |
| *railways* | 270 |
| Striker-out | 173 |
| Stringer; | |
| bag; paper | 299 |
| bead and bugle | 299 |
| pearl | 299 |
| racquet | 230 |
| Stringer- | |
| *footwear mfr.* | 175 |
| *piano mfr.* | 222 |
| *plastics goods mfr.* | 229 |
| *printing* | 295 |
| *sports goods mfr.* | 230 |
| Strip worker; copper | 270 |
| Striper (*fur dressing*) | 173 |
| Stripper; | |
| biscuit | 200 |
| bobbin | 199 |
| boiler; locomotive | 248 |
| brake | 248 |
| cable | 299 |
| car | 249 |
| card | 276 |
| cardboard | 227 |
| carriage and wagon | 248 |
| carton | 227 |
| cloth | 176 |
| cop | 199 |
| dog | 172 |
| engine | 248 |
| file | 276 |
| film | 227 |
| frame | L340 |
| gold | 270 |
| gut | 186 |
| ingot | 270 |
| leaf | 201 |
| leather lace | 175 |
| liquorice | 202 |
| locomotive | 248 |
| motor | 249 |
| paint; vehicle (*vehicle mfr.*) | 299 |
| paper | 227 |
| pirn | 199 |
| polish | 299 |
| rag | 176 |
| rubber | 228 |
| silver | 270 |
| spring | 248 |
| tin (*biscuit mfr.*) | 200 |
| tyre | 228 |
| wool | 199 |
| yarn | 199 |
| Stripper- | |
| *candle mfr.* | L340 |
| *cast stone products mfr.* | 223 |

| | Code number |
|---|---|
| Stripper- *continued* | |
| *ceramic mfr.* | L342 |
| *coal mine* | 314 |
| *metal trades-* | 244 |
| *electroplating* | 269 |
| *gold refining* | 231 |
| *wire drawing* | 234 |
| *mine, not coal* | 315 |
| *paper products mfr.* | 227 |
| *process engraving* | 206 |
| *railway workshop* | 248 |
| *textile mfr.* | 199 |
| *tobacco mfr.* | 201 |
| Stripper and buncher | 199 |
| Stripper and grinder | 276 |
| Stripper and setter (*soap mfr.*) | 184 |
| Stripper-assembler (*cast concrete products mfr.*) | L346 |
| Stripping hand (*hosiery mfr.*) | 226 |
| Stubber | 276 |
| Studder (*clothing mfr.*) | 299 |
| Student *see notes* p.4 | |
| Studhand | 172 |
| Stuffer; | |
| chair | 226 |
| cushion | 226 |
| soft toy | 226 |
| Stuffer- | |
| *mattress, upholstery mfr.* | 226 |
| *textile dyeing* | 297 |
| *toy mfr.* | 226 |
| Stuff worker; rough (*footwear mfr.*) | 175 |
| Stumper | 199 |
| Stunner | 186 |
| Stunt man | 059 |
| Stylist; hair | 159 |
| Stylist- | |
| *hairdressing* | 159 |
| *vehicle mfr.* | 056 |
| Sub-agent (*building and construction*) | 092 |
| Sub-contractor *see Contractor* | |
| Sub-editor | 054 |
| Sub-foreman *see Foreman-* | |
| Sub-ganger *see Ganger-* | |
| Sub-inspector- *see also Inspector-* | |
| *Min. of Defence* | M137 |
| *railway-* | F318 |
| *engineering* | 306 |
| Sub-Lieutenant- | |
| *armed forces-* | |
| *foreign and Commonwealth* | M136 |
| *U.K.* | M135 |
| Sub-officer (*fire service*) | F138 |
| Sub-postmaster- | 099 |
| self-employed | 101 |
| Sueder | 173 |
| Sugar worker | 202 |
| Sulphitation man | 202 |
| Sulphonator man | 184 |
| Sumper | 314 |
| Sundriesman | 101 |
| Superintendent; | |
| administrative (*insurance*) | F115 |
| advertisement | 014 |
| advertising | 014 |
| airport | 095 |
| ambulance room | 111 |
| assistant; | |
| overseas telegraph | 099 |
| progress | 115 |
| radio | 099 |
| assistant-*see also Superintendent-* | |
| *cemetery, crematorium* | 165 |
| *P.O.* | 099 |
| bath(s)- | 106 |
| *coal mine* | F165 |
| branch (*insurance*) | M134 |
| building | 157 |
| cargo | 097 |
| claims | M005 |
| cleansing (*local government*) | 111 |

| | Code number |
|---|---|
| **Tupper-** | |
| *building and contracting* | 313 |
| *steel mfr.* | 270 |
| Tupper at stripper and winch | 270 |
| Turf worker | 168 |
| Turn man; bye (*steelworks*) | L344 |
| Turncock | 310 |
| **Turner;** | |
| asbestos | 230 |
| axle | 239 |
| belt (*coal mine*) | 276 |
| billiard ball | 229 |
| biscuit | 200 |
| block; wood | 218 |
| bobbin- | 218 |
| metal | 239 |
| bowl (*tobacco pipe mfr.*) | 218 |
| brass | 241 |
| bush; axle | 239 |
| button | 230 |
| capstan | 241 |
| centre boss | 239 |
| collar | 226 |
| commutator | 239 |
| conveyor (*coal mine*) | 276 |
| copper band | 239 |
| core | 270 |
| cork | 230 |
| counter | 218 |
| crank | 239 |
| cutter | 239 |
| die | 239 |
| ebonite | 228 |
| engine; rose | 266 |
| engine | 266 |
| engraver's | 239 |
| frame (*shipbuilding*) | 276 |
| general | 239 |
| glove | 226 |
| graphite | 230 |
| gun | 239 |
| hand- | |
| *clothing mfr.* | 226 |
| *metal trades* | 239 |
| handle | 218 |
| heel (wood heels) | 218 |
| insulator | 193 |
| ivory | 230 |
| lathe; | |
| capstan | 241 |
| centre | 239 |
| turret | 241 |
| lathe (*metal trades*) | 239 |
| locomotive | 239 |
| loom | 239 |
| machine; pottery | 193 |
| maintenance | 239 |
| marine | 239 |
| mould; fringe | 218 |
| mould (*glass mfr.*) | 239 |
| optical | 241 |
| pan (*coal mine*) | 314 |
| patent (*clothing mfr.*) | 226 |
| pipe- | 260 |
| *tobacco pipe mfr.* | 218 |
| pirn | 218 |
| porcelain; electric | 193 |
| ring | 239 |
| rod (fishing rods) | 218 |
| roll | 241 |
| roller- | |
| metal | 241 |
| rubber | 228 |
| wood | 218 |
| *textile machinery mfr.* | 241 |
| rough | 239 |
| rubber | 228 |
| sheet- | |
| *galvanized sheet mfr.* | L344 |
| *rolling mill* | 299 |
| shell | 241 |
| shive | 218 |
| slipper | 225 |
| spiral | 218 |

| | Code number |
|---|---|
| **Turner;** *continued* | |
| spool | 218 |
| textile | 239 |
| tool | 239 |
| tube; steel | 239 |
| tyre (metal) | 239 |
| valve | 239 |
| vulcanite | 228 |
| wheel- | |
| *abrasive mfr.* | 230 |
| *ceramic mfr.* | L342 |
| *metal trades* | 239 |
| wire | 276 |
| wood | 218 |
| **Turner-** | |
| metal | 239 |
| plastics | 229 |
| rubber | 228 |
| stone | 301 |
| wood | 218 |
| asbestos-cement goods mfr. | 230 |
| brewery | 197 |
| canvas goods mfr. | 226 |
| cemented carbide goods mfr. | 230 |
| ceramic mfr. | 193 |
| clothing mfr. | 226 |
| coal mine | 239 |
| footwear mfr. | 225 |
| hosiery mfr. | 226 |
| leather dressing | 173 |
| metal trades- | 239 |
| *precious metal, plate mfr.* | 266 |
| plastics goods mfr. | 229 |
| process engraving | 206 |
| rubber goods mfr. | 228 |
| stone dressing | 301 |
| vulcanite goods mfr. | 228 |
| wood products mfr. | 218 |
| wood-wind instrument mfr. | 218 |
| Turner and fitter | 248 |
| Turner-down (*glove mfr.*) | 226 |
| Turner-engineer | 239 |
| Turner-fitter | 248 |
| Turner-in (*steel mfr.*) | 299 |
| Turner-out (*glass mfr.*) | 223 |
| Turner-over (*rolling mill*) | 299 |
| Turner-up (*rolling mill*) | 299 |
| Turnover man (*coal mine*) | 276 |
| Turnstile man | 140 |
| Turret hand | 241 |
| Tutor; private | 053 |
| Tutor- *see also notes p.4* | |
| *hospital service* | F043 |
| Twinder | 178 |
| Twiner (*textile mfr.*) | 177 |
| Twiner-joiner-minder | 177 |
| Twist hand; plain net | 180 |
| Twist hand | 180 |
| **Twister;** | |
| barley sugar | 202 |
| cap (*textile mfr.*) | 177 |
| cop | 177 |
| cotton | 177 |
| doubling | 177 |
| false | 177 |
| fancy cord | 199 |
| fly | 177 |
| gut | 204 |
| hat wire | 242 |
| machine | 199 |
| patent | 177 |
| *textile warping* | 179 |
| plain net | 177 |
| ring | 177 |
| silk | 177 |
| single | 177 |
| spinning | 177 |
| sprig | 177 |
| tube | 229 |
| twine | 199 |
| warp | 179 |
| wool | 177 |
| worsted | 177 |
| yarn | 177 |

| | Code number |
|---|---|
| **Twister-** | |
| *brush mfr.* | 230 |
| *textile mfr.-* | 177 |
| *rope, twine mfr.* | 199 |
| Twister and drawer | 179 |
| Twister-in (*textile mfr.*) | 179 |
| Twister-on (*textile mfr.*) | 179 |
| Twister-up (*textile mfr.*) | 179 |
| Tyer *see Tier* | |
| Tyer-on *see Tier-on* | |
| Tyer-up *see Tier-up* | |
| Tympanist | 060 |
| Typer (*textile mfr.*) | 227 |
| Typist; | 118 |
| copy | 118 |
| shorthand | 118 |
| superintendent | F118 |
| vari | 205 |
| Typist-clerk | 115 |
| Typographer | 205 |
| Tyreman (*railways*) | 233 |
| Tyre worker; rubber (*perambulator mfr.*) | 194 |

# U

| | Code number |
|---|---|
| Umpire (sports) | 063 |
| Uncoiler (*tinplate mfr.*) | 270 |
| Uncurler (*textile mfr.*) | 182 |
| Underbuyer (*retail trade*) | 015 |
| Underhand | 231 |
| Underbaster | 210 |
| Underground worker- | |
| *coal mine* | 345 |
| *mine, not coal* | 315 |
| Under-manager *see Manager-* | |
| Underpresser | 162 |
| Undersealer (vehicles) | 281 |
| Understripper | 226 |
| Understudy | 059 |
| Undertaker | 163 |
| Underwriter | 007 |
| Unhairer (*tannery*) | 173 |
| Unloader; | |
| autoclave (ceramics) | 338 |
| kiln (ceramics) | 338 |
| Unloader- | 335 |
| *docks* | 334 |
| Unloader and retort feeder; | |
| *blanching tank (fruit, vegetable preserving)* | 202 |
| Unreeler (*steel mfr.*) | 270 |
| Untwister (*hair dressing*) | 176 |
| Unwinder | 178 |
| Upholsterer | 213 |
| Up-twister | 177 |
| Urologist | 041 |
| Usher; | 165 |
| court | 165 |
| Usherette | 165 |
| Utility man- | L346 |
| *coal mine* | 345 |

# V

| | Code number |
|---|---|
| Vaccinator (poultry) | 172 |
| Valet- | 151 |
| car (*garage*) | 158 |
| Valuer | 005 |
| Valve and steam man (*coal gas, coke ovens*) | 348 |
| Valveman; hydraulic | 248 |
| Valveman- | |
| *cartridge mfr.* | 276 |
| *coal gas, coke ovens* | 348 |
| *steelworks* | 248 |
| *water works* | 310 |

| | Code number |
|---|---|
| Valver | 227 |
| Vamper | 175 |
| Van boy | 329 |
| Van lad; parcels | 329 |
| Van man | 128 |
| Varnisher; | |
| paper | 203 |
| spray | 281 |
| Varnisher- | 299 |
| *wallpaper mfr.* | 203 |
| Vat hand (*electroplating*) | 269 |
| Vatman- | |
| *brewery* | 197 |
| *paper mfr.* | 203 |
| *soft drinks mfr.* | 202 |
| *vinegar mfr.* | 197 |
| *wire mfr.* | 269 |
| Vatter (*brewery*) | 197 |
| Veiner | 230 |
| Veiner and marker (*artificial flower mfr.*) | 230 |
| Velourer | 226 |
| Vendor; | |
| horsemeat | 186 |
| ice cream | 128 |
| milk | 128 |
| news | 130 |
| newspaper | 130 |
| oil | 128 |
| pea and pie | 128 |
| pie | 128 |
| street | 130 |
| Veneer hand | 224 |
| Veneerer; | |
| tyre | 228 |
| wood | 203 |
| Venereologist | 041 |
| Ventriloquist | 059 |
| Verderer | 170 |
| Verderor | 170 |
| Verger- | 157 |
| *lace machine mfr.* | 241 |
| Verifier; | |
| card; punch | 119 |
| stock | 115 |
| Verifier (*rubber tyre mfr.*) | 291 |
| Versteller | 266 |
| Vessel man- | |
| *steelworks* | 231 |
| *textile dyeing* | 182 |
| Vest hand | 210 |
| Veterinarian | 051 |
| Vicar | 040 |
| Vicar-general | 040 |
| Vice man; | 244 |
| spring | 270 |
| Victualler; licensed- | 103 |
| off-licence | 101 |
| Viewer; | |
| ammunition | 299 |
| ball bearings | 286 |
| barrel (gun) | 286 |
| cloth | 289 |
| component (*metal trades*) | 286 |
| cycle | 286 |
| garment | 289 |
| glass | 299 |
| patrol (*metal trades*) | 286 |
| plastics | 292 |
| of bullets | 286 |
| Viewer- | |
| *cartridge mfr.* | 299 |
| *chocolate mfr.* | 290 |
| *clothing mfr.* | 289 |
| *electrical goods mfr.* | 286 |
| *film production* | 299 |
| *food products mfr.* | 290 |
| *hat mfr.* | 289 |
| *metal trades* | 286 |
| *plastics goods mfr.* | 292 |
| *rubber goods mfr.* | 291 |
| *sports goods mfr.* | 299 |
| *textile mfr.* | 289 |
| *wood products mfr.* | 293 |

| | Code number |
|---|---|
| Violinist | 060 |
| Violoncellist | 060 |
| Virologist; research | 065 |
| Viscose man (*man-made fibre mfr.*) | 196 |
| Visitor; | |
| district | 043 |
| health; | 043 |
| superintendent | F043 |
| home | 043 |
| housing | 039 |
| parish | 039 |
| school | 039 |
| sick | 043 |
| tuberculosis | 043 |
| under boarded-out order | 039 |
| Visitor (Children's Act) | 039 |
| Visualiser (*advertising*) | 055 |
| Viticulturist | 107 |
| Vitrifier (*artificial teeth mfr.*) | 191 |
| Vocalist | 059 |
| Voicer (organ) | 222 |
| Voicer and tuner (organ) | 222 |
| Volt boy | 276 |
| Vulcanizer | 204 |

# W

| | Code number |
|---|---|
| Wadder | 191 |
| Wageman (*coal mine*) | 345 |
| Wagon man | 327 |
| Wagoner- | |
| *coal mine-* | 331 |
| *above ground* | 338 |
| *farming* | 172 |
| *mine, not coal* | 327 |
| Wagoner's boy- | 329 |
| *farming* | 172 |
| Wagonwayman | 306 |
| Wagonwright | 268 |
| Waistcoat hand | 210 |
| Waiter; | |
| commis | 144 |
| head | F144 |
| service; | 199 |
| silver | 144 |
| wine | 144 |
| Waiter- | 144 |
| *stock exchange* | 124 |
| Waiter-on (*coal mine*) | 331 |
| Waitress | 144 |
| Walker; | |
| floor | F125 |
| shop | F125 |
| track (*railways*) | 306 |
| Walksman; river | 316 |
| Waller; dry | 300 |
| Waller- | 301 |
| *salt mfr.* | 184 |
| Warden; | |
| barrack | 157 |
| camp | 157 |
| castle | 157 |
| civil defence | 142 |
| club; youth | 039 |
| community centre | 039 |
| crossing (school) | 142 |
| dinner (school) | 151 |
| game | 172 |
| garage | 142 |
| range | 165 |
| resident (*L.T.E.*) | 157 |
| security | 140 |
| station | 157 |
| traffic | 141 |
| wood | F170 |
| Warden- | |
| detention centre | 108 |
| *caravan site* | 157 |
| *day nursery* | 150 |

| | Code number |
|---|---|
| Warden- *continued* | |
| *forestry* | F170 |
| *government* | 157 |
| *hostel* | 111 |
| *institution* | M037 |
| *L.T.E.* | 142 |
| *manufacturing* | 142 |
| *museum, etc.* | 142 |
| *nurse's home* | 111 |
| *old people's home* | M037 |
| *police service* | 111 |
| *school* | 142 |
| *social settlement* | 039 |
| *youth club* | 039 |
| Warder; | |
| chief | F139 |
| river | 172 |
| yeoman | 142 |
| Warder- | |
| *museum, etc.* | 142 |
| *prison service* | 139 |
| Wardrobe woman (*theatre*) | 165 |
| Ware room worker | 338 |
| Warehouse boy- | 333 |
| loading, unloading | 335 |
| Warehouse hand; lace | 338 |
| Warehouse hand- | 333 |
| loading, unloading | 335 |
| Warehouseman; | |
| biscuit (*ceramic mfr.*) | F223 |
| black | 191 |
| chief | F333 |
| glost (*ceramic mfr.*) | F223 |
| italian | 101 |
| stuff | 101 |
| Warehouseman- | 333 |
| loading, unloading | 335 |
| Warehouseman-clerk | 333 |
| Warehouseman-packer | 333 |
| Warehouse worker- | 333 |
| loading, unloading | 335 |
| Warehouser- | 333 |
| loading, unloading | 335 |
| Warmer; rivet | 276 |
| Warp hand | 181 |
| Warper | 179 |
| Warrener | 172 |
| Washman (*laundry*) | 162 |
| Washer; | |
| back (*textile mfr.*) | 199 |
| barrel | 348 |
| basket (*docks*) | L346 |
| benzol | 184 |
| blanket (*blanket mfr.*) | 199 |
| board | L342 |
| body (*hat mfr.*) | 199 |
| boiler | 276 |
| bone ash | 204 |
| bottle | 348 |
| box | 348 |
| brush | 199 |
| bulb (*lamp mfr.*) | 348 |
| cab | 158 |
| cake (*man-made fibre mfr.*) | 204 |
| car | 158 |
| carriage | 348 |
| cask | 348 |
| churn | 348 |
| cloth (*textile mfr.*) | 199 |
| coal (*coal mine*) | 198 |
| coke | 204 |
| cullet | 298 |
| dish (*hotels, catering, etc.*) | 147 |
| drum | 348 |
| feather | 199 |
| felt | 199 |
| fruit | 202 |
| glass- | L342 |
| *hotels, catering, etc.* | 147 |
| grit | 198 |
| hair; horse | 199 |
| hand (*coal mine*) | 198 |
| jar | 348 |
| keg | 348 |

# X

# Y

| | Code number | | | Code number | | | Code number |
|---|---|---|---|---|---|---|---|
| Yard man; | | Yardage hand ... ... ... 227 | | Youth-in-training- | | |
|   hotel ... ... ... ... L346 | | Yardsman- | | |   *P.O.*- ... ... ... ... 256 |
|   metal (*steelworks*) ... ... L344 | |   *blast furnace* ... ... ... 322 | |   motor transport ... ... 249 |
| Yard man- ... ... ... L346 | |   *dairy* ... ... ... ... L346 | |   *factories department* ... 253 |
|   *coal mine* ... ... ... 297 | |   *farming* ... ... ... 166 | | |
|   *farming* ... ... ... 166 | | Yarn man ... ... ... 199 | | **Z** |
|   *livery stable* ... ... ... 172 | | Yeast man ... ... ... 202 | | |
|   *vulcanised fibre board mfr.* ... 338 | | Yeast worker ... ... 197 | | Zinc worker ... ... ... 261 |
| Yard worker; ... ... ... L346 | | Yeoman ... ... ... 107 | | Zoologist ... ... ... 065 |
|   lime ... ... ... ... 173 | | Yoker (*shirt mfr.*) ... ... 212 | | |
|   tan ... ... ... ... 173 | | Youth worker ... ... ... 039 | | |

# Appendix F

## List of Conventional Codings

| Occupation | Code number | Occupation | Code number | Occupation | Code number |
|---|---|---|---|---|---|
| Agent | 101 | Furnace operator | 231 | Police constable | 137 |
| Assembler | 299 | Furrier | 101 | Policeman | 137 |
| Bailiff | 142 | Ganger | F316 | Police sergeant | F137 |
| Baker | 185 | Gas maker | 184 | Polisher | 243 |
| Banker | 006 | Gilder | 227 | Potman | 165 |
| Barman | 145 | Glass worker | 223 | Potter | 193 |
| Bleacher | 182 | Glove machinist | 212 | Power presser | 242 |
| Bookmaker | 164 | Grinder | 241 | Press operator | 242 |
| Buffer | 243 | Guillotine operator (female) | 190 | Press setter | 238 |
| Builder | 305 | Guillotine operator (male) | 276 | Press worker (female) | 162 |
| Cable maker | 230 | Hand press operator | 242 | Presser | 242 |
| Cap maker | 211 | Hatter | 101 | Process worker | 184 |
| Capstan lathe operator | 241 | Hewer | 314 | Representative | 133 |
| Carter | 338 | Houseman | 151 | Roadman | 308 |
| Caster | 270 | House worker | 151 | Roofer | 303 |
| Cellarman | 197 | Housekeeper | 149 | Salesman | 125 |
| Chain maker | 276 | Iron worker | L344 | Sawyer | 218 |
| Collector | 115 | Ironer | 162 | Seedsman | 101 |
| Collier | 314 | Jeweller | 101 | Sewing machinist | 212 |
| Commission agent | 164 | Jointer | 257 | Shearer | 276 |
| Concrete worker | 230 | Lathe operator | 241 | Shipper | 129 |
| Constable | 137 | Leather worker | 225 | Shop manager | 101 |
| Contractor | 316 | Lecturer | 033 | Signalman | 321 |
| Core maker | 235 | Lithographer | 207 | Smelter | 231 |
| Dairy hand | 202 | Machine setter | 238 | Spinner | 177 |
| Dairyman | 202 | Machinist (female) | 212 | Steward | 152 |
| Dairy worker | 202 | Machinist (male) | 241 | Stockman | 166 |
| Dealer | 131 | Matron | M043 | Tile worker | 223 |
| Designer | 056 | Merchant | 101 | Timberman | 316 |
| Driller | 241 | Milkman | 128 | Tin plater | 269 |
| Drilling machinist | 241 | Miller | 241 | Tool maker | 245 |
| Driver | 326 | Milling machinist | 241 | Tracer | 114 |
| Drop stamper | 242 | Miner | 345 | Tractor driver | 169 |
| Dyer | 182 | Model maker | 214 | Tube drawer | 234 |
| Engraver | 267 | Moulder | 235 | Tube maker | 270 |
| Fettler | 244 | Paper worker | 188 | Turner | 239 |
| Finisher | 212 | Pattern maker | 217 | Waiter | 144 |
| Fireman | 138 | Pickler | 270 | Waterman | 317 |
| Fish worker | 187 | Plant operator | 184 | Wirer | 273 |
| Furnaceman | 231 | Plater | 262 | Writer | 054 |

# Appendix G

## Relationship between the 1980 operational codes used in the alphabetical index and the 1980 occupation groups

| Operational Code | Employment status relationship to 1980 occupation groups | | | |
|---|---|---|---|---|
| | Self-employed | Managers | Foremen | Apprentices, etc. Employees n.e.c. |
| 001 | 001.0 | — | — | 001.0 |
| 002 | 002.1 | — | — | 002.1 |
| 003 | 002.2 | — | — | 002.2 |
| 004 | 002.3 | 002.3 | — | 002.3 |
| 005 | 002.4 | 002.4 | — | 002.4 |
| 006 | — | 002.5 | — | — |
| 007 | 002.6 | 002.6 | — | — |
| 008 | 002.7 | 002.7 | — | — |
| 009 | 003.1 | 003.1 | — | — |
| 010 | 003.2 | 003.2 | — | 003.2 |
| 011 | 004.1 | — | — | 004.1 |
| 012 | 004.2 | 004.2 | — | 004.2 |
| 013 | 005.1 | 005.1 | — | — |
| 014 | 005.2 | 005.2 | — | — |
| 015 | — | 005.3 | — | — |
| 016 | — | 005.4 | — | — |
| 017 | — | — | — | 006.1 |
| 018 | — | — | — | 006.2 |
| 019 | — | — | — | 006.3 |
| 020 | — | 007.1 | — | — |
| 021 | — | 007.2 | — | — |
| 022 | — | 008.0 | — | — |
| 023 | 009.1 | 009.1 | — | — |
| 024 | — | 009.2 | — | 009.2 |
| 025 | 009.3 | 009.3 | — | — |
| 026 | — | 009.4 | — | 009.4 |
| 027 | 009.5 | 009.5 | — | 009.5 |
| 028 | 009.6 | — | — | 009.6 |
| 029 | — | — | — | 009.7 |
| 030 | 009.8 | 009.8 | — | 009.8 |
| 031 | — | — | — | 010.1 |
| 032 | 010.2 | 010.2 | — | 010.2 |
| 033 | 011.0 | 011.0 | — | 011.0 |
| 034 | 012.1 | 012.1 | — | 012.1 |
| 035 | — | — | — | 012.2 |
| 036 | 012.3 | — | — | 012.3 |
| 037 | 013.1 | 013.1 | — | 013.1 |
| 038 | 013.2 | — | — | 013.2 |
| 039 | — | 013.3 | — | 013.3 |
| 040 | 014.0 | — | — | 014.0 |
| 041 | 015.1 | — | — | 015.1 |
| 042 | 015.2 | — | — | 015.2 |
| 043 | 016.0 | 016.0 | 016.0 | 016.0 |
| 044 | 017.1 | — | — | 017.1 |
| 045 | 017.2 | 017.2 | 017.2 | 017.2 |
| 046 | 017.3 | — | — | 017.3 |
| 047 | 017.4 | 017.4 | 017.4 | 017.4 |
| 048 | 017.5 | 017.5 | — | 017.5 |
| 049 | 017.6 | 017.6 | 017.6 | 017.6 |
| 050 | 018.1 | 018.1 | 018.1 | 018.1 |
| 051 | 018.2 | — | — | 018.2 |
| 052 | 018.3 | 018.3 | — | 018.3 |
| 053 | 018.4 | 018.4 | — | 018.4 |
| 054 | 019.0 | 019.0 | — | 019.0 |
| 055 | 020.1 | 020.1 | 020.1 | 020.1 |
| 056 | 020.2 | 020.2 | — | 020.2 |
| 057 | 020.3 | 020.3 | — | 020.3 |
| 058 | 020.4 | 020.4 | — | 020.4 |
| 059 | 021.1 | 021.1 | — | 021.1 |
| 060 | 021.2 | 021.2 | — | 021.2 |
| 061 | 022.1 | 022.1 | 022.1 | 022.1 |
| 062 | 022.2 | 022.2 | 022.2 | 022.2 |
| 063 | 023.1 | 023.1 | — | 023.1 |
| 064 | 023.2 | 023.2 | — | 023.2 |
| 065 | 024.1 | — | — | 024.1 |
| 066 | 024.2 | — | — | 024.2 |
| 067 | 024.3 | — | — | 024.3 |
| 068 | 025.0 | — | — | 025.0 |
| 069 | 026.1 | — | — | 026.1 |
| 070 | 026.2 | — | — | 026.2 |
| 071 | 027.1 | — | — | 027.1 |
| 072 | 027.2 | — | — | 027.2 |
| 073 | 028.1 | — | — | 028.1 |
| 074 | 028.2 | — | — | 028.2 |

| Operational Code | Employment status relationship to 1980 occupation groups | | | |
| --- | --- | --- | --- | --- |
| | Self-employed | Managers | Foremen | Apprentices, etc. Employees n.e.c. |
| 075 | 028.3 | — | — | 028.3 |
| 076 | 028.4 | — | — | 028.4 |
| 077 | 028.5 | — | — | 028.5 |
| 078 | 028.6 | — | — | 028.6 |
| 079 | 029.0 | 029.0 | 029.0 | 029.0 |
| 080 | 030.1 | 030.1 | 030.1 | 030.1 |
| 081 | 030.2 | 030.2 | 030.2 | 030.2 |
| 082 | 031.1 | — | — | 031.1 |
| 083 | 031.2 | — | — | 031.2 |
| 084 | 031.3 | — | — | 031.3 |
| 085 | 032.1 | 032.1 | — | 032.1 |
| 086 | — | — | — | 032.2 |
| 087 | 032.3 | 032.3 | — | — |
| 088 | 033.1 | — | — | 033.1 |
| 089 | — | — | — | 033.2 |
| 090 | 033.3 | 033.3 | 033.3 | 033.3 |
| 091 | — | 034.0 | 034.0 | — |
| 092 | — | 035.1 | — | — |
| 093 | — | — | — | 035.2 |
| 094 | — | 036.1 | — | — |
| 095 | — | 036.2 | — | — |
| 096 | — | 036.3 | — | — |
| 097 | — | 036.4 | — | — |
| 098 | — | 037.1 | — | — |
| 099 | 037.2 | 037.2 | — | — |
| 100 | 038.1 | — | — | — |
| 101 | 038.4 | 038.4 | — | — |
| 102 | 039.1 | 039.1 | — | — |
| 103 | 039.2 | 039.2 | — | — |
| 104 | 039.3 | 039.3 | — | — |
| 105 | — | 039.4 | — | — |
| 106 | 039.5 | 039.5 | — | — |
| 107 | 040.0 | 040.0 | — | — |
| 108 | — | 043.1 | — | — |
| 109 | 044.1 | 044.1 | — | — |
| 110 | 044.2 | 044.2 | — | — |
| 111 | 044.4 | 044.4 | — | — |
| 112 | — | — | 045.1 | — |
| 113 | — | — | 045.2 | 046.1 |
| 114 | 046.2 | — | 045.3 | 046.2 |
| 115 | 046.3 | — | 045.4 | 046.3 |
| 116 | — | — | 045.5 | 047.0 |
| 117 | — | — | — | 049.1 |
| 118 | 049.2 | — | 048.1 | 049.2 |
| 119 | 050.0 | — | 048.2 | 050.0 |
| 120 | — | — | — | 051.1 |
| 121 | — | — | 048.3 | 051.2 |
| 122 | — | — | 048.4 | 051.3 |
| 123 | — | — | 052.1 | 053.1 |
| 124 | 053.2 | — | 052.2 | 053.2 |
| 125 | — | — | 054.1 | 055.1 |
| 126 | — | — | — | 055.2 |
| 127 | — | — | 054.2 | 055.3 |
| 128 | 056.0 | 056.0 | 054.3 | 056.0 |
| 129 | 057.1 | 057.1 | — | — |
| 130 | 057.2 | 057.2 | — | 057.2 |
| 131 | 057.3 | 057.3 | — | — |
| 132 | 057.4 | 057.4 | — | 057.4 |
| 133 | 057.5 | 057.5 | — | 057.5 |
| 134 | 057.6 | 057.6 | — | 057.6 |
| 135 | — | 041.0 | — | 058.0 |
| 136 | — | 042.0 | — | 059.0 |
| 137 | — | 043.2 | 060.1 | 061.1 |
| 138 | — | 043.3 | 060.2 | 061.2 |
| 139 | — | — | 060.3 | 061.3 |
| 140 | 062.1 | — | 060.4 | 062.1 |
| 141 | — | — | 060.5 | 062.2 |
| 142 | 062.3 | — | 060.6 | 062.3 |
| 143 | 064.0 | 064.0 | 063.1 | 064.0 |
| 144 | 065.1 | — | 063.2 | 065.1 |
| 145 | 065.2 | — | 063.3 | 065.2 |
| 146 | — | — | 063.4 | 066.1 |
| 147 | — | — | 066.2 | 066.2 |
| 148 | — | — | 067.1 | — |
| 149 | — | — | — | 068.1 |
| 150 | 068.2 | — | — | 068.2 |
| 151 | 068.3 | — | 067.2 | 068.3 |
| 152 | 069.1 | — | 067.3 | 069.1 |
| 153 | — | — | 067.4 | 069.2 |
| 154 | — | — | 067.5 | 069.3 |
| 155 | — | — | 067.6 | 070.1 |
| 156 | — | — | 067.7 | 070.2 |
| 157 | — | — | 071.1 | 072.1 |
| 158 | 072.2 | 072.2 | 071.2 | 072.2 |
| 159 | 044.3 | 044.3 | 073.0 | 074.0 |
| 160 | — | — | 071.3 | 075.1 |
| 161 | — | — | 071.4 | 075.2 |
| 162 | — | 075.3 | 075.3 | 075.3 |
| 163 | 075.4 | 075.4 | — | — |
| 164 | 075.5 | 075.5 | — | — |
| 165 | 075.6 | 075.6 | 075.6 | 075.6 |
| 166 | 077.0 | — | 076.1 | 077.0 |
| 167 | 078.1 | — | 076.2 | 078.1 |
| 168 | 078.2 | 078.2 | 076.3 | 078.2 |

| Operational Code | Employment status relationship to 1980 occupation groups | | | |
|---|---|---|---|---|
| | Self-employed | Managers | Foremen | Apprentices, etc. Employees n.e.c. |
| 169 | 079.0 | — | 076.4 | 079.0 |
| 170 | 080.0 | — | 076.5 | 080.0 |
| 171 | 082.0 | 082.0 | 081.0 | 082.0 |
| 172 | 083.0 | — | 076.6 | 083.0 |
| 173 | 085.1 | 085.1 | 084.1 | 085.1 |
| 174 | 085.2 | 085.2 | 084.2 | 085.2 |
| 175 | 085.3 | 085.3 | 084.3 | 085.3 |
| 176 | 087.1 | 087.1 | 086.1 | 087.1 |
| 177 | 087.2 | 087.2 | 086.2 | 087.2 |
| 178 | 087.3 | 087.3 | 086.3 | 087.3 |
| 179 | 087.4 | 087.4 | 086.4 | 087.4 |
| 180 | 087.5 | 087.5 | 086.5 | 087.5 |
| 181 | 087.6 | 087.6 | 086.6 | 087.6 |
| 182 | 087.7 | 087.7 | 086.7 | 087.7 |
| 183 | 087.8 | 087.8 | 086.8 | 087.8 |
| 184 | 089.0 | 089.0 | 088.0 | 089.0 |
| 185 | 091.0 | 091.0 | 090.1 | 091.0 |
| 186 | 038.2 | 038.2 | 090.2 | 092.1 |
| 187 | 038.3 | 038.3 | 090.3 | 092.2 |
| 188 | 094.1 | — | 093.1 | 094.1 |
| 189 | 094.2 | 094.2 | 093.2 | 094.2 |
| 190 | — | — | 093.3 | 094.3 |
| 191 | — | — | 095.1 | 096.1 |
| 192 | 096.2 | 096.2 | 095.2 | 096.2 |
| 193 | 096.3 | 096.3 | 095.3 | 096.3 |
| 194 | 097.1 | 097.1 | 095.4 | 097.1 |
| 195 | 097.2 | 097.2 | 095.5 | 097.2 |
| 196 | — | — | 095.6 | 098.1 |
| 197 | 098.2 | 098.2 | 090.4 | 098.2 |
| 198 | — | — | 095.7 | 098.3 |
| 199 | 098.4 | — | 086.9 | 098.4 |
| 200 | 098.5 | — | 090.5 | 098.5 |
| 201 | — | — | 098.6 | 098.6 |
| 202 | 098.7 | 098.7 | 090.6 | 098.7 |
| 203 | 098.8 | — | 093.4 | 098.8 |
| 204 | 098.9 | — | 098.9 | 098.9 |
| 205 | 100.1 | 100.1 | 099.1 | 100.1 |
| 206 | 100.2 | 100.2 | 099.2 | 100.2 |
| 207 | 100.3 | — | 099.3 | 100.3 |
| 208 | 100.4 | 100.4 | 099.4 | 100.4 |
| 209 | 100.5 | 100.5 | 099.5 | 100.5 |
| 210 | 102.1 | 102.1 | 101.1 | 102.1 |
| 211 | 102.2 | 102.2 | 101.2 | 102.2 |
| 212 | 102.3 | — | 101.3 | 102.3 |
| 213 | 103.0 | 103.0 | 101.4 | 103.0 |
| 214 | 105.1 | 105.1 | 104.1 | 105.1 |
| 215 | 105.2 | 105.2 | 104.2 | 105.2 |
| 216 | 105.3 | 105.3 | 104.3 | 105.3 |
| 217 | 105.4 | 105.4 | 104.4 | 105.4 |
| 218 | 106.0 | 106.0 | 104.5 | 106.0 |
| 219 | — | — | — | 107.1 |
| 220 | 107.2 | 107.2 | 107.2 | 107.2 |
| 221 | 107.3 | — | 101.5 | 107.3 |
| 222 | 107.4 | 107.4 | 107.4 | 107.4 |
| 223 | 107.5 | — | 095.8 | 107.5 |
| 224 | 107.6 | 107.6 | 104.6 | 107.6 |
| 225 | 107.7 | 107.7 | 084.4 | 107.7 |
| 226 | 107.8 | 107.8 | 101.6 | 107.8 |
| 227 | 107.9 | 107.9 | 093.5 | 107.9 |
| 228 | 107.10 | 107.10 | 095.9 | 107.10 |
| 229 | 107.11 | 107.11 | 095.10 | 107.11 |
| 230 | 107.12 | 107.12 | 107.12 | 107.12 |
| 231 | 109.1 | — | 108.1 | 109.1 |
| 232 | 109.2 | 109.2 | 108.2 | 109.2 |
| 233 | 109.3 | 109.3 | 108.3 | 109.3 |
| 234 | 110.1 | — | 108.4 | 110.1 |
| 235 | 110.2 | — | 108.5 | 110.2 |
| 236 | 110.3 | 110.3 | 108.6 | 110.3 |
| 237 | 110.4 | — | 108.7 | 110.4 |
| 238 | 112.1 | 112.1 | 111.1 | 112.1 |
| 239 | 112.2 | 112.2 | 111.2 | 112.2 |
| 240 | 112.3 | 112.3 | 111.3 | 112.3 |
| 241 | 112.4 | — | 111.4 | 112.4 |
| 242 | 113.1 | 113.1 | 111.5 | 113.1 |
| 243 | 113.2 | 113.2 | 111.6 | 113.2 |
| 244 | 113.3 | — | 111.7 | 113.3 |
| 245 | 115.0 | 115.0 | 114.1 | 115.0 |
| 246 | 116.1 | 116.1 | 114.2 | 116.1 |
| 247 | 116.2 | 116.2 | 114.3 | 116.2 |
| 248 | 117.0 | 117.0 | 114.4 | 117.0 |
| 249 | 118.1 | 118.1 | 114.5 | 118.1 |
| 250 | 118.2 | — | 114.6 | 118.2 |
| 251 | 119.0 | 119.0 | 114.7 | 119.0 |
| 252 | 121.1 | 121.1 | 120.1 | 121.1 |
| 253 | 121.2 | 121.2 | 120.2 | 121.2 |
| 254 | 121.3 | 121.3 | — | 121.3 |
| 255 | — | — | 120.3 | 121.4 |
| 256 | 122.1 | — | 120.4 | 122.1 |
| 257 | 122.2 | — | 120.5 | 122.2 |
| 258 | 123.1 | 123.1 | 120.6 | 123.1 |
| 259 | 123.2 | 123.2 | 120.7 | 123.2 |
| 260 | 125.0 | 125.0 | 124.1 | 125.0 |
| 261 | 126.1 | 126.1 | 124.2 | 126.1 |
| 262 | 126.2 | 126.2 | 124.3 | 126.2 |

| Operational Code | Employment status relationship to 1980 occupation groups | | | |
| --- | --- | --- | --- | --- |
| | Self-employed | Managers | Foremen | Apprentices, etc. Employees n.e.c. |
| 263 | 127.1 | 127.1 | 124.4 | 127.1 |
| 264 | 127.2 | — | 124.5 | 127.2 |
| 265 | 128.0 | 128.0 | 124.6 | 128.0 |
| 266 | 130.1 | 130.1 | 129.1 | 130.1 |
| 267 | 130.2 | — | 129.2 | 130.2 |
| 268 | 131.1 | 131.1 | 129.3 | 131.1 |
| 269 | 131.2 | — | 108.8 | 131.2 |
| 270 | 131.3 | — | 108.9 | 131.3 |
| 271 | — | — | 129.4 | 131.4 |
| 272 | 131.5 | 131.5 | 124.7 | 131.5 |
| 273 | 131.6 | — | 129.5 | 131.6 |
| 274 | 131.7 | 131.7 | 129.6 | 131.7 |
| 275 | — | — | 111.8 | 131.8 |
| 276 | 131.9 | 131.9 | 131.9 | 131.9 |
| 277 | — | — | —.1 | — |
| 278 | — | — | — | —.2 |
| 279 | 133.1 | — | 132.1 | 133.1 |
| 280 | 133.2 | 133.2 | 132.2 | 133.2 |
| 281 | 133.3 | 133.3 | 132.3 | 133.3 |
| 282 | 133.4 | 133.4 | 132.4 | 133.4 |
| 283 | 135.1 | — | 134.1 | 135.1 |
| 284 | 135.2 | — | 134.2 | 135.2 |
| 285 | 135.3 | — | 134.3 | 135.3 |
| 286 | 137.1 | — | 136.1 | 137.1 |
| 287 | 137.2 | — | 136.7 | 137.2 |
| 288 | — | — | 136.8 | 138.1 |
| 289 | — | — | 136.2 | 138.2 |
| 290 | — | — | 136.3 | 138.3 |
| 291 | — | — | 136.4 | 138.4 |
| 292 | — | — | 136.5 | 138.5 |
| 293 | — | — | 136.6 | 138.6 |
| 294 | — | — | 136.9 | 138.7 |
| 295 | 138.8 | — | 134.4 | 138.8 |
| 296 | — | — | 134.5 | 138.9 |
| 297 | — | — | 136.10 | 138.10 |
| 298 | — | — | 136.11 | 138.11 |
| 299 | 138.12 | 138.12 | 138.12 | 138.12 |
| 300 | 140.1 | 140.1 | 139.1 | 140.1 |
| 301 | 140.2 | 140.2 | 139.2 | 140.2 |
| 302 | 140.3 | 140.3 | 139.3 | 140.3 |
| 303 | 140.4 | 140.4 | 139.4 | 140.4 |
| 304 | 140.5 | 140.5 | 139.5 | 140.5 |
| 305 | 140.6 | 140.6 | — | 140.6 |
| 306 | — | — | 139.6 | 141.1 |
| 307 | 141.2 | — | 139.7 | 141.2 |
| 308 | 141.3 | — | 139.8 | 141.3 |
| 309 | 141.4 | — | 139.9 | 141.4 |
| 310 | — | — | 139.10 | 142.1 |
| 311 | 142.2 | — | 139.11 | 142.2 |
| 312 | 143.1 | — | 143.1 | 143.1 |
| 313 | 143.2 | — | 143.2 | 143.2 |
| 314 | 145.0 | — | 144.0 | 145.0 |
| 315 | 146.1 | 146.1 | 146.1 | 146.1 |
| 316 | 146.2 | 146.2 | 139.12 | 146.2 |
| 317 | 148.0 | — | 147.0 | 148.0 |
| 318 | — | — | 149.4 | — |
| 319 | — | — | — | 150.1 |
| 320 | — | — | 149.1 | 150.2 |
| 321 | — | — | 149.2 | 150.3 |
| 322 | — | — | 149.3 | 150.4 |
| 323 | — | — | 151.1 | — |
| 324 | — | — | 151.3 | — |
| 325 | 152.1 | 152.1 | — | 152.1 |
| 326 | 152.2 | 152.2 | 151.2 | 152.2 |
| 327 | 152.3 | 152.3 | — | 152.3 |
| 328 | 153.1 | — | — | 153.1 |
| 329 | — | — | — | 153.2 |
| 330 | 155.1 | 155.1 | 154.1 | 155.1 |
| 331 | — | — | 154.2 | 155.2 |
| 332 | 155.3 | — | 154.3 | 155.3 |
| 333 | 157.1 | 157.1 | 156.1 | 157.1 |
| 334 | 157.2 | — | 156.2 | 157.2 |
| 335 | 157.3 | 157.3 | 156.3 | 157.3 |
| 336 | — | — | 156.4 | 157.4 |
| 337 | — | — | 154.4 | 158.1 |
| 338 | 158.2 | — | 158.2 | 158.2 |
| 339 | — | — | 159.1 | 160.1 |
| 340 | — | — | 159.2 | 160.2 |
| 341 | — | — | 159.3 | 160.3 |
| 342 | — | — | 159.4 | 160.4 |
| 343 | — | — | 159.5 | 160.5 |
| 344 | — | — | 159.6 | 160.6 |
| 345 | — | — | 159.7 | 160.7 |
| 346 | 160.8 | — | 159.8 | 160.8 |
| 347 | — | — | 159.9 | 161.1 |
| 348 | 161.2 | — | 161.2 | 161.2 |
| 349 | —.1 | —.1 | —.1 | —.1 |
| 350 | — | — | — | —.2 |

Printed in England for Her Majesty's Stationery Office by Hobbs the Printers of Southampton
(1122) Dd0698172 K40 12/80 G327